T0315048

ARRESTED DEVELOPMENT

ARRESTED DEVELOPMENT

The Soviet Union in Ghana, Guinea, and Mali, 1955–1968

Alessandro Iandolo

CORNELL UNIVERSITY PRESS   ITHACA AND LONDON

First published 2022 by Cornell University Press

Library of Congress Cataloging-in-Publication Data

Names: Iandolo, Alessandro, 1983– author.
Title: Arrested development : the Soviet Union in Ghana, Guinea, and Mali, 1955–1968 / Alessandro Iandolo.
Description: Ithaca [New York] : Cornell University Press, 2022. | Includes bibliographical references and index.
Identifiers: LCCN 2022003832 | ISBN 9781501764431 (hardcover) | ISBN 9781501764448 (pdf) | ISBN 9781501764455 (epub)
Subjects: LCSH: Economic assistance, Soviet—Ghana. | Economic assistance, Soviet—Guinea. | Economic assistance, Soviet—Mali. | Economic development—Ghana. | Economic development—Guinea. | Economic development—Mali. | Soviet Union—Relations—Ghana. | Ghana—Relations—Soviet Union. | Soviet Union—Relations—Guinea. | Guinea—Relations—Soviet Union. | Soviet Union—Relations—Mali. | Mali—Relations—Soviet Union. | Ghana—Economic conditions—1957–1979. | Guinea—Economic conditions—1958–1984. | Mali—Economic conditions—1959–
Classification: LCC HC1060 .I26 2022 | DDC 338.9667—dc23/eng/20220304
LC record available at https://lccn.loc.gov/2022003832

Contents

Acknowledgments

This was the most difficult section to write. Most academic colleagues and friends love acknowledgments. They find them funny, witty, sometimes moving, often cringy. Acknowledgments frighten me. How can one be sure to thank all without missing anyone, their absence forever recorded on paper? There are dozens, perhaps hundreds, of people who helped with this book. They all deserve a thank you and more. This is a task I could never hope to complete, and this is why I decided to take a minimalist approach, focusing on the most obvious institutional, intellectual, and emotional debts I owe to people and places.

Many institutions have made this book possible. I am thankful to Cornell University Press for publishing it. Roger Haydon believed in the project from the beginning. His engagement with the core ideas in the manuscript I initially sent him made it a much better book. Jim Lance took over the project at a later stage but worked with me with the same passion and dedication. Artemy Kalinovsky and Elidor Mëhilli, fellow Cornell authors, guided me in the process from day one. Both have been a huge source of intellectual inspiration, and both have helped me shape the book. I am also profoundly grateful to the two anonymous reviewers that read the manuscript for Cornell. They have given me crucial suggestions that I implemented in the final version. They have also saved me from a couple of embarrassing factual mistakes.

The idea for this book was born at the University of Oxford more than a decade ago and was assisted by a scholarship from the Economic and Social Research Council (ESRC). Generous financial support from the ESRC allowed me to conduct research in Russia and Ghana between 2009 and 2011. Anne Deighton and Alex Pravda at Oxford supervised a project that was highly unusual at the time when the historical study of development was far from an established field of research in the United Kingdom. It is thanks to their dedication, patience, and knowledge that my research idea came to fruition and eventually could be revised into a book. Many more people contributed to shaping my ideas in Oxford. I am especially grateful to Agnese Abrusci, Stephanie Brockerhoff, Charlotte Bruckermann, Stefano Caria, Emanuele Ferragina, Natasha Graham, Monika Hajdasz, Agostino Inguscio, Samuele Mazzolini, Michalis Moutselos, Dario Nappo, Salvatore Morelli, Andrea Polo, Ana Ranitović, Alberto Rigolio, Fabian Teichmueller, Rebecca Thomas, Piero Tortola, Peter Zeniewski, and Pegah Zohouri.

Later on, a fellowship from the British Academy allowed me to spend three wonderful years as a postdoc at the London School of Economics (LSE). The British Academy also generously funded research trips to Russia, Mali, France, and the United States. The LSE's Department of International History has long been a second home for me and many more UK-based historians interested in the Cold War. Arne Westad has been the best mentor I could hope for. A constant source of inspiration and intellectual stimulation, Arne created a real community of scholars at the LSE. He had started helping me when I was still writing my dissertation and continues to this day. I owe him so much. I met Matthew Jones on my very first day at the LSE. He has never stopped supporting me and my work since. As mentor, head of the department, and colleague, Matthew has helped me every step of the way. I feel so lucky to know him. At the LSE, I had the privilege of regularly attending and presenting twice at the contemporary history seminar series. It is an incredible resource for all scholars of international history in the UK and beyond. I also owe special thanks to many colleagues and friends in the LSE community, in particular: Roham Alvandi, Andrea Chiampan, Aurélie Dianara Andry, Vesselin Dimitrov, Matthew Hinds, Piers Ludlow, Tommaso Milani, Pete Millwood, Elizabeth Shlala, Natalia Telepneva, Simon Toner, Vladimir Unkovski-Korica, Laurent Warlouzet, and Vladislav Zubok.

I often feel that I learned more in less than a year at Columbia University than in all my previous years of higher education combined. I am grateful to the Fulbright Commission for granting me a fellowship, and to Mark Mazower and Małgorzata Mazurek for supporting me. I hope to be back soon.

Years after earning my PhD there, I returned to Oxford as a lecturer. It was a great home institution for a few years,and many colleagues engaged with my work and helped me advance my ideas. Paul Betts has encouraged me from the beginning. His comments on an early draft of the manuscript gave me the confidence and resolve to complete the project. I feel privileged to work with him. Many others in Oxford have been a great source of inspiration and constructive criticism, among them Kathrin Bachtleitner, Bill Booth, Puneet Dhaliwal, Enid Guene, Louise Fawcett, Friederike Haberstroh, Sudhir Hazareesingh, Hussam Hussein, Kasia Jeżowska, Eddie Keene, Miles Larmer, Juan Masullo, Neil McFarlane, Carlotta Minnella, Giuseppe Paparella, Marina Pérez de Arcos, Eduardo Posada Carbó, Andrea Ruggeri, Nelson Ruiz, and Ricardo Soares de Oliveira. I am also grateful to Paul Chaisty and Dan Healey for inviting me to present in the Russian and Eurasian Studies seminar series.

Since September 2021, I have been based at the Davis Center for Russian and Eurasian Studies at Harvard University. It is a wonderful place to work for someone interested in the Soviet Union. I am grateful to Donna Cardarelli and Alexandra Vacroux for their help and support.

One of the best aspects of writing this book has been traveling to many different places for research. Moscow is the place I have visited more often for this book, and one I never tire of visiting. Some colleagues I met there have provided tremendous help with the book. I first got to know David Engerman while we were both working in the same Moscow archive—one with particularly puzzling opening hours. David has been an incredible source of inspiration, help, and suggestions since then. It is difficult to express how indebted I am to his work, insight, and good humor. I have been fortunate to be able to follow the path David has forged in studying the Soviet approach to development. Likewise, I met Chris Miller while we were both based at the New Economic School in Moscow. Chris has been a fantastic friend since, and his feedback on a draft of the manuscript has made it into a much better book. In Moscow, I am also grateful to Alan Crawford, Liya Eijvertinya, JJ Gurga, Kristy Ironside, Hilary Lynd, Michelle Maydanchik, Colleen Moore, Aliide Naylor, Anna Nogina, Giovanni Savino, Samantha Sherry, Olga Skorokhodova, Olga Suchkova, Jonathan Waterlow, Shlomo Weber, Yuval Weber, and Andy Willimott. Many archivists and librarians in Moscow have greatly facilitated my research. I would not have been able to write this book without the help of Irina Tarakanova at the Archive of the Russian Academy of Sciences (ARAN), Sergei Pavlov at the Foreign Ministry Archive (AVP RF), Nadezhda Kostrikova at the Russian State Archive of the Economy (RGAE), and Liudmila Stepanich at the Russian State Archive of Contemporary History (RGANI).

In Accra, I am grateful to Kojo Bright Botwe for his help while working at the national archives (PRAAD). I am also indebted to Erin Braatz, Martí Roig Guardiola, and Martin Williams for their company and ideas while in Ghana. In Bamako, I owe special thanks to Fofana Sidibé at the Centre Nationale de la Recherche Scientifique et Technologique, Macki Samake at the Université des Lettres et des Sciences Humaines, and Ablaye Traoré at the Archives Nationales du Mali. I am also grateful to Bouréma Konate, Ylenia Rosso, and Rebecca Wall for the wonderful hospitality and company while I was in Mali. In Paris, I am thankful to Jean-Pierre Bat and Nicole Even for their help with the collections at the Archives Nationales in Pierrefitte-sur-Seine, and to all the reading room staff at the Archives du Ministère des Affaires Étrangeres in La Courneve. I am also grateful for the hospitality and ideas Mario Del Pero, Michele Di Donato, Veronik Durin-Hornyik, Massimiliano Gaggero, and Ophélie Rillon offered while I was in France.

Over the years, I have benefited from presenting my research and listening to so many great papers at many conferences and workshops. As a historian of the Soviet Union and the world—a field that counts many practitioners but sadly lacks official recognition—I have often felt I missed an obvious professional association to belong to and annual conference to go to. The Association for

Slavic, East European and Eurasian Studies and the Society for Historians of American Foreign Relations have both provided an intellectual home and an occasion to engage with the work of hundreds of brilliant historians. Both associations have become remarkably open to scholars whose research crosses approaches and geographical boundaries. Feedback and comments on various papers related to the content of this book have helped me immensely. I cannot wait to attend both conferences again.

I am also grateful to the organizers of a few workshops that allowed me to present my research work and receive great feedback on early and later drafts of sections of this book. In particular, fellow participants at the International Graduate Student Conference on the Cold War, organized jointly by the LSE, George Washington University and the University of California at Santa Barbara; and the European Summer School on Cold War History, organized jointly by the LSE and the University of Padua in Italy, gave me so many ideas and suggestions that helped me in completing this book. I am especially grateful to Frank Gerits, Elisabeth Leake, Emilie Menz, and Alanna O'Malley.

In October 2017, Elizabeth Banks and Robyn d'Avignon invited me to present at a terrific workshop on contacts between the Soviet Union and different parts of Africa at New York University. I learned so much from everyone that day, and for the first time I realized fully how much interest in Soviet-African relations has increased since I started my project. Nana Osei-Opare, whom I first met at the NYU workshop, read a draft of this book and helped me sharpen my argument and tighten my take on historiography. I owe him a lot.

The Laureate Program on International History at the University of Sydney offered me the perfect fellowship to focus on writing. I am grateful to Glenda Sluga for giving me this opportunity and for her constant engagement with my work since. While in Sydney, I also greatly appreciated conversations and discussions with Dave Brophy, Sophie Loy-Wilson, and Dirk Moses.

The biggest debt of all I owe to Philippa Hetherington. She has engaged with every section and every aspect of this book, from the general argument to minutiae about orthography and pagination. More important, she is the one who has shown me what it means to think and write like a historian. I have learned critical thinking from her. It is a debt I will never be able to pay back, but I can at the very least acknowledge it here.

For the time it took me to write this book, I know I have been a bad family member, friend, partner, and son. Over the past thirteen years, I have missed countless anniversaries, birthdays, celebrations, gatherings, holidays, and especially weddings, usually because I "really needed" to spend some more time in Bamako, Moscow, Paris, or someplace else. I hope the actual appearance of this book in print will give me at least a partial justification. My parents, Francesco Iandolo and Paola Silvestri, have given me everything they could. My family and friends of a lifetime, with whom I have been discussing some of this book's ideas since I was a teenager, have inspired everything in it. This book is dedicated to you. You know who you are.

Abbreviations

AN	Akademia Nauk SSSR (Academy of Sciences of the USSR)
CPP	Convention People's Party
CPSU	Communist Party of the Soviet Union
GKES	Gosudarstvennyi komitet po vneshnim ekonomicheskim sviaziam (State Committee for Foreign Economic Contacts)
IMEMO	Institut Mirovoi Ekonomiki i Mezhdunarodnykh Otnoshenii (Institute of World Economy and International Relations)
KGB	Komitet Gosudarstvennoi Bezopasnosti (State Security Committee)
MID	Ministerstvo Inostrannykh Del (Ministry of Foreign Affairs)
MO	Mezhdunarodnyi otdel (International Department of the CPSU)
NATO	North Atlantic Treaty Organization
PDG	Parti Démocratique de Guinée (Democratic Party of Guinea)
SSSR	Soiuz Sovetskikh Sotsialisticheskikh Respublik (Union of Soviet Socialist Republics)
TsK	Tsentral'nyi Komitet (Central Committee of the CPSU)
UN	United Nations
UP	United Party
US-RDA	Union Soudanaise-Rassemblement Démocratique Africain (Soudanaise Union—African National Rally)

Note on Transliteration

I have used the standard Library of Congress system to transliterate Russian names and words from Cyrillic.

ARRESTED DEVELOPMENT

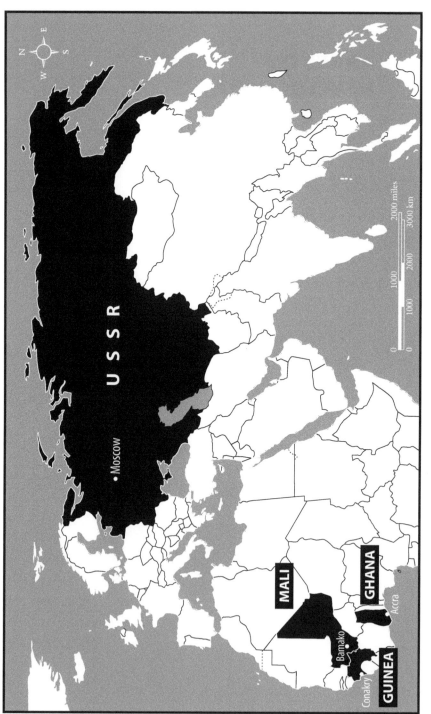

MAP 1. The Soviet Union and West Africa. Author: Mike Bechthold, 2021.

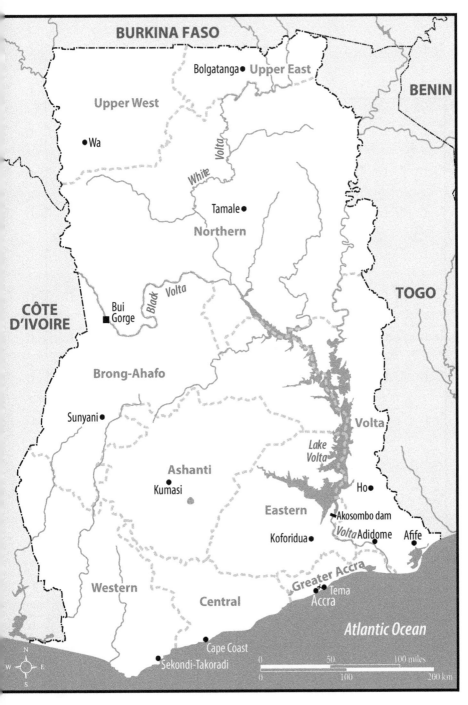

MAP 2. Ghana: major cities, regions, rivers, transport infrastructure, and sites of Soviet-sponsored development projects. Author: Mike Bechthold, 2021.

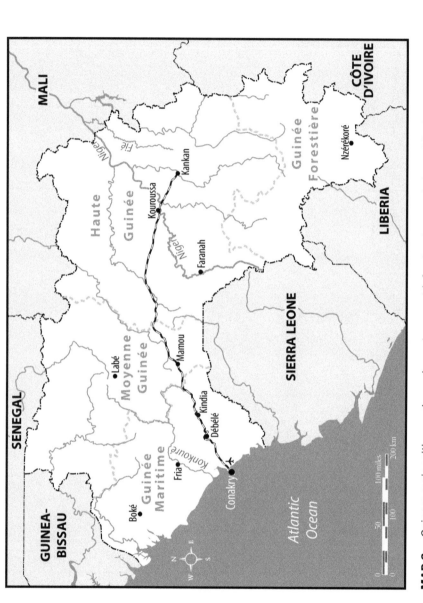

MAP 3. Guinea: major cities, regions, rivers, transport infrastructure, and sites of Soviet-sponsored development projects. Author: Mike Bechthold, 2021.

MAP 4. Mali: major cities, regions, rivers, transport infrastructure, and sites of Soviet-sponsored development projects. Author: Mike Bechthold, 2021.

INTRODUCTION

"Forty years ago, the Soviet Union was like Africa," Kwaku Akwei told a Soviet delegate to the All-African Peoples' Conference in Accra in December 1958. Akwei was a senior official in the Convention People's Party, the political movement that had led Ghana to independence and now ruled the country. He had recently visited the USSR with a delegation of trade unionists and was impressed by the "miracles accomplished by the Soviet people." Akwei had no doubts: "all Africa must follow this path."[1]

The path Akwei had in mind was that of socialism—building a prosperous, technologically advanced economy based on state investment, public ownership, and collective enterprise. It was a widespread dream among the first generation of postcolonial elites following the second wave of decolonization after World War II. The Soviet Union was the perfect guiding star to direct this process. A gigantic conglomerate of different lands, peoples, cultures, and traditions, the USSR had managed to turn itself into an industrialized superpower, following decades of revolution, war, and social and economic change, often extremely violent. The much-publicized Soviet narrative of victory over "backwardness," possibly the most important founding myth of the USSR itself, exercised an immense power of attraction over the first postindependence leaderships of West Africa. As Akwei told his Soviet interlocutor, many in Ghana and elsewhere aspired to replicate the Soviet success, using similar instruments.

This book examines the process that was expected to fulfill this ambition. Its core concept is development, as an ideal end goal to be achieved through a process of "modernization." Specifically, the book looks at the Soviet attempt to export a model of development based on socialist principles to Ghana, Guinea, and Mali between the mid-1950s and the late 1960s. In West Africa, as in most of the Third World at the time, the Soviet way to development was not the only possible approach. The USSR and its allies held a vision of development that tended to prioritize building up the state as the main instrument of modernization. By contrast, the Western world, including both the United States and the European former colonial powers, espoused a vision centered on market competition and private investment. The contest between these two archetypal approaches to modernization constitutes the analytical backbone of the book.

Following Joseph Morgan Hodge's invitation in an influential state-of-the-field review and works by David Engerman, Artemy Kalinovsky, and Timothy Nunan that look at the USSR specifically, this book focuses primarily on the practice of development.[2] Although the "elusive origins of development"—its intellectual roots—are explored with regard to the Soviet tradition, the book investigates development as a work of shovel, brick, and mortar. It does not follow specific modernization projects as case studies to investigate the Soviet-West African road to development. Rather, the book looks at the search for development as a holistic phenomenon whose many branches are impossible to understand separately and must be taken as parts of a whole. The construction of a road made no sense without considering the need to transport agricultural commodities, whose production had to be boosted through collective farms and whose workers had to be trained in a newly built polytechnic institute. The capital, expertise, and organizational principles for such enterprises came from the Soviet Union. The book investigates the initial ambition that led to the design of joint Soviet-West African development projects, their implementation on the ground, and their eventual abandonment.

Politics was at the center of this search for modernity. In the Soviet Union, just as much as in Ghana, Guinea, and Mali, policymakers, economists, engineers, and agronomists involved in modernization projects were not content with simply finding solutions to technical problems. Their goal was to build a specific form of development based on socialist ideas. This was not the same as replicating Soviet communism abroad. On the contrary, the model the USSR recommended in West Africa mixed elements of a planned system with surviving pillars of a traditional market economy. State investment and collective organization dominated the Soviet vision of development in West Africa, but private property was not abolished, agriculture was never fully collectivized, and heavy industry remained on the sidelines. The Soviet strategy mirrored import-substitution development efforts pioneered in capitalist contexts but did so with a socialist orientation, always prioritizing state over market. This is the core argument of the book.

Les mots et les choses

This book deals with ideas, terms, and concepts whose meaning, use, and intellectual tradition are supremely contested. "Development" is the most obvious case. What is it, and why does it matter? An immense anthropological literature has explored the uses and misuses of the concept of development. Recent historical works have investigated the relationship between international politics and the search for development in the wake of decolonization. Both traditions have highlighted the hypocrisy and inherent racism in the idea of developed societies inspiring and guiding underdeveloped ones. Moreover, anthropologists and historians have detailed the boundless political, economic, social, cultural, and environmental destruction wrought on the peoples and lands of Africa, Asia, and Latin America (and beyond) in the name of development during the twentieth century.[3]

This book has a more restricted scope. Here, development is understood and used in the way the main actors at the time did. The Soviet and West African approach to development was quantitative: boosting agricultural production, increasing basic industrial output, improving living standards measured using traditional indicators (life expectancy, number of houses, schools, roads, hospitals, etc.). In essence, the Soviet and West African leaders equated development with economic growth. It was possibly Nikita Khrushchev, the Soviet leader until 1964, who best captured this materialistic vision. At a time when the Soviet economy and society were undergoing profound changes, abandoning the rigidities of high Stalinism, Khrushchev summed up his approach to modernization rather crudely: "It is not bad if in improving the theory of Marxism one throws in also a piece of bacon and a piece of butter."[4]

Khrushchev's counterparts in West Africa, while more sophisticated, shared his vision of what development was. Kwame Nkrumah, Ghana's first postindependence prime minister and later president, harbored no doubts about what his country's priorities should be. "We shall measure our progress by the improvement in the health of our people; by the number of children in school, and by the quality of their education; by the availability of water and electricity in our towns and villages, and by the happiness which our people take in being able to manage their own affairs."[5] The key to success was creating a national economy, independent from predatory businesses and detached from the former colonizers. Fodéba Keïta, a prominent intellectual and a member of Guinea's first government, declared during a visit to Egypt in early 1959: "Our main task is to free our economy, our culture, and all our life. Our country is 85% agricultural. We are trying to establish some very basic cooperatives of producers and consumers in the agricultural regions. We shall succeed. National industry is basically still non-existent. Our bauxite is exported by French, American, Italian,

Swiss and Canadian firms, which transform it into aluminum in their own countries. In the future, we want this transformation to happen entirely in Guinea."[6] It was here that the Soviet model appeared particularly attractive, building up the state as the key constituent of national development. Modibo Keïta, the first president of independent Mali, explained this position particularly well. In September 1962, talking to his political party two years after having achieved independence, Keïta reminded his audience that Mali faced a "double imperative"; ending "the economic pillaging" of Mali by the former colonizers and ensuring sufficient provision of goods and services in a context in which a national private sector was virtually nonexistent. "Faced with this dilemma, there was only one solution: to make the state the instrument of the reorganization of our economy, and to operate in such a way that our economy is balanced, no longer as a complementary economy of the French economy, but as an independent one, based on the sole interest of our country and of the working people."[7]

In this context, modernity referred to the ideal end-stage of the development process. This very process was modernization: the application of new ideas, models, and technology to the organization of society and production. Soviet participants in the search for modernity in West Africa, be they Presidium members in Moscow or technicians deployed on the field, habitually called it *razvitie*, which could refer both to development as process and development as stage. Nkrumah and his people in Ghana used development and modernization interchangeably, as is the case in this book. Likewise, in Guinea and in Mali, both government documents and workers in all capacities treated the terms *développement* and *modernisation* as synonyms. Often, they preferred the word *croissance* (growth). This material, relatively straightforward idea of development as transformative economic growth (benign, according to its proponents) is how the term is used in the book.

If development and modernization can be used as actor's categories, the same cannot be said about the expression Third World, which is used in this book to refer to the countries of Africa, Asia, and Latin America. Popular in the 1950s and 1960s following its coinage by the French scholar Alfred Sauvy in 1952, the expression Third World has gone out of fashion. After many variations and permutations have waxed and waned over the years, developing countries and the Global South are the most used terms to refer to the same group of states and regions of the world today.

Third World, banned from the parlance of international organizations and intergovernmental meetings, is still popular in academic literature. It is normally assumed to have a hierarchical meaning. The First World was that of the capitalist West, developed and modern. The Second World comprised the USSR, its European satellites, and perhaps (but perhaps not) Cuba, China, and other socialist countries in Asia and Africa. Everyone else belonged to the Third World—the poor, downtrodden, underdeveloped.

The phrase Third World was not popular in the Soviet Union. According to the *Bol'shaia Sovetskaia Entsiklopediia* (Great Soviet Encyclopedia), the closest to an official repository of Soviet knowledge, the expression *Tretii Mir* was defined simply as a synonym of *razvivaiushchiesia strany* (developing countries). Those were the "countries of Asia, Africa, Latin America and Oceania, in the past in their majority colonies and protectorates of the imperialist powers or countries dependent from them, that enjoy political sovereignty, but, entering the orbit of the world capitalist economy, remain to a certain extent unequal (*neravnopravnyi*) partners of the highly developed capitalist states."[8] The Soviet preference for developing countries over Third World derived from the classic Marxist idea that different societies were at different stages of development, but all converged toward industrial capitalism and eventually revolution and communism. Moreover, the Soviet leadership was understandably wary of accepting a terminology that seemed to relegate the USSR and the rest of the socialist world to Second World, and therefore second-best.

In West Africa, Third World was just as unpopular. The leaders of Ghana, Guinea, and Mali seldom used it in their speeches and writings. Afro-Asian and Non-Aligned (after the formation of the Non-Aligned Movement, of which all three states were members) were convenient, and more precise, alternatives. Nkrumah had no qualms about claiming to speak for all of Africa but was more careful to associate Ghana with countries in other regions of the world. Guinea's president Ahmed Sékou Touré and Modibo Keïta did not have a problem with calling Guinea and Mali less-developed or even *sous-développés* (underdeveloped) but rarely referred to their countries as part of a *Tiers Monde*.

Why then using Third World in this book if it was not an actor's category? Precisely because Third World is a loaded expression. It implies a political definition rather than a purely economic one. Sauvy coined the phrase thinking of the Third Estate, which in prerevolutionary France was "nothing" but wanted to become "something."[9] The essence of Third World was revolutionary change. Hannah Arendt famously wrote that the "Third World is not a reality but an ideology." Decades later, Vijay Prashad opened his "people's history" of the Third World, paraphrasing Arendt: "The Third World was not a place. It was a project." Arendt scorned the idea that the peoples of Asia, Africa, and Latin America could be new revolutionary subjects. In her view, this ideology was wishful thinking, detached from the reality of backwardness in the Third World that prevented any real revolutionary manifestation. Prashad, on the contrary, aimed to retrieve and resurrect the radical tradition of thinking about the Third World as a revolutionary category.[10]

Whether an ideology, a project, or an idea, Third World was more than the sum of its geographical components. As Georgii Mirskii (the author of the entry in the *Great Soviet Encyclopedia*) understood, what Third World countries had in common was the consciousness of "not enjoying equal rights" vis-à-vis other states and, crucially, the willingness to overcome this inequality. The Third World project was about changing the world, starting with the global political economy. The colonial relations based on dependency that characterized the old world of empires had to be cut in favor of a new order that prioritized independence and equality. Obtaining this change without development was impossible. This is why Nkrumah, Sékou Touré, and Keïta, together with other first-generation postcolonial leaders such as Gamal Abdel Nasser in Egypt, Jawaharlal Nehru in India, and Sukarno in Indonesia, tended to regard the conquest of modernity as an integral part of the struggle for independence. This is also why the Third World could not be defined by simple geography. In his definition, Mirskii made a point of excluding Israel, Japan, New Zealand, Rhodesia, and South Africa—states that may have had something in common with Third World countries, but not necessarily the wish to change the world order. Thus, the Soviet government may have been suspicious of the phrase Third World, but it understood its political meaning and, to an extent, supported the project that derived from it. Likewise, the leaders of Ghana, Guinea, and Mali preferred other expressions, but in their action shared both the assumptions and the goals of the Third World project. This is why this book uses the phrase Third World.

The New Cold War

The Cold War is the book's inescapable analytical framework. In West Africa, the Soviet Union was part of a contest, a competition, to provide economic aid and technical assistance superior to those offered by the United States and its European allies. The motivation to enter this contest, its modalities, and the projected end goal were determined by the Cold War, as a global clash between two rival but related ways to organize society and the economy.

This is a relatively new way of thinking about the Cold War. Traditionally, the period between 1945 and 1991 was interpreted as a competition between the United States and the USSR to secure resources and obtain strategic advantages. It was in this context that the first studies of the Soviet Union's engagement with the Third World appeared. Already in 1970, Robert Legvold offered a pioneering analysis of Soviet policy in West Africa. Detailed and insightful, the book focused on what was assumed to be the Soviet objective at the time: the transformation of African societies into communist regimes. Given West Africa's relative lack of natural resources and generally low strategic importance, this appeared as the only viable goal that could justify significant Soviet investments in the region. Nonetheless, Legvold concluded that while the Soviet government assumed a flexible attitude toward the West African leaders, who were far from communists, in the end most West African states lost interest in the USSR and in what it could offer them. The relationship, though deep at times, did not produce anything of consequence.[11]

Forty years later, Sergei Mazov published the first major historical study of the USSR's interactions with Ghana, Guinea, and Mali. Now able to access a vast array of Soviet primary sources, which were previously unavailable, Mazov followed an analytical trajectory similar to Legvold's and other Sovietologists'. Soviet engagement in West Africa is presented as a "distant front of the Cold War"—a significant but secondary episode of the superpower rivalry, whose main theatre remained Europe and whose main battlefields remained diplomatic and military. Mazov pays attention to development cooperation, which is discussed in detail, but generally understood as instrumental to other, more traditional Cold War objectives. Similar to what Legvold had argued four decades earlier, Mazov concluded that "the Africans could not find in the Soviet literature the formulas to solve their urgent economic problems."[12]

Both these monographs contributed to creating and then reviving a field of scholarly inquiry, and both have stood the test of time. However, historiography on the Cold War since has evolved in a different direction, one in which development and modernization in the Third World have taken center stage, replacing the traditional focus on Europe and on strategic issues. Since the publication of Arne Westad's *The Global Cold War*, the literature has tended to frame the Cold War as a geoideological conflict, in which the Soviet Union and the United States attempted to reconstruct Third World polities, economies, and societies in their own image and likeness.[13] As Westad argues, the Soviet and American Cold War postures were essentially two parallel colonial projects, a "continuation of colonialism through slightly different means."[14]

Ideology was at the core of the Cold War. Both the American and Soviet projects were based on sets of beliefs and assumptions about history, the state of the world, and its future. American liberalism was shaped by a belief in the superiority of individual freedom, democratic rule, and free markets. Soviet socialism, by contrast, was founded on equality, collective organization, and state oversight over the economy. As Engerman explains, both ideological systems were "universalistic" and "messianic."[15] The United States and the USSR were not content to cultivate the pursuit of happiness or the march toward communism at home. Both required the transformation of other societies in the same direction to fulfill their respective project. After the end of World War II and the onset of the second wave of decolonization, the transformation of Third World states and societies became the main activity (or at least ambition) of the Cold War rivals. Traditional Cold War scholarship recognized the importance of ideology but tended to look at the transformation in terms of establishing or overthrowing governments or of supporting communist parties or conservative movements. Newer literature tends to look at economic development as the kernel of Cold War transformation. According to this view, the American and Soviet ambition was not to control or influence but to shape the path toward modernity of emerging societies.

Although this is the dominant paradigm, some of the literature has taken issue with the depiction of the USSR as an economic power able and willing to transform others. The Soviet economy was weak, the argument goes, and therefore it could not sustain a global Cold War against the much stronger United States. The USSR had no chance of becoming an autarkic economy, a dream that was quickly abandoned in favor of integration in the global capitalist system. The Soviet Union's only chance of economic survival was obtaining technology from the advanced capitalist economies. The Soviet economic imperative was therefore maintaining and ideally boosting trade links with the rest of the world. In this context, the USSR's interest in the Third World, which peaked with Khrushchev in power, was far from an attempt to establish an economic system alternative to capitalism. On the contrary, cultivating relations with Third World states was simply a way to engage in international trade and to obtain raw materials and resources that the Soviet economy needed.[16]

Pathbreaking, fascinating, and controversial, all these approaches have informed this book. However, the case of Soviet engagement with Ghana, Guinea, and Mali remains somewhat elusive. All grand narratives require some refinement to understand change in the short term. As the book shows, the USSR's aim in West Africa was not to replicate itself or to lay the foundations of communism. In line with the prevailing thinking in Moscow about the prospects of real socialism in the Third World, the agreements signed with Guinea, Ghana, and Mali aimed to build a large state sector in the economy and to disrupt existing trade links with the West. Trade with West Africa hardly made the Soviet Union more integrated into the global economy. The volumes of trade were too limited, and the commodities acquired were not valuable enough. Trade was instrumental to a vision based on development. This vision was ambitious, but it was neither transforming the world in the USSR's image nor transforming the USSR in the capitalist world's image. Rather, the Soviet government aimed to export what the Khrushchev leadership thought it was best at—fostering rapid growth through state investment to catch up with more advanced economies in the short term. This was what the Third World (including Ghana, Guinea, and Mali) was after, and without much thought about communism or even the global economy. What mattered was economic growth.

Ghana, Guinea, and Mali were ideal candidates to receive Soviet assistance. Newly independent states with small populations, they emerged from decades of colonial domination anxious to affirm themselves as modern economies and as actors on the international stage. The radicalism of their leaders made them receptive to the Soviet vision of development based on state ownership and collective organization. Their small sizes made Soviet investment significant, even if relatively small in absolute terms. To the Soviet leadership, the value of Ghana, Guinea, and Mali was symbolic and relational. A confident, prosperous West African state, which successfully modernized with Soviet money and assistance, was worth more to the USSR than any commodity it could acquire from them. This projected success story would inspire other Third World countries in similar situations to follow the Soviet example, to embrace development with a socialist bent. The world would become a much friendlier place for the Soviet Union, with many more opportunities for fruitful collaboration in all fields. Eventually, this process may even lead modernized Third World states to take the road of communism, as Marxism-Leninism would posit. This was a transformation that Soviet leaders and analysts projected into a distant future.

In the short run, the Soviet project was the establishment of a model of economic development based on the state, of which Ghana, Guinea, and Mali represented ideal test cases. This was different from classic Soviet-style communism. Most important, state and market were expected to coexist. Soviet economic and technical assistance aimed to build up the West African state apparatuses. Basic infrastructure would be built with state funds, new farms and factories would be organized collectively, and the government would be in full control of both the money supply and foreign trade. At the same time, there was ample space left for the private sector and individual investors. Retail and distribution would largely remain in private hands, as did the bulk of smaller businesses. Moreover, the type of economic modernization sponsored by the USSR in West Africa differed from the classic Soviet model in one crucial respect: heavy industry did not feature in it. The element that is most associated with the USSR was instead relegated to the sidelines of what Soviet specialists recommended in Ghana, Guinea, and Mali. The projects the Soviet Union supported focused primarily on transport and energy infrastructure and on boosting agricultural productivity. Some also aimed to develop a few light industrial sectors, such as textiles and food processing. However, traditional heavy industry (metals, chemicals, mining)—the backbone of the Soviet economy—was judged impossible to develop in West Africa, with few exceptions. Contrary to the common view that sees the Soviet Union always pushing for industrial development, in West Africa the USSR prioritized agriculture, in line with what Soviet experts believed the region's most pressing necessities were.

The Soviet model for West Africa is difficult to situate on the Cold War divide. Soviet analysts and scholars themselves struggled with how to define and understand what they were doing in West Africa and elsewhere. Most agreed that the conditions in the Third World were not suitable for the establishment of so-called scientific socialism. Although socialism was still assumed to be the end point, a transitional phase was necessary first. The most conservative in the USSR estimated that the construction of capitalism and its maturation would take at least a century before Third World societies could hope to transition to socialism. Others, following Khrushchev's rise to power, argued that the process could be shortened if the direction of economic development in the Third World was steered toward a noncapitalist course. As the case of Soviet involvement in Ghana, Guinea, and Mali shows, this transitional noncapitalist stage was essentially "state capitalism."[17]

Although hazy, this formulation guided Soviet economic policymaking abroad during the Khrushchev era. The model deviated from Soviet-style communism in several significant ways, but it was still far from the type of capitalism sponsored by the West. The contest between these hybrid models was more complex than a simple Cold War between two ideal types of societies. At heart, however, it remained an economic Cold War between a vision founded on the state and one based on the market. In Moscow, they ended up calling their model of development for the Third World simply noncapitalist. In West Africa, as this book shows, it found one of its most fascinating and challenging applications.

On Agency

This is a book about the Soviet Union. The primary focus of the analysis is on the USSR, its vision of development for the Third World, and its attempt to construct it in West Africa. The newly independent states of Ghana, Guinea, and Mali were the coprotagonists of this project. Representing vibrant and complex societies, the governments of Ghana, Guinea, and Mali aspired not only to improve living standards at home but also had ambitious and multifaceted foreign policies. Their visions of modernity and development were based on a mix of politics, ideology, and economics as elaborate and fascinating as the Soviet one. This book presents the fullest possible picture of this complex entanglement of Soviet and West African ideas, hopes, projects, and failures. The book's central arguments, however, pertain to the USSR, its history, and its place in the world.

This is not an issue of giving or denying agency. As Walter Johnson argued, the whole discourse of framing historical analysis in terms of agency is fraught with contradictions.[18] In this case, Ghana, Guinea, and Mali were ambitious newly independent states in the early 1960s, whose foreign policies and push for economic development deserve dedicated studies, for which this book cannot be a substitute. Some such studies have already appeared, and more are on the way as more sources become available. The link between politics and economics in West Africa and the global Cold War is well established. Ghana, and Nkrumah especially, has received the most scholarly attention from this point of view. Waiting for a new history that takes full advantage of now-declassified primary sources, Willard Scott Thompson's 1969 study remains the most comprehensive general history of Ghana's foreign relations under Nkrumah.[19] Since the 2010s, a new generation of scholars started to explore independent Ghana's distinctive ideological posture, its pursuit of economic and social modernization and their legacy, and its fascinating blend of symbols of the past and ambitions for the future.[20] In particular, Nana Osei-Opare examined Soviet-Ghanaian relations in the first few years after independence, showing the extent to which Nkrumah and others in Accra feared a potentially neocolonial Soviet Union.[21]

Likewise, Mali has been the object of several studies that explored its path to independence, the troubled relationship between the search for development and the establishment of sovereignty, the evolution of science and technique, and the impact of modernization on culture and society.[22] On the contrary, Guinea has traditionally presented the biggest challenge to researchers due to the difficulty of obtaining primary sources. Elizabeth Schmidt is among the few historians who have investigated Guinea's path to independence in 1958. She showed that it was the local labor movement, shaped by its ties to international socialism, that made a clean break with France possible.[23] André Lewin's monumental biography of Sékou Touré is probably the most detailed general history of Guinea since the interwar era.[24] Using a combination of oral histories and case studies, Mike McGovern explored the construction of a new identity for Guineans under Sékou Touré and the legacies of this socialist experiment today.[25]

This book builds on these pioneering and pathbreaking studies, and it aims to further a dialogue between historiography on the USSR and on West Africa. It cannot, however, replace historical analysis focused specifically on Ghana, Guinea, and Mali.

North, South, East, West

The source base for this book is necessarily international. It is based on primary sources from archives, libraries, and private collections in France, Ghana, Mali,

Russia, the United Kingdom, and the United States. The aim is to cover the points of view of virtually all actors involved in the search for economic modernization in West Africa. This includes not only the governments of the USSR, Ghana, Guinea, and Mali but also leading economists who acted as consultants, international organizations, private businesses, and the governments of Britain, France, and the United States.

The Soviet Union was a complex actor in both domestic and international affairs. Soviet sources reflect this complexity. Numerous agencies, organizations, and bureaucracies, sometimes with overlapping competencies, participated in the decision-making process. The most basic division among them was between bodies that belonged to the Communist Party of the Soviet Union (CPSU) and agencies that were part of the standard state apparatus. Their respective remit was often all but clear, and membership frequently spanned both ends of the divide, but in general terms the CPSU dealt with the overall political and ideological direction of the country while the state carried out policy in practice. Documents produced by the Central Committee of the CPSU, itself divided into commissions and subcommittees, allow to gauge the general Soviet position toward the Third World and West Africa in particular. Further, reports and dispatches from the Ministry of Foreign Affairs, from the Ministry of Foreign Trade, and from the state agency that coordinated foreign aid activities make it possible to follow the evolution of development projects on the ground. Academic think tanks and research institutes, which occupied a liminal space between state and party, routinely acted as consultative bodies for both and often provided ex-post analyses of what went wrong. Their documents are equally important for this book.

As in the USSR, in Ghana, Guinea, and Mali ruling parties took over many of the functions traditionally associated with state bureaucracies. Luckily, at least some of the documents that both party and state agencies produced in West Africa are now available to researchers. The national archives of Ghana and Mali offer a unique window into one of the most formative decades for both countries. No historical work on West Africa after independence can disregard their rich collections. Minutes from parliamentary committees, reports from fact-finding missions, letters from powerful politicians all convey the sense of urgency that the search for development took and the fascination with the USSR. At the time of writing the holdings of the national archives of Guinea are still undergoing a lengthy cataloging process, made more challenging by a severe lack of resources. Though undoubtedly a significant issue, symbolically as well as methodologically, necessity dictates that Guinea be analyzed through documents from France, the USSR, and the rest of West Africa.

Britain and France, the former colonial powers, had dominated West Africa for more than a century. After most colonies obtained independence, their presence was still strong in the region. The governments in London and Paris kept a close eye on their former colonial subjects, especially the most rebellious ones. British and French diplomats, soldiers, spies, businessmen, consultants, and simple visitors observed what was going on in Ghana, Guinea, and Mali with great attention, particularly whenever the USSR was involved. Even though their uncertain finances did not allow Britain and France to launch development programs on a par with the Soviet or American ones, both former imperial powers had all the intention of retaining (or regaining) as much influence as possible in West Africa. The relative openness of British and French archives allows using this remarkable mass of information on Ghana, Guinea, and Mali, which helps to fill some of the gaps left by the patchiness of Soviet and West African records.

The United States was routinely described in Soviet diplomatic, military, and intelligence circles as "the main adversary" (*glavnyi protivnik*). In West Africa, Dwight Eisenhower's America was a somewhat reluctant adversary, at least as far as economic aid was concerned (John Kennedy changed this to an extent). Nevertheless, the United States' overwhelming military and economic power, coupled with its growing cultural capital throughout Africa, made it a strong presence everywhere in the region. Even though this presence was sometimes only imagined, for the Soviet Union the United States was the ideal benchmark against which to measure itself and its action. For its part, the US information apparatus—gigantic and resourceful, if occasionally distracted—looked at the USSR's flirtations with the radical leadership of Ghana, Guinea, and Mali with a mix of fear, scorn, and curiosity. Most of the products of this encounter are now available in the *Foreign Relations of the United States* series.

Besides bureaucracies, many individuals connected to the era of Soviet engagement in West Africa left memoirs and recollections. These include prominent political leaders from all sides, as well as economists, journalists, technicians, intelligence officers, and foreign observers who traveled to Ghana, Guinea, and Mali during the 1950s and 1960s. Rich in details and anecdotes but generally poor in analytical depth, these memoirs are used sparingly in this book. Collected speeches and interviews by Nkrumah, Sékou Touré, and Keïta are useful sources to explore their ideologies. Likewise, the memoirs of Khrushchev and other Soviet leaders can give useful insight into their worldview and the workings of the apparatuses they headed. Conversely, the memories of disaffected diplomats, vainglorious spies, haughty businessmen, and superficial journalists should not be given more credit than they deserve. As a rule, this book relies on archival documents. Memoirs serve to add color or texture.

Poor Numbers

A word of warning about the numbers and figures used in this book is necessary. Statistics about the Soviet Union are problematic, regardless of their source. Official Soviet statistics were notoriously unreliable. In a country where the state budget was long an impenetrable state secret, obtaining data themselves was challenging. Once data on the USSR's economy became more available—generally after 1956—problems remained. Besides the use of different methodologies and intellectual traditions in the generation of figures, the agencies tasked with producing Soviet numbers had little incentive to make them reliable. Every branch of the USSR's economy strived to show that it was fulfilling, or overfulfilling, its production quota in a planned system. The raw data that Soviet statisticians processed and aggregated were therefore misleading. Moreover, figures about the economy formed an important part of the Soviet Union's image abroad. The Soviet government had all the interest in showing the world that the USSR was a powerful and prosperous country, with an economy that grew at breakneck speed. Consequently, Soviet numbers grossly overestimated production, progress, and growth. Similarly, the USSR's enemies had an obvious interest in exaggerating Soviet economic prowess. The Central Intelligence Agency (CIA) dedicated ample efforts to measuring the Soviet economy. The CIA produced economic indicators that were more reliable than the USSR's own figures, but that still tended to overestimate everything. The assumption was that the Soviet Union was a dangerous and powerful threat for the United States, and that the American security apparatus consequently needed vast resources to counter it. Producing conservative numbers made little sense in this context.

Where are the real numbers, then? Sadly, they do not exist. However inaccurate, the official figures were the ones that Soviet planners themselves used. With the partial exception of the large military sector, there was no double bookkeeping between what was published and what was used internally. Does this make those awfully misleading numbers more real? Many Western and Russian historians and economists have produced different estimates of the Soviet Union's GDP and other indicators. Using more sophisticated methodology than their Soviet or CIA predecessors, these figures correct for latent inflation, revealing far less impressive numbers that look reassuringly conservative. However, measuring actual prices in the Soviet system is not an easy—and uncontroversial—matter. Different assumptions lead to a different set of figures. Which ones are the real ones? One may have to accept that the economy is also a product of the mind and that the value of numbers, figures, estimates, and debates about them depends in no small part on the eye of the beholder.[26]

The Soviet Union was certainly not the economic behemoth that official propaganda depicted, and that Western security agencies were more than happy to confirm. At the same time, it was also not an unmitigated economic disaster. Few would dispute that in the two decades between 1945 and 1965, the Soviet economy grew at relatively high rates. The USSR was visibly more prosperous in material terms in the mid-1950s and mid-1960s than it had been before the war. While the Soviet Union did not even come close to its stated goal of catching up and overtaking the West, Soviet economic growth captured the attention of intellectuals, politicians, and leaders in the postcolonial world. Many of them aspired to replicate Soviet growth in their countries, using similar instruments. They may have been misled by inaccurate figures and blatant propaganda. Perhaps, they were more interested in ideas than numbers. Chapters 1 and 2 deal with Soviet economic growth and its reception in the Third World in more detail.

The originality of the Soviet idea of development is a matter of debate. Was it an alternative to global capitalism, or was it simply derivative of it? This is one of the main questions in the book, albeit one that has no clear answer. As long as Khrushchev was in power, the Soviet leadership believed it was exporting a distinctive approach to modernization. Likewise, West African elites regarded cooperation with the USSR as qualitatively different from engagement with the West. Whether the Soviet model really was different, or whether everything was in the eye of the beholder, is not a matter this book can aim to solve.

In terms of methodology, the book refrains from making arguments based on numbers. When figures are used, this is usually to give the reader an idea of magnitude, intensity, or scope—purely descriptive in nature. In these cases, figures refer only to the specific context in which they were created. When the book makes comparisons over space or time using numbers, these are taken from the same source—usually from Angus Maddison's monumental statistical handbook.[27] Any such comparisons remain incredibly problematic and should be taken as a rough indication.

Outside the Box

The foci of this book are economic cooperation and the political exchanges that made it possible. By necessity, this leaves out some fascinating aspects from the analysis of Soviet interactions with Ghana, Guinea, and Mali. The cultural and gender politics of Soviet-West African cooperation are among the themes that could not be developed further in this book but which warrant additional study.

Culture, both high and low, was an important part of the USSR's engagement with the outside world. The tension between the Soviet government's anxiety that the USSR's culture was backward and its desire to present it to the rest of the world as better than other cultures has long been an object of academic study. Since the late 2000s, cultural exchanges between the Soviet Union and the Third World have become a major field of inquiry. At the time of writing, studies that address Soviet-African cultural cooperation are still relatively rare (with the exception of student exchanges, which have been explored in detail), but many more are on the way. Areas as disparate as Soviet radio, literary exchanges, the teaching of Russian as a foreign language, African literature and films in the USSR and vice versa, and relations between women's organizations in the Soviet Union and in Africa have been or will soon be explored in forthcoming articles and books. When discussing aspects of cultural cooperation, this book relies on this formidable and expanding body of knowledge.[28]

Gender is an equally complex theme. Although there is no space in this book to do justice to the construction of gender norms in Ghana, Guinea, and Mali after independence, or among the Soviet specialists who worked in and with West Africa at the time, these are intriguing and extremely important topics. Considerable effort went into remaking men and women both in the USSR and in West Africa at the time, which was often conceptualized as one of the elements necessary to achieve modernity. The focus of the book is on tangible aspects of development. This is a compromise, imperfect but necessary for reasons of space. Many excellent studies exploring the connection between gender and development have already appeared. More are on the way, including some that will focus specifically on the USSR and Africa.[29]

Quantitative gender imbalance is perhaps a less complicated issue to address. Most individuals discussed or mentioned in this book in connection to their role in Soviet relations with West Africa were male. This is hardly surprising given the patriarchal structure of virtually all societies discussed in the book. The analysis of economic cooperation and its diplomacy requires focusing on government-level exchanges. During the 1950s and 1960s, high politics and economic ministries were dominated by men to an even larger extent than they are today. Between 1954 and 1964, Khrushchev's Presidium—the top decision-making body in the USSR—counted between ten and fifteen members, of which only one was a woman, Ekaterina Furtseva, who also served as the USSR's minister of culture between 1960 and 1974. Furtseva was an exception rather than the rule. About 20 percent of CPSU members at the time were women, but only 3.3 percent were in the Central Committee (or about 5–6 women of almost 200 members in the Khrushchev era).[30] The Ministry of Foreign Affairs, the Ministry of Foreign Trade, and the aid agencies had more women working there, but they were routinely relegated to lower-ranking positions, and their career progression tended to be much slower than men's. There were a few prominent exceptions in the 1960s (albeit not in West Africa), but foreign policy and matters of economic and financial cooperation with the Third World were by and large masculine arenas in the Soviet Union.[31] As a consequence, most Soviet primary sources discussed in this book were authored by men. In this context, the Institute of Africa of the USSR's Academy of Sciences stood out. Though still in the minority, some of the Institute's women did occupy positions of relative power, and a couple of them even managed to travel to Africa—a relatively rare privilege for Soviet academic researchers at the time.[32]

Most of the Soviet personnel involved in development projects on the ground in West Africa were men. Some areas of cooperation, such as healthcare and education, tended to involve a larger proportion of Soviet women, for nursing, teaching, and interpreting were highly feminized professions in the Soviet Union. The book deals mostly with international cooperation that involved jobs and professions traditionally performed by men—planning, construction, trade, and finance. Yet the Soviet Union produced thousands of women agronomists, economists, engineers, and geologists each year. Why did so few of them end up in West Africa as specialists working on development projects? A thorough answer would require more research, but the generally patriarchal structure of the USSR certainly did not help. Traveling abroad, even on assignment working on a construction project in a remote region of West Africa, was a privilege in the Soviet Union. A posting abroad usually brought better remuneration, potential access to goods unavailable in the USSR, and simply the excitement of an experience far away from home. Soviet men were allowed these privileges more often than Soviet women. Moreover, work assignments abroad, especially in the Third World, were considered not free from risks and generally low on comfort. In a society that still predominantly regarded women as family-focused, this made postings to Ghana, Guinea, and Mali even less available to Soviet women in not especially feminized sectors of employment. Future studies that address these questions directly will be able to provide a more nuanced picture.

In terms of the number of women in government positions, the West did not fare much better than the Soviet Union in the 1950s and 1960s. This is reflected in the individuals discussed in this book and in the authorship of primary sources from Britain, France, and the United States that are cited. Neither the Eisenhower and Kennedy administrations in the United States nor Harold Macmillan's cabinet in Britain included any women. Charles de Gaulle's government in France was unusual in having a woman in a ministerial position—Nafissa Sid Cara, who acted as State Secretary for Social Questions in Algeria between 1959 and 1962. In general, despite big social changes in Western societies during the 1960s, women in areas such as foreign policy, intelligence, international economic co-operation, and journalism were rare. In the period examined in this book, there were no women in senior positions in the State Department, the Foreign Office, or the Quai d'Orsay working in or with Ghana, Guinea, Mali, and the USSR. Therefore, Western observers of Soviet engagement in West Africa were by and large male. In this, as in all other cases, the authorship of primary sources cited in this book reflects the strong gender imbalances of the time.[33]

In this context, West Africa presented more diversity. Keïta's first government in Mali was entirely male, but Aua Keïta—a leading militant for independence and later member of parliament—was a prominent woman in Bamako high politics. Both Nkrumah and Sékou Touré appointed women in their cabinets. Susanna Al-Hassan held various ministerial positions in Ghana between 1961 and 1966, and Loffo Camara became Guinea's minister for social affairs in 1961. Despite these prominent exceptions, women in executive, managerial, and leading administrative positions were still generally rare in Ghana, Guinea, and Mali, reflecting the structural imbalance in access to education and career opportunities in West Africa at the time. Nonetheless, the ruling political parties in Ghana, Guinea, and Mali had large, professionalized, and relatively well-funded women's organizations. Some were inherited from the days of anti-colonial organizing and had played an instrumental role in the fight for independence. Others were formed after independence and often followed the Soviet model. They were important players in the politics of the time and were the most obvious manifestation of the Accra, Conakry, and Bamako governments' will to create a "new" West African woman. In general, women's organizations were rarely involved in the most technical aspects of economic cooperation with the socialist bloc, which remained the prerogative of male-dominated government bodies. This is why they do not feature prominently in this book. However, contacts between Soviet and West African women organizations were frequent and deep, as Christine Varga-Harris shows.[34] New studies in this field will no doubt contribute to revealing even more the vibrancy of West African societies at the dawn of independence, including in gender relations.[35]

The Order of Things

The book is organized into six chapters, plus a conclusion. Chapter 1 looks at the Soviet Union in the mid-1950s, emerging from decades of Stalinism and ready to launch a series of political and economic reforms that captured the attention of many newly independent nations. Chapter 2 investigates the USSR's rediscovery of the Third World under Khrushchev, both in terms of theoretical speculation and practical engagement. Chapter 3 explores the path that led Ghana, Guinea, and Mali to become radical Third World states and the birth of the relationship with the Soviet Union. Chapter 4 analyzes the elaboration of a model of development for the region, looking at modernization projects in infrastructure, agriculture, and light industry. Chapter 5 deals with the implementation of the said model and, crucially, with everything that went wrong. Chapter 6 details the abandonment of the model and the USSR's disengagement from the region. Finally, the conclusion discusses the general themes of the book and offers some reflections on the long-term legacy of Soviet engagement with West Africa.

A FAREWELL TO ARMS

De-Stalinization, the Soviet Economy,
and the Global Cold War

In July 1954, the French photographer Henri Cartier-Bresson boarded a train headed from Paris to Moscow. He was the first Western photojournalist allowed to take pictures on the streets of the Soviet capital. Cartier-Bresson's *Magnum* colleague Robert Capa had been able to do something similar back in 1947, but since then the USSR had been all but closed to Western photographic eyes. Cartier-Bresson's trip signified that outsiders were interested in looking at the Soviet Union, and that the USSR was now less anxious about being looked at. This new confidence showed in Cartier-Bresson's photos. He captured the most obvious aspects of life in Moscow—the huge avenues, the gray buildings, the soldiers on parade. At the same time, Cartier-Bresson was captivated by the variety and diversity of people he encountered from all corners of the Union. He photographed shoppers in a department store, taxis waiting by a busy railway station, a young couple moving into a new apartment, women attending a fashion show, children playing in Gor'kii Park, and university students enjoying a break from their classes. The image of the Soviet Union one gets from Cartier-Bresson's pictures is that of a normal country, in which people lived, worked, and consumed like elsewhere. In the mid-1950s, the streets of Moscow and Leningrad were no doubt shabbier than those of New York, Paris, or London. However, the Soviet Union had reached a level of material comfort that was at least comparable to that of the advanced economies in the West.[1]

Cartier-Bresson was only one among many who were fascinated by the Soviet experiment. Observers from Asia, Africa, and Latin America had never stopped being interested in the USSR. A few years after Cartier-Bresson, Walter

Rodney arrived in the Soviet Union. At the time, he was still an undergraduate student at the University of the West Indies and had only just turned twenty years old. Rodney's visit to the USSR was brief but formative. It left a lasting impression on one of the most radical voices of the global Black liberation movement. Rodney was impressed by the level of economic development and cultural sophistication he saw in the USSR of the early 1960s. He idealized the fact that ordinary Soviet citizens took airplanes to travel across their vast country. The USSR had managed to transcend the airport as a quintessential "bourgeois institution." Books were available everywhere in the Soviet Union, including on the sidewalks, whereas in the United States one could only buy "hot dogs and hamburgers" on the streets. The Bol'shoi Theatre was affordable for ordinary Muscovites, unlike the West End theatres in London, which Rodney remembered being patronized only by the "upper classes." Many experiences contributed to making Rodney a radical and an activist, but the things he saw in the USSR in the 1960s "remained with me and still do."[2]

For Rodney, as for many others in the Third World, the USSR became an economic success story, despite a history of war, revolution, and social upheaval, with the potential to represent a model of development alternative to Western capitalism. This chapter explores the roots of the USSR's economic success and its reception abroad. It looks at the long-term trajectory of Soviet growth, which made it into a potential model for the outside world. It charts the changes at the top of Soviet politics that made the mid-1950s different from the past. Finally, it presents an overview of the individuals, institutions, and groups that drove Soviet engagement with the Third World in general and with Africa especially.

History's Locomotive

The economic prospects of the Russian Empire before the 1917 revolutions have long been the object of a lively and occasionally heated debate. The Bolsheviks were famously critical of the Russian Empire's backwardness (*otstalost'*). Lev Trotskii opened his *History of the Russian Revolution* with a sentence that left no doubts: "The fundamental and most stable feature of Russian history is the slow tempo of her development, with the economic backwardness, primitiveness of social forms and low level of culture resulting from it. . . . The conquest of nature went wide and not deep."[3] The others agreed. Lenin built much of his Marxist analysis on the notion that Russia had a pre-modern, backward type of capitalism.[4] Iosif Stalin was possibly even more extreme in his views on the matter. "One feature of the history of old Russia," he told Soviet industrial managers in 1931, was the continual beatings she suffered because of her backwardness. She was beaten by the Mongol khans. She was beaten by the Turkish beys. She was beaten by the Swedish feudal lords. She was beaten by the Polish and Lithuanian gentry. She was beaten by the British and French capitalists. She was beaten by the Japanese barons. All beat her because of her backwardness, military backwardness, cultural backwardness, political backwardness, industrial backwardness, agricultural backwardness.[5]

Modern historians tend to take a more nuanced approach to Russia's prerevolutionary economic history. Alec Nove opened his pioneering economic history of the USSR, writing that "the Russian Empire had reached a level of development which, though leaving it well behind the major industrialized Western powers, was none the less appreciable."[6] Nove credited the major reforms of the second half of the 1800s with boosting industrialization and literacy in the empire. Cliometric economic historians have pushed this argument even further. According to this view, the Russian Empire at the dawn of the twentieth century was about to begin a major economic take-off. It was the October Revolution and the establishment of the flawed Soviet system that prevented the empire from entering the club of Western-style democracy and fully developed capitalism. Predictably, this argument has caused great controversy among historians of different methodological persuasions.[7]

Overcoming the supposed backwardness of the Russian Empire was one of the main tasks that the Bolsheviks set for themselves upon obtaining power. The fight against *otstalost'* took many forms over the years. In principle, the Bolsheviks' success in late 1917 meant the abolition of private property and the nationalization of the means of production, in accordance with the most basic precepts of Marxism. In fact, the hardships of the revolution and a long Civil War led to the adoption of a more moderate approach in economics—*Novaia Ekonomicheskaia Politika* (New Economic Policy, NEP), which allowed for a mix of state control with market incentives. NEP was abandoned in the late 1920s in favor of virtually total state control over the economy. The first five-year plan, which specified the production goals and centrally allocated resources to all sectors of the Soviet economy, was launched in 1928. Stalin, by then in control of the Soviet Union, aimed to turn the country into a technologically advanced, modern industrialized economy in record time, and with little regard for human life. Agriculture was forcefully collectivized, and most resources were channeled toward the establishment and expansion of heavy industry. These policies wrought cataclysmic destruction on the Soviet people. Millions, perhaps tens of millions, lost their lives as a direct or indirect consequence of forced collectivization, incompetent or deliberately murderous allocation of resources, and draconian waves of repression that the Soviet system employed to maintain discipline and hunt for saboteurs, real or imagined. Despite the indescribable violence of Stalinism, and the staggering casualties, by the 1940s the Soviet economy was sufficiently industrialized to be able to resist the productive might of Nazi Germany. The USSR not only managed to defeat Germany but emerged from World War II as one of the two superpowers, supposedly rivaling the United States in political prestige, military might, and economic potential.[8]

The difference between the US and the Soviet economy in the second half of the 1940s was huge. GDP per capita in the United States, for example, was at the very least six times that of the USSR.[9] Nevertheless, the Soviet experiment in economics—the first socialist country with a fully planned economy—never failed to attract the attention and capture the interest of foreign observers since the early days of the Bolsheviks' rise to power. In his influential *How Europe Underdeveloped Africa*, Rodney was full of admiration for the Soviet economy. He argued that a society that had been ravaged by capitalism through colonialism could "resume its own independent development only if it proceeds to a level higher than that of the economy which had previously dominated it." That was what the USSR seemed to have achieved. "As far as the two biggest socialist states are concerned (the Soviet Union and China)—Rodney wrote—socialist development has already catapulted them beyond states such as Britain and France, which have been following the capitalist path for centuries." Africa should do the same: develop without capitalism following the Soviet and Chinese lead.[10]

Even before Rodney, many intellectuals and activists in what was still the colonial world wondered whether the trajectory of the Soviet economy was something their own countries, once liberated from imperial domination, could replicate. Dozens of communists from Africa, Asia, and Latin America traveled to the USSR to participate in the construction of the new socialist society and to see the experiment with their own eyes. George Padmore, who would later become one of the leading theorists of Pan-Africanism, was among them. Born in Trinidad (then a British colony), Padmore went on to study in the United States and joined the Communist Party there. In 1929, he traveled to Moscow and became one of the representatives of the international trade union movement within the Communist International (Comintern). Padmore left the USSR a couple of years later with mixed feelings about the country, its leadership, and its line in foreign policy. He remained convinced that the Soviet Union represented a model to overcome colonial exploitation and that "socialist planning 'sublimated' the political and economic differences of diverse communities, [and] could end racial chauvinism." However, the brutality of Stalinism and the

Comintern's ambivalent attitude toward the fight to liberate the colonies profoundly disappointed him.[11]

Padmore's disappointment was not unusual. This was representative of the early Soviet approach to the colonial world, which remained ambiguous at best as long as Stalin was in charge, even as decolonization began following World War II.

The Death of Stalin

Iosif Vissarionovich Dzhugashvili, better known as Stalin, died on March 5, 1953. The death of the man who more than anyone else had shaped Soviet domestic and foreign policy since the mid-1920s had a profound effect on all aspects of life in the USSR. Government and the direction of Soviet foreign policy were, of course, among them. The first issue that confronted Stalin's heirs was a basic one—who was to succeed him at the helm of the Soviet Union. This succession struggle was not just a clash of personality but also a struggle between different ways of understanding the Soviet Union, its economy, and its place in the world. The reformists Lavrentii Beriia and Georgii Malenkov advocated change at home and abroad, whereas the hardliner Viacheslav Molotov preferred not to deviate from the Stalinist tradition. In the end, it was the least well-known among Soviet leaders to succeed Stalin at the top of the USSR: Nikita Sergeevich Khrushchev, the head of the Communist Party apparatus.[12]

Born in a peasant family from a small town in Western Russia in 1894, Khrushchev found employment as a metal worker and miner in the Donbas region. Like Beriia and Malenkov, he joined the Bolsheviks during the Civil War. Uneducated and brusque, but intelligent and ruthless, Khrushchev did well in the Communist Party. He rose rapidly through party ranks, like many new recruits un-compromised with the old tsarist regime, and managed to win Stalin's favor all the way to his inner circle in the Presidium. Khrushchev's colleagues generally looked down on him. It was a miscalculation they lived to regret.[13]

Khrushchev managed to outsmart his rivals in the space of a few years. Beriia was executed in 1953. Malenkov was forced to resign in February 1955, and Khrushchev took from him the post first secretary of the Tsentral'nyi Komitet (TsK, the CPSU Central Committee), traditionally the most important position of leadership in the USSR. Marshal Nikolai Bulganin, an ally of Khrushchev who was previously minister of defense, became the Soviet premier. In June 1957, Malenkov, Molotov, and a few more conservative Soviet leaders attempted to oust Khrushchev in a coup. The plot backfired. Once again, Khrushchev outmaneuvered them, securing a majority in the CPSU Central Committee and expelling his rivals from the party. Following the defeat of the "Anti-Party group"—as the plotters became known—Khrushchev's leadership was consolidated. He could dedicate himself fully to implementing a bolder foreign policy and sweeping domestic reforms.[14]

Khrushchev was convinced that Stalin had badly mishandled foreign affairs, generating the standoff with the Western powers. As a result, the USSR suffered politically and also economically, because of the amount of resources directed to the defense sector. He also believed that it was possible, and that it was his duty, to change the direction of Soviet foreign policy, bringing about some sort of mutual understanding with the US government, as to guarantee peace and thence the possibility for the socialist countries to seek economic prosperity.[15]

This new approach culminated in the Twentieth Congress of the CPSU, in February 1956. The congress is most famous for Khrushchev's secret speech, in which the first secretary launched himself in a scathing denunciation of Stalin's faults and numerous crimes, both against individuals and against the Soviet Union as a whole. The speech, which was to be made known only to a select few attendees but was quickly leaked to the press, had a momentous effect not only on the politics and society of the USSR but of the entire socialist world. The Twentieth Congress represented the beginning of de-Stalinization, the process that aimed to do away with Stalin's ideas and methods in all aspects of Soviet life and gave birth to the so-called Thaw (*ottepel'*). Many political prisoners were released from the Gulag, the names of many of those killed during the purges of the 1930s were rehabilitated, and the whole repressive apparatus of the Soviet Union was scaled down a few notches. Moreover, the Thaw inaugurated a brief and contested period of relative opening in education, the arts, journalism, and social and cultural life in general.[16]

Profound as they were, these were not the only changes introduced with the Twentieth Congress. As well as denouncing Stalin, at the congress Khrushchev inaugurated a new course in foreign policy. In his report to the Central Committee, he introduced the notion of "peaceful coexistence" (*mirnoe sosushchest-vovanie*), which was to dominate the next decade of Soviet foreign relations. Peaceful coexistence meant "the rejection of the 'inevitability of global war' and of the violent revolutionary transition between the opposite social systems capitalism and socialism." As Margot Light wrote, Khrushchev could hardly claim originality for the development of peaceful coexistence, a concept formulated by Lenin. Indeed, in his report to the congress, the first secretary insisted that peaceful coexistence had been the line of conduct of Soviet foreign policy, and that this continued to be a fundamental principle for the USSR. Mutual understanding, and perhaps even cooperation in some areas, was supposed to replace hostility in the Soviet Union's relationship with the West.[17]

However, renouncing war did not mean renouncing ideological struggle. Khrushchev expressed this point clearly years later:

> We Communists, we Marxists-Leninists, believe that progress is on our side and victory will inevitably be ours. Yet the capitalists won't give an inch and still swear to fight to the bitter end. Therefore, how can we talk of peaceful coexistence with capitalist ideology? Peaceful coexistence among different systems of government is possible, but peaceful coexistence among different ideologies is not. It would be a betrayal of our Party's first principles to believe that there can be peaceful coexistence between Marxists-Leninist ideology on the one hand and bourgeois ideology on the other.[18]

William Hayter, the British ambassador to Moscow, put it in similar terms in a contemporary report to Prime Minister Harold Macmillan. "Neither of them [Khrushchev and Bulganin] are messianic or in hurry to establish world communism. They are intelligent enough to want international peace and to realize that a price must be paid for it. But fundamentally they remain convinced communists and believers in the necessity for world communism."[19]

Khrushchev hoped to expand socialism beyond the USSR and Eastern Europe using means other than war. The Third World would be an integral part of this new approach. When in India on an official visit in 1955, Khrushchev made his intentions clear: "Let us verify in practice whose system is better, . . . We say to the leaders of the capitalist states: let us compete without war." What he meant was to "demonstrate that Soviet policy stemmed from the noble principles of 'fraternal solidarity and internationalism,' in contrast with the colonial powers of the West."[20]

Khrushchev had confidence in socialism as an economic system. He believed that it was the best possible system to organize society and production, and that it had the potential to replace liberal capitalism. Khrushchev had great trust in the achievements of the Soviet Union, and he was convinced that these could be repeated in other countries. The USSR could act as a model and inspiration for the rest of the world.

> Over the years the Soviet Union has gained great prestige in the eyes of all people who fight for peace, progress, and liberation from colonialism. The goal of our foreign policy hasn't been to enrich our own state at the expense of other states; we have never believed in the exploitation of man by man, of state by state. On the contrary, both by our stated policies and by our deeds we have encouraged countries not only with our counsel and by the example we have set, but we have also given

them gratuitous material aid or sold them goods and equipment at reduced prices. Our foreign policy is rooted in our conviction that the
way pointed out to us by Lenin is the way of the future not only for the
Soviet Union, but for all countries and all peoples of the world.[21]

The new Soviet leader wanted to confront the West on a terrain where he
believed the USSR had better chances of prevailing. The point was not to defeat
the West on the battlefield, but in terms of living standards and technological
achievements. The Soviet Union was ready to compete with the capitalists in
terms of the kind of progress and modernity their respective social systems could
bring about. Khrushchev "counted on the ability of Soviet foreign policy to generate 'soft power': a reputation as a peace-loving country, friendly to small nations,
generous to friends, eager to set disputes with opponents."[22]

The historians Constantine Pleshakov and Vladislav Zubok accuse Khrushchev of suffering from what Lenin famously dubbed "leftist disease," which in
Khrushchev's case caused an emotional attachment toward Third World nationalists.[23] Khrushchev's romanticism was boosted by the atmosphere of the mid-1950s,
when a growing number of countries in Africa and Asia became independent and
were eager to break with the colonial past and push for accelerated economic development. As the next chapter shows, African and Asian leaders found much to
like in the Soviet experience of rapid modernization. Khrushchev was not the only
one to think that the USSR was a model the newly independent countries would
want to imitate.

Thawing the Economy

The idea of imitating the Soviet Union may appear surprising given the trajectory of the Soviet economy in the last decades of the twentieth century. In the
mid-1950s, however, things looked different. One of the main sources of international interest in the Soviet Union at the time was indeed its economy. When
Khrushchev came to power, the USSR was doing very well, and there were few
reasons to doubt that it would continue to do so in the future.

The Great Patriotic War to defeat Nazi Germany had wrought unprecedented
destruction on the Soviet Union. Human and material losses were staggering—
more than twenty-million deaths and one-quarter of the USSR's entire capital
stock destroyed by the war. Yet the Soviet productive model had not only with-
stood total war with a technologically superior enemy but also rebuilt the economy afterward. In 1956, at the time of the CPSU Twentieth Congress, the Soviet

Union had enjoyed a decade of uninterrupted growth at record rates. In aggregate terms, Soviet output was back at pre-war levels by 1950 and became significantly higher (by a good 20 percent or above, depending on different GDP estimates) in the mid-1950s. In the second half of the twentieth century, the Soviet Union managed to become a middle-income society. This was no small achievement for a country with vast resources, but whose first half of the century had been dominated by the destruction of the First World War and Civil War and by the horrors of Stalinism.[24]

Despite this progress, living standards in the Soviet Union lagged considerably behind those of most Western countries. The Stalinist model, which continued in the first decade or so of the postwar era, traditionally privileged heavy industry and, particularly, anything that had to do with the defense sector. In the 1950s, Soviet technology, especially in the military sector, seemed more competitive than ever before. In 1949, the USSR had tested its first atom bomb. In 1953, it tested its first H-bomb. Khrushchev was determined to alter this balance and focus more on raising living standards and improving conditions in the consumer side of the Soviet economy.

Already at the 1955 Presidium meeting that ousted Malenkov, Khrushchev embraced some of his rival's enthusiasm for economic reform. He harshly criticized Malenkov for questioning the primacy of heavy industry, necessary for the USSR's defense, but at the same time Khrushchev reassured his audience that the Soviet government cared about living standards: "One more question, about heavy and light industry. Of course, we also need printed cotton; we need boots, and other things. Some might say that, here they removed Malenkov and it means now, goodbye boots and other goods [laughter in the hall]." One moment later, Khrushchev added: "And here's the proof for you: The Plenum of the Party Central Committee just finished work on the questions of developing animal husbandry. What does that say about this? It's just that there are questions of the production of consumer items. What the consumer items are, they are meat, potatoes, bread, butter, and other articles."[25]

To deliver this new vision to Soviet citizens, Khrushchev focused primarily on improving Soviet agriculture, removing some of the bottlenecks, and easing the restrictions of the Stalin era. Shortly after Stalin's death, the procurement prices for agricultural products (the price at which the Soviet state bought agricultural commodities from collective and state farms) were increased. Moreover, compulsory deliveries from private plots (small allotments that Soviet farmers could plow autonomously from collective agriculture to obtain extra food, extra income by selling their products, or both) to the state were reduced significantly. The remuneration of agricultural workers was also generally increased. These measures improved the incentives to produce more in the agricultural sector, which in the USSR had been traditionally exploited to transfer resources to industry, making the output of Soviet farms generally higher.[26]

To boost agricultural production further, Khrushchev resorted to some notorious schemes. His conviction that growing corn (*kukuruza*) was the key to plenty is often mocked, given the obsessive force with which Khrushchev embraced it and the mixed results it generated. Aaron Hale-Dorrell called it a "crusade" for corn, which involved virtually all levels of Soviet society.[27] In addition, the first secretary was a firm believer in the necessity to adopt new technologies in agriculture and to expand arable land in the Soviet Union. Khrushchev's most famous (and controversial) pet project was probably the "Virgin Lands" campaign that started in 1954. The idea was simple: claiming large swathes of uncultivated land (*tselina*) in Western Siberia and Northern Kazakhstan to make them fertile. Tractors, modern irrigation techniques, chemical fertilizers (another obsession of Khrushchev), and the enthusiasm of Soviet youth coopted to cultivate the virgin lands were expected to boost agricultural production in the USSR. For the first few years, Khrushchev's idea seemed to work. Between 1954 and 1959, Soviet agricultural output was generally good, and the Virgin Lands yielded record harvests in 1954, 1956, and 1958.[28]

The introduction of new technology and techniques was not limited to agriculture. The expectation that innovation in both things and ideas would improve the lives of Soviet citizens was widespread after Stalin's death. This had a profound effect on the ways in which the USSR understood itself and related to other societies. In the early Khrushchev era, the realm of Cold War competition was extended to new areas. The traditional Soviet preoccupation to catch up and overtake (*dognat' i peregnat'*) the West no longer applied only to steel production, chemical fertilizers, and nuclear weapons. Guaranteeing Soviet citizens a standard of living comparable to that of Westerners became a priority for the USSR and one of the benchmarks with which to measure its success in the Cold War. Khrushchev's heated debate with Richard Nixon about the merits of a model kitchen at the opening of the 1959 American National Exhibition in Moscow captured this moment. To win the Cold War, the kitchen now mattered just as much as (and perhaps even more than) the battlefield.[29]

This is not to say that more traditional military-related technology was neglected. Missile technology, in particular, made significant progress during the 1950s, leading to the development of the first Inter-Continental Ballistic Missile in the USSR. Progress in this field allowed the Soviet Union to achieve some spectacular successes in the so-called Space Race. In October 1957, the USSR became the first country to launch an artificial satellite into space—the *Sputnik*, which orbited around the earth for a couple of months. A few years later, in 1961, the Soviet cosmonaut Iurii Gagarin became the first human to travel into space, followed by Valentina Tereshkova—the first woman in space—in 1963.[30]

These exploits caused consternation, incredulity and even soul-searching in most Western capitals. The US president Dwight D. Eisenhower was not the only one to fear—mistakenly—that the USSR was ahead of the West in science and technology.[31] On the contrary, the same Soviet successes generated awe and admiration in Africa, Asia, and Latin America. Tobias Rupprecht wrote that "newspapers from the Rio Grande to Tierra del Fuego and from Chile to the Caribbean led with reports of the space program" following the *Sputnik* flight.[32] In Southern Africa, "thousands in Bulawayo, Salisbury [Rhodesia] and elsewhere were reported to have 'tried to catch a glimpse' of the satellite, many of whom 'were disappointed.'"[33] In Ghana, which had become independent only a few months before, the poet Geormbeeyi Adali-Mortty pointed at the *Sputnik* as an example of what the country's education system should aspire to. About a year later, the Soviet ambassador Mikhail Sytenko reported that the "launch of the Soviet cosmic rockets" generated a "significant growth of interest in the Soviet Union" among Ghanaians.[34]

Space mattered, but it was things closer to earth that really captured the imagination of the first postcolonial leadership in West Africa. During the Khrushchev era, the Soviet government launched ambitious infrastructure projects. Large dams, in particular, came to define the age. In 1954, the Presidium approved the construction of the Bratsk dam on the River Angara in Eastern Siberia. Bratsk, celebrated in Evgenii Evtushenko's eponymous poem, was a colossal project.[35] More than three kilometers long, more than one hundred meters tall, and with a reservoir of more than 5,000 square kilometers, the dam was the largest one of its kind when fully completed in 1966. For about a decade, the hydroelectric power station connected to the Bratsk dam was the largest producer of electricity in the world.[36] A few years later, in 1961, the Soviet government initiated the construction of the Nurek dam on the River Vakhsh in Soviet Tajikistan. As ambitious as Bratsk, and located in an even more challenging environment, the Nurek project was conceived as a model to guide development efforts in what was then the USSR's poorest republic, but also in the postcolonial world.[37] Official delegations and individual visitors to the Soviet Union from Asia, Africa, and Latin America were routinely taken to tour the dams. They did not fail to impress. A Malian delegation who visited Bratsk in 1964 reported back to Bamako that "everywhere, the Soviets are taming nature. So far considered a region of steppe and tundra, Siberia will become a very important industrial center thanks to the Bratsk hydro-electric power station, the largest one in the world, built on the River Angara in the Irkutsk area."[38]

The same dream of taming nature ("deep," as Trotskii put it three decades earlier) and building material progress in regions often considered wild and backward would soon dominate the push for development in West Africa too.

Who, What, Where

While Khrushchev and his colleagues in the Presidium were interested in issues of development assistance and certainly determined its general direction, many Soviet agencies and institutions dealt with equally crucial aspects. Both party and state organizations gathered information, prepared plans and projects, discussed them with foreign diplomats and technicians, physically carried out development work on the ground, and reported back to the Soviet leadership in Moscow. In each of these passages they could shape the terms of the debate, advise on implementation, and often even decide the fate of a project. Each organization had its own culture, network of alliances and rivalries, and budget. Most were interested in boosting their power and resources. Often, they were just as interested in reducing those of their institutional competitors.

The Presidium of the Central Commission of the Communist Party of the Soviet Union, known as Politburo before 1952 and after 1966, was the highest governing body of the CPSU, and therefore of the whole Soviet system. The Presidium was the most important authority of Soviet political life. Every important question was discussed at the Presidium level, which took the most crucial decisions in domestic as well as foreign policy. A CPSU Central Committee member became a Presidium member through a vote by the existing Presidium members. Since the Presidium was technically part of the Central Committee, its head was the first secretary of the TsK. The first secretary was, since Stalin's times, the most powerful Soviet leader. Khrushchev occupied the post of first secretary of the CPSU Central Committee from September 1953 until October 1964. The number of Soviet leaders who were members of the Presidium was not constant. During the Khrushchev era there were approximately fifteen members, divided into full members—who enjoyed voting rights—and candidate members—who participated in the discussions but could not vote. All the most prominent Soviet leaders were part of the Presidium.[39]

Despite what they would later claim, the Presidium leadership was generally supportive of Khrushchev's policies, especially after 1957. Anastas Mikoian was especially involved in opening up to the Third World and the provision of economic aid. Born in Armenia, then part of the Russian Empire, at the end of the nineteenth century, Mikoian joined the Bolsheviks a couple of years before the 1917 Revolution, making him an Old Bolshevik. A strong supporter of Stalin during the 1920s and 1930s, he had no hesitations about becoming a close Khrushchev ally. Mikoian was generally interested in foreign relations, and he was a strong believer in supporting national liberation movements and newly independent countries in the Third World. He traveled to Africa, Asia, and Latin America relatively often (by Soviet standards). The Presidium relied on him to establish or consolidate contacts with new potential allies and to solve diplomatic crises. Khrushchev held his opinion in these matters in high regard. This did not prevent Mikoian from supporting Khrushchev's enemies in the 1964 coup that removed him from power. It brought him little good; in 1965, Mikoian was forced to resign and lived the rest of his life far from politics.[40]

Directly under the Presidium and the Central Committee in the CPSU hierarchy was a plethora of party committees, subcommittees, commissions, and sometimes ill-defined groupings, responsible for a particular area of Soviet policy. The International Department of the Central Committee (Mezhdunarodnyi Otdel TsK KPSS, MO) was by far the most important for foreign policy and especially relations with the Third World. A direct heir of the Comintern, the International Department's task was to manage day-to-day relations with other communist parties. After the 1956 turmoil in Poland and Hungary, the Presidium decided to split it up in two. One branch, headed by Iurii Andropov, was responsible for coordination with ruling communist parties (mostly in Eastern Europe), while the other looked after relations with nonruling communists and movements worldwide. In particular, foreign economic aid "was largely to be supervised through the I[nternational] D[epartment], which was given responsibility for liaison with National Liberation Movements around the world."[41]

The International Department was headed by Boris Ponomarev, a long-serving Cominform (the organization that succeeded the Comintern after World War II) official and a protégé of Mikhail Suslov, a senior Presidium member. Ponomarev was an influential figure in Moscow. His organization often determined the agenda of meetings, and Suslov often acted as the "voice" of the International Department in the Presidium. Ponomarev himself arguably "wielded greater practical policy influence than some full Politburo members from outside Moscow."[42]

The MO was a relatively large organization, with a permanent staff of about 150 people in the Khrushchev era. It was organized geographically and consisted of many desks, headed by a deputy head, each dealing with a specific area of the world. Rostislav Ul'ianovskii headed the division that worked on sub-Saharan Africa ("black Africa" in Soviet parlance). Both Ponomarev and Ul'ianovskii were instrumental in the definition and consolidation of the Soviet approach to the Third World and specifically to economic development. Karen Brutents, whose memoirs provide useful information on the MO and its people, started working for the Africa desk in these years.[43]

The Soviet agency that more than any other was responsible for shaping the Soviet vision of economic development abroad was Gosudarsvennyi komitet po vneshnim ekonomicheskim sviaziam (State Committee for Foreign Economic Relations; GKES). GKES was created in 1955 in response to the USSR's growing involvement in providing economic aid to India. As the name suggests, the new organization was a state one rather than a party one, under the authority of the USSR's Council of Ministers. However, GKES relied on personnel and consultants who came from all sides of Soviet politics—the CPSU, but also ministries and academic research institutes.[44]

GKES was active at all stages of thinking, planning, and implementing development. GKES specialists tended to have a technical background—economists, engineers, and agronomists. They were usually the first to travel to a country that could become a new economic partner to study the situation on the ground, evaluate resources and needs, and formulate a proposal with concrete projects that the Soviet government could sponsor and supervise. Once the Kremlin leadership approved the projects, it was normally GKES that negotiated the terms of the agreement with the partner government, including the exact quantities of materials needed, the cost and extent of Soviet supervision, and often the management of the completed project too. It was GKES that elaborated, reelaborated, and exported the practicalities of the Soviet vision of economic development under Khrushchev.

For most of the Khrushchev and Brezhnev era, the head of GKES was Semën Skachkov. A mechanical engineer by training, Skachkov had worked in both metallurgical factories and agricultural management before landing at GKES in 1958. The technocratic, can-do, ethos of GKES—believers in machines and fertilizers more than economic theory—certainly owed something to the background of its chairman, who remained in his post until the early 1980s. Besides Skachkov, the individual who most notably shaped the Soviet response to West Africa's development needs was Dmitrii Degtiar'. An influential GKES official since 1957, Degtiar' (born in 1904) belonged to the relatively new professional figure of planners. Following his training at the Moscow Planning Institute, he worked as a planner for the Russian Soviet Republic for nearly two decades. He became deputy head of GKES in 1960. Degtiar' traveled to West Africa more often than any other Soviet leader, and met with counterparts in Ghana, Guinea, and Mali frequently. He invested his personal prestige trying to make economic cooperation work, to the point that he was made Soviet ambassador to Guinea in 1962.[45]

Parallel to GKES, which focused on cooperation and aid, a different state organization supervised the other crucial dimension of Soviet engagement with West Africa—trade. The Ministry of Foreign Trade (Ministerstvo Vneshnei Torgovli, MVT) was created in 1953, when responsibility for domestic and foreign exchanges in the USSR was handed over to two separate institutions. The MVT managed everything that had to do with commercial exchanges that involved foreign governments or businesses. Given the planned nature of the Soviet economy, the MVT mostly operated in terms of exchanges of goods and commodities with other goods and commodities that came from abroad. This involved negotiating trade agreements, evaluating unit prices, assessing the quantities to be exchanged, and coordinating the logistics. Nikolai Patolichev was the minister of foreign trade from 1958 until 1985. A long-serving CPSU member with a technical education and a long stint in the military, Patolichev was perhaps less influential in shaping the Soviet approach to economic development than some of his colleagues. However, he was an active minister, who met frequently with representatives from the Third World, including from West Africa, to negotiate treaties and agreements.[46]

Last, and possibly least, was the Ministry of Foreign Affairs (Ministerstvo Inostrannykh Del, MID). Housed in the distinctive Stalinist "skyscraper" on Smolenskaia Ploshchad' in central Moscow, MID was probably more interesting from the outside than from the inside. On the surface, it operated like any other ministry of foreign affairs. Its core task was maintaining diplomatic relations with other states, socialist and nonsocialist. MID was responsible for over one hundred embassies and consulates worldwide, plus analytical departments in Moscow, each dedicated to a specific country or region. Despite its size, MID had relatively little say in the USSR's foreign policy, which was traditionally the remit of the top CPSU leadership. Much depended on the status and personal prestige of the minister. Someone with a permanent post in the Presidium/Politburo could make MID's voice heard, sometimes directly with the first or general secretary of the CPSU. Nevertheless, this tended to reflect more individual preferences than an institutional take on foreign policy. In many ways, MID functioned more like a giant information-gathering machine than an executive body.

For most of Soviet history, the post of minister of foreign affairs was occupied by prominent personalities. During the Khrushchev era, Molotov, Dmitrii Shepilov, and Andrei Gromyko succeeded one another at the helm of MID. Molotov and Khrushchev disagreed widely on many things, including the conduct of the USSR's foreign policy. Molotov resented Khrushchev's policy of peaceful coexistence and was ambivalent on the opportunity of an alliance with nationalist, but not communist, leaders in the Third World. Khrushchev had little time for Molotov's conservatism.[47] He lost his post of foreign minister in 1956 and, after the failed Anti-Party coup in 1957, Molotov's influence in the Kremlin waned.

Molotov's successor, Shepilov, represented a major change for MID. Much younger than his predecessor, Shepilov used to be the editor-in-chief of *Pravda* and enjoyed a good personal relationship with Khrushchev. He accompanied the first secretary on delicate state visits to China in 1954 and to Yugoslavia in 1955. Later in 1955, Shepilov traveled to Cairo to meet with Gamal Abdel Nasser and help negotiate an arms deal between Egypt and the Soviet Union. He shared Khrushchev's interest in the Third World and was a supporter of the new policy of opening up toward Asia, Africa, and Latin America. Referring to the new agreement with Egypt, Shepilov thought that "we had a genuine interest. We really wanted to help Egypt. I proved to Khrushchev, and he had faith in this, that this help would be to our advantage. And Nasser, when he came to visit us, confirmed it."[48] The idyll did not last long. In June 1957, Shepilov joined the Anti-Party plotters, unwittingly causing his dismissal from MID and the end of his political career.

He was succeeded by Gromyko, who was a career diplomat. Among the first recruits to enter the new MID after the purges of the late 1930s, Gromyko's area of expertise was relations with the capitalist world, and especially with the United States and Britain. He had served as ambassador to Washington, London, and the United Nations. The West remained Gromyko's primary interest throughout his long career in Soviet politics. He was personally skeptical of the possibility of exporting some form of socialism to the Third World. He regarded countries in Africa, Asia, and Latin America as too backward and excessively economically dependent on the West for the USSR to be able to establish meaningful cooperative relations with them.[49] Anatolii Dobrynin, a high-flying Soviet diplomat who served as ambassador to the United States for two decades, remembered that: "The Third World was not his [Gromyko's] prime domain. He believed that events there could not decisively influence our fundamental relations with the United States; . . . More than that, our Foreign Ministry traditionally was not really involved with the leaders of the liberation movements in the Third World, who were dealt with through the International Department of the party, headed by Secretary Ponomarev. He despised Gromyko; the feeling was mutual."[50]

Regardless of his personal convictions, Gromyko did not have much power to interfere with Khrushchev's plans. Although respected by the top Soviet leadership, he did not become a Presidium member until 1973. Under Gromyko's tenure, MID interpreted its role conservatively. Embassies and delegations met with foreign representatives, kept an eye on current developments, and reported everything back to Moscow. On Smolenskaia ploshchad', the analytical departments carried out little analysis. MID's approach to reporting was factual and contained little contribution from whoever authored the documents. Risk-aversion was the rule. MID reports rarely gave an indication of whether a certain policy would be convenient or risky for the Soviet government. This was usually framed in such a way that MID could never be blamed for whatever happened afterward. It worked: Gromyko remained in his post of Foreign Minister for nearly thirty years, until Mikhail Gorbachev fired him in 1985.

Outside of the traditional policy-making agencies in the CPSU and the Soviet state, there were research institutes and think-tanks that participated in shaping the USSR's novel approach to the outside world. Stalin's death in 1953, and the abandonment of some of his most restrictive ideas, allowed the establishment, reestablishment, and revamp of many academic and research bodies dedicated to the study of international politics and economics. Formally, they were disconnected from either party or state. They could be self-standing bodies, such as the Institut Mirovoi Ekonomiki i Mezhdunarodnykh Otnoshenii (Institute of World Economy and International Relations, IMEMO). More often, the new institutes of the mid-1950s tended to be under the umbrella of the Soviet Academy of Sciences (Akademiia Nauk SSSR, AN), each dedicated to the study of a specific region of the world. In theory, their work was purely academic. In reality, both IMEMO and the area studies institutes actively participated in conversations and debates on the direction of Soviet policy toward their area of competence. The institutes were often asked to prepare background materials on regional political or economic trends, particular countries with which the Soviet government was conducting negotiations, and sometimes even on specific political or intellectual leaders. Moreover, the doors between the academic institutes and the party/state apparatus were revolving ones. It was not unusual for a party official to become the head of one of the academic institutes and, vice versa, for an academic to serve in some capacity in the International Department of the CPU or in a ministry that dealt with foreign relations.

For obvious reasons, the Institute of Africa (Institut Afriki) contributed the most to Soviet engagement with West Africa. Created in 1959, the institute was a novelty. The study of Africa was not a particular strength of Soviet, and previously Imperial, academia. The institute could not rely on a preexisting tradition, let alone resources. The director of the Institute of Africa was Ivan I. Potekhin. He was previously the deputy director of the Academy of Sciences' Institute of Ethnography and coordinated the small group of Africanists within the Institute of Oriental Studies (Institut Vostokovedeniia). A Siberian from Krasnoiarsk, Potekhin was a product of the 1930s. Born in a peasant family, he was selected to pursue higher education first in Leningrad, at the so-called Eastern Institute, and later at the University of the Toilers of the East in Moscow, the Comintern school for foreign communists. His area of specialism was the history of African liberation movements in the British colonies. In 1957, Potekhin became the first-ever Soviet scholar to visit sub-Saharan Africa, traveling to newly independent Ghana to conduct research and meet with government officials.[51]

The institute's task was to improve the USSR's knowledge and understanding of Africa through academic research. This officially included participating in propaganda efforts and producing books and brochures to facilitate mutual understanding between Africa and the Soviet Union. Expertise focused mostly on history and the social sciences. At the moment of its establishment in October 1959, the Institute of Africa had seventy-two people. Two had the title of *doktor nauk* (roughly equivalent to full professor)—Potekhin and Irina Iastrebova, who worked on Southern Africa. Besides five *kandidaty nauk* (postdoctoral researchers) and a few admin staff, the bulk of the institute was made up of *aspiranty* (doctoral researchers) and graduate students. Few had received any specific training in African matters, fewer spoke a language other than English or French and, except for Potekhin, none had been to Africa.[52]

Despite virtually no expertise and limited material resources, the Institute of Africa set out on the task of providing knowledge and context to the Soviet government. For better or worse, the institute was the best existing cluster of knowledge about Africa in the USSR, and it embodied the aspiration to train a new generation of Africanists for a new era of engagement with African nations and peoples. Especially in the early days of Soviet opening to West Africa, the institute was very involved in defining Soviet objectives in Ghana, Guinea, and Mali. Potekhin was considered one of the few reliable experts on the region, and his opinion mattered to the International Department, GKES, and MID. He and other researchers at the institute were frequent participants in conferences and debates organized by party or state bodies to evaluate Soviet policy. Moreover, people like Degtiar' and Patolichev occasionally took part in events organized by the institute, bringing the perspective of operative agencies on the ground. Alas, the possibility of carrying out fieldwork in Africa remained an impossible dream for all but the luckiest of the institute's researchers.

In July 1957 Godfrey Meynell, a Cambridge undergraduate from a well-to-do British family traveled to Moscow to take part in the Sixth World Festival of Youth and Students. The festival was a major event. With more than 30,000 participants from 130 countries, it was meant to showcase the USSR to the world. The Khrushchev leadership aimed to project a new, friendlier image of the Soviet Union, able to win over the world's youth.[53]

Meynell's time in Moscow was however unpleasant. Like most other participants in the youth festival, he engaged in numerous discussions and debates with his peers, both formal and informal. As he recalled in an article for the magazine *Time and Tide*, Meynell was surprised by the vehemence of the anticolonial sentiment he found in Moscow. The scion of a family whose male members had traditionally served in the British Army in India, he was shocked and alarmed that his peers from former British colonies did not have much time for Britain's imperial legacy. Used to thinking of his empire as a benign builder of railways and civilizer of peoples, Meynell was not prepared for what awaited him in Moscow. Spurred and supported by their Soviet hosts, young Africans, Arabs, and Indians rebuffed with open hostility his attempts at defending Britain's record in the colonies. "The Russians—he concluded—were hugely successful."[54]

Meynell and many of his conservative readers in Britain were no doubt wondering whether a much-feared alliance of Soviet communism with anticolonial thinking had finally materialized. The USSR was indeed about to give them much to worry about. The Soviet Union of the mid-1950s was a confident country. A new, bold, political leadership, sweeping reforms, and remarkable economic results and technological exploits made the USSR willing to jump into the cauldron of decolonization, anti-imperialism and—above all—the search for development in the former colonies. They found many attentive listeners in Asia and especially Africa.

BRAVE NEW WORLD

The Soviet Union and the Making
of the Third World

The years between Stalin's death in March 1953 and Khrushchev's consecration as
top Soviet leader in June 1957 were formative for the USSR's foreign policy. Initially drawn toward the Third World more by hazy ideas of anti-imperialism and
vague plans of cooperation than by a fully thought-out strategy, the Soviet government progressively came to understand what common ground it shared with the
postcolonial world. Economics was the key. The Soviet Union's economic success
at home generated interest abroad. The feeling of attraction in the newly independent countries of Africa and Asia for the Soviet economy and for socialist development was undeniable. Leaders of different countries, including Nehru in India,
Nasser in Egypt, and Sukarno in Indonesia, looked at the USSR attracted by the
combination of central state planning and collective enterprise that had allowed
the Soviet Union to turn into an industrialized country. The Soviet economy appeared to the leadership of colonized people seeking independence as a concrete,
feasible alternative to liberal capitalism. Like prerevolutionary Russia, in Third
World countries a large proportion of the population was employed in agriculture,
capital was scarce, and rapid industrialization was the prime aspiration for political as much as economic reasons. Therefore, the USSR's experience of economic
development—centered on a forced march to modernization through rapid industrialization, import substitution, and rejection of Western imperialism (at least in
official rhetoric)—greatly appealed to Third World countries. Once the Kremlin
embraced the notion that the Soviet economy was its best asset to win friends in
Africa and Asia, economic cooperation and development aid dominated the
USSR's foreign policy toward the Third World for the next decade.

The Discreet Charm of the Bourgeoisie

"I share not the opinion of those who believe in a golden age of Hindostan," Karl Marx wrote in the *New-York Daily Tribune* in June 1853.[1] "There cannot, however, remain any doubt"—Marx continued—"but that the misery inflicted by the British on Hindostan is of an essentially different and infinitely more intensive kind than all Hindostan had to suffer before." India, "an Italy of Asiatic dimensions" according to Marx, was not new to invasions, revolutions and foreign despots motivated by greed only. However, British colonialism was different. "England has broken down the entire framework of Indian society, without any symptoms of reconstitution yet appearing." By neglecting traditional agriculture and forcing British-made industrial textiles into the Indian market, the British had destroyed the long-established local economic and civic institutions, epitomized in Marx's view by the village, ancient and immutable in both power relations and production techniques. British rule was the beginning of a revolution. Marx wrote: "English interference having placed the spinner in Lancashire and the weaver in Bengal, or sweeping away both Hindoo spinner and weaver, dissolved these small semi-barbarian, semi-civilized communities, by blowing up their economical basis, and thus produced the greatest, and to speak the truth, the only social revolution ever heard of in Asia."[2]

The village communities, "the solid foundation of Oriental despotism," were the root of what Marx regarded as India's structural plight. They fostered an "undignified, stagnatory, and vegetative life," in which humankind was enslaved by superstition, fear, and the brutal authority of the ruling castes. In the Indian village, "man, the sovereign of nature, fell down on his knees in adoration of Kanuman, the monkey, and Sabbala, the cow."[3] By destroying these old social structures, Britain was nothing but "the unconscious tool of history," planting through steam, guns, and the free market the seeds of future capitalist development and eventually of revolution and socialism.

Marx's vision of economic development was schematic. His theory of the "stages of history" (a theory of economic development) stipulated that primitive "slave societies" would be replaced by "feudalism"—roughly the stage in which Marx believed India was in 1853—and then by capitalism, following a bourgeois revolution led by owners and merchants. In turn, capitalism would be swept away by the proletarian revolution, the first step of the inexorable advance toward communism. Human ingenuity guaranteed a steady improvement in the technology of production from one stage to the next, to which corresponded a higher degree of class consciousness and therefore revolutionary potential in the masses. Under capitalism, society would reach the highest level of capital productivity.

As the capitalists' rate of profit would inevitably start to decline, generating conflict and instability, the road to revolution would open.[4]

The progression from one stage to the next was rigid. All the steps needed to be reached and then overcome before communism could be established. India, still a feudal society dominated by traditional beliefs, had no chance of advancing to communism in the mid-1850s. In Marx's view, the traditional order restrained human ingenuity, forcing it to bow to monkeys and cows, and shackled India's productive potential. Before a proletarian revolution could become thinkable, India needed to reach capitalism first. The same was true for every other colony. Before the specter of communism could begin haunting Africa and Asia, the steam engine and the stock exchange needed to take hold. Therefore, however ugly, Western colonialism was convenient inasmuch as it facilitated the passage from feudalism to capitalism.

Marx's disciples from the Russian Empire deviated widely from his vision. Lenin's understanding of the stages of history was much more flexible than Marx's, not least because the Bolshevik revolution he had helped to inspire took place in a society that fell short of that advanced capitalist economy Marx viewed as an essential prerequisite for the proletarian revolution. In his *Imperialism, the Highest Stage of Capitalism*, Lenin argued that capitalism's constant need for new markets overseas was accelerating its demise through international conflict, offering radical new prospects for the liberation of the "peoples of the East."[5] In 1920, speaking at the Second Comintern Congress (the Communist International that had been resurrected by the Soviet government in 1919), Lenin declared that "we, as communists, must and will support the bourgeois liberation movements in the colonial countries only when these movements are actively revolutionary, when their representatives will not prevent us from educating and organizing in the revolutionary spirit the peasantry and the vast masses of the exploited."[6] Lenin was convinced that the communists' superior organization would allow them to replace the nationalists in power and fulfill the transition to socialism. Recent events in the Soviet Union offered the best proof. Lenin compared the situation of the European colonies to that of Turkestan (the collective name given to the Central Asian provinces of the Russian Empire). Both were preindustrial societies, at first sight unsuitable for communism and lacking a working class. However, as the experience of Russian communists who operated in Central Asia showed, a dedicated vanguard could instill the revolutionary spirit even in a precapitalist society, as had happened in Turkestan according to Lenin.[7] The road toward an alliance between the communist and national-liberation movements, which Marx rejected, had been opened.

Lev Trotskii went further. In a 1938 conversation with the Argentinian trade-unionist Mateo Fossa, Trotskii answered a question on Latin America evoking an imaginary war between Britain, the Western imperialist state par excellence, and Brazil, a developing economy run by a nationalist regime.

> In Brazil there now reigns a semi-fascist regime that every revolutionary can only view with hatred. Let us assume, however, that on the morrow England enters into a military conflict with Brazil. I ask you on whose side of the conflict will the working class be? I will answer for myself personally—in this case I will be on the side of "fascist" Brazil against "democratic" Great Britain. Why? Because in the conflict between them it will not be a question of democracy or fascism. If England should be victorious, she will put another fascist in Rio de Janeiro and will place double chains on Brazil. If Brazil on the contrary should be victorious, it will give a mighty impulse to national and democratic consciousness of the country and will lead to the overthrow of the Vargas dictatorship. The defeat of England will at the same time deliver a blow to British imperialism and will give an impulse to the revolutionary movement of the British proletariat.[8]

Trotskii almost reversed Marx's theory. In his view, the revolution, rather than depending on a high level of economic development to be possible, could begin from the underdeveloped periphery, and then spread to the core of the imperialist system. A good revolutionary would support whoever was fighting the imperialists, pace the stages of development. Trotskii's idea of the revolution was global in nature.

Alas, neither Lenin nor Trotskii had much chance to influence Soviet foreign policy. Lenin died in 1924, and Trotskii was already living in exile in Mexico by the time he exposed his views on Brazil and Britain to Fossa. Stalin, who succeeded Lenin and banned Trotskii, had little interest in the Third World and in revolutionary experiments. For the three decades Stalin was in power, Marx's original vision informed Moscow's relations with the Third World. True, between 1917 and 1927 some timid attempts were made at involving communists from the colonial world in the Comintern, and concrete aid was given to the communist movements in Mongolia and China. The experience of China was particularly traumatic for Stalin, and it changed his understanding of the extra-European world. Not one for theoretical speculation, Stalin was initially happy to tag alongside Lenin in his turn toward the Third World during the last years of his life. Therefore, he supported the idea of Soviet involvement on the side of the Communist Party in the Chinese civil war. In line with Lenin's ideas, and in contrast with Trotskii and the Indian communist M.N. Roy, Stalin advocated an alliance between the Chinese communists and the nationalists (the Kuomintang). Following Lenin's reasoning at the Second Comintern Congress, the plan was to use the nationalists to win the war, and then to outmaneuver them to let the communists take power. The plan went awfully wrong. On April 12, 1927, Kuomintang troops rounded up about 1,000 communist militants and trade unionists in Shanghai. Several hundred were executed. The Shanghai massacre initiated a series of large-scale purges of communists in the territories held by the Kuomintang, delivering a nearly fatal blow to the Chinese Communist Party.[9]

After the Shanghai disaster, Stalin defaulted back to Marx's restrictive interpretation of the stages of development. "One cannot trifle with the laws of historical development," he reportedly concluded in the aftermath of the fiasco in China.[10] What Stalin meant was that there could be no revolution without an advanced capitalist economy and a large industrial working class. No more concessions were to be made to ideologically unreliable nationalists. Thus, for the next two decades, Moscow stuck to a conservative view of the world that recognized only two categories, or "camps," to classify nations.[11] A country could either be socialist, and therefore friendly toward the Soviet Union and worthy of support from Moscow, or bourgeois and capitalist, and therefore inherently hostile. The socialist category fit comfortably only the Soviet satellites in Eastern Europe. China, North Korea, and North Vietnam struggled to qualify as socialist, despite their best efforts. Colonies, as territories dominated by imperial powers, were squarely in the hostile capitalist camp. Newly independent countries were dominated by bourgeois leaders, who were nothing but "lackeys of imperialism" that helped maintain the fiction of independence when in fact the imperial powers continued to dominate the politics and economies of their former colonies.[12] As long as Stalin was in charge, the Third World could never be a priority for the Soviet Union. When Stalin died, things began to change.

Red Dawn

In August 1953, less than six months after Stalin's death and almost exactly one century after Marx published his views on British colonialism, the renowned US diplomat George F. Kennan addressed an audience of leading policymakers at Johns Hopkins University. The topic was "Soviet imperialism." Kennan wrote off the chances of a possible Soviet expansion toward Western Europe, but he warned his audience that in Asia and the rest of the Third World "the pattern is reversed."[13] "I think we in the West—Kennan continued—must face the fact that for a great many of these people the repulsion that Soviet realities hold for us is not operable in anywhere near the same degree. Their accumulated resentment of Western patterns is apt to appear commendable in their eyes by that very fact. . . . The Western world, and our country in particular [the United States], must be extremely careful how it deals with this phenomenon of the Soviet appeal to the peoples of the underdeveloped areas of Asia and elsewhere."[14]

Kennan was not the only one worrying about possible Soviet gains in the post-colonial world. A British crash course on the Soviet Union and its foreign policy for students at the Joint Services Staff College concluded that: "Her [the USSR's] propaganda has found an inexhaustibly rich theme in the struggle for South-East Asia. Britain and France, in their efforts to restore order and protect their legitimate commercial interests in countries which were in any case guaranteed continually expanding self-government, have been made to appear, in the eyes of ill-informed Asians, brutal re-conquerors of peoples who had rejected their rule. The Soviet Union on the other hand can pose as the champion of national self-determination."[15]

A new trend had begun in the USSR, one that put the Third World closer to the center of Soviet foreign policy. Kennan and the British military understood that in Moscow the assumption that socialism would gain at the expense of imperialism had not changed, despite the change of leadership in the Kremlin and the ideological shift brought about by the adoption of "peaceful coexistence." Following the change of doctrine, it was clear that the Soviet leadership no longer believed that socialism could be imposed on the world after a war with the capitalists. However, it could still be exported as a social and economic model for the newly independent countries to imitate. Rather than as the backwater Stalin saw, the extra-European world was now considered important for the future of socialism and the Soviet Union. In a 1955 memorandum to Khrushchev and Bulganin, Soviet deputy foreign minister and *Pravda* editor Ivan Maevskii wrote: "The next stage of the struggle for the global hegemony of socialism will focus on the liberation of the colonial and semi-colonial peoples. In Africa, Asia, and Latin America there are more prospects of winning the next stage than in Europe or America. Moreover, the loss of their colonies and semi-colonies should hasten the victory of socialism in Europe and eventually in the US as well."[16]

Kennan believed that Soviet communism could only bring misery and poverty to the Third World. As Maevskii's memorandum shows, ideas in Moscow were quite different. Given that in the nuclear age a full-scale war between the West and the Soviet bloc could lead to the annihilation of humankind itself, the competition against the capitalists had to change. At the Twentieth Congress of the CPSU in February 1956, Khrushchev declared that

> The new period in world history which Lenin predicted has arrived, and the peoples of the East are playing an active part in deciding the destinies of the whole world, [they] are becoming a new mighty factor

in international relations. In contrast to the pre-war period, most Asian countries now act in the world arena as sovereign states which are resolutely upholding their right to an independent foreign policy. International relations have spread beyond the bounds of relations between the countries inhabited chiefly by peoples of the white race and are beginning to acquire the character of genuinely world-wide relations.[17]

Khrushchev's attention to the Third World needed a new Soviet approach, a new policy. Under his leadership the USSR started to give special attention to some key Third World countries. The Foreign Office in London believed that

There are signs that the Soviet Union is paying increasing attention to the needs of underdeveloped countries. Delegations of industrialists and agriculturalists from several South-East Asian countries are at present being feted in the Soviet Union. Selective Soviet aid on more generous terms than is the usual Soviet practice could do much to further Communist aims in South-East Asia. The Soviet appeal for underdeveloped countries has not been confined to Asia. Soviet propaganda is also being carefully directed to trouble spots such as Brazil and Chile at the U.S.'s own backdoor.[18]

In France, the Quay d'Orsay took the same view. In the annual review for 1954, French analysts wrote that the search for consensus in Asia, Africa, and Latin America and the willingness to detach Third World countries from the West "will remain one of the main weapons used by the Soviet government." The French Foreign Office came to the conclusion that the earlier Soviet "discretion" in the field of "colonial subversion" would be abandoned in favor of a more active stance.[19] They were right.

The Globalization of Soviet Foreign Policy

In April 1955, twenty-nine delegations from independent states and colonial territories in Africa and Asia gathered in Bandung, Indonesia, to agree on a common approach to the Cold War, decolonization, and economic development. The Bandung conference was the first large-scale political and diplomatic initiative that came from the Third World. Its genealogy and legacy are contested, but the conference contributed to creating a stable coalition of newly independent states with similar needs and compatible goals. A few years later, in 1961, the Non-Aligned Movement (NAM) was born at the second Afro-Asian conference in Belgrade, Yugoslavia.[20]

Excluded from both Bandung and Belgrade, despite some timid attempts to take part, the Soviet government was ambivalent about the nascent NAM. Before Bandung, Molotov had expressed careful praise of the initiative, highlighting its anti-imperialist dimension.[21] However, future developments had multiple unpalatable aspects for the Soviet Union. The idea of nonalignment stemmed from the ambition to keep equidistant from the United States and the Soviet Union—a tough sell in both Washington and Moscow. Moreover, the main animators behind the NAM—Burma, Egypt, India, Indonesia, Pakistan—were traditionally regarded with suspicion in the USSR. According to Moscow, these were bourgeois regimes, in some cases still close to the old imperial powers. They tended to be hostile to communists at home and not particularly friendly toward the Soviet Union abroad. China and Yugoslavia—socialist but not necessarily aligned with the USSR—represented an even bigger problem for Moscow. Moreover, at the Bandung conference some delegates argued that Soviet colonialism in Eastern Europe should be condemned just as Western colonialism in Africa and Asia. The final statement issued at Bandung called for the end of "colonialism in all its manifestations," implicitly acknowledging that the Soviet Union too engaged in imperial practices.[22]

The official Soviet take on Bandung and other Third World initiatives was predictably negative. The press routinely criticized the participants for being still in thrall of the imperialists. Soviet observers were particularly keen to point out that some of the signatories of the Bandung declaration were also members of military alliances with the United States—the Baghdad pact and the Southeast Asia Treaty Organization. Yet the Soviet government understood that anticolonialism as a foreign policy was on the rise, and that the USSR should not waste this opportunity. Attempting to redirect the international struggle against empires in a more obviously socialist direction, the Soviet Union inspired the creation of the Afro-Asian Peoples' Solidarity Organization (AAPSO). Contrary to the NAM, AAPSO's membership was made up of social organizations—trade unions, women's groups, youth federations, and so on—rather than government delegations. The Soviet Solidarity Committee with the Countries of Asia and Africa, technically a civil-society organization while in fact controlled by the CPSU, represented the USSR at AAPSO. The first congress took place in Cairo, Egypt, in 1957, followed by a second one in Conakry, Guinea, in 1960. Both Egypt and Guinea were at the time Soviet allies. However, despite Soviet efforts and an extensive membership, AAPSO congresses failed to make the same splash as those of the NAM. The organization lived on but did not quite make a difference.[23]

The Soviet government was more successful in building bridges with the Third World in more traditional ways. In June 1955, Jawaharlal Nehru went for an official visit to the Soviet Union. The Indian prime minister was the first Third

World leader to tour the USSR in the postwar era. During those two weeks, Nehru exchanged cordial speeches with his hosts, toured the country from Crimea to Central Asia, via Moscow and Leningrad, visiting the best the Soviet Union had to offer in terms of factories, farms, dams, and public buildings. The diplomatic meetings between Nehru and the top Soviet leadership did not achieve anything concrete, other than an invitation to Khrushchev to visit India. Nonetheless, Nehru's visit was a first, destined to be repeated many times with more Third World leaders, following a similar itinerary.[24]

On September 27, 1955, Gamal Abdel Nasser announced that Czechoslovakia would provide his government with Soviet weapon systems, including jet fighters, armored vehicles, and tanks. Nasser's announcement "sent shockwaves around the world," not least because the USSR was clearly behind the arms deal.[25] For the first time since the end of World War II, the Soviet Union was active in the Middle East, normally dominated by American and British influence. Egypt and the USSR had been "flirting" since the early 1950s, but it was only with Khrushchev's rise to power that the Soviet government switched gear and started engaging Egypt with conviction.[26]

Khrushchev viewed the arms deal as a first step. Discussing a further request for weapons from Cairo at the Presidium, he said that fulfilling it was "a risk," but one that was "paying off" (*okupaetsia*). Egypt followed an independent policy, and this made it a worthy investment.[27] The idea that bourgeois, but radical and potentially anti-Western, Third World regimes could become important partners for the USSR was destined to change Soviet foreign policy.

Shortly after the closing of the arms deal with Egypt, Khrushchev and Bulganin (at the time premier of the Soviet Union) set off on an official state tour of India, followed by visits to Afghanistan and Burma, in November and December 1955. The visits signaled that the Third World now occupied a prominent place in Moscow's thinking. Khrushchev was convinced that the USSR could build a common front with India against the imperialists and he did not mince his words during his tour. According to the Foreign Office, the first secretary "opened with a fierce onslaught on our [British] colonial policy in India, accusing us of allowing some twenty-three million Indians to starve, and quoting at length from books by Nehru and other Indians."[28] Khrushchev's "disgraceful tirade" was spoken with "arrogant self-confidence," making the Foreign Office conclude that he was "dizzy with success after his Asian tour and may be now so confident of the effect he has made in Asia as to believe that he can afford to disregard Western susceptibilities."[29] As the diplomatic row grew during the next few weeks, neither Khrushchev nor Bulganin toned down their rhetoric against Western colonialism, showing the Soviet resolve to court the newly independent countries even at the cost of upsetting the West.[30]

Khrushchev's assessment of his travels was enthusiastic. India left an especially strong impression on him. "The portrayal of India in our literature and
cinema is primitive," Khrushchev announced to his colleagues in the Presidium
on his return. The first secretary told them about the great sights of old and new
India that he had seen (the Taj Mahal in Agra, the palaces in Jaipur). At the same
time, he recalled the poverty and dilapidation he noticed around him (the crowds
in Calcutta, the stench of rotting seaweed in Bombay). Khrushchev was impressed by the reception he and Bulganin received—someone climbed a col-
umn to greet them in Madras; on their final night in Calcutta, dozens of people
gathered outside their residence to wave goodbye. Nehru and other Indian leaders made a good impression on Khrushchev. Their meetings went well, and the
Indians seemed to understand Soviet foreign policy and share some of the USSR's
preoccupations with regard to the West. Yet Khrushchev complained that the
Soviet Union understood India and its culture "poorly." Few books about India
were translated in the USSR, and *Novoe Vremia*—the Soviet magazine published
in multiple languages for a foreign audience—was "boring." Khrushchev expected many things to change.[31]

A better understanding of India and the rest of the Third World was necessary because Soviet engagement with them was already a reality. Shortly after
Khrushchev and Bulganin's trip, the Soviet government agreed to fund the construction of the Bhilai steel plant in Chhattisgarh. The Bhilai project inaugurated a long era of Soviet-Indian economic cooperation.[32] The same was true for
Afghanistan and Burma. During their visit, Khrushchev and Bulganin discussed
with the Rangoon government the possibility of sponsoring the construction of
a polytechnic institute, and potentially a stadium and a hospital too. In Afghanistan, Prime Minister Mohammed Daoud Khan approached the Soviet delegation with a request for military equipment. Khrushchev recommended that it
be given to him "free of charge."[33] The Presidium raised no objection, accepting
that aid was now a key component of competition with the West. Mikoian had
argued as much already before Khrushchev and Bulganin returned from their
visits when the possibility of granting aid to Third World countries was first discussed. "If we want to engage in more serious competition with the USA, we
need to give aid to some states." "This money will pay off," Mikoian concluded.[34]

The State Department agreed with him. At the time of Khrushchev and Bulganin's visit to India, the US embassy in Delhi wrote to Washington that "nothing is likely to help Russians more in their current objectives in India than actions
in Washington suggesting reduced interest in welfare of free Asian countries at
very moment when Bulganin and Khrushchev are hinting broadly at increasing
aid they are already providing, and openly challenging West to 'compete for India's friendship.'"[35]

"Competing" not just for India but for the Third World at large became one of the main dimensions of the Cold War in the second half of the 1950s. In this, the Soviet government was facilitated by the prevailing Western attitude at the time. The West's response to the Soviet diplomatic offensive in India was somewhat clumsy. The British government seethed but chose not to produce a statement addressing the merit of Khrushchev's accusations of colonial crimes. The US government did respond. On December 2, 1955, Secretary of State John Foster Dulles produced a joint declaration with Portugal's foreign minister Paulo Cunha denouncing Soviet statements. The document referred to Goa as a Portuguese "province," which infuriated the Indian government, and emphasized "the interdependence of Africa and the Western World."[36] Predictably, the joint declaration hardly won Washington any sympathy in the Third World. George Evans, the *Daily Telegraph* correspondent who followed the Soviet delegation in its tour of Asia, told Foreign Office officials that "Khrushchev's success had been enhanced by Mr. Dulles' statements on Goa." The British journalist "considered that this had been disastrous in that it had revived all the suspicions of America which were beginning to disappear."[37]

In Egypt, Western intransigence led to even bigger gains for the USSR. Nasser was looking for international sponsors to help finance his government's most ambitious project: the Aswan Dam, a large dam on the Nile to provide Egypt with better control over floods and with hydroelectric power. Nasser had received promises of forthcoming funding from the US and the British government. However, following Egypt's arms deal with Czechoslovakia and official recognition of the People's Republic of China, the Western offer was withdrawn. The USSR was quick to step in. In June 1956, the Soviet government granted Egypt a loan of 400 million US dollars (twice what the Americans had promised) for the project. The Aswan Dam, completed in 1964, became the best-known Soviet development project in the Third World.[38]

Following Nasser's nationalization of the Suez Canal, Britain, France, and Israel attacked Egypt in October 1956. The Soviet government stood firmly by Nasser's side, condemning the invasion and urging the invaders to stop the attack. Egypt survived the onslaught and moved even closer to the Soviet Union. Moreover, the USSR acquired prestige in the eyes of Third World governments. Its uncompromising support for Egypt contrasted favorably with Britain and France's latest colonial adventure. The United States may have been as vocal as the Soviet Union in ending the Suez crisis, but its reputation suffered from its association with the Europeans and their unrepentant imperialism.[39]

The Soviet leadership played its cards well. Khrushchev understood that winning the trust of the leading non-aligned countries was in the USSR's best interests. During the international talks that attempted to solve the Suez issue, he insisted with his colleagues in the Presidium that the Soviet line should be "worked out in collaboration with India, Indonesia."[40] Likewise, Khrushchev made a point of keeping Nehru informed of what the Soviet government's take on the Suez crisis was. Likewise, Nehru's opinion mattered in the Kremlin.[41] Thus, the USSR by 1956 had managed to carve out for itself a significant role in extra-European affairs, thanks to a combination of vision and opportunism.

Out of Africa

Africa stood out as a prominent exception. The USSR had found new friends from the Middle East to Southeast Asia, but the African continent appeared impervious to Soviet influence. Historically, the Comintern had an ambiguous relationship with Africa. The initial interest in black liberation and African affairs of the 1920s turned into indifference since the mid-1930s, with the partial exception of the communist movement in South Africa. Rhetorically, Soviet officials had always denounced racism against Africans and African Americans in the West. The official line was that racism was a degeneration of the capitalist system. On the contrary, the USSR was presented as a raceless society. This contrasted with the everyday reality of the Soviet Union, in which people with darker skins—whether Soviet citizens or foreign visitors—regularly faced abuse and discrimination.[42] Soviet analysts and scholars generally refrained from framing the USSR's engagement with the outside world in terms of racial liberation. They preferred to employ the tried and tested categories of resistance to capitalist exploitation, as per classic Marxism. Since the 1960s, following the growth in interest in the Third World, racial analysis became more prominent in Soviet academia and in official discourse. As Nikolai Zakharov has written, "foreigners"—normally depicted as "spies" in Soviet discourse—came to be represented as "exotic and attractive people" in the Khrushchev era, with open reference to their racial background. Of course, this racialization of the "foreigner" in the USSR was itself often the product of prejudice and stereotyping.[43]

Besides discourse, the Soviet Union was hardly present in Africa at the dawn of the Khrushchev era. Egypt looked at the Middle East more than at Africa, and the USSR was only peripherally involved in the Algerian War of Independence.[44] More than North Africa, it was sub-Saharan Africa that seemed to offer new opportunities for the Soviet Union in the second half of the 1950s. Traditionally overlooked by Moscow's foreign policy, the African continent was now in turmoil, and West European domination appeared poised to end. It was time for the USSR to look at Africa with more attention.

In 1954, the first major Soviet academic publication dedicated to contemporary Africa came out. Dmitrii Ol'derogge and Ivan Potekhin—two of the few Africanists in the USSR—edited *Narody Afriki* (The Peoples of Africa), a pioneering ethnographic study.[45] Although *Narody Afriki* was hardly at the edge of academic research on Africa at the time, its publication signaled newfound interest. The Foreign Office in London was concerned. It reported that the Soviet Academy of Sciences was striving "to improve its study of African peoples and is creating more research posts in the field. Evidently a long-term project is afoot which will lay a solid foundation for eventually greater political activity on the continent." The British embassy in Moscow noticed that a "delegation of African trade unionists visited the USSR in July. Diplomatic and trade feelers have been extended, particularly in Libya and the Sudan. At least ten substantial articles and broadcasts have been issued during the year, chiefly with a colonial-liberation slant."[46]

In January 1956, the first ever Soviet delegation traveled to sub-Saharan Africa. They attended the inauguration ceremony of William V.S. Tubman, who had been reelected president of Liberia in May 1955. It was more than a symbolic gesture. As Tubman himself revealed to the American ambassador, the Soviet representatives had been "instructed by their Government to have a confidential talk with me on several subjects, one being the exchange of diplomatic representation between our two countries." Tubman was staunchly pro-Western, and he assured his American interlocutor that "he was not going to let the Soviets come into Liberia." Moreover, "with respect to economic aid, Mr. Tubman asserted that he did not want aid, and would not receive it even if they offered $100,000,000."[47] A few days later, Tubman wrote a personal message to Eisenhower, confirming that the Soviet delegation had offered economic aid. However, "our patent regard for the agreement entered into between our two governments for economic assistance in our development programs cannot be bartered nor sold by any new traducing ideology and the visit of the Soviet delegation to Liberia seeking to effect arrangements for exchange of diplomatic representatives and economic assistance will have no effect on the Liberian Government's attitude and policy."[48]

The first Soviet venture into sub-Saharan Africa ended in disappointment for Moscow. Tubman, whether personally suspicious of Soviet ideology or simply worried about upsetting his American friends, showed great resolve to resist all openings that came from the USSR. West Africa would soon offer new opportunities. Liberia may have snubbed Moscow's offers but, as new territories in the region became independent between 1957 and 1960, their governments proved more interested in the possibility of receiving aid from the Soviet Union.

History of Noncapitalism

Soviet engagement with the Third World during the early Khrushchev era took a variety of forms. Diplomatic roundtables, state visits, and military assistance played an important role in establishing the USSR as a potential partner for radical governments in Africa and Asia. It was economic aid and development cooperation, however, that determined the course of Soviet involvement. The transformation of Third World societies became the essence of Cold War competition in these years. The USSR could not compete with the level of development achieved in the West. However, leaders like Mikoian and Khrushchev grasped that the Soviet Union's claim to the status of superpower in the Cold War depended on its ability to provide economic assistance to developing countries. The USSR needed its own blend, its own recipe of development, comparable but at the same time different from (and hopefully better than) what the West could offer.

Khrushchev's peaceful coexistence did not mean renouncing the competition with the West. It meant moving it from the military sphere, where the USSR was both unable and unwilling to compete, to the sphere of economic development and modernization, in which at least it could try. According to Westad, "it was Soviet modernity that would win people for Communism abroad, as socialism—freed from Stalin's shackles—showed its full productive potential."[49] This Soviet modernity was attractive in the Third World. Leaders in Africa and Asia looked at the Soviet experience of central planning, state investment, and closed markets to find inspiration to solve the problems their countries faced after independence. As Engerman put it, "enthusiasm for rapid industrialization through central planning prevailed throughout the Third World in the 1950s and 1960s. The power of the Soviet model was so strong that those swayed by the romance of economic development typically assumed that planning was the sole means to that end."[50]

The Soviet Union's relative "backwardness" compared to the Western world offered some advantages in this context. The USSR's own search for modernity had parallels and commonalities that resonated with many Third World leaderships, who faced comparable problems. Analyzing Soviet foreign policy in 1956, the British Foreign Office wrote that: "The countries of Asia and particularly the uncommitted ones tend to judge us—and the Russians and the Chinese—by what we are and what we do and above all by what help we can afford them in the solution of their own pressing domestic problems on which their attention is concentrated. There is inevitably a feeling that the problems with which the Russians and the Chinese have to deal are rather more closely related to their own problems than there are the problems of Europe."[51]

The first manifestation of the USSR's provision of development aid for the Third World was the large-scale assistance program toward the People's Republic of China (PRC), launched in 1953–1954. The scale was gargantuan. "In every department of every ministry, in every large factory, in every city, army, or university there were Soviet advisers, specialists, or experts who worked with the Chinese to 'modernize' their country and move their society toward socialism."[52] This was an important turning point. Even though Moscow had recognized the PRC in 1949, the CPSU apparatus still did not consider it a fully socialist state. The CPSU International Department officially classified China as an Asian noncommunist country; something that changed only in 1957.[53] The assistance program was the most important sign yet of the Kremlin's growing interest in non-European countries. "Not just the First Secretary, but the whole party leadership was convinced that the socialist transformation of the most populous country on earth was a task that the Soviet Union had to engage in—it not only confirmed their Marxist worldview, but also highlighted the universal centrality of the Soviet experience in building socialism."[54]

Soviet aid to China was a precedent that inaugurated a new course. The road was open to seek more cooperation agreements with other countries in Africa and Asia. In the summer of 1956, Modest Rubinshtein, a prominent economist, published a two-part article in the international edition of New Times that introduced a new idea: the "non-capitalist path for developing countries." Rubinshtein's point was simple: contrary to Stalin's conservative interpretation of Marx's thought, Third World countries did not need to build "full" capitalism before beginning the transition toward socialism. What they needed was development, and specifically the development of "state capitalism," a Leninist concept based on the establishment of a large state sector to dominate the economy. This, according to Rubinshtein, was what the USSR should foster in its interactions with the developing world. Transition to "real" socialism would come over time. The introduction of the notion of "non-capitalist path of development" was destined to revolutionize the Soviet understanding of development in the Third World.[55]

Unanswered questions remained. What kind of economic aid should the USSR provide, and with what aim? Who would Moscow's interlocutors in the Third World be? By the late 1950s, these questions needed answers. The Soviet government needed a policy if its push in the Third World was to be successful. It took a while for the CPSU to come up with satisfying answers, which required some degree of ideological twisting. One of the first and possibly most important analytical formulations was produced by the recently established CPSU Central Committee commission for "Questions of Ideology, Culture and International Party Contacts" in October 1958. The commission prepared a long and detailed document on current Soviet policies in Africa and Asia, analyzing the state of affairs and advancing practical suggestions for the future. The CPSU started from the very basics. The commission foresaw that many countries were destined to gain independence from their colonial masters, and this was a positive development from the Soviet point of view. The main trend of decolonization was the growth of "nationalism," interpreted in the Kremlin as the "liquidation of the colonial structures" of the newly independent countries' polities and economies and the creation of national states. Independence, however, carried numerous problems, which the commission related to "underdevelopment" (*slaborazvitie*): poverty, lack of capital, absence of even the most basic facilities. Capitalism, with its exploitative nature, could not be the answer. "Not one of these problems can be solved with the path of capitalist development," the commission concluded. "The peoples of the countries of Asia and Africa will therefore step by step turn to the socialist side and, after finding a complete understanding of their interests from the socialist camp, will all be more and more convinced that their future is to be linked not with capitalism, but with socialism."[56]

The Soviet Union could be the vehicle for the establishment of a form of socialism in the Third World. The struggle against imperialism required Moscow's active support for progressive postcolonial leaders of the nationalist variety who could become important allies for the USSR. Soviet policy should begin with highlighting the positive role that the USSR could play for economic and social development in the Third World.[57]

The problem was that the Third World elites that showed interest in the Soviet model—leaders like Nasser, Nehru, and Sukarno—were nationalist and bourgeois, not communists. In fact, they tended to lock up communists in their countries. Could they be reliable partners for the USSR? The role of the national bourgeoisie (as postindependence leaders were referred to in the official Soviet parlance) in the Third World was the subject of an important conference, organized jointly by the Ideology and Culture Commission and the Academy of Sciences from October 31 to November 1, 1958. It gathered academics who worked on Africa and Asia and policymakers involved in foreign policy. Its official aim was to analyze the current situation and provide the Soviet government with a coherent set of recommendations for policy. The proceedings were sent to the CPSU Central Committee and to its International Department to be reviewed by the likes of Mikoian and Boris Ponomarev.[58]

The unspoken goal of the discussion was finding an ideologically acceptable way for the Soviet Union to pursue a more active engagement with the Third World, despite the lack of real communist parties as partners. This was the line that Khrushchev and the Presidium had taken since at least 1954; now it was time to give it official party sanction. Most conference delegates did not have a

problem with the national bourgeoisie. They agreed that leaders of newly independent countries tended to profess generically socialist ideas and were not opposed to having friendly relations with the socialist camp. Their priority was
independence, but once this was secured the nationalist leaders were preoccupied with the modernization and the economic development of their countries.
This offered the USSR a significant opportunity to shape their future toward
socialism through international cooperation and economic aid. This was the
most contentious issue. A few conference speakers raised objections to the idea
of supporting the national bourgeoisie. The ghost of Shanghai in 1927 loomed
large. They were worried that once in power nationalist leaders would adopt
"antidemocratic" policies that hindered the "natural development of the working class" (outlawing communist parties and imprisoning their members). However, they were in the minority. Most participants agreed that investing in the
Third World was worthwhile. The struggle against imperialism required new alliances, and the Third World bourgeoise could represent a key ally as long as it
remained anti-Western. The key task for the socialist camp was to promote economic development with socialist characteristics. With time, socialist development would "unleash the revolutionary energy of the masses," pushing forward
the transition of newly independent countries toward real communism.[59]

This was a long-term goal. In the short run, the Soviet government did not
intend to waste time building communism in Africa, Asia, or Latin America.
Although the Khrushchev leadership was much more optimistic about the prospects of socialism in the Third World than Stalin, few in the Presidium and
other Soviet bureaucracies thought that a Soviet-style command economy could
be replicated in the Third World. Khrushchev and his colleagues had abandoned
Stalin's restrictive view of the colonies and their successor independent states
but still shared part of Marx's original skepticism. Communism required a mobilized working class, which in turn required an industrialized society. In Moscow's view, the Third World—some countries more than others—may have been
moving in the right direction but was not quite there yet. Khrushchev used the
word *kerenshchina* to describe India after his 1955 visit. The term derived from
Aleksandr Kerenskii, the Socialist Revolutionary leader who headed Russia's
Provisional Government between the February and October revolutions in 1917.
What Khrushchev meant was that India was in a transitional phase. By obtaining independence from the British Empire, India had achieved much, but it
was still a society modeled on a bourgeois system—that of the former colonial
master. The same was true in every other Third World country. The inevitable
transition toward a truly revolutionary, socialist society had to go through an
intermediate stage that mixed elements of capitalism and socialism to achieve
a sufficient level of economic development. Facilitating the progression to this

stage became the overarching goal of Soviet engagement in the Third World during the Khrushchev era. Economic aid and development cooperation were the prime instruments of this engagement.[60]

Others elaborated this basic notion to create the ideational foundations of Soviet involvement in the Third World. Rostislav Ul'ianovskii, the deputy head of the Institute of Oriental Studies, argued that the national bourgeoisie in the Third World was already successfully resisting Western economic imperialism. The key was the creation of a large state sector in the local economies, which promoted development. Industrialization contributed to the creation of a growing working class, which in time would acquire class consciousness. Ul'ianovski called this "state capitalism" and argued that it was the first step toward socialism. Hence, it was in the Soviet Union's best interests to provide capital and expertise for the development of Third World countries led by radical national bourgeois leaders.[61]

Ul'ianovskii's personal history illustrated the broader trend in Moscow. This was not the first time he had dealt with political economy in the extra-European world. As a young academic in the early 1930s, Ul'ianovskii published a series of works on the national liberation movement in India, and in particular on the decay of the imperial economic system in the country. His unorthodox enthusiasm for the working masses of India cost him dearly. In January 1935, Ul'ianovskii was arrested by the NKVD, accused of being a supporter of a Trotskiist organization, and sentenced to five years in a labor camp. Released in 1940, he was sent to work for the Ministry of Light Industry in provincial towns. In 1955, Ul'ianovskii was officially pardoned and allowed to return to Moscow, where he resumed his academic activities. Twenty years after his arrest, Ul'ianovskii's unorthodox views had become useful for the CPSU. Khrushchev's push for the Third World needed a theoretical framework to prop it up, and Ul'ianovskii was among the leading ideological workers for the task. He rose as rapidly as he had fallen. In 1958, he became the deputy director of the prestigious Institute of Oriental Studies (Institut Vostokovedeniia) of the Academy of Sciences and was made deputy director of the reformed International Department of the CPSU Central Committee, focusing on relations with Africa and Asia. His oft-repeated take, borrowed from Rubinshtein's earlier work—that the creation of state capitalism in the Third World was a desirable step toward socialism—was now the official Soviet position.[62]

It was Ponomarev, the influential head of the CPSU International Department, who officially sanctioned the positive role of state capitalism in the Third World in Soviet doctrine. In a 1961 article in *Kommunist*, the CPSU ideology journal, Ponomarev stated that "the position of the national democratic state is a Marxist-Leninist theoretical position." Moreover, "the point is not to pigeonhole all liberated countries and then to state: these belong to one category, and these other ones to a second or a third. Such approach would be schematic and detrimental." According to Ponomarev, achieving independence opened the way toward the establishment of "social progress." This was achieved through introducing "limitations for the development of capitalism," driving "the imperialist monopolies out of the economy," and—crucially—creating and strengthening "a state sector in the economy." Some newly independent countries were already on the right track; making use of Soviet help and expertise, radical Third World states aimed to replicate the USSR's "world-famous historical successes" in the fields of industrialization, agricultural development, education for the masses, healthcare, and so on. Ponomarev mentioned Ghana, Guinea, and Mali among them.[63]

This did not mean that these societies were going to become communist states any time soon. Ponomarev wrote that "Marxism-Leninism teaches that all countries proceed toward socialism. However, each chooses their own path of transition." In the Third World, national democracies were the first stage of the path to socialism, but exactly how long this process would take was not clear. The Soviet leadership was perfectly comfortable with this indeterminacy: neither capitalist nor socialist, but noncapitalist. Khrushchev espoused this view. Speaking at the Higher Party School in Moscow in early 1961, he announced that "at present, Asia, Africa and Latin America are the most important centers of the revolutionary struggle against imperialism." It was the duty of the USSR, the other socialist countries, and the international working class to help them carry out this struggle. Economic assistance was essential. As Khrushchev put it, "the aid extended by the USSR and the other socialist states to the countries which have won independence has but one aim—to help strengthen the position of these countries in the struggle against imperialism, to further the development of their national economy and improve the life of their people."[64]

However, "the correct application of Marxist-Leninist theory in the newly-independent countries consists precisely in seeking the forms that take cognizance of the peculiarities of the economic, political and cultural life" of Third World countries. "Communists support the general democratic measures of the national governments," Khrushchev explained. "At the same time, they explain to the masses that these measures are far from being socialist."[65]

The point was not to recreate Soviet communism in the Third World. State capitalism was a more realistic short-term goal, both for Third World states and for the USSR as their sponsor. The Soviet government had found a policy: the noncommunist national bourgeoisie of the Third World could and should be supported by the USSR, not to establish socialist regimes but to create a large state sector in their economies.

Brothers in Aid

Transforming principles into action was another issue the Soviet leadership needed to solve. The USSR was ill-prepared to respond to growing interest from the Third World. Soviet knowledge was scarce. There were not enough specialists who spoke the necessary languages and were familiar with the history, politics, and cultures of Africa, Asia, and Latin America.[66] The deputy head of the CPSU Ideology and Culture commission, Georgii A. Zhukov, lamented that Soviet diplomats routinely switched from posts in Europe to appointments in the Third World, which prevented them from developing an understanding of the countries in which they worked. Potekhin, the coauthor of *Narody Afriki* whom the commission consulted as an Africa expert, added that gaining field experience for would-be Soviet Africanists was practically impossible. It was generally difficult for Soviet academics to travel abroad, funding was limited, and Soviet institutions had no existing partners in Africa and Asia.[67]

This had to change if the USSR was to win new friends in the Third World. Over the course of 1958, British observers noticed that Soviet academic institutions considerably increased the number of foreign languages they taught, including vernacular African languages. In July 1958, the MID created a specialized African and Asian department, separate from the West European desks that had dealt with the colonies in the past.[68] Between 1958 and 1960, virtually all major Soviet policymaking institutions equipped themselves with departments dedicated to specific regions of the Third World. Several academic institutes were also set up to build expertise.[69]

At the same time, public diplomacy organizations were given new tasks. Soviet diplomatic representatives and information agencies had to stress the advantages of socialism over capitalism, by focusing on the historical achievements of the Soviet Union. In particular, what they presented as the successful modernization of the Caucasus and Central Asia was judged to be especially relevant in the context of the Third World. By contrast, Western economic aid had to be unmasked as exploitative in nature. It served no other purpose than opening the way for the expansion into Third World markets of Western monopolies and for the formation of aggressive military blocs. Contemporary economic imperialism was not that different from traditional colonialism, according to the CPSU propaganda commission. Socialist aid, on the contrary, created an economic brotherhood among countries founded on peaceful relations and mutually advantageous exchange.[70]

The provision of aid was the pillar of Soviet engagement with the Third World. During the Khrushchev era, the USSR extended financial aid and technical assistance to many countries in Africa, Asia, and Latin America. The CIA calculated that between 1955 and 1964 the Soviet Union gave about 4 billion US dollars to the Third World. Countries such as Egypt (which received 1 billion), India (more than 800 million), and Afghanistan (about half a billion) were the largest beneficiaries. Sub-Saharan Africa received about 500 million US dollars, most of which went to Ghana, Guinea, and Mali.[71]

In absolute terms, Soviet aid was generally lower than Western economic assistance. Soviet aid was nonetheless sought after for it tended to have fewer "strings attached." At the Twentieth Congress of the CPSU in 1956, Khrushchev announced that developing countries no longer needed to "go begging for modern equipment from their former oppressors." Fraternal aid from the USSR and the rest of the socialist world would take care of that, "free from any conditions of a political or military nature."[72]

By and large, Khrushchev kept his word. The deals the Soviet Union offered were attractive for Third World governments. The Soviet government seldom gave grants, preferring loans. These loans, however, carried favorable conditions. When discussing the arms deal with Egypt at a Presidium meeting, Khrushchev made this point clear. He told his colleagues that the possibility of giving help free of charge "is not worth it," while a "favorable [l'gotnyi] credit" was instead possible.[73] As a rule, loans from Moscow carried low interest rates and could be paid back over a long period of time, usually after the completion of the project. Furthermore, the entirety or at least part of the loan could be repaid in local currencies, or even using traditional exports (rice, cotton, cocoa, etc.). This was a real blessing for Third World governments that lacked hard currency reserves. Finally, the Soviet government generally let its partners decide what they wanted to do with Soviet help. Once the project was completed, the recipient government was left in charge of it.[74]

This policy had a clear and immediate appeal for a number of governments in the Third World. In late 1960, the leadership of Mali, which had just become independent, was evaluating different options to receive aid from abroad by looking at agreements signed between Third World countries and foreign states and agencies. The Soviet-Guinean cooperation agreement, signed the year before, was among the ones taken into consideration. The Malians approved of it because it envisaged cooperation "on the basis of equality and mutual benefit." Two elements stood out in Soviet assistance to Guinea: "(1) the USSR undertakes to respect the independence of the Republic of Guinea and its freedom of choice in the economic field; (2) The state that receives Soviet aid enjoys full freedom of determination in the use of such aid." As the next chapter shows, this freedom of choice that the USSR granted its partners in the Third World was what convinced the government of Mali, and many others, to cooperate with the Soviet Union.[75]

The West looked on worriedly. The US National Intelligence Estimate for 1955 warned of a "new cold war offensive" carried out by the USSR and the PRC. "The Bloc is offering expanded trade and economic and technical assistance, often on highly favorable terms, to a numbers [*sic*] of countries."⁷⁶ The Europeans, whose colonial interests were threatened by Soviet activism in the Third World, were even more worried. In late 1955, a British diplomat called Soviet loans "a sinister new phenomenon very attractive to small countries." In the same report, the Foreign Office lamented the tendency in London to "underestimate what the USSR can do for underdeveloped countries," concluding that "this financial industrial penetration . . . is gravely more menacing than the supply of armaments."⁷⁷ A few weeks later, the House of Lords was informed that: "Soviet economic penetration through selected offers of capital equipment, technical assistance and armaments, is likely to play an increasingly important role out of all proportion to the volume of the trade involved. Present developments cannot be regarded as a flash in the pan. It seems probable that the Russians will be able to honour the commitments they have already undertaken and shoulder new ones as and when they think necessary."⁷⁸

The French were just as concerned. The economics and finance department of the Quai d'Orsay reported how Third World countries were "seduced by the recent Soviet proposals to buy agricultural surplus and to provide long-term credits with very low interest rates and without any obvious political conditions." Maurice Dejean, the new French ambassador to Moscow, believed that "the USSR presents itself more and more as the supplier of under-developed countries." In his view, Soviet loans and commercial treaties would "make it possible to obtain the progressive conquest of the world market."⁷⁹

Western anxiety may have been excessive, but the USSR did have an ambitious vision. Soviet aid policy made few distinctions based on politics or geography. Plans for assistance to Africa, Asia, or the Middle East were founded on the same ideas. Despite the increasingly sophisticated analyses produced by research institutes in Moscow, Soviet leaders tended to see the Third World as homogeneous and characterized by the same problems. Similar principles were applied everywhere: Soviet aid and advice aimed to expand the role of the state in the national economy through direct control over agricultural and industrial enterprises and the realization of ambitious infrastructure projects. These were the bases of the "non-capitalist path of development" in practice.⁸⁰

It is commonly assumed that the United States was the pioneer in the field of modernization theory and development assistance on the ground. The USSR was not far behind. Even though their work did not have the theoretical sophistication of Walt Rostow or Immanuel Wallerstein, Soviet academics and party officials also developed a set of basic ideas and concepts concerning development in theory and practice. At the same time, Soviet policymakers began to put them into practice, in some cases even before the US was seriously engaged in the provision of aid. The Soviet leadership did not take long to realize what Third World leaders wanted: a blueprint for modernization. By the late 1950s, the Soviet Union had developed one to offer, mixing elements of the USSR's own historical experience with principles borrowed from market systems. The Soviet aim was not turning the masses of Africa and Asia to communism but convincing the elites of the newly independent countries to adopt socialism as a state-led development model. The noncapitalist model of development was born and ready to make its debut in Africa.

FIRST CONTACT

Anthropologists use the expression "first contact" to describe the "initial encounters between peoples of different societies."[1] Even though the Soviet Union was aware of decolonization and had had contacts with African states in the past, Ghana's independence in March 1957, followed by Guinea in October 1958 and Mali in September 1960, represented a first both for decolonization and for Soviet foreign policy. Karen Brutents, who started working for the CPSU International Department in 1961, remembered that "we were ill prepared for the Black continent's [sic] exit from colonial oblivion."[2] He was among the few in the African section of the International Department able to speak English and some French. Describing a Ghanaian delegation that visited the USSR in late 1961, Brutents reminisced that: "They looked at us inquisitively [izuchaiushche], as we did with them, observing everything around them with clear interest and even sympathy, but they remained cautious, avoiding whenever possible to express their opinion: this was because of a first acquaintance situation and also because the position of their party was not yet fully determined."[3]

What Brutents described was typical of Soviet relations with West Africa at the time. There was obvious interest, but the two parties were only just getting to know each other. Ghana, Guinea, and Mali were among the very first sub-Saharan African territories to win independence from a European colonial empire. The Soviet Union pursued them as partners in the Third World. Moscow's previous attempts to establish relations with independent African states had not been particularly successful. This time, the USSR had a better proposal. It approached Ghana, Guinea, and Mali offering a blueprint for modernization, based on the

Soviet Union's own experience, but combining elements of central planning with a market-based economy.

The USSR found responsive partners in Nkrumah's Ghana, Sékou Touré's Guinea, and Keïta's Mali. The three countries found themselves in difficult economic conditions following independence, and all leaders saw a push for economic development as essential for the future of their states. The Soviet Union seemed to offer the best recipe for economic modernization. Moscow's approach to development not only appeared to offer the fastest route to prosperity, but it also coincided with Nkrumah, Sékou Touré, and Keïta's vision—one based on the conquest of economic independence from Britain and France, and on the tempering of capitalism.

Soviet ideas took time to penetrate West Africa. The links between the newly independent states and their former colonial masters were still strong, particularly in the case of Ghana. West European politicians and businessmen were the first to react to the risk of losing influence and markets to the USSR. Soon, the Americans, too, made their imposing presence felt in the region. The Cold War in West Africa thus took shape.

A New African in the World: From Gold Coast to Ghana

The British colony of the Gold Coast was formally established in 1867. This was the last step in a process that over four centuries transformed a once-powerful West African empire into a European colony. Attracted first by gold deposits, since the fifteenth-century multiple groups of European colonists settled on the coast of modern-day Ghana. They soon switched from gold to the slave trade. Through warfare and diplomacy with other empires and local kingdoms, the British became the rulers of the Gold Coast by the late nineteenth century.[4]

With the decline of the slave trade, the Gold Coast reverted to gold mining and agriculture as its main economic activities. The British colonial administration kept the production of gold firmly in its hands. The need for a skilled workforce in the mining industry created the need to build a network of schools and a limited number of technical colleges. Graduates from these institutions soon filled the ranks of the colonial administration as well as of the mining industry. It was among them that ideas of self-rule and independence began to develop.[5]

The majority of the population worked in the agricultural sector. Cocoa, introduced to the Gold Coast in the late nineteenth century, proved particularly well suited to local conditions. Boosted by steady growth in demand from Europe and driven by West African farmers, cocoa production increased during the early twentieth century. By the mid-1920s, it had outstripped gold as the main source of revenue for the Gold Coast. Thanks to profits from the sale of both gold and cocoa, the colonial administration could afford to invest in a modernization program in the Gold Coast. The British focused on transport networks first—useful to move export commodities from the interior to the ports on the coast—and then on the provision of some basic services, such as irrigation and limited healthcare. These policies are usually credited with making the Gold Coast one of the most prosperous colonies in West Africa and in the whole continent.[6]

As in other European colonies in Africa, the two world wars had a profound impact on society in the Gold Coast. After 1945, veterans who had served in the British Army returned home with new ideas and larger ambitions. If people from the Gold Coast could fight and die for their colonial masters, why could they not run their own country too? Their grievances found support among the educated elite who worked in the colonial administration and aspired to parity with British personnel. The marked increase in demands for pensions from veterans and social benefits from African workers made the British government realize that keeping colonies in Africa would be financially unwise in the long run. The road to independence was open.[7]

In this context, a young intellectual and activist founded a new political movement destined to change the history of the Gold Coast. Born in 1909 in Nkroful, a small town on the Southwestern coast, Kwame Nkrumah had trained as a schoolteacher before leaving to study in the United States in 1935. As a student at Lincoln University and then the University of Pennsylvania, Nkrumah became increasingly more politicized. He befriended and corresponded with several leading left-wing expatriates, such as the Marxist philosopher C.L.R. James and Trotskii's former secretary, the philosopher Raia Dunaevskaia. In 1945, Nkrumah moved to London, where he became one of the leading figures in the African student organizations that demanded decolonization. He returned to the Gold Coast in 1947, after the approval of a new constitution that allowed African citizens to be elected in an advisory council. Following a series of disturbances in early 1948, which culminated in the shooting of three protesters by the police on February 28, Nkrumah realized that the Gold Coast's existing political movements were too elitist to convince the British authority to grant the Gold Coast independence. Only mass support could.[8]

In 1949, Nkrumah founded the Convention People's Party (CPP), whose ranks were filled not only by the educated urban class, but also by disgruntled veterans, cocoa farmers, youths, and women. In 1950 the CPP started a campaign of strikes and nonviolent resistance. The British reacted by imprisoning Nkrumah, whose prestige with the people of the Gold Coast grew even more. The colonial administration, however, also created an elected legislative assembly. The CPP won resounding electoral victories both in 1951 and 1954, leaving little choice to the British colonial administration, which was forced to relinquish more of its powers in favor of local government. Nkrumah was nominated prime minister and had to be released from jail. Despite the rise of an Ashanti opposition movement, which questioned the CPP's vision of a centralized government, the CPP-dominated assembly requested full independence in the summer of 1956. The British government accepted the request, and March 1957 was set as independence date.[9]

Nkrumah named the newly independent country "Ghana," after a powerful West African empire that existed between the fourth and the thirteenth century but whose territory did not include modern-day Ghana. Besides the change of name, the new constitution stipulated that independent Ghana would be a member of the British Commonwealth and that the British monarch would remain the head of state, represented by a governor-general. Nkrumah would keep his post of prime minister.

The CPP government inherited what many regarded—and some still regard—as a so-called model colony. According to available estimates, Ghana's GDP per capita at the moment of independence was the second highest in West Africa after Senegal's, and among the highest in Africa. Its reserves of foreign currency were higher than its neighbors' due to the cocoa and gold trade. Infrastructure included a network of roads, a functioning port, and an international airport. Ghana's population was relatively well educated, thanks to the schools the British had established.[10]

The new government, however, was not content. Addressing the nation on the night of independence, Nkrumah made a passionate appeal to the people of Ghana and the whole of Africa for the future. Independence—as he often repeated—was only the first step. "Today," Nkrumah announced, "from now on, there is a new African in the world and that new African is ready to fight his own battle and show that after all the black man is capable of managing his own affairs. We are going to demonstrate to the world, to the other nations, young as we are, that we are prepared to lay our own foundation."[11]

Ghana's biggest battle after independence was for economic development. This was necessary, most important, to improve living standards for Ghanaians. Whatever relative prosperity the colonizers had left was not sufficient for Nkrumah. Ghana aspired to look at the former colonial masters from a position of parity and not to be snubbed as backward or underdeveloped. Moreover, Nkrumah was a committed Pan-Africanist. He believed in the necessity to decolonize and unify Africa, and he hoped Ghana could lead this process. His aspiration was a modern, prosperous country, whose political and economic achievements would exceed whatever colonialism had brought, so to inspire a new wave of newly independent countries in Africa to follow the same path. Soon, Ghana's ambitions encountered Soviet ideas.[12]

Great Expectations

Looking at the guests of honor at Ghana's official proclamation of independence ceremony on March 5–6, 1957, one might be forgiven for concluding that the Soviet government looked at the newly independent state with little interest. Richard M. Nixon, Eisenhower's shrewd vice president, and his wife represented the United States. Princess Marina, the duchess of Kent, was Queen Elisabeth II's emissary in Accra. Several notable statesmen, activists, and politicians attended the celebrations. Among them, there were a young Martin Luther King Jr., Nobel prize winner Ralph Bunche, and US congressmen and civil rights activists Charles Diggs and Adam Clayton Powell. The head of the Soviet delegation was Ivan A. Benediktov, a name unknown to most visitors to Accra that day. The absence of a top Kremlin leader at the independence celebrations has been taken as an indication that the Soviet government paid no particular attention to Ghana.[13] The contrast with Nixon, who had been chosen as the official representative of the American government to demonstrate Washington's dedication to Africa, was evident.[14]

This, however, is a superficial assessment. Benediktov was no equivalent of a vice president in the Soviet hierarchy, and he had no royal glamour or civil rights credibility to compensate, but his selection as Soviet representative reflected a precise choice. He was a leading figure in the field of agricultural policy, and specifically agricultural mechanization. At the time of his trip to Accra, Benediktov was the minister of state farms (sovkhozy), a post he had occupied since 1955, after having been minister of agriculture from 1947 to 1955. He was one of the key Soviet officials who had elaborated and launched Khrushchev's Virgin Lands campaign.[15] This was what made him the ideal representative of the Soviet Union in Accra. The Soviet leadership was convinced that the mechanization of agriculture and the increase in production that followed the Virgin Lands campaign were precisely the kind of results that a state like Ghana was looking for on its way toward modernization. The ability to export such positive outcomes in developing economies was believed to be the key to winning influence with the newly independent countries of Africa and Asia.

Benediktov's task was to show off Soviet progress in agriculture to the new Ghanaian government. He met with Nkrumah several times in Accra. The Soviet representative tried to obtain from Nkrumah the promise that Ghana would quickly establish formal diplomatic relations with the Soviet Union. He proposed that a goodwill delegation from Ghana visit the USSR in the near future and invited the Ghanaian minister of agriculture, Boahene Yeboah-Afari, to take part in the visit.[16] Moreover, the Americans had "unverified intelligence to the effect that the Russians plan to make a major purchase of cocoa at the time of the ceremonies."[17]

The Ghanaian government, however, reacted coldly to Soviet openings. Benediktov's initial mission was only half successful. Ian Maclellan, the British high commissioner in Ghana, reported that "after vacillation the Ghana Government replied that they did not wish at present to extend the range of direct diplomatic relation so far agreed."[18] Moreover, Nkrumah ruled out the possibility of a visit of Ghana's minister of agriculture to the USSR. The Ghanaian prime minister wrote to Moscow that his cabinet was reviewing the whole economic policy for the future, and the minister could not leave the country at such a crucial moment. The door was left open for "a similar opportunity to see and learn from the agriculture of the USSR in the future," but the timeframe was left deliberately unspecified.[19]

The Soviet side reiterated similar offers several times between late 1957 and early 1959. Moscow's Ambassador to Britain, Iakov Malik, made contact with Ghana's high commissioner in London, Edward Asafu Adjaye, stressing Moscow's readiness to receive a high level Ghanaian delegation in the USSR and extending a personal invitation to Nkrumah to visit the country as a guest of the Soviet government.[20] The main purpose of a "trade and goodwill mission to the USSR, led by a Minister" would be to discuss trade and development aid, and also to let Ghanaians see and study how small industries in rural areas were run in the Soviet Union.[21] Malik requested to meet Nkrumah personally when the Ghanaian prime minister visited London in August 1958, repeating the same proposals.[22]

Despite the Soviet ambassador's efforts, Ghana showed some interest in the Soviet offers but little willingness to make concrete arrangements and commit to precise dates. Asafu Adjaye insisted on restricting the numbers of Ghanaian delegates visiting the USSR to no more than three (whereas Moscow wished for a larger group) and stated that Nkrumah would visit the Soviet Union only when he "feels free."[23] On the contrary, he immediately accepted Eisenhower's invitation to visit the United States in July 1958.[24]

Nkrumah himself was noncommittal during his meeting with Malik. The US embassy in Accra reported that the Ghanaian prime minister "had had difficulty in countering Malik's pressure for exchange of diplomatic missions soon."[25] Nkrumah confirmed that an exact date for the opening of official relations with Moscow had not yet been set, and that it would most likely take place after the

Ghanaian delegation's goodwill visit to the USSR, which was intended for 1959. Even cultural exchanges between the USSR and Ghana proved to be complex to establish. The Accra cabinet decided that any cultural contact with communist countries should be first authorized by the Ministry of Defense and External Affairs. Even though exchanges between individuals or organizations and socialist countries were not prohibited, the Ghanaian government did not trust the USSR and its allies, and desired to keep an eye on all the activities that involved the socialist world.[26]

Nkrumah's resolve to prioritize relations with the West was the main obstacle for the Soviet Union. Since the early days of independence, the Ghanaian prime minister had kept close contact with the Americans and the British, informing them of any interaction with Moscow. Conversing with Nixon just before the independence ceremony, Nkrumah said that "Ghana might find it necessary to establish some kind of representation with the Soviet bloc."[27] A couple of months later, he told a group of foreign diplomats, including US ambassador Wilson C. Flake, that a definitive decision concerning Ghana's relations with the USSR had not yet been taken, that Moscow was exercising significant pressure for a prompt opening of official exchanges, and that he "saw little way to hold the USSR off much longer."[28]

Both Washington and London pressured Nkrumah and his cabinet to prevent Ghana from establishing closer links with the Soviet Union. Ambassador Flake thought that "we might persuade Prime Minister [to] use [a] new formula to postpone indefinitely USSR exchange." His idea was to convince the Accra government that the United States was ready to provide significant aid, thus reducing Ghana's temptation to look for potential alternative donors, such as the Soviet Union.[29]

Likewise, Accra kept the Foreign Office in London informed about its dealings with the Soviet government.[30] Although the Foreign Office seemed resigned to the idea that sooner or later the USSR would obtain permanent representation in Ghana, British diplomacy still deemed advantageous to continue "our efforts to bring home to the Ghanaians the danger this implies and, if possible, to offer them advice discreetly on dealing with a Soviet mission once it is established." To maximize the effect on the Ghanaian prime minister, the British thought of using African friendly contacts to talk to Nkrumah and convince him of the risks connected to an official opening to the Soviet government, a strategy that had allegedly been employed with success since 1957.[31]

Until 1959, the only success the USSR enjoyed in pursuing the establishment of official relations with Ghana was sending Ivan Potekhin, one of the few Soviet Africanists, for a research trip to Ghana in late 1957. Moreover, Oleg Orestov, a journalist previously based in India and then briefly in Cairo, became the resident correspondent for *Pravda* in Accra.[32] Both spent time in Ghana trying to understand the country's politics, society, and economy. They met some of Ghana's most prominent leaders and visited different areas of the country. Both reached similar conclusions: Ghana was still too dependent on Britain for the USSR to be able to do business with the Accra government.

Potekhin, who visited Ghana from October to December 1957, met Nkrumah and several other members of the Ghanaian government. He reported his impressions back to Moscow in early 1958. Potekhin described his meeting with Nkrumah as "rather frank." Although the Soviet academic had come to see the Prime Minister primarily as a scholar interested in the history of national liberation movements, he "soon switched the conversation to contemporary themes." The African leader complained about the current Ghanaian constitution, drafted by Britain, which, according to Nkrumah, did not grant Ghana real independence. The constitution would need to be changed but at a later stage since Ghana was then still in a phase of "political stabilization." Even though Nkrumah did not specify "in which direction the constitution will be changed," Potekhin was able to deduce from meetings with other Ghanaian political leaders that the proposed amendments aimed to reduce London's influence. The main point was that Ghana should become a republic, severing the formal link with the British crown. Furthermore, an "anti-feudal" reform was necessary to modernize the country's economy and abolish the landowners' privileges.[33]

Nkrumah's personality and ambition struck Potekhin. The Soviet academic agreed with Nkrumah that Ghanaian society needed modernization and that British influence should decrease. The changes to the constitution that Nkrumah envisaged could lead Ghana "on the path of further limitation of democracy and the establishment of a dictatorship of Egyptian type. Nkrumah told me that the ways of bourgeois democracy limit him, tie his hands. He manifestly dreams about autocracy."[34] Given Nkrumah's interest in the socialist world—he confidentially told Potekhin that he was interested in visiting the USSR as early as 1958—this was positive news for Moscow.

In a June 1958 report, Orestov largely confirmed Potekhin's impression of Nkrumah and the domestic situation in Ghana. Orestov added that Nkrumah was extremely popular after the achievement of independence, and his ruling Convention People's Party was firmly in control of the country. Although part of Ghana's intelligentsia was skeptical of some of Nkrumah's policies, especially the more "socialist" ones, the opposition United Party (UP) did not have a real political program. It simply opposed everything Nkrumah did. The UP relied mostly on the discontent among the Ashanti population in the central region of the country, where the production of cocoa was mostly concentrated. Therefore, for the time being the UP did not constitute a serious threat to Nkrumah and the CPP.[35] N.S. Makarov, an attaché to the Soviet embassy in London who was tasked with commenting on Orestov's "raw" report before transmitting it to the MID in Moscow, felt the need to stress the "bourgeois" nature of the CPP. Nkrumah's party focused on the achievement of independence first, and now on the consolidation of the new state, but was not a socialist or communist party.[36]

Both Potekhin and Orestov highlighted the negative role played by some of Nkrumah's closest advisers. In particular, Potekhin saw George Padmore as "a renegade, in the mood for anti-Communism."[37] Padmore was one of Nkrumah's closest and most trusted mentors and advisers since his days in the United States and now worked in Ghana. His thinking was heavily influenced by Marxism, but he remained ambivalent with regard to the Soviet Union and its policies.[38] He was convinced that for Ghana to become the leading force of Pan-Africanism, it had to maintain distance from both Cold War blocs. Ghana could be friendly toward the Soviet Union and other socialist countries but should by no means become entangled in the socialist camp.

The first All-African Peoples' Conference, held in Accra from December 5 to December 13, 1958, offered a new opportunity for the Soviet government to probe Ghana. The conference was the culmination of Nkrumah and Padmore's initial efforts to make Ghana the center of Pan-Africanism. Besides delegates from more than thirty African countries, including many that were still colonies, international observers from the Soviet Union, the PRC, and the United States also participated. The Soviet delegation was composed of members of the Afro-Asian Solidarity Committee (Sovetskii Komitet Solidarnosti stran Azii i Afriki). Nkrumah made sure to impress his Soviet guests. The Ghanaian Prime Minister met the head of the Soviet delegation, P. Azimov, and discussed Ghana's current policy. He stressed the need to make the country a republic, totally independent from Britain, and then to focus on economic development. Relations with the socialist bloc would play an important role, but at the moment the West's economic pressure was too strong for Ghana to consider taking any further step in this direction.[39]

Despite Nkrumah's best intentions, the Soviet delegation reported negatively on the conference. In their view, most participants were pro-Western, and Nkrumah's speeches, although anticolonial, always leaned toward compromise with the colonialists, to the chagrin of the Algerian and Egyptian delegations. The culprit was obvious: "the conductor of influence from the imperialist powers toward Nkrumah is the notorious renegade George Padmore." To be a "notorious renegade," Padmore seemed to go out of his way to charm the visitors from the USSR. Before their return to Moscow, he treated the Soviet delegation to dinner, and discussed Ghana's economic prospects together with officials from the central bank who were also present. Whether or not Padmore's efforts were sincere

(Azimov thought Padmore agreed to spend time with them only on Nkrumah's insistence), he showed little real interest in furthering Ghana's relations with the Soviet Union. When Azimov complained of the lack of progress with regard to the exchange of diplomatic representatives between the two countries, Padmore mentioned financial concerns and the difficulty of finding a suitable candidate to send to Moscow as Ghana's ambassador given the unappealing weather in Russia ("quite possibly an exaggeration," in Azimov's words). All in all, nothing concrete came out of contacts between Soviet delegates and Ghanian officials at the All-African People's conference, other than the impression that Ghana's foreign policy was still work in progress.[40]

Padmore's suspicion of the Soviet Union did not so much derive from his past experience in Moscow, but rather from preoccupation about Ghana's place in the world. Soviet offers of economic aid were potentially appealing but also problematic. Accepting them, the first independent sub-Saharan African state risked entering into a new unequal relationship with an external white power, not unlike the previous colonial relationship with Britain. In Padmore's, and Nkrumah's, view Ghana should avoid economic dependency on the USSR, the socialist world, or any other white power. As Nana Osei-Opare argued, racial considerations mattered more in Padmore's thinking than purely economic ones at this point in time.[41]

Padmore's influence on Nkrumah was undeniable, but the two men did not see things in the same way when it came to Ghana's current and future policy. They shared the same vision of an independent and united Africa, able to stand its ground in world affairs without being part of one or the other Cold War blocs. They both aspired to make Ghana the leading force of Pan-Africanism, the example that other newly independent countries would follow. Nkrumah and Padmore agreed that Ghana's independence was only the first step, but their foreign policy outlook differed. Whereas Padmore, who worked in the newly formed Bureau of African Affairs in Accra, focused on Africa and the preexisting networks of Pan-African activists in Europe and the United States, Nkrumah had to think globally. Nkrumah was genuinely convinced of the importance of neutrality for Ghana, but he also realized that he had to deal with the Cold War and with the superpowers' respective positions on Africa.

Hence, Ghana's foreign policy was difficult for Soviet observers to interpret. Orestov considered it akin to Nehru's India: "active neutralism" was the key concept, although "Ghana was ready to accept help from any nation," as long as it was not politically charged. Nkrumah staunchly supported national liberation movements everywhere on the continent. He also tried to co-opt other countries in the region in a sort of Ghana-led West African federation, although this project was still at a very early stage.[42]

All Soviet observers agreed that Ghana's relations with the West were more than cordial. In particular, British influence in the country was still strong, especially in key areas such as the armed forces. Ghana's army was commanded by a British general, and British officers occupied prominent positions in it. Moreover, London's grip on the Ghanaian economy was strong, given the dominant position that British businesses maintained in the country after independence. Makarov drew the obvious conclusions: "Nkrumah's government followed and still follows a policy of reduced speed with regard to the establishment of Soviet-Ghanaian relations. Such a position of Ghana's government is explained, first of all, by the strong dependency of Ghana from Britain, and, secondly, by the fear of Nkrumah's government to 'spoil' its relations with Britain and the USA and most of all to diminish the chances of receiving economic aid as a result of establishing normal diplomatic, trade and other relations with the Soviet Union."[43]

The Empire of Cocoa

The most significant achievement of Benediktov's mission in 1957 was a temporary increase in trade between Ghana and the Soviet Union. The USSR, which had been buying cocoa from Ghana since 1955, purchased 36,700 tons in 1957, a large increase from 12,200 tons purchased in 1956. Soviet cocoa imports fell sharply in 1958 and 1959, to less than 10,000 tons.[44] The remarkable increase in imports from Ghana in 1957 aimed to show Ghana that the Soviet Union was interested in expanding its trade links with Africa. However, this was also the real root of the problem between the USSR and Ghana.

Cocoa was the core issue. According to Orestov, Ghana was a "typically colonial" economy based on the production and export of a single commodity—cocoa. After independence, the cocoa trade remained Ghana's main economic activity. Most of Ghana's population worked in the agricultural sector, which accounted for more than half of the country's GDP. Cocoa farming employed about one-third of agricultural workers, and the cocoa trade generated between 15 and 20 percent of total GDP. Furthermore, the sale of cocoa beans abroad was by far the country's main source of hard currency. More than 80 percent of Ghana's cocoa beans were sold to British businesses. Independence could not change the basic structure of the Ghanaian economy, which remained dependent on Britain.[45]

The Soviet government was aware of Ghana's situation. Already in February 1957, the Ministry of Foreign Trade asked the British department of MID to prepare a report on the cocoa trade in the then-Gold Coast. S. Chenchikovskii, the head of the British department at MID, described to his colleagues at the Ministry of Foreign Trade (MVT) a system in which "the sale of the Gold Coast's cocoa beans is conducted by the monopolistic organization 'Gold Coast Marketing Board,' controlled by British capital. Representatives of the Ministry of Trade and Work and the Ministry of Finances of the Gold Coast participate in the governing of the organization. The Gold Coast Marketing Board deals with the purchase of cocoa beans from the producers. Its sale organization on the international market is the 'Cocoa Marketing Company Ltd' in London, which establishes the selling price."[46]

The system described by Chenchikovskii was the legacy of imperial trade practices. Its origins lay in the conflict between buyers and producers over price. In 1937, Ghanaian cocoa farmers refused for several months to sell their beans in protest against the falling prices they were offered by the colonial administration. To solve the conflict, London created a marketing board to manage the sale of cocoa from local producers to buyers in Britain. The outbreak of World War II facilitated the creation of a West African Produce Board, whose task was to buy the entire output of West African commodities such as cocoa and coffee, and then sell it to British manufacturers. When the war ended, the structure was maintained. The Gold Coast Cocoa Marketing Board was established in 1947. Like its predecessor, it operated by buying the entire yearly crop of Ghanaian cocoa beans at a stable price. The board then marketed the beans to buyers. After independence, the organization was renamed Cocoa Marketing Board and continued to function as before.[47]

Although the board's ostensible purpose was to protect Ghanaian producers against price fluctuations on the international market, it looked after British buyers as well. The existence of the Marketing Board and its London subsidiary, the Cocoa Marketing Company, made sure that Ghanaian cocoa beans were sold to British buyers at a price that was convenient enough for them. The board had been established with capital from British manufacturers, and several of its executives came from them. The relationship between the board, the company, and its customers in Britain was tight. In January 1956, the board brought in Paul Cadbury, the president of the chocolate maker with the same name and the company's best customer, to discuss the implications of the global decline in the price of cocoa. They all agreed that the response should be coordinated between the board and its customers, in the same way as manufacturers agreed to consider the needs of the board before developing cocoa production in other regions of the world. Moreover, already before Ghana's independence, the board was worried by the new government's plans to establish centralized planning for development. The board had traditionally acted as sponsor for rural development projects, prioritizing those that facilitated the production of cocoa, and looked with suspicion at Nkrumah's pursuit of development in other areas too. Relations between the cocoa apparatus and the government in Accra would be tense.[48]

Ghana's cocoa trade was a very distant scenario from a perfect competition market in which new buyers could enter and exit as they pleased. Potential international buyers could not approach local producers in Ghana directly but had to organize purchases through the company in London. Thus, large non-British chocolate makers, such as the American Hershey's and Kraft, and the German Hechez and Stollwerck bought Ghanaian cocoa beans from the Cocoa Marketing Board via the British-run Market Company. In this way, British chocolate makers could influence the board and maintain at least some degree of control over the price and quantity of Ghanaian cocoa beans sold on the international market.[49]

This situation was problematic for Ghana. The country did not produce much else for export besides cocoa beans and was dependent on foreign imports for some key goods and commodities. Ghana's main source of foreign currency—needed to pay for imports—was the sale of cocoa beans. Any attempt to break the British dominance on Ghana's economy required making sure to provide sufficient guarantees to be able to buy a significant part of the cocoa production. It was important for Ghana to sell its cocoa at a sufficiently high price for the country to buy the imports it needed. Trading cocoa beans with British buyers, who dominated the market for Ghana's cocoa, was therefore of vital importance for the survival of Ghana. At the time of independence in 1957, the world price of cocoa was still relatively high. However, there was no guarantee for the future.

The Soviet Union aimed to end London's virtual monopsony on Ghanaian cocoa. This is why the USSR repeatedly proposed to increase Soviet purchases of Ghanaian cocoa since Benediktov's first mission to Accra in 1957. Any interference in the system of cocoa trade risked compromising the hegemony that British businesses enjoyed over Ghanaian cocoa, which guaranteed them easy and cheap access to the raw material they needed to remain competitive against potentially larger businesses in Western Europe and the United States. Predictably, British chocolate makers put up stiff resistance to avert the rise of a rival buyer. This was easy to do. When discussing the possibility of selling larger quantities of cocoa to the USSR, the Ghanaian cabinet acknowledged that the final word rested with the Cocoa Marketing Company in London. Eric Tansley, general manager of the company, let the Accra government know that he had no objection to the possibility of selling to the Soviet Union, "provided that the Government of Ghana was in no way committed in advance to the price of any quantity of Ghana cocoa to be purchased by the USSR."[50] Thus, the company would remain in control of Ghana's supply of cocoa beans, being able to negotiate one price with Moscow while selling to the usual buyers at a different one. For large British chocolate manufacturers influencing the Cocoa Marketing Company was not difficult. They had operated in symbiosis for more than a decade, and the company's capital came mostly from those same businesses. Tansley had long worked for the United Africa Company before switching to the Cocoa Board.[51] Keeping the USSR away from large purchases of cocoa was therefore child's play. Consequently, in 1958 and 1959 the USSR bought relatively small quantities of beans at prices higher than what British buyers paid. British influence on the price of Ghana's cocoa had an especially detrimental effect on Soviet plans. As the next sections will show, Moscow's hopes to establish cooperative relations with Ghana were based on offering development aid through barter agreements, which were virtually impossible to manage without fixed prices.

The Tyranny of Foreign Investment

At the time of independence, a debate that went beyond the structure of the cocoa trade was going on in Ghana. The country's declared goal was to show the world that the "new African" was "able to manage his own affairs," as Nkrumah had declared in his independence speech. This meant creating a viable economy that would guarantee Ghana prosperity and end dependency on foreign goods. To that end, Ghana faced important choices. The new government had to lay the foundations of the economic policy the country would adopt in the following years.

Nkrumah was sure that capitalism was not the only way. In the introduction to his autobiography, published in 1957, he wrote that "capitalism is too complicated a system for a newly independent nation. Hence the need for a socialistic society." Furthermore, Nkrumah believed that "economic independence should follow and maintain political independence." In his view, the development of a newly independent country must be rapid. "What other countries have taken three hundred years or more to achieve, a once dependent territory must try to accomplish in a generation if it is to survive."[52] Nkrumah belonged to the same generation of nationalist leaders like Nasser, Nehru, and Sukarno who, without being communists, resented colonialism, and desired full independence for their countries, including in the economic sphere. British observers had no time for such distinctions. Discussing Ghana's independence, the Foreign Office remarked "the fact that many of the colored leaders against colonial domination have fallen under Communist (or, more precisely, in Dr. Nkrumah's case Marxist) influence."[53]

Nkrumah understood that Ghana needed to reduce its dependency on the cocoa trade to guarantee itself a prosperous future. The country needed basic infrastructure to allow some differentiation in the economy. Developing an agricultural sector that went beyond cocoa farming and encouraging the birth of small-scale industry depended on the provision of energy, transport, and irrigation facilities. These were expensive. Newly independent Ghana, however, lacked the resources to finance such investments. There was no alternative to looking for donors and partners abroad.

Some ministers in Nkrumah's cabinet shared Nkrumah's lack of enthusiasm for Western capitalism. Kojo Botsio, minister of trade and labor until 1958 and then minister of foreign affairs, was known as a leftist and favored establishing cooperative relations with the Soviet Union and the rest of the socialist bloc. Others disagreed. Komla Agbeli Gbedemah, a founding member of the CPP and the influential minister of finance in Nkrumah's first government, always argued in favor of building strong relations with the West, and primarily with the United States.[54] Gbedemah advocated approaching the American government to obtain financial and technical aid to realize the most ambitious project of the Nkrumah government—the Volta River dam and hydroelectric complex. Nkrumah had long dreamt of reviving an old project of the British colonial administration: building a dam at Akosombo, in Southeastern Ghana, flooding part of the Volta River basin, and generating electricity thanks to a hydroelectric power station to be built on the same site. The British had abandoned the project due to its high costs, but Nkrumah's ambition went farther than London's. He wanted enough electricity to power a smelter to produce aluminum, creating a new sector in Ghana's economy. Nkrumah mentioned the project to Nixon in 1957, and then directly to Eisenhower at the White House in 1958.[55] Both president and vice president responded politely but coldly. Eisenhower's take was that Washington may consider making a financial contribution for the Akosombo Dam only if Ghana made sure to look for the bulk of the funding elsewhere. He suggested the International Bank for Reconstruction and Development and private investors.[56] It was clear that Eisenhower had little time for Nkrumah's schemes, to the point that Ambassador Flake was instructed by the State Department not to mention the Volta dam when discussing with the Ghanaian government projects that the US might consider funding.[57] Even the usually pro-American Gbedemah declared to the *Manchester Guardian* that if the West was not ready to offer sufficient funds toward the realization of the Volta project, then the government of Ghana would look in "another place," a fairly obvious reference to the Soviet Union.[58]

The Akosombo Dam was not the only point of contention with regard to the future of Ghana's economy. As the entire economic strategy was being worked out, a clash between two alternative visions took shape in Accra. Shortly before independence, Nkrumah chose W. Arthur Lewis as chief economic adviser of the new government. Lewis was in many respects the ideal adviser for Ghana.

Born in Saint Lucia from a family of Antiguan descent, Lewis had become the first black member of staff to teach at the London School of Economics immediately after World War II. In 1948 he moved to the University of Manchester, where he became the first Black professor to hold a permanent chair in a British university. In Manchester, Lewis pioneered the study of the patterns of growth in developing countries and of economic development in general. Thanks to his academic and personal background, the Colonial Office sought his advice on the future of British trade policy toward soon-to-become-independent colonies. In 1957, Lewis began his work for Ghana.[59]

Grounded in anti-imperialism and a firm belief in the necessity of rapid modernization in the former colonies, Lewis's worldview partly coincided with Nkrumah's. Both looked at Ghana's development as a task of historical significance, and both believed the country needed to boost agricultural production and establish a local industry. Similarities, however, ended here. An early draft of Lewis's development plan was presented to the Ghanaian government in June 1958. In it, Lewis recommended granting unlimited access to the Ghanaian market to foreign enterprises for the next five to ten years. The goal was to create in Ghana an industry that would work in close collaboration with the businesses that already operated in connection with the cocoa trade. Lewis saw no alternative to attracting investments from foreign private operators to supply Ghana with the capital it needed. The cocoa trade was the only sector of the economy developed enough to attract them.[60]

Not every member of the cabinet reacted with enthusiasm to the proposed plan. Several ministers, including Botsio, manifested their unhappiness with Ghana's overreliance on the export of cocoa beans, which in their opinion was destined to grow even more if Ghana followed Lewis's recommendations. Nkrumah himself, who held Lewis in great esteem, was not entirely convinced by his development plan and spoke in favor of reducing the role of private enterprise in favor of more state control.[61] Nkrumah had shown signs of disagreement with Lewis's ideas even before the official unveiling of the plan. In December 1957, the Ghanaian prime minister asked Potekhin to comment on the plan for economic development, implying that he was not convinced by it. Potekhin found the plan unsatisfactory and, urged by Nkrumah, proposed strengthening the cooperation with other African states and opening relations with the socialist world instead.[62] Potekhin's comments were too banal and vague to be an actual alternative strategy. Nonetheless, it was obvious that the Ghanaian leader harbored doubts about the future of his country, and he was aware that the socialist world might represent an alternative model of economic and social development—one that Nkrumah was at least willing to consider. In the end, the Ghanaian government agreed that Lewis's draft plan needed to be revised to allow for some areas of the national economy to be developed without private enterprise.[63] Ghana had not made a precise choice yet; its economic future was all to be determined. However, influential voices in its leadership questioned the wisdom of adopting a capitalist system as a model and the international market as a guide. This was an opportunity the Soviet Union was not going to let slip.

A Diplomatic Revolution

In April 1959, the Ghanaian government finally yielded to Moscow's protracted pressure. Mikhail Sytenko became the USSR's first ambassador to Ghana, and a Soviet embassy began operating in Accra the following August, after nearly two years of unsuccessful Soviet attempts to establish diplomatic relations with Ghana. It was hardly a breakthrough. The Accra government imposed a strict quantitative limit on Soviet personnel (no more than eighteen people could work at the embassy), as advocated by Britain and the United States.[64] Moreover, the Special Branch of the Ghanaian police, with the active collaboration of MI5, the British internal security service, planned to keep an eye on the Soviet embassy. They even considered tapping telephone lines and intercepting correspondence.[65]

As Orestov wrote, Ghana was still in a "spiritual, cultural and psychological dependency on Britain."[66] Ghanaian institutions were modeled on British equivalents, and the Ghanaian ruling class had been by and large trained in the United Kingdom. Many key posts in government and administration—from the army commanding officer to the chairman of the central bank—remained occupied by British officials. London's grip on the cocoa trade completed the picture, making the extent of Ghana's independence a matter of debate, and not only in the Soviet Union. Franz Fanon, who was the Algerian provisional government's ambassador to Accra between 1960 and 1961, also harbored doubts. He respected Nkrumah as a Pan-Africanist and commended Ghana's achievement of independence. The two, however, disagreed on the methods. Fanon advocated the necessity to use violence to free Africa from imperialism, whereas Nkrumah at the time still subscribed to the complete rejection of violence against the European colonialists. Fanon hoped to make Ghana a base from where to recruit and train Africans to fight for independence, both ideologically and militarily. What he saw around him in Accra did not fully convince him, though. In the *Wretched of the Earth*, Fanon complained that "the Assembly of Chiefs in Ghana hold its ground against Nkrumah." This was an expression of continuing colonial power in the country, for in Fanon's view it was the colonialists that mobilized the most conservative elements of the population against the national government.[67]

Soviet observers were on the same line. In Orestov's view, complete independence would be achieved only when the Accra government managed to rule the
country without relying on Western advisers and Western money. Yet he was
not completely negative about the state of Ghana. The Soviet correspondent remarked that Ghana's leadership remained strongly hostile to British colonialism. Nkrumah's government had to be formally pro-London in order not to "risk
economic chaos in the country," given Ghana's current state of dependency.
Nonetheless, since independence Nkrumah had been slowly, but constantly,
working to curtail the influence of British advisers and councilors in the state
apparatus. The government had been critical of London's policies, and there were
several "progressive elements" in the CPP and in the trade unions that pressured
Nkrumah to be even more anti-British. Orestov approved the prime minister's
repression of political opposition, for, in his judgment, the United Party was simply London's puppet. If Nkrumah's personal power grew, then things in Ghana
were destined to change.[68]

The Soviet government was willing to bet on Ghana. Immediately after the
establishment of diplomatic relations in April 1959, a Soviet delegation arrived
in Ghana to discuss the terms of a trade agreement between the two countries.
Part of the Ghanaian government knew nothing of it. Patrick Quaidoo, who had
replaced Botsio as minister of trade in 1958, reported to his cabinet colleagues
that he had been surprised by the arrival of the delegates from the USSR. A program of meetings and visits for the Soviet visitors was put together in a rush.[69]

Whether the Accra government really did not know the Soviet intentions, or
they feigned ignorance not to upset their Western partners, Nkrumah and his
ministers certainly were not able to make the most of the USSR's offers. The Soviet delegation came with concrete proposals. The core idea was the establishment of a barter agreement, similar to the one the Soviet Union had recently
signed with Guinea. Machinery and technology from the USSR and the rest of
the Soviet bloc could be exchanged with Ghanaian cocoa beans. As a demonstration of interest in Ghana, the Soviet Union was ready to make additional purchases of cocoa paying in hard currency—a sign of goodwill from Moscow,
which normally preferred barter agreements.[70] However, Ghana was unable to
accept Soviet proposals. The Ministry of Trade and Labor's official position was
that "during the discussions it became obvious that, in view of the international
obligations of Ghana, the terms of any formal agreement on trade between the
two countries would require careful consideration, and that the departmental
and other consultations necessary before the conclusion of such an Agreement
would entail more time than is available during the present visit of the Representatives of the U.S.S.R. Ministry of Foreign Trade to Ghana."[71]

The mention of "international obligations" hinted at Accra's lack of control over the cocoa trade. As long as the final say on the selling price of cocoa beans rested with Tansley and the Cocoa Marketing Company in London, working out a barter agreement with Moscow was out of the question. As a consequence, in 1959 the Soviet Union imported 7.5 million rubles of cocoa from Ghana, paid for in hard currency, and exported only 600 thousand rubles worth of machinery. For the time being, imports from the USSR were relegated to the margins of the Ghanaian economy.[72]

Not all was lost from the Soviet point of view, however. If some observers in MID viewed British influence in Ghana as too strong and US influence on the rise, others noted that the Ghanaian government never ruled out closer relations with the USSR. If Ghana did not receive the aid it expected from the Western powers, then it would not be unreasonable to think of an opening toward the socialist bloc. Should the Americans drag their feet on funding the Volta project, Nkrumah was ready to look East. The future of Soviet-Ghanaian relations depended on the direction that the executive in Accra decided to take; embracing the special relationship with London and Washington, or reforming the structure of the country's economy? As the next chapter shows, Nkrumah's vision, aided by a series of circumstances, pushed Ghana closer to the Soviet Union. Until then, two former French colonies seemed to offer better prospects from the Soviet point of view.

Learning to Say No: From French West Africa to Independent Guinea and Mali

Stable European colonization came to Guinea and Mali relatively late. Similar to Britain in Ghana, another major European power—France—established a colony in West Africa at the end of the nineteenth century through a series of military campaigns against local kingdoms.[73]

Both Guinea and Mali (with the name Soudan Français, French Soudan) were part of the Afrique Occidentale Française (AOF; French West Africa), a large swathe of land that besides Guinea and Mali comprised modern-day Benin (Dahomey), Burkina Faso (Haute Volta, Upper Volta), Côte d'Ivoire, Mauritania, Niger, Senegal, and, after 1919, Togo. The entire territory was under the administration of a governor-general, based in Dakar. Beyond some historic settlements in Senegal (the so-called Quatre Communes, whose inhabitants were French citizens and could elect deputies to the Assemblée Nationale), French presence on the ground was thin. The colonial administration in Guinea and Mali relied on hundreds of local functionaries and intermediaries for most run-of-the-mill tasks, including tax collection, policing, and labor recruitment.[74]

As in most of colonial Africa, the main economic function of the AOF was exporting commodities to the *métropole*. In Guinea there was no single product, such as cocoa in Ghana, that dominated exports and needed a separate administrative structure to manage its production and sale. Guinea exported fruit and vegetables and limited quantity of minerals to France through well-established colonial networks. The case of Mali was slightly different. In the 1920s, French Soudan had been chosen to become the prime source of cotton for the French textile industry. The colonial administration launched its most ambitious modernization project in West Africa, which aimed to transform the Niger valley into one of the world's largest cotton plantation through intensive cultivation and modern irrigation techniques. Created in 1932, the Office du Niger was the agency responsible for running the project. The plan did not produce the expected results. The office was plagued by poor productivity, which the brutal methods to recruit and discipline workers did not help to improve, attracting widespread criticism instead.[75]

French domination over its colonies in West Africa began to change in the mid-1930s. First, the impact of the Great Depression was particularly strong in the AOF. The volume of West African exports to France contracted significantly due to much lower demand in the *métropole*. Deprived of its source of revenues and desperate for resources, the colonial administration resorted to higher taxes and lower remuneration for African farmers and workers. Discontent among the local population was the obvious consequence. Meanwhile, in 1936 the Front Populaire won the elections in France. The new government authorized the formation of trade unions in the French empire, as well as allowing freedom of movement between the colonies. The resentment born out of the economic crisis and the brutal treatment of West African workers found an outlet. A wave of strikes hit the AOF in 1936–37, which the colonial administration repressed using armed troops, leading to yet more resentment. On the eve of the war, the situation in the AOF seemed back to normality, with the turmoil completely quashed and the colonial territories ordinarily contributing troops to the French war efforts. Following the fall of Paris in 1940, French West Africa chose to stay in the Vichy camp. The new colonial administration rolled back the limited reforms introduced by the Popular Front, extending the practice of forced labor and further limiting the privileges of the West African elites. The AOF's switch from Vichy to the Free French in 1943 did not alter the exploitation of West African workers.[76]

After the end of the war, growing resentment at racial discrimination and thousands of colonial soldiers who returned home with ideas of independence put considerable pressure on the French colonial administration in West Africa, as well as elsewhere in the empire. West African elected representatives took part in France's Constituent Assembly in 1945–1946, and the newly born Fourth Republic granted West African citizens the right to elect representatives in local councils. In 1946, the Rassemblement Démocratique Africain (RDA) was created at a congress in Bamako. The RDA was a political party that aimed to bring together the various movements in French West and Equatorial Africa that were associated with the French Communist (Parti Communiste Français, PCF) and Socialist (Section Française de l'International Ouvrière) parties. Amid pronounced differences in attitudes and political sympathies, the RDA's goal was to present a common front to demand increased autonomy and better economic conditions for the French colonies in Africa. It was in this context that the future leaders of Guinea and Mali took their first steps toward independence.[77]

Ahmed Sékou Touré was born in 1922 in a small town in central Guinea. His family was not well off, but they were descendants of Samory Touré, one of the tribal chiefs who had resisted French colonization in the late nineteenth century. Sékou Touré finished school and found employment with the Postal Service. During his early working years he became radicalized, joining the trade union of postal workers and eventually ascending to the post of General-Secretary of the same union in 1945. Sékou Touré's political career took off after the end of World War II. He was one of the founding members of the Parti Démocratique de Guinée (PDG), the Guinean branch of the RDA, in 1947 and was elected party leader in 1952. In 1956, thanks to the new Loi-Cadre that allowed colonies to elect representatives at the Assemblée Nationale, he was elected Guinea's representative to the French parliament. Whereas the RDA moved away from the PCF and communism in general as a result of France's position in the Cold War, the PDG in Guinea remained committed to the collective organization of labor and mobilization of the masses. Independence, not autonomy, was the goal.[78]

Modibo Keïta's background was different. Born in 1915 in Bamako from a family whose roots stretched back to the Mali Empire, Keïta attended the École Normale Supérieur William Ponty in Dakar, the leading French educational institution in the AOF that formed the West African elite. After qualifying and working as a teacher, he joined one of the first Communist groups in French Soudan and was among the leading figures behind the establishment of the RDA at the Bamako conference in 1946. At the same time, Keïta helped found the Union Soudanaise (US-RDA), the RDA's branch in French Soudan. In 1956, he was elected to the National Assembly in Paris. He later served as Secretary of State for Overseas Territories in two French governments. Keïta's political career brought him closer to the French establishment than Sékou Touré. Even though he remained a socialist and a convinced anticolonialist, Keïta was willing to cooperate with the French authorities and reach independence through gradual steps.[79]

The Empire Strikes Back

The collapse of the Fourth Republic gave both Sékou Touré and Keïta the opportunity they needed. In late 1958 Charles de Gaulle was called back to government, with the aim of drafting a new constitution that would give birth to the Fifth Republic. Colonial issues, especially the ongoing war in Algeria, were at the forefront of the crisis that had engulfed and swept away the Fourth Republic. The new constitution proposed to create a Communauté Française to replace the imperial system. Being part of the Communauté meant remaining in the French orbit, but members were given the possibility of requesting complete independence in the future. A referendum with universal suffrage was scheduled on September 28, 1958 in order to approve or reject the new constitution in France and in all its colonial possessions.[80]

The RDA was generally supportive of the new constitution, which received virtually unanimous support across French Africa.[81] In French Soudan, following the approval of the constitution in September 1958 (with 97.54 percent of votes in favor), an intergovernmental conference was called in Bamako in December 1958 to establish a new union under the umbrella of the Communauté. Keïta and Léopold Senghor, the Senegalese leader, decided to merge French Soudan and Senegal together, whereas Haute Volta and Dahomey abandoned the project. The Fédération du Mali, a clear reminder of the past glories of the Mali Empire, was officially formed in January 1959.[82]

Developments in Guinea were far more dramatic. The country was the only one in the French empire to vote "no" in the referendum. The PDG, which controlled an absolute majority since 1957, campaigned for immediate total independence and the rejection of all links to the *métropole*. The result was overwhelming. More than 95 percent of Guinean voters dismissed de Gaulle's constitution, with the second-highest turnout in West Africa and the third highest in the whole empire. It was a victory for the leftists in the PDG and a slap in the face of the newly born Fifth Republic.[83]

The French government reacted to the outcome of the referendum in Guinea with anger. Paris ordered the withdrawal of all French personnel from the country and the removal of whatever equipment that could be transported—medicines, lightbulbs, telephones, and vehicles were taken back to France. Some fixed infrastructures, such as buildings and plants, were deliberately damaged during the withdrawal. As Elizabeth Schmidt wrote, the French even cracked state dishes "in a gesture laden with pettiness and symbolism." Moreover, France suspended all forms of economic exchange with Guinea, cutting aid and imposing a trade embargo with the collaboration of the rest of the French community in Africa. The young Guinean Republic, lacking qualified personnel to run the administration and dependent on imports for the most basic of necessities, risked being strangled at birth.[84]

The only way for Guinea to make independence from France viable in the long term was to seek help from abroad, which required obtaining formal diplomatic recognition first. Immediately after independence, Sékou Touré sent a telegram to several governments, including the Soviet and American ones, announcing the result of the referendum and signaling Guinea's readiness to establish diplomatic relations.[85] The French, however, put pressure on Washington not to recognize Guinea. The Ministère de la France d'Outre-Mer feared that recognizing Guinea "could complicate France's policy with regard to other territories in French Africa" and advised caution. Hervé Alphand, the French ambassador to the United States, recommended that the United Nations take time to reflect before admitting Guinea as a new member. Paris played the communist card, stressing Sékou Touré's supposedly socialist ideas and his apparent willingness to work with socialist countries. Washington hesitated. On the one hand, American officials were concerned that not recognizing Guinea might throw the newly independent state directly into the Soviet Union's arms. On the other, the US administration found it difficult to resist French insistence. The establishment of relations between Guinea and the West was therefore delayed.[86]

Contrary to the West, the Soviet government wasted no time. Following the receipt of Sékou Touré's telegram, MID deputy director Kuznetsov reported to the Central Committee that exchanging diplomatic representatives with Guinea would be consistent with the Soviet policy of friendship and support toward newly independent African states. Kuznetsov also anticipated that Guinea would soon try to obtain a seat at the United Nations and expressed the view that the Soviet Union should support its request. The Presidium discussed the matter on October 4, approving a resolution that followed the Foreign Ministry's recommendations. A positive reply was sent to Sékou Touré on the same day.[87]

The establishment of relations between Guinea and the USSR, nevertheless, was not as smooth as anticipated. On November 8, Foreign Minister Gromyko wrote to the Central Committee signaling that a month after the initial promising start the Soviet Union had not "managed to establish a direct contact with the government of the Guinean Republic" yet. Moreover, the *Pravda* correspondent in Paris, who was planning to visit Guinea, was prevented from reaching the country by the French authorities, which refused him permission to travel through the French territories in West Africa. Even though Gromyko did not mention it, it was clear that the Guinean government was dragging its feet in the hope of securing recognition from the West before officially opening to the Soviet Union. Gromyko repeated that, in the MID's opinion, establishing contacts with Sékou Touré's government was a suitable policy, and suggested sending Pavel Gerasimov, a counselor at the Soviet Embassy in the United Arab Republic, to Guinea to discuss "the perspectives of Soviet-Guinean relations and to probe the Guineans' reaction to the possibility of setting up a Soviet embassy in Conakry." The Foreign Ministry proposed to send somebody from the State Committee on Foreign Economic Relatons (GKES) and a *Pravda* journalist along with Gerasimov. The Presidium agreed with Gromyko's proposal. It was decided that Gerasimov would reach Conakry via Accra in late 1958.[88]

Gerasimov's visit to Conakry took place from December 1 to December 13, 1958. "The goal of this trip"—Gerasimov wrote back to the MID in his report— "was the establishment of a direct contact with the government of the Guinean Republic, an exchange of opinions about the prospects of development of Soviet-Guinean political, economic and cultural relations and a study of the internal situation and the foreign policy of the country." The Soviet delegation met President Sékou Touré, as well as various government Ministers and representatives of the leading Democratic Party of Guinea.[89]

The visit was a success. Sékou Touré and his ministers expressed interest in developing relations with Moscow, and they seemed certain of the Soviet Union's friendly support in the struggle for full independence. However, the exchange of diplomatic personnel between the two countries was still problematic: the Guinean Minister of Cooperation stated that "at the moment, Guinea is forced not to be tacked, not to join one bloc." Apparently, Sékou Touré judged it more convenient to establish formal diplomatic relations first with a capitalist country, and only then with the socialist world. In this way, Gerasimov reported, the Guinean president wanted to avoid irritating France, which otherwise would form a "united front with Britain and the USA" and "try to strangle the Guinean Republic." The Guinean leader insisted that this was only a tactical expedient, and that Guinea would soon turn its attention toward the Soviet Union. Gerasimov reported that special attention had been given during the meetings to showing how building diplomatic relations with the socialist camp would help Guinea in its struggle with the imperialists, pointing out as examples Soviet support for Egypt, Syria, and Iraq.[90]

Several Guinean ministers made informal inquiries about obtaining equipment for the newly formed Guinean army. They were told that the Soviet Union did supply weapons to some countries, such as Egypt and Syria, and "should such a request arrive from the Guinean government, it will be examined with attention." Guinea also showed readiness to sell fruit to the Soviet Union, partly in exchange for Soviet industrial goods. Moreover, the Minister of National Education "expressed a wish about the concession of some scholarships for Guineans students in Soviet institutes of higher education (mainly technical)."[91]

On December 12, Gerasimov met Sékou Touré for the last time, and they agreed on a few crucial points. First, the Guinean president sought to establish commercial and cultural agreements with the Soviet Union. Therefore, a Soviet delegation was invited to travel to Conakry at any time to prepare such agreements. Second, the Guinean government would send to Moscow the Secretary of State for Foreign Contacts, Diallo Abdulaye, with the main purpose of discussing Soviet economic aid to Guinea. Finally, Sékou Touré repeated that formal diplomatic relations between the two countries would be established in the near future. All talks of economic aid or bilateral trade were held off until the following year.[92]

Things moved quickly in 1959. Guinea finally managed to obtain diplomatic recognition from the United States. However, it was far less successful in convincing the Americans to grant aid or to lobby Paris to change its policy of noncooperation with Guinea.[93] Any reservation Sékou Touré might have had about veering toward one side in the Cold War evaporated in the face of American dithering and Soviet resolve to act rapidly. In January 1959, the CPSU Central Committee authorized a delegation to travel to Guinea to arrange the opening of a Soviet embassy in Conakry and to negotiate the terms of an economic cooperation agreement between the two countries.[94] Shortly thereafter, Guinea received small arms from Czechoslovakia, free of charge, together with a small group of military advisers. As British and French intelligence noted, the number of weapons was far above the limited needs of Guinea's small army. The Czechoslovak supplies included: 6,000 rifles, 6,000 hand grenades, 1,000 automatic handguns, about 500 bazookas, 20 heavy machine guns, 6 mortars, 6 small cannons, as well as 10 large tents, 10 sidecars, 5 field kitchens, and 2 armored Škodas. At the time, the Guinean army comprised only about 3,500 soldiers, who were able to use only French-made weapons. According to French intelligence, "the value of only the first batch [of Czechoslovak weapons] exceeds Guinea's entire military budget." The Soviet bloc was clearly going to great lengths to signal its readiness to do business with Guinea.[95]

The Conakry government realized that the opportunity offered by the USSR was too useful to let it pass. On April 16, Gerasimov—the same diplomat who had made the first trip in 1958—arrived in Conakry to become the Soviet Union's first ambassador to Guinea. He was received at the airport by Secretary of State Cissé Fonde with great pomp, including an orchestra playing the national anthems and an escort of motorcyclists. Gerasimov's inaugural speech was broadcast on the national radio and then published in the local press. Sékou Touré's welcome speech stressed the fact that Guinea had cut all links to France. In his words, independence was only the first step of a "revolution" that he intended to carry out on the "economic, social, political, and moral" levels.[96] The Guinean government wanted to show how important the establishment of formal links with the USSR was. A few months later, in September 1959, Seydou Conté was nominated Guinean ambassador to Moscow.[97] A new era of cooperation was about to begin.

Guinea offered more promising prospects for the USSR than Ghana because its links to France had been severed. Sékou Touré himself told a visiting Soviet official that "Guinea and Ghana are two completely different states. Ghana received independence only nominally: now as before the British hold complete sway, the feudal elite and the government are bought and bribed by the British, corruption thrives in the country, the 'comprador bourgeoisie' propagates itself."[98] Because of its vote in the independence referendum, Guinea now faced political isolation and economic difficulties. The new government needed political support and, most of all, economic aid from a foreign sponsor. Moscow knew it could provide both, and by doing this it could establish a base from which to spread its ideas and promote its model of development in Africa. Sékou Touré may or may not have been a real Marxist (the French communists seemed to think he was), but this was not the point.[99] From Moscow's point of view, Guinea deserved attention because it had rejected the West.

A New Hope: Mali Breaks with the West

The formation of the Mali Federation in early 1959 aroused scarce interest in Moscow. As part of the Communauté Française, the new territory was assumed to be autonomous only in name. The first secretary of the Soviet embassy in Conakry, V.I. Ivanisov, called the creation of the Federation "reformist," as opposed to Guinea's "revolutionary" choice to leave the Communauté. The Federation leader—Senegalese president Senghor—was described as a convinced Catholic who nurtured anti-Soviet feelings. The Soudanese leader, Modibo Keïta, had more progressive ideas but his party, the Union Soudanaise, played only a "secondary role in the national movement," therefore offering little hopes of an opening toward the socialist world.[100]

Ivanisov underestimated Keïta's determination to create an independent state free of French influence, with or without the union with Senegal. In less than one year, thanks to his inflammatory rhetoric and seeming unwillingness to compromise on matters of principle, Keïta managed to become one of the most prominent leaders of the Mali Federation. In June 1960, the Federation was meant to become fully independent from France. Keïta was the most popular leader and was poised to become the president of the nascent constituent assembly—a promising development from the Soviet point of view. The MID changed its assessment of the Mali Federation, and now advised the Central Committee to write to Keïta proposing formal recognition of the Federation and the exchange of diplomatic representatives.[101] The Foreign Ministry believed that supporting an independent Mali Federation would speed the process of creation of a larger Federation encompassing all former French colonies in the region and the emergence of more radical leaders.[102] On June 20, the day of independence, Khrushchev sent an official message to Keïta, extending his congratulations and offering formal recognition and the possibility of future cooperation with Moscow. Keïta replied favorably on July 8.[103]

Once again, MID's judgment of the situation in Mali was somewhat off the mark. As expected, Keïta was elected president of the constituent assembly on July 20. However, the Mali Federation itself was not to survive much longer: On August 20, two months after independence, Senegal seceded from the union to form an independent, autonomous state as a result of a prolonged standoff with the Soudanese leadership over the organization of power in the Federation. This contrasted with MID's hopes, which maintained that the Mali Federation was the first step toward the creation of a French-speaking West African "super state." The Soviet embassy in Guinea, which followed events in French West Africa, blamed foreign intervention for the break-up of the Federation. According to the embassy, French and American agents had acted together with Senghor to make the project of integration between the two countries fail, so that France could keep its colonial interests in Senegal and Senghor could obtain more power at the expense of Keïta. The independent Republic of Mali, formerly Soudanese Republic, was officially created on September 22, with Keïta as president.[104]

The end of the Mali Federation turned out to be favorable to Moscow. The uneasy cohabitation of moderate Senghor and leftist Keïta was over, and newly born Mali was able to pursue a more radical foreign policy. Keïta had nothing to envy Nkrumah or Sékou Touré in terms of anticolonial feelings and interest in socialism. He opposed the idea of keeping some sort of relationship with France and had since a young age gravitated toward socialist organizations and movements. Moreover, his US-RDA had a large and well-organized structure in the country, able to engage virtually all strata of the population. Building a bilateral relationship with Keïta's Mali was therefore in line with Khrushchev's policy of looking for allies among radical nationalists in the Third World.[105]

Keïta was open in his decision to follow Guinea's course and call on the socialist world for help. As early as September 4 a delegation from Mali visited Conakry and met with representatives of the socialist countries, including the Soviet ambassador. The Malians made it clear that their goal was to create a fully independent state, free from all French influence, and "arrange cooperation with Guinea and the socialist countries, in the first place with the Soviet Union."[106] On October 5 the Presidium recognized Mali as an independent state. A few days later, Khrushchev sent Keïta a telegram signaling the USSR's readiness to establish diplomatic relations and exchange ambassadors, to which the Malian leader replied positively. Diplomatic relations were formally established in December.[107]

Once again, Moscow faced limited competition from the West at this stage. The French government had no problems with recognizing the new Mali in September 1960, even if it had left the Communauté. However, as the Bamako government began to pursue a more radical line both in foreign and domestic policy, Paris wavered on previous offers of aid. The French agreed with the British that most of their economic aid should focus on those territories that had remained members of the Communauté/Commonwealth and generally maintained friendly relations with the former colonial powers. As for the more radical states, such as Ghana, Guinea, and Mali, both London and Paris thought that aid competition with the socialist bloc made sense only if the Americans were behind it.[108]

Despite European hopes, US interest in Mali was relatively low. The State Department was "particularly anxious to avoid a repetition of the Guinean experience" and thus encouraged Eisenhower to recognize Mali immediately and suggest that the United States was interested in cooperation in the near future.[109] Local pro-Western governments, such as Félix Houphouët-Boigny's in Côte d'Ivoire, urged the Americans to extend aid to Mali as soon as possible, lest the Bamako government become too close to the USSR. This time, the French raised no objections. However, it was Eisenhower, whose days in office were approaching the end, who had reservations. He saw little point in committing the US to Mali, absent a larger aid framework that involved the whole of sub-Saharan Africa. He also made it clear that he preferred aid to be channeled through the UN, or even through the former *métropole*, rather than coming from the US government. The treasury was in full agreement with Eisenhower. Granting aid to Mali would constitute a precedent that may in the future tie the United States to offer the same treatment to more newly independent countries. In the end, it was agreed that the United States would accord only limited sums to Mali, and then try to get the UN involved for longer-term aid in an unspecified future.[110]

Confronted with American indifference, the Bamako government wasted no time in developing further the first promising contacts it had had with the Soviet Union. At the end of September 1960, before the USSR and the nascent Republic of Mali had even established official diplomatic relations, Usman Ba, minister of civil administration, work and social affairs of the provisional Mali government, visited Moscow to probe the possibility of receiving help from the Soviet Union. As soon as Mali became independent, a delegation from the Soviet Ministry of Foreign Trade and from GKES was sent to Mali for two months (October and November 1960) to prepare a trade and cooperation agreement with the new state. Mali was immediately granted a credit of eight million rubles, and it was decided that 25 percent of Malian exports to the Soviet Union would be paid for in hard currency—a way to transfer much needed resources to the Bamako government. A more comprehensive aid and trade package was under study. Keïta was grateful. In November he wrote to Khrushchev thanking him for the USSR's help and announcing that Mali was ready to undertake profound social and economic reforms, with the goal of improving the living standards of the population through central planning and state control. After Guinea and Ghana, a third radical West African state entered the Soviet orbit.[111]

In November 1959, the Service de Documentation Extérieure et de Contre-Espionnage (SDECE), France's main intelligence agency, reviewed Soviet "penetration" in Africa. Its assessment was worrying. "Behind all the nice words pronounced by the current master of all Russias—SDECE explained—hides the firm will to banish the influence of the Western world from the entire African continent—including from Algeria."[112] French intelligence was alarmist. The USSR had after all just managed to establish a foothold in a continent otherwise still dominated by the colonial powers. The Soviet Union was now a factor in West African politics and, crucially, economics.

Three factors helped the Soviet government establish relations with newly independent Ghana, Guinea, and Mali between 1957 and 1960. First, Moscow pursued its aim with perseverance and occasionally insistence. Even in the case of initial delays and difficulties, the USSR pressed for diplomatic recognition and stressed its readiness to start economic cooperation. The Soviet leadership knew that Ghana, Guinea, and Mali initially did not particularly favor the USSR, and in some cases openly preferred building relations with the West first. This did not prevent Moscow from courting Nkrumah, Sékou Touré, and Keïta, and it shows the extent to which Khrushchev and his Presidium colleagues believed in establishing new contacts with the Third World. They were confident in the economic strength of socialism. It did not matter that the Soviet Union started from a position of relative weakness compared to the United States, with its political and economic might, and to long-established colonial powers, which had operated in West Africa for over a century. The attractiveness of Soviet assistance as a fast-track modernization project compensated for the initial disadvantage.

Second, the West moved slowly and clumsily. The Americans looked at West Africa as a backwater that offered little rewards. The Eisenhower administration was wary of committing American resources to the region and preferred delegating to London and Paris. The British were overconfident of their position of power in Ghana and overlooked both Nkrumah's determination to break free from colonialism and the USSR's interest in the country. The French seemed more interested in punishing Guinea for its decision to reject the Communauté than in maintaining their influence in Conakry. By the time the French government changed its policy, the Soviet Union had already established a foothold in West Africa, and Mali followed Guinea's example rather than privileging its links to France.

Third, and perhaps most important, the preferences and decisions of local elites in West Africa mattered. Nkrumah, Sékou Touré, and Keïta were not forced to choose the Soviet Union. They did so willingly. As the next chapter shows, the new leaders in Ghana, Guinea, and Mali shared with each other not only a strong dislike of the colonial West but also an equally strong interest in the USSR and the socialist bloc. Their common ambition was to make their countries politically independent and economically prosperous. The Soviet Union seemed to offer the perfect recipe.

4

THE HEART OF THE MATTER

In the spring of 1959, West German intelligence assessed Soviet presence in Guinea. Its conclusions were indicative of European paranoia about "communist penetration" in Africa. Pavel Gerasimov, the Soviet ambassador to Conakry, was defined as "one of the best specialists in African affairs of Soviet diplomacy." Gerasimov—who had received a technical education in Leningrad—had ended up in Guinea more by coincidence than because of his expertise. Previously a high-ranking diplomat in the Cairo embassy, his knowledge of sub-Saharan Africa was tangential. Soon, Gerasimov would leave Conakry and return to his real area of competence: the Middle East.[1] Furthermore, German intelligence noted that: "Among Gerasimov's collaborators there are a few Soviet Muslims who until now worked in Mukhitdinov's staff. They operate under the cover of economic experts and try to gain the trust of Sékou Tourè's collaborators through attractive offers of aid."[2]

Little did West German intelligence know that those agents under the cover of economic experts really were economic experts. Nuritidin Mukhitdinov was the first secretary of the Uzbek Communist Party and also a Presidium member. He benefited greatly from Khrushchev's opening to the Third World. Mukhitdinov presented Uzbekistan and the rest of Soviet Central Asia as potential models of development for the newly independent countries of Africa and Asia. Khrushchev appreciated and made him a key figure of Soviet foreign policy toward the developing world. That is why Central Asians were routinely chosen as Soviet economic experts in Africa and Asia: The Kremlin leadership assumed that they would be the most effective in selling the Soviet model, based on their knowledge and experience at home. Their offers of economic aid were not a pretext to obtain something else but rather the core activity of Soviet engagement with Guinea. The point was not communist subversion, as the Europeans expected. The Soviet government's ambition in West Africa was the construction of a new type of development.[3]

By the end of 1960, the Soviet Union had gained three new allies in West Africa and was ready to commit significant resources for their modernization. Moscow yearned to show the world that exporting state-led development abroad was not only possible but also more effective than traditional capitalism. Why West Africa? Size was key. Being relatively small, Ghana, Guinea, and Mali offered opportunities that other, larger, Third World countries did not. In 1948, following independence and partition, India had a population of 350 million, which rose to 418 million in 1958, and to nearly 450 million by 1961. This was more than twice the population of the Soviet Union in the same period. Indonesia had a population of slightly less than 80 million in 1949, the year of independence. By the early 1960s, it reached 100 million inhabitants, a size comparable to that of the entire Russian Soviet Federative Socialist Republic (Rossiiskaia Sovetskaia Federativnaia Sotsialisticheskaia Respublika), by far the largest Soviet republic. India and Indonesia—both recipients of Soviet aid—were giant countries, where Soviet economic assistance, however extensive, could have only a limited impact. Even much smaller Soviet partners in the Third World were still large countries. For example, in the 1960s Egypt's population was comparable to that of Soviet Ukraine, the second largest republic in the Union, on a scale of 30–40 million inhabitants.[4]

West Africa presented a completely different picture. In 1957, the year of independence, Ghana counted fewer than 6.5 million inhabitants, a size comparable to that of Soviet Uzbekistan (7.5). In the early 1960s, Guinea and Mali had populations of respectively approximately 3 and 4.5 million (Moscow's population in 1960 was roughly 5 million).[5] Imagining that the Soviet Union could economically sustain a Russia or Ukraine in South Asia or the Middle East was unthinkable. Helping to create an economic area the size of Moscow in West Africa, on the contrary, appeared a decidedly more manageable, if still ambitious, task.

However, creating a whole new Uzbekistan, or even just a new Moscow, was not the Soviet objective in West Africa, despite Moscow's extensive engagement in the local economies. The goal was instead to design a model of development that would prove effective given the existing conditions on the ground in Ghana, Guinea, and Mali. As economic and commercial relations deepened, Soviet policymakers, economists, and advisers needed to work out in practice how to reach the ambitious targets set out for Soviet development aid: the creation of mechanized agriculture, the development of small-scale industry, and independence from Western imports for basic goods and commodities. The only solution was mixing elements of central planning with a market system. This chapter analyzes the steps that the Soviet Union took toward this hybrid model, leading to the application in practice of the noncapitalist—but also noncommunist—model of development. West Africa was the ideal testing ground, thanks to its size and the willingness of its leaders to experiment with the boundaries of state and market.

Captains Courageous

Guinea was the country that needed Soviet aid the most, and Sékou Touré was the leader with the most radical attitude. Guinea was severely hit by the economic sanctions imposed by France and its allies in West Africa, which prevented Guinea from receiving economic aid from Paris and from trading with its neighbors. Cooperation with the Soviet Union was a possible way out of economic isolation and was therefore welcomed by the Guinean leadership. However, need was not the only reason to seek Soviet assistance. Sékou Touré and his government were fascinated by the Soviet Union as a model of society and were interested in imitating it in Guinea.

In January 1959, the CPSU Central Committee authorized a Soviet delegation to visit Guinea to sign a preliminary commercial agreement. Every other topic, the TsK specified, would be discussed once a Soviet embassy was operative in Conakry.[6] The deputy head of the Africa department at the MVT, Leonid Ezhov, traveled to Conakry in January–February 1959. He met representatives of the Guinean government and conducted preliminary talks about the establishment of extensive commercial relations. Ezhov reported that the Guineans were interested in studying the Soviet Union in the most disparate fields, from the mechanization of agriculture to the eradication of illiteracy, and from the formation of cooperatives to the organization of the Party and of the army. In particular, Sékou Toureé wished to make use of the Soviet experience to "organize the economy," with the aim of limiting the influence of foreign companies and foreign capital. Sékou Touré's plans fit Khrushchev's hopes for the Third World. Guinea was looking for a model to follow, and the USSR promised the type of modernization the Conakry government aspired to.[7]

The pioneering trade treaty between the Soviet Union and Guinea was signed in February 1959. It was essentially a barter agreement, and it was onerous for the Soviet Union. Guinea could acquire relatively expensive technology from the USSR in exchange for agricultural products valued above their market price.[8] As a contemporary British intelligence report on the situation in Guinea explained, Guinea's agricultural exports were uncompetitive. Importing them did not make economic sense but was uniquely useful as a "political premium." Buying Guinea's bananas and pineapples at prices above the market average was after all what France had long been doing before independence. The Joint Intelligence Committee in London reckoned that there lay the key to gaining influence in Conakry, for Guinea was dependent on foreign trade to obtain the essential primary goods it did not produce.[9]

A few months later, following the opening of the Soviet embassy in Conakry, Gerasimov extended to Sékou Touré an official invite for a Guinean delegation to visit the Soviet Union and work out the terms of a comprehensive economic cooperation treaty between the two countries.[10] The visit took place in August 1959. Led by two of Sékou Touré's closest aides, his half-brother Ismaël Touré and Saifoulaye Diallo, president of the National Assembly and secretary of the PDG, the Guinean delegation spent nearly two weeks in the USSR. They met with Khrushchev while he was vacationing in Crimea, where they admired the sanatoria and chatted with Soviet holidaymakers. The delegates then visited Kiev, where they were shown a nearby kolkhoz and a garment factory, before reaching Leningrad and Moscow, where they discussed politics and economics with Mikoian. In Moscow, Diallo told a non-committal Mikoian that "communism does not scare us at all" and that "they say we have the economy of a People's Democracy, that we are communists, this must be because we did everything the people wished for."[11]

The Guinean delegates also spent a few days in Soviet Azerbaijan, which had been chosen by their hosts because it was largely Muslim like Guinea. This visit was especially significant. It was organized to impress the Guinean delegates with Soviet modernity. The aim was to show Touré, Diallo, and the other delegates what Guinea could look like in a few years' time, if it chose the noncapitalist way. The Guineans met local CPSU representatives in Baku, who impressed their guests by boasting that Azerbaijan had better technical cadres than France. The delegates then toured a factory that produced laminated tubes, and some of the oil platforms in the Caspian Sea. The visit was a success. According to the report sent to Mikoian, the Guineans were excited by the successes of Soviet development. Diallo agreed that there were many similarities between his country and Soviet Azerbaijan, and Touré must have delighted his Azeri hosts by stating that "this is how I imagine the future Republic of Guinea, when she firmly stands on her feet." Both requested materials in French to be able to study "the experience of Azerbaijan."[12]

Throughout the visit, the delegates from Guinea praised the "abundance and prosperity" they saw in the USSR and warmly congratulated Khrushchev on his leadership. During the conclusive speeches in Moscow, Mikoian reinforced the same concepts, describing the Soviet Union as a modern, developed nation, whose people were busy realizing the grandiose seven-year plan. Nonetheless, the USSR was ready to offer a helping hand to the peoples of Africa. Diallo reciprocated by repeatedly praising the "great achievements" of the Soviet Union. Another member of the delegation promised that once back home they would "tell the Guinean people all the truth about the Soviet Union, their loyal and certain friend." As some among the first African explorers of the postwar Soviet Union, Diallo and Touré's visit was especially significant. Its purpose was not just to study the USSR, its economy, and its leadership, but also to launch concrete cooperation between Moscow and Conakry. Their trip inaugurated an era of Soviet involvement in West Africa.[13]

On August 24, Diallo signed the first comprehensive economic cooperation agreement between the Soviet Union and a sub-Saharan African country. It comprised development aid, technical cooperation, and trade, and it would become the blueprint for future Soviet economic engagement in West Africa. The terms were simple. The Soviet Union granted the Republic of Guinea a loan of 140 million rubles, repayable in twelve years with a 2.5 percent annual interest rate. These were favorable conditions for, according to the Soviet government, the United States and other Western countries usually applied a 5 percent interest rate to similar loans. The credits would be used "in the construction of several industrial enterprises, in the development of agriculture and the building of roads, geological surveys for useful materials, and also in the field of healthcare and the preparation of national engineering-technical cadres." Aid was connected to trade. The Conakry government could use the loan to buy Soviet technology and machinery, which could be paid back using Guinean commodities, such as fruit and coffee, as established in the February treaty.[14]

Cooperation between the Soviet Union and Guinea picked up pace quickly. Sékou Touré became the first sub-Saharan African head of state to visit the Soviet Union. He arrived in Moscow in late November 1959.

> The reception accorded to M. Sékou Touré was out of all proportion to the size and present importance of Guinea. With the exception of Mr Khrushchev, who was on holiday, and Mr Mikoian, who was in Mexico, nearly all the members of the Party Presidium, a large number of ministers and a galaxy of Marshals attended the various social functions and ceremonies. In spite of the cold, the inhabitants of Moscow were turned out in force to welcome and see off M. Sékou Touré, and his activities were reported at length in the Soviet press, usually on the front page.[15]

After Moscow, Sékou Touré was taken to Gagra, on the Black Sea, where Khrushchev received him. The visit showed how much importance the Soviet leadership gave to building solid relations with Guinea. Sékou Touré was treated as a close and important ally, even though he always pointed out in his official speeches that Guinea did not belong to any bloc. Frol Kozlov, an influential Presidium member, declared that the Soviet Union was glad to "share with them our versatile experience in economic and cultural organization." "The development of the young Republic of Guinea—Kozlov continued—confirms once more that the nations that freed themselves from colonialism have true friends in the Soviet Union and the other socialist countries."[16]

Sékou Touré was delighted by the attention and made clear that he was after more than just cordial relations: "We are sure that the experience of the USSR will prove to be useful for us and our path will be based on the path taken by your country. Our visit, as also our relations with your country, is not purely sentimental. Your country and its historical path offer us a purport of our existence, a new example in history and therefore they play an enormous role in terms of the choice of the direction that our country will take."[17]

As a further sign of interest in Guinea, in March 1960 Gerasimov was replaced by Daniil Solod as Soviet ambassador to Conakry. Before Guinea, he had worked in Syria and Lebanon, and had been ambassador to Egypt at the time of the arms deal with the USSR and the agreement on the Aswan Dam. Sékou Touré made sure to receive the new ambassador—whose inaugural speech was broadcast on the national radio—with all honors, including a motorcade and a Republican Guard salute. By then, Guinea was already the USSR's closest associate in Africa, and one of Moscow's most important allies in the Third World. Soviet economic assistance, as Touré wanted, would shape Guinea's path to modernity. Guinea, however, was only one part of a larger project. Guinea's neighbors in West Africa were about to join it.[18]

Wind of Change

In January 1960, Harold Macmillan went on his first official visit to Ghana. At the end of his stay in Accra, the British prime minister could not help admitting that "Britain and Ghana do not always see the situation with the same eyes." The exchanges between Macmillan and Nkrumah had been cordial on the surface, but the Soviet embassy believed that tension between the two leaders was palpable. In conversations with Macmillan, Nkrumah repeatedly stressed Ghana's firm intention to support African liberation movements, even if it meant going against Western interests in Africa. Moreover, Nkrumah criticized Britain and the West for not condemning the French nuclear tests in the Sahara, which the Soviet Union had censured several times. Such firmness in criticizing British policy was unusual on Nkrumah's part, and it captured Moscow's attention.[19]

Many things had changed in Ghana since independence. In December 1958, Arthur Lewis had resigned from his post as chief economic adviser to the Ghanaian government. The reason indicated in his letter of resignation—disagreement with the government on how to treat a plant infection—hid a much vaster discomfort. Since the discussion of Lewis's draft development plan the previous June, his personal relationship with Nkrumah had deteriorated. Lewis and Nkrumah were at odds about Ghana's development strategy and openly resented each other. The Ghanaian government significantly modified Lewis's initial draft of the development plan. They now envisaged a total expenditure of 100 million pounds, to include undertakings that Nkrumah and others believed to be essential. Lewis was shocked by what he saw as the Accra cabinet's willingness to waste resources on useless prestige projects. He blamed Nkrumah. In August 1958, he wrote to Nkrumah that: "The idea of spending money on embassies, air forces, yachts, making Ghana's voice heard all over the world, and other such boastfulness is downright sinful so long as 80 percent of the people still have no water and so long as one baby in every three still dies before it is five years old. You belong to the class of great leaders of small countries like Masaryk, Ben Gurion, Muñoz Marín, Cardenas, and U Nu, none of whom would for one moment consider spending £18 million on such baubles."[20]

The problem was that embassies, air forces, and especially making Ghana's voice heard in the world were precisely what Nkrumah wanted. His vision of development and modernization differed from that of his main economic adviser quite substantially. Lewis was a technocrat, who saw his task as overseeing the transition from the colony of the Gold Coast to independent Ghana in the smoothest possible way, favoring the attainment of basic development goals. Nkrumah was a dreamer, whose ambition was to make Ghana a great nation and to unify all other soon-to-be independent African countries under its aegis. The issue that divided Nkrumah and Lewis was time. As was made clear by the draft of his development plan, Lewis believed that modernization could come to Ghana only slowly. In his view, Ghana should not hurry to discourage the production of cocoa, even in the face of declining prices. "To abandon cocoa while it is still profitable is like committing suicide now because if one doesn't, one will only die at some future date." Although he was generally in favor of developing industry in Ghana and of protecting it against foreign competition, the British economist also thought that "for the time being, if we are to have more factories, we must rely on foreign private enterprise." Foreign investment was essential to Ghana's strategy, according to Lewis, and the only way to guarantee a steady influx of capital was making sure that foreign investors found in Ghana the prospect of profit and a favorable economic environment. The most obvious investors to attract were the ones already active in the country. Thus, the surviving structures of imperial trade had to continue, at least for a while. Moreover, Lewis thought that the government needed to maintain a friendly outlook toward other potential foreign investors who may want to operate in Ghana, even though he knew that "some Ghanaians still find this cross a little hard to bear." He was skeptical of the possibility of replacing Western private capital with loans from the socialist world. "There are foolish housewives who buy everything that is offered to them on credit—Lewis quipped—but theirs is hardly a model for this Government to follow."[21]

Nkrumah thought differently. First, he resented the idea that Ghana would continue to operate as a colony. Second, he was suspicious of foreign businesses setting up shop in Ghana. At independence, Nkrumah had promised autonomy, not a compromise. Moreover, his vision of pan-Africanism and African unity required a strong, independent Ghana to lead independent Africa. With regional rival Nigeria, a much larger country than Ghana, to become independent in 1960, and Ethiopia, never tarnished by European colonization, also vying for leadership, Ghana's bid was anything but certain to succeed. The only way to lead the pan-African movement Nkrumah dreamed of was showing Africa and the world that Ghana was on the way to becoming the most modern, the most developed country on the continent. That is why the symbols of power—the embassies abroad, the airplanes, the voice that Lewis despised as extravagances—were so important to him. No time could be wasted following a careful development strategy that would take decades to bear the first visible fruits. Development needed to proceed at breakneck speed. Nkrumah openly talked of a "forced march" to progress, to be achieved in one generation. In terms of ambition, his vision was not unlike that of the Soviet Union of the 1930s, at the time of the first five-year plan. The rest of the government in Accra was less radical than Nkrumah. Nonetheless, they tended to side with him rather than Lewis in the numerous arguments on Ghana's future that took place over the summer of 1958. Even Gbedemah did not fully agree with Lewis. Given the scale of ambition in Accra, the Soviet experience was too obvious an example for the Ghanaian government to ignore it for much longer.[22]

Less than one year after Lewis's resignation, another major obstacle to the establishment of closer relations with Moscow fell. On September 23, 1959, George Padmore died. Long suffering from cirrhosis of the liver, he had traveled to London to seek treatment, where he passed away following severe complications. Padmore's death was both a major blow for Nkrumah's ambitions and a personal tragedy. He lost not only a key adviser, but also a close friend and an unparalleled inspiration for his ideas about Africa and the world. The Soviet government, on the other hand, was delighted. Given his past in the Comintern, Padmore, more than Lewis, had long been identified as the main enemy of the

Soviet Union in Ghana. He had always advocated a neutralist line for Ghana, equidistant from the two Cold War blocs. Even though Soviet assessments of him were comically inaccurate in describing a Cold Warrior bent on smearing the USSR, Padmore certainly had no desire to see Ghana moving closer to the Soviet Union. Now that he was out of the way, the Soviet embassy in Accra believed that Nkrumah would be more responsive to Moscow's offers.[23]

Changes in Ghana were not limited to top advisers alone. In 1960, the country underwent a major political transformation. On April 27, a constitutional referendum was held to decide whether Ghana should remain formally under the British Crown or become a republic. The results were overwhelmingly in favor of the latter, the one Nkrumah had campaigned for. Moreover, presidential elections were held at the same time, which Nkrumah won easily. On July 1, 1960, he was inaugurated president of the Republic of Ghana, replacing Elizabeth II as head of state. Nkrumah took the official title of *Osagyefo*, meaning "redeemer" or "savior" in the Akan language, which was used in all official correspondence.[24]

It was much more than a symbolic second declaration of independence. The proclamation of the republic signaled Ghana's desire to experiment, to push the boundaries of what was possible for a small Third World country. The CPSU International Department saw the proclamation of the republic as an unequivocal signal that Nkrumah's personal power was growing at the expense of British influence in Ghana. The new constitution granted him much more direct control over both the legislative and executive branches of government in Ghana.[25]

Nkrumah's rhetoric had taken a sharp turn to the left. Soviet observers highlighted how in recent speeches he had stressed the importance of fighting against foreign economic interests in Ghana and in Africa in general. The nationalization of Ghana Airways and the Black Star Line shipping company were hailed as concrete signs of progress.[26] In February 1961, the Kwame Nkrumah Ideological Institute was inaugurated in Winneba, a town between Accra and Cape Coast. The Institute had the task of consolidating and propagating the ideas of Ghana's leader. Although its formulations were not always in line with Soviet thinking, Marxism-Leninism occupied a prominent role in the intellectual history of the Institute. Moreover, some of its personnel came from the Soviet bloc or had spent time in educational institutions in the socialist world.[27]

In the economic sphere, just weeks after his presidential inauguration Nkrumah announced to his cabinet that Ghana needed more control over the cocoa trade, and that the center of operations needed to move from London to Accra. As part of this process, the CPP government planned to tax the profits of the cocoa buying agencies that operated in Ghana as branches of the mother company in Britain. This had consequences for the British chocolate manufacturers. Cadbury's expected that in the fiscal year 1961 "most of the cash balances accruing in Accra will be required for taxation." The company resolved to sell some property in Ghana and increase the availability of funds in the local office to meet its financial obligations to the government.[28]

Direct conciliatory signals were sent from Accra to Moscow too. In January 1960, the limit on the number of Soviet personnel authorized to work at the Embassy in Accra was lifted. The following March, a Ghanaian embassy was finally established in Moscow. The new ambassador was John Elliot, considered a left-winger by MID. Everything was ready for the beginning of economic cooperation.[29]

The Volta Conundrum

The Soviet option gained ground in Accra because Ghana's experience of dealing with Britain and the United States over aid and trade was dispiriting. Nkrumah regarded control over the cocoa trade as a priority, but progress was slow. The Volta project quickly turned into the second thorn in Nkrumah's side. Despite the Eisenhower administration's lack of enthusiasm for the project, Accra insisted that the Americans provide funds and guidance to build the dam and the hydroelectric complex. Washington, however, did not change its policy. The United States was ready to consider a Ghanaian application for a loan to finance part of the expenses for the Volta project, and Nkrumah was advised to seek support from the IBRD too. However, no agreement could be reached that did not involve the private sector. The US government and the IBRD could lend Ghana about half of the estimated 168 million US dollars necessary for the project, applying standard market interest rates (about 5 percent). The rest of the funds needed to come from Ghana itself and from a private operator willing to invest in the Volta project. It was a matter of principle on which there could be no compromise. Nkrumah, who had hoped to secure a more favorable deal on the loans from Eisenhower, did not object to a private foreign investor.[30]

Despite Nkrumah's optimism, finding and managing an investor proved to be the most problematic and controversial aspect. The US government facilitated talks between the Ghana government and Kaiser Aluminum, an American aluminum producer headed by the tycoon Henry J. Kaiser, whom Eisenhower knew since World War II. Kaiser was interested in investing, with the idea of creating an aluminum smelter powered by the Akosombo hydroelectric complex. However, VALCO (Volta Aluminum Company, the consortium that reunited Kaiser and a few minor investors) demanded some conditions before agreeing to invest.

The Kaiser group wanted a formal pledge from the Ghanaian government that VALCO would be exempted from corporate tax, and that it would be able to buy electricity from the government at a subsidized price. Essentially, Kaiser was not willing to invest without the certainty of profit. Nkrumah personally asked Eisenhower to intercede with Kaiser or to grant Ghana additional funds to finance the subsidies but to no avail.[31] Despite the unpopularity of the deal with part of the government and with the public, and despite signals that Moscow was ready to offer Ghana a loan to finance the Volta project, Ghana went ahead with VALCO.[32]

The agreement with Kaiser left Ghana in an awkward position. The government needed to borrow vast amounts of money to finance the Volta project but would draw limited income from it because of the voracity of a private business. Discontent in Ghana was widespread and often voiced in the CPP's official outlets. However, the US government was not going to tolerate any dissent. In October 1960, US ambassador to Ghana Wilson Flake let Nkrumah know that:

> If he and his supporters did not want private enterprise to undertake the Volta or some other project for the purpose of making a profit he should say so at this time and the American companies would go elsewhere; but if the President wanted the consortium to proceed under conditions mutually agreed upon, then it was the President's responsibility to stop some of his supporters from their campaign of hate against American and other "economic imperialists." I assured the President that I myself would advise Kaiser when he is here next week to get this question settled clearly before signing any final agreement.[33]

Nkrumah and the CPP had to swallow their pride. Work on the Volta project began in 1961. Nkrumah's decision to stick to the US to finance a project in which he had invested so much personal prestige carried a very high price. He had offered the Americans, who were otherwise not particularly interested in Ghana, both a reason and a way to meddle in Accra's foreign policy. As Thomas Noer wrote, "the decision to fund the Volta project was made quite reluctantly and only after Nkrumah was forced to accept a set of conditions that bound him to accept at least verbally American principles in economics, politics, and international relations."[34] Whenever Ghana deviated from the established principles, Washington could remind the Accra government that the Volta project was dependent on American goodwill. Kaiser himself put it quite bluntly, reminding Nkrumah that if he "had to say some nice things about USSR, he should at same time be equally complimentary of USA." This humiliating situation made Nkrumah more determined to test the limits of US tolerance.[35]

Georgia on Their Minds

Throughout the Volta project negotiations, Nkrumah and his ministers were aware that the Soviet Union represented a potential alternative source of funding and inspiration for Ghana's development. If shortly after independence Ghana was too connected to Britain to consider Soviet overtures seriously, now Accra had gained more room for maneuver to pursue Nkrumah's ambitious goals.

Moscow was ready to compete with the Americans for the Volta complex. Soviet experts had already studied the project and made a first estimate of the costs. Nkrumah, however, was too committed to his idea that the US finance the complex, and preliminary contacts with Moscow went nowhere.[36] Other areas of cooperation proved more fruitful. In April-May 1960, a Ghanaian parliamentary delegation visited the USSR for the first time. Ostensibly, the purpose of the visit was to foster the friendship between the two countries. In Moscow, the Ghanaian delegates were treated to a session of the Supreme Soviet, during which they "listened with great attention" to Khrushchev's speech and "often joined in the rounds of applause by the participating members" of the Supreme Soviet. On the same occasion, they learned that the previous May 1 an American U2 spy plane had been shot down while flying over Soviet airspace (Khrushchev's announcement "made a great impression on the delegation"). The guests from Ghana also visited Moscow State University and met representatives from the "USSR-Africa" friendship society.[37]

The Moscow mundanities were misleading. The composition of the delegation revealed a very different purpose. Former foreign minister Kojo Botsio, now minister of agriculture, was the head of a party that included Krobo Edusei, minister of transport and communication, and Francis Yao Asare, who had only just stepped down as minister of agriculture. Botsio was the most left-leaning among Nkrumah's close collaborators in the CPP, and he had advocated seeking better relations with the socialist bloc since 1957. Botsio carried with him a letter from Nkrumah addressed to Khrushchev in which the newly elected president made formal requests for economic aid. Botsio hoped to go back to Ghana with a formal commitment from the Soviet government. During his visit to the Supreme Soviet, he told one of its members that Ghana was now ready to move toward socialism—a statement that was reported to the CPSU Central Committee.[38]

A few days later, Botsio met Nikolai Patolichev, the Soviet minister of foreign trade. He told him that Ghana hoped to negotiate a credit of about 100 million pounds from the Soviet Union to finance a series of modernization projects in agriculture and infrastructure, possibly including the Volta complex too. Moreover, Botsio announced that Ghana was prepared to sell much larger quantities of cocoa, signaling Nkrumah's willingness to challenge the status quo. Patolichev confirmed Moscow's availability to assist Ghana, but the exact details could be worked out only once a Soviet technical delegation was allowed to carry out a full assessment of the projects on the ground. In early June, Nkrumah wrote to Khrushchev to confirm that the government was preparing to receive Soviet specialists. Ghana was ready to begin economic cooperation with the Soviet Union. "My objective—the Ghanaian President wrote to Khrushchev—is the rapid industrialization and electrification of the country, but also accelerated development and mechanization of agriculture."[39]

As with the Guinean delegation the previous year, a visit to the Caucasus was the highlight of Botsio, Edusei, and Asare's trip to the USSR. This time, Georgia was chosen. The results were impressive. The British High Commission in Ghana reported that the "visitors received the very best of treatment." "They returned starry-eyed," the report continued. "Mr Edusei was impressed by the size of everything; Mr Asare by the efficiency of those collective farms he was shown; Mr Botsio by the capacity of the Russians to produce results; and all three by what they took as a visible demonstration of the merits of the one-party system."[40] During the visit, Asare declared that his government needed to study the example of Georgian agriculture, so to learn how to boost productivity and improve the living standards of the Ghanaian peasantry.[41]

From then on, Soviet-Ghanaian cooperation quickened. On August 4, the agreement between the USSR and Ghana was signed. It was nearly a carbon copy of the one signed with Guinea less than twelve months before. The USSR would grant Accra a credit of 160 million rubles repayable over twelve years with an interest rate of 2.5 percent. The funds would be used to finance development projects in industry and agriculture. The agreement also specified that Soviet advisers and technicians would help draft a list of priorities for Ghana's development strategy. Nkrumah had clear priorities for Soviet-Ghanaian cooperation. With the Volta project firmly in Western hands, there were two other areas of development in which he was keen to draw Soviet assistance. The first was agriculture. Nkrumah admired Soviet collective agriculture and was impressed by what Botsio and Asare told him about Georgia. He hoped that Moscow would be able to supervise the establishment of large state farms in Ghana, which would not only be more productive than private farms but also more compatible with what Nkrumah regarded as African traditional values. Moreover, Nkrumah wanted the Soviet Union to be involved in the construction and development of modern port facilities in Tema, a small town not far from Accra. The Tema project, which required transforming a small fishing village into a modern industrial center, was judged essential to boost trade (the Tema harbor was supposed to become the new import-export hub) and give Ghana the possibility of developing the fishing sector.[42]

In August 1960 the two parties could not sign a trade agreement as well, as had been the case with Guinea, because Ghana was still negotiating its position in the cocoa trade. It took Nkrumah another year to increase Ghanaian control over the Cocoa Marketing Board, and thus to be able to finalize a commercial treaty with the USSR in November 1961. The deal established that the Soviet Union would buy large quantities of Ghanaian cocoa beans for five years. However, the necessity to accommodate the London branch of the Cocoa Board, which still had a strong influence on sales on the international market, prevented Ghana from using all the cocoa destined to Moscow to pay for Soviet credits, as Guinea did with its exports. The Soviet Union had to pay for part of the cocoa using hard currency, while the remaining part would be considered payment for the loans. However, the agreement stipulated that the proportion of cocoa to be purchased in hard currency would progressively diminish over time (from 55 percent in 1962 to 30 percent in 1966), reflecting the Ghanaian government's confidence that it would be able to increase its control over trade even more.[43]

Even though this was not a particularly convenient arrangement for the USSR, which always preferred barter agreements to acquire commodities from the Third World, it was the only possible way to trade with Ghana. The final result was what mattered the most. The Soviet embassy in Accra was delighted when Nkrumah announced on the national radio that Ghana would follow "a socialist policy in economics." After Guinea, a second West African state had entered the Soviet orbit. The West looked on with preoccupation as Ghana, thus far a firm ally, slid toward the Eastern bloc.[44]

The Third Man

Where Nkrumah and Sékou Touré had hesitated or taken time, Keïta had no doubts. Independent Mali was going to take a socialist path, and the Soviet Union would be a key partner. In January 1961, the US-RDA government demanded the complete evacuation of all French military personnel from the military bases in the country, a move that Moscow welcomed. At the same time, a Soviet embassy was established in Bamako. Shortly thereafter, a Malian delegation—headed by the minister of internal affairs and information Madeira Keïta—traveled to the USSR to negotiate the terms of an economic cooperation agreement and a trade deal. Negotiations proceeded swiftly, and the agreement was signed in March. As usual, the USSR granted Mali 40 million rubles in credits payable over twelve years with a 2.5 percent annual interest rate to finance development projects in agriculture and industry.[45] The treaty left ample space for Soviet supervision. Indeed, the Bamako government regarded the agreement as a way for the Soviet

side "to provide the Malian organizations with technical assistance in the selection of areas of construction and priorities of the projects, in the organization
and execution of construction work of infrastructure, as well as supervision in
the realization of a project by the authors of the preliminary studies."[46]

As in other countries in West Africa, the trade agreement allowed the Malian government to exchange local products with Soviet goods, while Moscow
was going to pay for part of its imports in hard currency. In 1961 the Soviet Union
exported to Mali 7.7 million rubles in machines and tools and imported 3.4 million rubles worth of peanuts, Mali's main export commodity. At the same time,
Mali continued to receive aid from France and limited assistance from the United
States.[47]

Despite continued Western presence, the general direction of Mali's economic
policy was clear: socialism. Modibo Keïta, speaking at the US-RDA congress in
September 1962, declared that following independence in 1960: "The Congress,
the supreme body of our party, opted for a socialist planned economy. The Congress gave the Party and the Government the mandate to take all the decisions
aimed to lay the foundations of our economic independence, and this through the
organization of a socialist planned economy." Keïta identified two main challenges
for the Bamako government: ending the "economic plundering" connected to international trade and developing a nationalized economy able to provide the population with the essentials. "Confronted by this issue, there is but one solution:
making the State the instrument of the reorganization of our economy."[48]

Among Malian elites, admiration for the Soviet example was tangible. The
Mali embassy in the USSR, reporting on the adoption of the new party program
at the Twenty-Second Congress of the CPSU in October 1961, reported that "it
suffices to compare the projected figures of Soviet production in 1980 with those
of any other country in the same group to see the enormity of the goals of the
long-term plan." The Malian representatives expected that the Soviet *semiletka*
(the seven-year plan that began in 1959) "will not only be fulfilled in 1965 but
also surpassed." According to the embassy in Moscow, "the organization of the
Soviet economy gives it two advantages: the power and unity that in this way
allow the concentration of all efforts on one objective." The well-known pitfalls
of Soviet bureaucracy "cannot hide the indisputable general effectiveness of a system that has been perfecting itself constantly for forty years and has not stopped
arousing the interest of Western economists."[49]

Mali's interest in the USSR went beyond economic performance. It encom-
passed all aspects of Soviet society. In 1964, a Malian delegation headed by Madeira Keïta spent most of the summer traveling around the Soviet Union. They
visited Moscow first—"sunny, with its large avenues"—and then went across Siberia to Alma Ata (Almaty) in the Kazakh Soviet Republic, stopping at Bratsk to visit

the hydroelectric complex. Keïta was impressed by what he saw in Kazakhstan. "A backward region before 1917, it [Kazakhstan] is a classic example of liberation from the colonial yoke. It has switched directly from feudal and patriarchal relations to the stage of socialism." It was the standard of living in Central Asia that left the most vivid impression on the Malian visitors. "At the level of each *sovkhoz*, each *kolkhoz*, there are schools, community health centers, nurseries for children, recreational clubs, cinemas, etc." Before returning to Mali, the delegation was taken to Sochi and then to Leningrad, where they visited the famous mosque built in 1913. "During a one-month visit, we have been able to see the Soviet people from close up and we could see for ourselves some of its immense achievements and some of its possibilities for the future. What we have seen, what we have experienced, felt, has convinced us even more that the Soviet Union is marching resolutely toward a better kind of society—communism."[50]

Fair Trade

Once aid agreements and commercial treaties were in place with all three countries, economic exchanges between West Africa and the USSR could begin. In comparative terms, Ghana, Guinea, and Mali were poor countries. In 1959, Guinea had both the highest natality rate and the highest mortality rate in the world. Life expectancy at birth in the country was thirty-four years, half that of the Soviet Union. In neighboring Mali, life expectancy was the lowest in the world at the time: twenty-seven years.[51] In 1960, the GDP per capita of Ghana, one of Africa's richest states, was 1,378 US dollars, comparable to that of Soviet Turkmenistan (1,585 US dollars), one of the poorest Central Asian republics of the USSR. Guinea and Mali were considerably worse off. Mali's GDP per capita in 1960 was 535 US dollars. Guinea, then arguably Africa's poorest independent country, was theoretically at a level of GDP per capita (392 US dollars) lower than that estimated for the Grand Duchy of Muscovy at the end of Ivan III's reign in 1505 (499 US dollars).[52]

The comparison with medieval Europe is misleading. Yet this was precisely how Soviet scholars working on Africa framed the situation. During one of the first staff meetings of the newly established Institute of Africa, Director Potekhin described Africa as a premodern society, where economic conditions—with few exceptions—were still "like in the fifteenth century." The blame was placed on European colonialism. Indeed, the "sacred duty" of Soviet Africanists was to debunk the myth of colonialism as harbinger of civilization. In practical terms, "the countries of the socialist camp are ready to provide African peoples with all possible (*vsemernyi*) help."[53]

Potekhin's description of Africa was simplistic. However, the conditions that the first postindependence governments faced in Ghana, Guinea, and Mali were not easy. All three countries were agricultural societies, in which most of the population relied on subsistence agriculture to survive. In Ghana, by far the most advanced economy of the three, Soviet scholars attached at the Institute of Africa reported that 61.7 percent of the population worked in agriculture. In Guinea and Mali, this percentage rose to more than 80 percent. Ghana and Mali more or less corresponded to the colonial stereotype of monocultures—cocoa beans (in Ghana) and peanuts (in Mali) were cultivated to be sold to producers in the respective *métropole*. Ghana produced about 250 to 300 thousand tons of cocoa yearly, equal to one-third of the world's total production. Monocultures had led the colonial governments to make some investments into infrastructure for agriculture. Investment, however, was limited to the few farms that produced export commodities, while large-scale farms in other sectors were limited. Mechanization was limited too: in 1960, there were only 138 tractors in the whole of Mali. No significant attempt at developing Guinea's agriculture had ever been made, to the point that one of the first Soviet expeditions to survey the country could not find a single functioning water well. Ghana, Guinea, and Mali all needed to import basic goods and commodities from abroad—from salt to soap, from shoes to fuel, from bricks to spades. Twenty percent of Ghana's total imports were basic foodstuff, signaling the inability of the country's agriculture to feed the population.[54]

Infrastructure was scarce and of poor quality. Ghana had a decent network of roads, a functioning international airport, and some limited port facilities in Takoradi, which the government judged insufficient. Guinea's airport in Conakry was not operative, its port was underdeveloped and decaying, and many roads became unusable during the rainy season. Mali, a landlocked country, depended entirely on the Dakar-Niger railway, built by the French in the 1900s to link the Atlantic Ocean with the Niger River. The two-thirds of the country north of Mopti, a harsh desert zone, were largely isolated from the South. Energy was insufficient everywhere. Ghana had a few diesel-powered stations that supplied electricity to the major towns, and the project of a hydroelectric power station in Akosombo. Guinea had one small power station outside of Conakry and, like Mali, relied on small generators in the regional capitals, leaving large parts of the two countries in the dark. Water supply and sanitation created problems everywhere, including in the largest towns.[55]

Given the circumstances, jumpstarting Ghana, Guinea, and Mali's economies, transforming them into modern, self-sufficient states was a titanic enterprise. Doing it in the "space of one generation alone," as Nkrumah wanted, was a visionary endeavor that required effort and help from outside.

Addressing trade dependency was conceptually the easiest step. All three countries traded almost exclusively with their former colonial masters. All three, as Sékou Touré explained to the *Pravda* correspondent Orestov, wanted a "complete reform of the colonial structure of trade."[56] The Soviet Union offered this opportunity. The Soviet government proposed to replace Britain and France as the principal trade partner, guaranteeing the supply of those numerous basic goods and commodities that Ghana, Guinea, and Mali did not produce at home.

The Soviet plan offered to bypass the international market and the need to pay for imports using convertible currency. The commercial treaties signed with Ghana, Guinea, and Mali were, in fact, barter agreements. Rather than selling cocoa (Ghana), peanuts (Mali), and fruit (Guinea) to Britain or France, the West African governments could now exchange their commodities directly with Soviet products and materials, and thus obtain the agricultural machinery, the consumption goods, and the energy they needed. Barter through clearing accounts was based on fixed exchanges of prearranged quantities of goods, whose value was established in advance by the MVT together with its counterparts in West Africa. All three treaties stipulated that, if for whatever reason one of the parties did not fulfill its preestablished quota of exports for the year, then the government of that party would transfer an amount of hard currency equivalent to the value of the missed exports to the other party—a situation that both the USSR and its West African partners much preferred to avoid.[57]

Generally, the terms of the agreements were quite favorable to Ghana, Guinea and Mali. With the partial exception of Ghanaian cocoa beans, the value of West African agricultural products was deliberately estimated above market rate (usually between 15 percent and 20 percent higher than the international price at the time). Indeed, exchanges with the socialist countries were meant to safeguard the balance of payments of Ghana, Guinea, and Mali. By exchanging overpriced agricultural products with machines, technology, technicians, and industrial goods, the governments in West Africa were able to obtain the capital they needed without fueling a massive trade deficit, which was feared to generate an unsustainable rate of inflation. For example, in 1958 the value of Guinea's exports was only 35 percent of the value of its imports. Following the signing of the commercial agreements with the Soviet Union and other socialist countries, this ratio grew to 47 percent in 1959 and 84 percent in 1961. Moreover, the barter arrangement was a lifesaver for Guinea, which was initially under embargo by France and its neighbors in the Communauté, and in desperate need of obtaining supplies from abroad. Ghana and Mali, although still able to trade with other countries, saved some of their limited hard currency reserves through the barter agreements with the USSR.[58]

The details and clauses of the three commercial treaties were similar, reflecting each country's particular predicament. Mali, which maintained relatively good relations with France, continued to trade with it and other members of the West African Franc zone, such as Senegal and Côte d'Ivoire. Guinea, by contrast, was entirely reliant on exchanges with the Soviet Union and other socialist countries. The most complex case was Ghana. The Accra government insisted on selling part of its cocoa for hard currency only to satisfy the Cocoa Marketing Board and appease those government members that did not look at the USSR with favor. This caused problems in Moscow, with Gosbank (the USSR's central bank) often complaining about using expensive hard currency for cocoa instead of the usual clearing accounts. The price of cocoa beans was also the object of frequent discussions between Soviet and Ghanaian officials. The Ghanaian side was adamant that prices could be lower only if the USSR agreed to buy larger quantities of cocoa, which the Soviet government was willing to do using clearing accounts. Nkrumah promised to look into the possibility of expanding barter exchanges with the USSR, but negotiations went on for more than two years without ever reaching a real conclusion. As the next chapter shows, Soviet-Ghanaian trade entered a severe crisis before a mutually agreeable compromise could be reached.[59]

Another striking difference between Ghana and the two former French colonies was the degree of government control on foreign trade. Whereas the Nkrumah government struggled to control the London-based branch of the Cocoa Marketing Board, Guinea and Mali were able to bring all trade under state supervision. In 1958, shortly after independence, Guinea created the Comptoir Guinéen du Commerce Extérieure (CGCE), a state agency that controlled all commercial exchanges with foreign countries.[60] As Sékou Touré explained to Modibo Keïta, the creation of the CGCE "had the goal of reaffirming the system in which the monopoly is always exercised by the state."[61] According to the Ministry of Overseas Territories in Paris, "foreign trade centered on exchanges with the Eastern-bloc countries aims to progressively eliminate the capitalist European commercial firms" that operated in Guinea.[62] In 1961, the Malian government adopted the same model, creating the Société Malienne des Importations et Exportations (SOMIEX), which was explicitly modeled on its Guinean predecessor and dubbed "the most decisive instrument of our independence" by Keïta.[63]

Both the CGCE and SOMIEX shared the same goal: "eliminating foreigners from the national economy."[64] For countries like Guinea and Mali, where dependence on French imports and capital was absolute (the Bamako government estimated that until 1960 nine-tenths of Mali exports went to France, and three-fourths of Malian imports came from France), this represented an inescapable necessity on the way to economic independence. "It is some French companies that control the economic life of the country," Louis Lansana Beavogui declared. "The important decisions that condition the economic life of the country are not taken in Bamako or in Dakar, but in Paris in the secrecy of managerial offices. And the managers in charge of taking these decisions are European managers, strictly controlled by the board of the company. How can we be surprised that in their minds the preoccupations of developing the Malian economy come way after the interests of their company?"[65]

Decolonization in West Africa did not just mean political sovereignty for the state. It also meant decolonizing the private sector: ensuring that both citizens and local businesses could obtain what they needed regardless of British or French commercial interests. Compared to trade with European partners, who were after profit, exchanges with the Soviet Union offered the promise of a relationship seemingly built on solidarity and based on acceptable terms for Ghana, Guinea, and Mali.

In Guinea and Mali especially, once commercial relations with the socialist world replaced existing ties with French providers, attitudes became defiant. When in early 1959 the issue of existing contracts with French sugar companies was raised at the Conakry chamber of commerce, the CGCE director Habib Niang responded: "we laugh at your contracts. Only ours matter." The French Ministry of Overseas Territories concluded that no defense of the private sector was possible at the time, lamenting the "dictatorial" decisions taken by the Guinean government, which aimed to replace French products with equivalents from the socialist world. "The agreements signed with the four communist countries entail ipso facto the prohibition to import from the *métropole* those products whose importation is provided for from those countries."[66] Thanks to Soviet involvement, French commercial hegemony in Guinea and Mali was over.

The quality and quantity of goods and commodities exchanged with the Soviet Union followed the same scheme in Ghana, Guinea, and Mali. Technological products, processed food, and household items were sent from the USSR to West Africa, while fruits and other agricultural products (together with the odd raw material) went the other way. The lists of products that Moscow agreed to sell Ghana, Guinea, and Mali starting in 1959–61 included such disparate goods as trucks and window glass, chemical fertilizers and clocks, haberdashery and tractors, movies and ferrous metal, medicines and matches, frozen fish and cement, tires and optics. Ghana sent to the USSR cocoa beans, coffee, and tropical fruit (bananas, pineapple, and kola nuts). Guinea exported coffee and fruit, and Mali nearly only peanuts.[67] Between 1958 and 1961, "fraternal trade" between West Africa and the socialist world became larger in volume than "exploitative trade" with the capitalists. As of June 1963, the USSR bought 30 percent of Guinea's bananas and 67 percent of its pineapples. Moscow also purchased 33 percent of Mali's peanuts. On the contrary, due to the difficulty of breaking into the cocoa market, the Soviet government was still behind Western buyers of Ghana's cocoa beans.[68]

Farm First, Factory Later: Soviet Agriculture in West Africa

If trade was a necessity, aid contained the real vision. Khrushchev's idea of development was typically bread-and-butter. "Keep in mind—the Soviet leader told Sékou Touré in 1959—that people want to eat, they want clothes, shelter, and if you do not provide these, you will not keep your influence in the country." If Guinea was to pursue a noncapitalist path to development, then the Soviet Union must be the obvious point of reference. "Do not expect that the Rothschilds and the Rockefellers will help you build socialism," Khrushchev admonished Sékou Touré.[69]

The Soviet Union believed itself to be ready and capable to help. As GKES reported to Khrushchev in late 1959, the USSR was exceptionally well-placed to act as both inspiration and donor given its recent history of economic development. The goal, the GKES specialists stated plainly, was to distinguish Soviet aid from Western aid.[70] V.S. Baskinyi, an economist at the Institute of Africa, offered an overview of how the Soviet Union should favor modernization in the Third World as an alternative to Western capitalism: "Soviet technical and economic aid needs to facilitate those internal processes in the economic and social life of developing countries that would objectively contribute to their transition to a non-capitalist path of development. In this respect, it is possible to identify three main functions of the Soviet credits: favor the creation of a state sector in industry, transport, trade; favor the development of cooperatives in agriculture; facilitate the creation and the strengthening of concentration centers of industrial proletariat."[71]

In Ghana, Guinea, and Mali, the USSR was directly involved in defining the objectives of development cooperation. For example, shortly after the signing of the cooperation agreement with the Conakry government in the summer of 1959, seventeen specialists from GKES traveled to Guinea to work on a list of priorities to be realized with Soviet assistance. Many other similar missions followed, in Guinea as well as in Ghana and Mali. Soviet experts were supposed not only to assess whether or not a particular project made economic sense, but also to specify the exact requirements to carry it out, including: "The number of workers required, and the duration of the construction; the necessary quantity of specialists from the USSR with the duration of their stay; how many Guinean specialists it is necessary to send to the USSR for training; what quantity of construction materi-

FIGURE 4.1. Ahmed Sékou Touré, right, and Nikita Khrushchev, left, shake hands during Sékou Touré's official visit to the USSR. September 1960. Credit: Sputnik.

als and equipment from the USSR will be required; how much tin will be required for a canning factory and how much raw material for a leather factory."[72]

Nonetheless, Soviet ideas did not come across a clean slate in West Africa. For the leaderships in Accra, Conakry, and Bamako, the first term of reference to think about development was the colonial experience. The British and French administrations in West Africa had engaged in development, especially during the last decades of imperial rule. Infrastructure projects, modernization of export-oriented agricultural sectors, and also the establishment of educational, healthcare, and generally charitable institutions had a long history in Ghana, Guinea, and Mali. Indeed, colonialism was often justified as a way to improve the lives of colonial subjects. Questionable as these claims were, the practice of colonial development left a long-lasting impression on Nkrumah, Sékou Touré, and Keïta. Modernization projects that the colonial administrations had initiated, or at least considered, were the first to be submitted for study to the foreign specialists that surveyed Ghana, Guinea, and Mali after independence, including Soviet ones. Damming the Volta in Ghana, building an aluminum smelter in Guinea, and extending the railway links in Mali were among the many projects conceived as colonial plans that would become symbols of postindependence development.

Reclaiming these colonial modernization projects became one of the main tasks of the Soviet specialists who worked in West Africa in the 1950s and 1960s. Despite its colonial origin, development now needed to affirm the power and prestige of the new states. Jeffrey Ahlman has shown how the Tema project in Ghana came "to embody the procedural nature of the decolonization process itself for the emergent country."[73] Originally a project of the British colonial administration, modernizing the harbor facilities and creating a new industrial center in Tema became a cornerstone of the CPP's development strategy, in conjunction with the Volta project. It was Padmore who warned Nkrumah not to rely on the British in Tema. The Soviet government eventually agreed to supply funds and expertise. In the case of Tema, as in other development projects in West Africa, the very concept of economic modernization was rooted in the search for independence, with a collectivist tinge. According to Louis Lansana Beavogui, at the time minister of planning in the Guinean government, "our main task is to free our economy, our culture, our entire life. Our country is an agricultural country with a ratio of 85 percent. We are trying to establish some fundamental Cooperatives of producers and consumers in the agricultural regions. We shall succeed."[74]

The former colonizers were conscious of this process of reappropriating colonial development and tried to delay it. Jacques Foccart, de Gaulle's influential adviser on Africa, was worried by the possibility that the new government in Conakry (or worse, a foreign power) would get their hands on the French colonial project to build a dam on the Konkouré River in western Guinea. A couple of years before independence, the French government had sent drafts and preliminary reports to the World Bank for consideration. Foccart asked Michel Debré, the Prime Minister, to ensure the Bank would not transmit those to any other party. "These studies cost the French government nearly 700 million francs," Foccart reminded Debré. "They took five years."[75] Despite Foccart's efforts, the Konkouré project was among the ones the Soviet Union agreed to fund and supervise. It did not matter that the idea could be traced back to France.

The goal, in Konkouré, as in many other former colonial development projects that the USSR took over, was to refashion them as socialist.

"Socialism" was a fashionable word in West Africa during the late 1950s and early 1960s. Nkrumah, Sékou Touré, and Keïta did not hesitate to define their ideas for the development of their countries socialist. In practice, what they had in mind was significant state intervention in the economy in the form of both government investment in infrastructure and the creation of state-run farms and factories. The development projects undertaken by the colonial administrations, if completed, remained under the control of the European colonizers. Likewise, projects supported by the US or international organizations tended to involve private investors, who naturally would retain at least some degree of control over the completed project. On the contrary, what the new governments of Ghana, Guinea, and Mali aspired to was to maintain virtually total control over development. In their view, the national government had to be able to control and manage all modernization projects on West African soil. That was the essence of Nkrumah, Sékou Touré and Keïta's conception of socialism. This coincided with Soviet ideas on development in the Third World and made cooperation between the Soviet and West African governments relatively smooth.

Other aspects of the West African leaders' approach to socialism and politics in general were more problematic for the USSR. Soviet observers usually looked at Nkrumah, Sékou Touré, and Keïta's ideological formulations with skepticism, if not open suspicion. Pan-Africanism, for example, was regarded as a potentially dangerous idea, with elements of progressivism and bourgeois nationalism mixed together. In a similar fashion, the Soviet government tended to regard ideologies specific to West Africa—such as Nkrumahism in Ghana or African socialism in French-speaking Africa—as little more than a form of basic collectivism centered around the cult of a charismatic leader. However, as academics and members of the Central Committee agreed in 1958, as long as Pan-Africanism and African socialism remained fundamentally anticolonial and anti-Western, it was in the USSR's interest to support them.[76]

In practical terms, the backbone of socialism (or noncapitalism) in West Africa was to be economic planning. It was very much in the spirit of the times, and the governments of Ghana, Guinea, and Mali fretted to produce plans that indicated the exact measures to push modernization. Planning, and generally strengthening the state, served two purposes in West Africa. On the one hand, it was supposed to produce development. On the other, as Fred Cooper wrote, "the stress on state planning coincided with many politicians' distrust of groups within their countries that could provide a base for counter-organization, farmers' associations and labor unions in particular." The state, development, and planning were instruments of political power just as much as of the economy, as they had been during the colonial era.[77]

Ghana, which had a history of planning already in colonial times, was the first to move. In March 1958, the CPP government presented its five-year development plan, which would cover the period between 1959 and 1964. Guinea followed suit: in April 1960 the PDG government unveiled a three-year development plan with great fanfare. It organized a three-day conference in Kankan to present the plan. Last but not least, Mali launched its own five-year plan in October 1961. All three plans were the result of extensive consultations between the governments and foreign economists. These external advisers were selected according to their unconventional ideas and willingness to experiment. Arthur Lewis was a radical, although not of the Marxist variety, reflecting Ghana's hesitation between socialism and enlightened capitalism. Guinea and Mali had no such doubts. The Conakry government relied on Charles Bettelheim, a leading French Marxist economist, as its principal economic adviser. Mali chose Jean Bénard, a disciple of Bettelheim.

Bettelheim was an influential figure. Before working with Guinea, he had advised the Egyptian, Indian, and Algerian governments. In 1958, he founded the Centre d'Études sur les Modes d'Industrialisation, attached to the École des Hautes Études en Sciences Sociales in Paris. An academic scholar of the Soviet economy, Bettelheim had spent time in Moscow in the 1930s and spoke fluent Russian. He was critical of Stalinism but maintained that the USSR's approach to planning, industrialization, and fast economic growth held many lessons for newly independent countries. Bettelheim favored a more practical approach rather than full central planning, arguing that Third World countries should focus on agriculture first and industrialize only slowly, rejecting the forced pace of the USSR's first Five-Year Plan. Moreover, he was convinced that several elements of a market economy should survive in newly independent countries, although tempered by state intervention and planning, both at the central and regional level. Although unorthodox from a standard Soviet point of view, Bettelheim's ideas were compatible with Moscow's approach to economic assistance to West Africa. The result was a Guinean development plan "totally soaked in Marxist theory," according to French observers.[78]

Bénard, a professor in the faculty of law at the University of Poitiers, was less well-known than Bettelheim but no less influential in Mali. He headed a team of radical economists—including a young Samir Amin, who would later become one of the leading figures of the "dependency theory" school—that advised the Bamako government on its development plan.[79] Already before secession from the Soudanese Federation, Bénard framed the economic choices Mali faced in terms of a dichotomy between state and market. As he put it, "it is necessary to know if we give priority to the intervention of foreign private capital and if consequently we need to seek their confidence or if, on the contrary, the Soudanese government decides to take in its own hands the essential tasks of supplying the country and building the principal instruments of production while accepting foreign aid, preferably public, consistent with national independence." The risk with the first option, private capital, was a repetition of what had happened under French rule: Mali would be dominated by "foreign monopolies" guided by profit alone, and certainly with no interest in the development of the country. Bénard had no doubt. "Thus, the second solution is the only option."[80]

Ghana, Guinea, and Mali's development plans presented numerous similarities. They all aimed to transform the countries into prosperous economies in record time, and they all focused on large state investments, rather than private capital, to finance agricultural modernization, new infrastructure, and the creation of industry. Guinea's three-year development plan stated that "progresses in production will fall as much as possible within the scope of the collective and social property of the means of production (expansion of the public sector). The State sector and the cooperative sector will rapidly need to play a dominant role in every field." In macroeconomic terms, the plan aimed to generate an annual GDP growth rate of between eight and ten percent. At the same time, it was expected to produce a considerable increase in both the rate of accumulation of capital and in consumption broadly defined, thanks to "the expansion and improvement of collective and social services." The Guinean government expected the total volume of investment necessary for the three-year plan to be in the region of thirty billion CFA francs (roughly 120 million US dollars in 1960), half of which needed to come from foreign aid. Investment would be divided into agriculture (30 percent of the total), industry (20 percent), infrastructure (20 percent), and the social sector (20 percent), including healthcare, public housing, education, and professional training.[81]

This vision corresponded entirely to Soviet ideas. Soviet economists agreed that the first priority was agriculture. Moscow and the West African governments shared the conviction that local agriculture needed to become more productive to be able to feed the population, thus reducing the need to import basic foods from abroad. Ghana and Mali also shared the imperative to diversify their production, reducing the cultivation of cocoa and peanuts in favor of crops destined for domestic consumption. Moreover, the governments in Ghana, Guinea, and Mali hoped to be able to export some of their agricultural products to improve their balance of payments.[82]

The common belief in Moscow and in West Africa was that agriculture needed to move beyond subsistence and become a modern sector based on a few large mechanized farms, together with many smaller cooperative farms. Guinea's development plan foresaw an increase of 4 percent per year in agricultural production, both for the domestic market and for exports. This would be achieved thanks to the combined effect of mechanization and a projected expansion of arable land. The government foresaw the creation of no fewer than 500 new cooperative farms in three years. During the same time, the production of all traditional crops—rice, bananas, coffee, pineapple, palms—was expected to increase from four- to seven-fold. The mechanization effort would be huge. The Guinean government estimated it needed nearly 800 new tractors, more than 500 wheeled carts, about 230 threshing machines and about as many hullers, for a total value of 2 billion CFA francs. Given Guinea's limited resources, Soviet financial assistance and technical supervision would be essential in all areas.[83]

In all countries, rice was judged a particularly important crop to develop in order to guarantee food security. The coastal plains in Guinea, the Volta basin in Ghana, and the Niger basin in Mali represented especially promising environments for rice, and a significant expansion of cultivation was expected to take place in nearly all regions in the three countries. Guinea expected to increase rice production by 13 percent by 1963; the Soviet Union was to organize state rice farms on a surface of seven thousand hectares, thanks to a credit of 20 million rubles. In Ghana, the government aimed to increase the production of rice to 10,700 tons per year, so to end its dependency on imports. The USSR would provide half of the necessary funds—3.5 million out of the estimated seven million rubles. In Mali, there were only nine functioning rice farms at the time of independence. Most of the rice Malians consumed had to come from abroad. Thanks to Soviet and Chinese assistance in developing more farms, the Bamako government hoped to be in a position to stop importing rice by 1962. Irrigation, essential for rice cultivation, was a challenge in tropical countries with long dry seasons and harsh geographies. Soviet experts set to study how to exploit existing water resources, whether it made sense to deviate the course of rivers or to build new canals. Besides rice, cattle farming could provide another way to improve living standards through the production of meat and dairy products, for which Moscow committed 4 million rubles in Guinea. Mikoian and Nkrumah agreed to raise the yearly production of meat to 290 tons a year, from Ghana's initial negligible levels.[84]

The Soviet Union provided machinery and technology—tractors, fertilizers, seeds, irrigation systems—as well as expertise, in the form of agronomists and managers who would help identify the best possible crops to grow and the best possible ways to organize both large state farms and small cooperatives. However, agricultural modernization was not just a matter of adding tractors and new crops to the existing system. Modernization, as understood both in Moscow and in West Africa, required new infrastructure and novel forms of organization. All three governments agreed that their countries' agriculture had to be organized in collectives and largely controlled by the state. The inspiration was the USSR. Nonetheless, collectivization was not going to be absolute, as had happened in the Soviet Union. Speaking to Mali's ambassador to Moscow, Mikoian explained that in the 1930s Stalin insisted for the complete liquidation of all commercial enterprises in Soviet villages, including small farms. This had been a mistake, which Mikoian claimed to have tried to resist. "The solution—he continued—is not dogmatic." In a country like Mali, where the vast majority of the population worked in agriculture, small cooperative farms represented a useful and "democratic" instrument to improve production and distribution through commerce.[85] Therefore, Soviet planners that worked in West Africa were happy to leave space for the formation of a large number of small agricultural cooperatives, which were technically private and for-profit even though they could access capital (both physical and financial) provided by the government. The mix of a few large state farms and many smaller cooperatives became the Soviet template for agricultural modernization in West Africa. For example, eighty-five new cooperative farms were created in Ghana as of 1960, all growing crops other than cocoa and all organized on the model of the socialist countries. At the same time, the Soviet Union helped Ghana set up three large state farms (*goskhoz*)— two that grew rice and one that grew corn. The Ghanaian state farms built with Soviet funds and supervised by Soviet experts occupied a total area of about 6,000 acres, or 17 percent of the total arable land in Ghana. This was about twice the combined size of the four US-sponsored and the one Israeli-built farms that existed in the country at the time (3,500 acres).[86]

The Soviet approach to agriculture in West Africa was not too different from what Lewis had recommended for Ghana; he believed that "agriculture in Ghana depends, and will continue to depend, mainly upon small-scale farming," but reckoned that a few larger scale "plantations" would be useful to spread new cultures and experiment with mechanization. However, in accordance with his views, Lewis believed that any form of large-scale farming should have been left to foreign private enterprise, bringing in capital and expertise. The USSR promised to replace private capital and know-how with public funding, "fraternal" loans, and Soviet agronomists.[87]

The government of Mali elaborated similar ideas. Several ministers discussed industrial development, but most agreed with the need to modernize agriculture first. Using semi-Marxist terminology, Seydou Badian Kouyaté, the minister of development and a close collaborator of Keïta, captured the vision of the Bamako government speaking at the 1962 conference on African socialism in Dakar. "Agricultural modernization," he declared, "is the first step toward economic development, but agriculture must not maintain the colonial traits, that is to say remaining the supplier of raw materials for extra-African industries. . . . Small and medium industry will realize the valorization of agricultural products subject to the principles of accumulation in the context of the imperatives of self-development. This is the way that seemed to us the most appropriate for this period in which we live."[88]

Cooperation with the socialist bloc was an essential component of Mali's approach to agricultural modernization. Shortly after the dissolution of the Mali Federation, Salah Niaré, the Secretary of State for agriculture, spoke to Soviet representatives about the possibility of setting up cooperatives farms in Mali and lamenting the government's lack of financial means for modernization.[89] Mali's government plan was to revamp the Office du Niger, making it the prime instrument of agricultural development. A large chunk of Soviet aid was channeled through it (35–40 million rubles, about one-fourth of the total). According to Mali's development plan, the office was to take center stage in the collectivization of agriculture, its mechanization, and the realization of irrigation infrastructure. The US-RDA government in Bamako hoped to greatly expand Mali's production of both rice and cotton with Soviet assistance. The goal was to expand arable land in Mali from 50,000 hectares in 1961 to 65,000 hectares in 1965, the final year of the five-year plan. Cotton output was expected to increase fivefold, and Keïta hoped to build a cotton mill to be able to refine some of the harvest in Mali.[90]

Throughout West Africa, mechanization could be achieved only by ensuring that each farm, large or small, received the technology and equipment it needed. Regional distribution and agricultural research centers, modeled on those created by the Khrushchev reforms in the USSR only a few years before, were established and often run with the help of Soviet advisers. Guinea planned to create thirty such new regional centers in the first three years of the country's development plan. Each center would dispose of between 300 and 600 hectares of land to test new cultures and try out new techniques using modern equipment. Mali planned to do the same, and the USSR's contribution was judged so crucial that the Bamako government explicitly asked that the Soviet Union send not only technical experts but also managers to supervise some of the new centers.[91]

Soviet agriculture was plagued by low productivity and poor management for most of the USSR's history. However, around 1960 the Soviet approach to agriculture appeared a promising way forward. The signs of crisis in the Soviet Union were still a few years ahead, and collective agriculture was producing remarkable results, including in large-scale flagship projects such as the Virgin Lands campaign. Visitors from Ghana, Guinea, and Mali looked at Soviet agriculture as a remarkable example of modernization. The mechanized, state-of-the-art farms they saw in Azerbaijan, Georgia, Kazakhstan, and Tajikistan convinced them that the same model could be replicated at home.

The Infrastructure of Industrial Revolutions

Agriculture was the first preoccupation of both Soviet experts and European consultants, but large-scale construction projects attracted the attention of the local governments just as much. In Guinea, Sékou Touré and his ministers wanted to realize a few large projects to improve living conditions in the country. In particular, they wanted at least one large dam with a hydroelectric power complex to be built on the Konkouré River—the old French colonial plan. In their hopes, this would provide Guinea with enough electricity to supply most of the country. The project had been studied in detail by the French colonial administration, which had even submitted its technical dossiers to the World Bank as a preliminary step before formally applying for a loan. Following Guinea's rejection of the Communauté in 1958, however, the French government lost all interest in the project. Given the frosty relations with France, the PDG government in Conakry looked around for new sponsors. Sékou Touré wrote to Khrushchev in July 1960, asking for Soviet help. The Soviet government showed its willingness to become involved in the Konkouré project in September 1960, during the Guinean president's second visit to the USSR.[92] Sékou Touré told his hosts that he did not want the French or the Americans involved because they would impose a "monopoly" on the energy produced, probably making a reference to the situation with the Volta complex in Ghana. He also proposed to share with Soviet engineers the French plan that Foccart was so eager to keep hidden from them. Sékou Touré's offer spurred both Khrushchev and Mikoian to remind their guest about the USSR's own extensive experience in building dams and hydroelectric complexes. Soviet engineers needed no French plan.[93]

Despite Khrushchev and Mikoian's boastfulness, it was not until Leonid Brezhnev's official visit to Guinea in early 1961 that an official promise to build the dam was made. A couple of preliminary surveys conducted by Soviet and East European engineers concluded that the project was going to require a major effort. Soviet experts estimated that building a fairly small hydroelectric complex (450,000 kilowatts) would cost about 300 million rubles (75 million 1960 US dollars)—a sizeable investment. For this reason, the Soviet government approached all its Eastern European allies to survey what they would be able to contribute. The results were not encouraging. Despite some goodwill from Poland and Czechoslovakia (while Romania and the German Democratic Republic refused even to consider contributing), GKES concluded that: "The Soviet Union will need to provide for the bulk of the financing and a significant part of the supply of equipment and materials. It should also be noted that at Touré's request the Guinean side expects that the socialist countries will provide a loan for the full cost of construction, including the necessary internal costs in local currency."[94]

The Guinean government offered to repay the loan by giving the USSR and other socialist countries part of the aluminum it hoped to produce in a smelter connected to the power plant. The aluminum smelter would be built by a Western consortium, which was already active in the region of Fria with a smaller refinery. Nonetheless, the Conakry government insisted that "the dam in Guinea on the Konkouré River must be built with help from the Soviet Union, for this is the most important objective in the development of the national economy, and our hope." Despite the cost and relative lack of clarity about the repayment of the loan, the Soviet government gave the go ahead for the construction of the Konkouré dam. Preliminary surveys were scheduled to start in 1963, and the works were estimated to be completed in 1967.[95]

In Ghana, Nkrumah considered reviving another colonial project for a dam in addition to Akosombo. The Accra government asked the Soviet Union to study the feasibility and cost of realizing a dam on the Black Volta at the Bui gorge in Central-Western Ghana. Soviet specialists traveled to the region in late 1961 and began to work on the project of a 200,000-kilowatt power station and a 250-kilometer transmission line to transport electricity toward the north of the country. The works were estimated to be completed in 1964–1965. Mali followed suit. In the spring of 1961, the Bamako government requested Soviet help in studying the possibility of building a dam and a power plant on the Senegal River at Gouina, in the southwestern portion of the country, not far from the borders with Senegal and Mauritania.[96]

Industry was no less important than infrastructure. In Guinea, industrialization was Sékou Touré's open ambition. Responding to a journalist from the West German weekly *Der Spiegel*, who had asked him if Guinea really did not need Europe anymore, Sékou Touré declared: "We can industrialize Guinea independently of Europe and much more rapidly, much more effectively and under conditions more socially favorable to our population than it would have been the case under French direction. What is more, we have found in Eastern Europe partners that have made and still make us offers."[97]

In its quest to affirm independence and sovereignty, the Guinean government was especially concerned with control over natural resources and their transformation. While traveling between Prague and Warsaw in early 1959, Beavogui complained that "national industry is still basically non-existent." The extraction of Guinea's bauxite was managed by Western companies, which then transformed it into aluminum. Beavogui hoped that this process could be completed in Guinea soon.[98]

Bauxite came to embody Sékou Touré's vision of independence through development for his country. Guinea was endowed with some of the world's largest reserves of bauxite, which had been exploited since the 1920s. A US-French consortium was active in Fria, where the Konkouré project was to be realized, while the French-Canadian company Société Bauxites du Midi operated near the town of Boké in the northwest of the country. In 1961, after lengthy but unsuccessful negotiations on the development of the Boké mine, the Guinean government decided to nationalize Bauxites du Midi. As of 1962, production was run by the Guineans with help from Polish and Hungarian specialists. The Soviet government agreed to look into the possibility of taking over the further development of the Boké site.[99]

Apart from bauxite, the Conakry government expected to see the production of processed food, textiles, clothes, and household items to expand significantly over the five years following independence. The initial three-year plan listed fruit conserves, dried rice, kitchen utensils, wooden furniture, shoes, and basic transportation means such as carts and wheelbarrows as some of the priorities for light industry, to be produced with help from foreign firms. Moreover, Guinea looked at fishing as a promising industry to develop, both as a basic source of food and a potential new export sector.[100] The USSR provided funding, equipment, and specialists to build a fruit and vegetable conserve factory in Kindia, with a capacity of 3 million jars per year, a footwear factory in Kindia able to produce half a million shoes each year, and a sawmill and timber processing factory in Nzérékoré to make wooden furniture. In Conakry, Soviet technicians prepared to install a large refrigerator to store up to 100 tons of fish in accordance with the government's wish to develop the fishing industry. Moreover, a few leather factories would be realized with the help of Soviet money and Czechoslovak expertise. Repair workshops to keep vehicles functioning (which depended on spare parts and tools imported from the socialist world) would be established in Conakry and the major regional centers.[101]

Concerning infrastructure and industry, the strategy in Mali largely resembled that of Guinea, including the focus on small projects to decrease dependency on imports. Keïta was especially keen that the Soviet Union be involved in the development of light industry in Mali. Following the visit of the first Soviet delegation in late 1960, the Malian Prime Minister wrote to Khrushchev outlining the priorities for his country's modernization and hoping for Soviet involvement. Keïta hoped to obtain Soviet assistance in the construction of a concrete plant in Gao (vital for other construction works in the region), a modern slaughterhouse equipped with refrigerators in Bamako, and a dairy factory and a soap factory in locations to be determined. In total, Soviet investment in light industry in Mali was projected to be about 10 million rubles.[102]

Despite small-scale industrialization, however, imports would remain necessary for the country's survival in the foreseeable future. For Mali, a landlocked state, access to the ports on the Atlantic Ocean was vital. Traditionally, supplies destined to Mali came through the Dakar port in Senegal. Between 1900 and 1924, the French had built a railway line that linked Dakar to Bamako, and then to Koulikoro on the banks of the Niger, from where goods could be transported on barges to the Mopti, Timbuktu, and Gao regions. Mali's independence complicated the country's supply routes. The Bamako government needed to balance its desire to detach itself from France and its Communauté with the necessity to continue trading with Senegal and Côte d'Ivoire, both steady French partners. The Malian Ministry of Commerce identified the most pressing problem as "transport, which constitutes a bottleneck. . . . Indeed, Mali used to import about 14,000 tons of goods per month through the Dakar-Niger railway—the Conakry-Niger [railway] and the Conakry port not being sufficiently equipped to intervene effectively, basic imports and exports were redirected through Abidjan. The Abidjan-Niger [link] also rapidly became clogged, and forces us to seek the solution to our problems in a rail-road combination."[103]

Guinea, given the radical course it had taken, seemed to represent an ideal alternative to the established commercial routes. In theory, goods could travel to Mali from the Conakry port, removing the dependency link to what remained of the French empire in West Africa. The reality, however, was much more complicated. The necessary infrastructure was almost completely nonexistent, to the point that the roads that crossed from Mali into Guinea were little more than trails, impossible to use for half the year when heavy rains all but erased them. The only solution was for the USSR to develop the Conakry port, and to provide assistance to improve transport infrastructure in both Guinea and Mali. Soviet engineers worked on the possibility of improving and expanding the navigability of the Niger, which normally depended on water levels. Moreover, to link Mali with the ocean, the Bamako government proposed the construction of a railway line that stretched from Bamako all the way to Kankan in Guinea, then joining the existing but decaying line from Kankan to Conakry via Mamou and Kindia. In Mali's proposal, the Malian and Guinean governments would divide expenses equally. The Soviet government agreed to finance part of the project and to provide experts and construction materials. Work on the first section of the railway (the 300 kilometers from Conakry to Mamou) began in earnest, and most of it was completed in late 1961. The two countries then agreed to split expenses proportionately to continue the construction of the remaining part of the railway from central Guinea to Bamako.[104]

Besides the railway, the Guinean government expected more investment in transport infrastructure. New roads needed to be built to provide better east-west links, and existing ones needed to be resurfaced, offering a better connection from Conakry to Nzérékoré, Guinea's third-largest city. The three-year plan envisaged the construction of 1,800 kilometers of roads, and Moscow contributed 4 million rubles worth of road construction equipment. Moreover, with Soviet assistance, Conakry's airport needed to become functional and modern—a new international gateway to a new country. Besides refurbishing the runway, the Guinean government asked the Soviet Union to construct twenty warehouses to store import-export goods and at least one large hangar for maintenance and repairs of aircraft. Guinea would buy Iliushin-14 and Iliushin-18 from the USSR to equip the newly formed Air Guinée. Nearly one hundred Soviet specialists worked on the Conakry airport in 1961.[105]

Ghana, richer than most of its regional neighbors and better endowed with existing infrastructure than Guinea and Mali, had different needs. As in Guinea and Mali, the production of energy and effective management of water resources for agriculture and consumption were essential items in Ghana's development plan. The improvement of transport infrastructure was not as pressing a need as elsewhere for Ghana's roads were generally better than those in Guinea and Mali.[106] The country also had a functioning international airport in Accra and reasonably modern port facilities in Takoradi. Ghana's problem was differentiating its economy, promoting crops other than cocoa, and developing local industry. Nkrumah believed in the necessity to create a second major port in Tema, which the government hoped would stimulate fishing and create a local canning industry. Moscow approved the project, and Soviet advisers began working on a construction plan, which included port facilities, complete with refrigerators, factories to process the catch, workshops to keep the boats in function, and also living quarters for the fishermen and the industrial workers that were to be based in Tema. The Accra government and GKES hoped that the project could be finished by 1964. Like the bauxite industry in Guinea, Tema and the fishing industry came to embody Nkrumah and the CPP's idea of development independent from the old colonial masters. The Soviet government agreed. Visiting the building sites in Tema in January 1962 and addressing local workers, Mikoian commented that "old Ghana, the old Africa is dying away, and the road is open for a new Africa with a great future ahead."[107]

The Soviet contribution to the development of the Tema port and of the fishing industry was very significant. The Soviet government would build two large accommodation blocs in Tema for a total of 12,000 people (the town's total population at the time was about 25,000 people).[108] The design of the blocs would be entirely Soviet, and Moscow would provide all materials, equipment, and machinery for construction, together with expert supervision, and cover 80 percent of the cost. Regarding fishing, Accra expected Soviet experts to conduct no less than "a survey of the entire industry with particular emphasis on the types of fishing boats and gear, methods of making the catch, storage, processing both on board ship and ashore, and marketing, and offering suggestions as to ways of introducing the improvements that may be recommended." The USSR would also provide Ghana with ten modern trawlers and train each crew, which would be composed of eighteen people each, including engineers, refrigerator technicians, hydro-acoustic specialists, and commanding officers. Moreover, the Soviet government agreed to assist the Ghanaian government in the construction of a fish processing complex in Tema, comprising of a fish canning factory, a fish smoking factory, a fish cookery shop, and a rendering plant for waste and grease. Soviet experts would draw the building plans, Soviet engineers would direct the works, and the USSR would provide both the materials and the training for Ghanaian workers. The total cost, which was approved in December 1962, was estimated at approximately 1.5 million rubles.[109]

In all three countries, the Soviet Union financed and supervised generic small-scale industrial projects, such as leather tanning and footwear factories, textile manufactories, dairy farms, vehicle repair workshops, and canneries. Factories to produce cement and concrete, necessary for nearly all other construction work, were an especially urgent priority in West Africa. Likewise, the USSR funded the creation or expansion of existing small factories that produced bricks and tiles to facilitate local construction projects (Guinea, for example, planned to build 250 new homes in 1962 alone). Soviet involvement followed the gradual approach of the development plans—the priority was the creation of the basic small-scale industry, to be followed at a later stage by more advanced industry. For instance, Guinea's development plan focused first on small factories to transform basic agricultural products, such as dried rice, meat, leather shoes, fruit juices, and palm oil. In the future, Guinea would be able to set up the production of goods that required additional processing, such as dairy, sugar, soap, flour and starch, textiles, wood pulp, and cigarettes, for which the USSR was expected to contribute capital and expertise.[110]

The Soviet Union also sponsored geological surveys and expeditions to look for oil, natural gas, gold, diamonds, and other precious metals, and any useful minerals. In Ghana, Soviet and Polish specialists studied how to exploit a large deposit of iron ore in the North-East of the country, Soviet technicians helped the government to extract manganese ore, and Soviet engineers helped run a metallurgical plant that would make use of both iron and manganese. The Soviet government promised Ghana up to 21 million rubles for more geological exploratory works. Likewise, Moscow was ready to support the Guinean government's search for oil and gold, with a projected total cost of 13 million rubles, which was expected to require nearly 120 Soviet geologists. In Mali, the

USSR provided a loan of 3.5 billion francs to finance surveys to look for oil, gold, and diamonds in the north of the country. In all cases, "the Soviet Union will sustain almost all of the expenses: the provision of equipment, of specialized personnel and the necessary funds."[111]

Soviet aid also was requested to support infrastructure for education and the training of technical specialists. In Guinea, the Soviet government agreed to build a Polytechnic Institute, which would train engineers, geologists, road technicians, and agronomists. The project included the construction of facilities such as a large library and workshops, but also a stadium with a capacity of 25,000 spectators, a swimming pool, and a gym. The exact same project for a polytechnic was to be replicated in Mali, complete with a large stadium in Bamako. The Ghanaian government liked the idea and in May 1961 made a formal request to the Soviet Union for help in the realization of a "technical institute" to train 5,000 students, but with no stadium attached this time. The USSR agreed to "provide, on credit terms, technical designs, documentation schemes and plans for training, equipment and materials, and technical assistance in constructing and initiating the training courses."[112]

FIGURE 4.2. A delegation from Ghana visits the Tashkent Textile Factory in the Uzbek SSR. August 1963. Credit: Sputnik.

As of 1961, the USSR financed and supervised approximately twenty major projects in Guinea in agriculture, industry, and infrastructure, for an estimated value of 226 million old rubles (about 60 million 1960 US dollars, or 57 million new rubles). This represented nearly 40 percent of total capital investment in Guinea.[113] Even when Guinea began receiving aid from the West, Soviet assistance remained larger. For example, American and West German aid combined (a commitment of approximately 40 million US dollars) was about two-thirds of the USSR's alone.[114] At the same time, Soviet overall engagement in Mali totaled slightly less than 50 million new rubles (45 million US dollars, or about 13 billion CFA francs), distributed over approximately fifteen major projects.[115] Figures for Ghana are slightly more complex to calculate given the large number of projects still at the drawing stage by 1961. Combining the initial August 1960 agreement with the additional one signed in late 1961, the total Soviet formal commitment to Ghana was in the region of 55–60 million US dollars to finance about twenty major projects, including farms, factories, the Tema port, and scientific and geological cooperation.[116]

These were significant sums. In Guinea, funds from the socialist countries equaled 70 percent of all investment, 42 percent of which came from the Soviet Union alone.[117] Soviet aid at its peak equaled about 15–18 percent of Guinea's GDP.[118] Mali and much more so Ghana were richer countries, and thus the relative impact of Soviet aid was not as pronounced. However, the USSR was still by far the largest foreign donor in both countries. In 1960–1961, the Soviet Union gave Mali slightly less than 13 billion West African francs, more than the value of aid that came from all West European countries combined (11 billion CFA). The second largest donor, France, gave about 5.5 billion CFA, just slightly more than the People's Republic of China (4.9 billion CFA). Czechoslovakia, one of the most active European socialist countries in Africa, contributed 2.5 billion francs, considerably less than the United Arab Republic (4.2 billion CFA).[119] In Ghana, the West had agreed to contribute about half the funds necessary for the construction of the Volta project—84 million US dollars out of the estimated 168 million US dollars. The World Bank would contribute 40 million US dollars, the US government 30 million, and the UK government 14 million.[120] The Soviet Union alone gave Ghana more than 55 million US dollars, making it the single largest donor. The total aid Ghana received from the whole of the Soviet bloc in 1961 surpassed 80 million US dollars.[121]

Besides the figures, the importance of Soviet aid cannot be underestimated. In practical terms, Soviet aid gave Ghana, Guinea, and Mali the possibility of obtaining some of the essential supplies that ensured the countries' economic survival. Moreover, it provided the local governments with the funds and part of the expertise they needed to pursue their developmental agenda, which granted

Nkrumah, Sékou Touré, and Keïta political legitimacy. In the early 1960s the economies of Ghana, Guinea, and Mali could hardly function without the Soviet Union.

Free Money

The cost of the development plans devised by Ghana, Guinea, and Mali was high. It far surpassed the resources any of them could hope to obtain in the short term. Guinea envisaged a total investment of about 30 billion CFA francs in three years, Ghana of more than 100 million pounds in five years (almost 250 million pounds, including the Volta project), and Mali of about 80 billion CFA francs in five years. Foreign assistance was vital, and Soviet loans were more than welcome. However, part of the necessary investments needed to come from domestic sources. All countries, according to the "most optimistic estimate," expected to be able to raise about half of the necessary funds at home.[122] In this area, control over the money supply (the ability to print money and set the interest rate through a central bank) and banking (to regulate access to credit in the country) were judged vital by all three governments.[123]

Before independence, Ghana, Guinea, and Mali belonged to currency unions managed by the respective *métropole*. Ghana used the West African pound, whose value was set by the London-controlled West African Currency Board, and Guinea and Mali were part of the West African franc zone, which united all French territories in the region under the same currency. The Gold Coast already had a national bank set up in 1953. Shortly after independence, the new government in Accra created an independent Bank of Ghana that assumed all functions of a central bank, including printing money (the new Ghanaian pound, introduced in 1958). All new Ghanaian coins and banknotes were minted with the effigy of Nkrumah, and not that of the Queen of England as was customary in Commonwealth countries. The image of Nkrumah was circled by the Latin motto *Civitatis Ghaniensis Conditor* ("Founder of the State of Ghana"). It was a clear message: the new government aspired to monetary independence.[124]

The reality of managing the new central bank was more challenging. Even though it was technically independent, the Bank of Ghana maintained connections to Britain. The first chairman of the Bank of Ghana, Alfred Eggleston, was a Scottish imperial functionary who had been transferred to Ghana from India, following nomination by the then British Governor-General. Moreover, at least four of the most important officials in the Bank of Ghana were British. Their fears were probably exaggerated, but Soviet analysts looked at the Bank of Ghana as yet another instrument of London's continuing influence over its former colony.[125]

The new Ghanaian pound remained in the sterling area, meaning that it kept a fixed exchange rate to the British pound and indirectly to other currencies. In theory, this meant that the value of the Ghanaian pound should have followed that of the British pound, appreciating or depreciating according to decisions taken in London rather than Accra. Lewis, who regarded membership of the sterling area as an unavoidable necessity, was aware of the potential problems this may have presented and proposed that the government use all possible means to avoid devaluing its currency at an "awkward" moment, even if the pound sterling did so. Ghana ended its currency's fixed exchange rate with the pound sterling in 1965, when the government introduced the cedi as the country's new currency.[126]

As in several areas of public life, for the first few years following independence Nkrumah's control over Ghana's money supply was limited. Whether because of British influence or simply because of economic convictions, the Bank of Ghana was more interested in maintaining price stability and preserving the fixed exchange rate with the pound sterling than pursuing the expansionary monetary policy Nkrumah's plans would have required. As a consequence, Ghana did print money to finance its development agenda, which contributed to bringing the inflation rate from near zero during the Currency Board years to about 8 percent in the early 1960s, but not at a level sufficient to finance the development plan.[127]

Exports and taxation remained key to finance development in Ghana, but they did not bring in enough revenues to pay for the most ambitious objectives the Nkrumah government had set. Writing to the Accra government just a few days before leaving his post, Lewis argued that some projects were too expensive and should be scrapped. Ghana simply could not afford them. "We desire everything that richer and larger nations have," Lewis wrote, "but we cannot afford as much as they can. At present we are in the same position as if an elementary school teacher were trying to put his son through Cambridge University, entirely out of his own earnings. The object is laudable, but the means will not support it, so the policy is mistaken."[128]

Soviet loans and more control over the money supply offered a way out. However, it was only after 1963, when the Accra government tightened its control over the Bank of Ghana, that the growth rate of the money supply expanded twofold.[129] At the same time, the government created the National Investment Bank, a body designed to finance economic development with a focus on industry. Seventy-five percent of the Bank's shares belonged to the Accra government, and both the Minister of Finance and the Minister of Industry were members of the board of directors.[130] In a similar fashion, the Nkrumah government also created an International Bank, based in the City of London, to manage international capital flows, and a Social Security Bank, to manage the savings of Ghanaian citizens. Thanks to these new banks, the government became the largest operator in Ghana's financial sector, otherwise dominated by British-run banks, such as Barclays and the Bank of West Africa (formerly the Bank of British West Africa).

Guinea took a more radical path. Even though it had broken relations with France and its Communauté, Guinea continued to use the West African franc for about a year after independence. During this time, Soviet advisers pressed the Conakry government to drop the franc and issue Guinea's own currency. Bettelheim agreed. In early 1960, after some hesitation, Sékou Touré announced the creation of the Guinean franc, which officially replaced the CFA franc on March 1, 1960, keeping an exchange rate of one to one with the old franc. The Soviet bloc had been instrumental in the currency reform. Czechoslovak experts oversaw the transition to the new legal tender, including the physical printing of the new money.[131]

The effects of the currency reform in Guinea were complex. It can be easily described as an unmitigated disaster. Even the Czechoslovak ambassador to Guinea was dubious about the possibility of introducing a new currency, and early reports showed that the newly established Banque de la République de Guinée was unprepared to manage the transition. Basic tasks such as printing and distributing the new francs—let alone the more complex operation of managing the money supply—could not be performed without constant supervision by experts from Czechoslovakia or other Soviet bloc countries. The sudden switch to a new currency also caused severe problems to private firms and businesses, and also occasionally government agencies, which were unable to pay wages and other expenses. Moreover, the new franc was inconvertible, meaning that neither its neighbors in West Africa nor France were willing to trade with Guinea. The country became even more reliant on exchanges with the Soviet Union, its satellites in Eastern Europe, and the socialist world at large. Trade was essentially fully nationalized, with the CGCE in control of all foreign transactions. Not unlike the Bank of Guinea, the Comptoir for trade was ill-prepared to coordinate and manage the exchanges that were essential to Guinea's economic survival. Numerous witnesses at the time, including several Soviet observers from MVT, reported a wide range of wastes, delays, incompetence, bureaucratic chaos, and extensive corruption. Shortages of basic goods and commodities, including food and medicines, were the immediate consequences.[132]

The transition to the Guinean franc was certainly problematic. However, blaming the decision to introduce a new currency as the main cause for Guinea's economic malaise is not entirely accurate. Guinea's economic isolation was already a reality, well before the reform. Remaining in the West African franc zone would have required mending relations with Paris, and the French government sent Guinea mixed signals in this respect. More important, Sékou Touré's economic strategy was already well defined: Guinea was to pursue an ambitious development plan that required a large amount of resources. Monetary sovereignty was an absolute necessity. Soviet advisers remained supportive of Guinea's decision to quit the franc zone and print its own currency.[133]

Following the currency reform, the Conakry government gained virtually total control over money and finance in Guinea. The few foreign banks operating in the country were nationalized shortly after the introduction of the Guinean franc. In the summer of 1961, the functions of the Bank of Guinea were split among the newly created Banque Centrale de la République de Guinée, which issued and managed the Guinean franc, the Banque Nationale de Développement Agricole, for investment in agricultural modernization, the Banque Guinéenne du Commerce Extérieur, which helped the CGCE manage the few financial transactions with foreign countries, and finally the Crédit National pour le Commerce, l'Industrie et l'Habitat, which operated as a commercial bank for both individuals and firms.[134]

All aspects of banking were in Sékou Touré's hands. In theory, Guinea was free to print as much money as it needed to pursue agricultural modernization and industrialization. Moreover, the government controlled access to credit, making it possible to finance the creation of agricultural cooperatives and small firms. Sékou Touré referred to the government's fiscal and monetary policy as a "humanist philosophy" of the national budget, which allowed the PDG to translate into practice its revolutionary aims. The obvious problems were that Guinea possessed no hard currency reserves, that the new franc was worthless abroad, and that the country's porous borders challenged the CGCE's already precarious monopoly on foreign trade because of smuggling. As long as the Soviet Union was willing to provide physical capital and expertise, and to accept either local commodities or even the Guinean franc as means of payment, Sékou Touré's plan could go ahead.[135]

Mali followed a path similar to Guinea. Just like Guinea, after independence Mali stayed in the franc zone for about a year and a half, while the government considered what to do. France's interference in the management of Mali's finances was a problem for the US-RDA government, which hoped to be able to raise resources for its development plan. The Soviet Union and its allies, primarily Czechoslovakia, firmly believed that Mali could not launch such a plan without full monetary sovereignty. Moreover, the Czech advisers saw monetary reform as a possible first step toward the creation of a monetary union with Guinea and possibly Ghana too.[136] Bénard agreed: "a nation that wants to plan seriously its economy in order to secure independent development, needs to have both internal and external monetary powers."[137] In the end, the development plan unveiled by the Keïta government in late 1961 was as ambitious and as expensive as Ghana's or Guinea's, and pursuing it without control over the money supply was unthinkable. Thus, in July 1962 Keïta announced that Mali would be issuing its own currency—the Malian franc. Nevertheless, the Bamako government officially did not see the birth of the Malian franc as the end of Mali's participation in, or at least association with, the franc zone. Displaying a certain flair for verbal acrobatics, Keïta wrote to de Gaulle that "it is evident that our departure from the monetary union does not call into question the very principle of our membership of the very same franc zone."[138] The new Malian franc was inconvertible, and it was only thanks to the French government's intercession and financial aid that Mali could continue exchanges with the franc zone. Commercial banking in Mali was managed by the Banque Malienne de Crédits et de Dépôts, a state bank created in 1961 with the participation of French private capital.[139] As in Ghana and Guinea, the new currency was a powerful instrument to pursue Mali's modernization agenda, but at the same time the process generated inflation, whose deleterious effects on both state finances and living standards would become evident in the longer run.[140]

With Soviet inspiration and Soviet supervision, the governments of Ghana, Guinea, and Mali obtained nearly full control over money and finance. In their vision, money and finance were simply instruments in the hands of the state, which needed resources to jumpstart modernization. Private entrepreneurship and foreign direct investment, which in liberal economic theory provide capital for modernization, clashed with the ultimate goal of economic independence. Therefore, monetary policy had to be completely subordinated to government control. In banking and finance, as in virtually all other areas of economic policy, the Soviet approach in West Africa mirrored what had been and would be done in other developing countries that applied an import-substitution development strategy.

A Soviet ISI

Cooperation with the USSR and the socialist bloc determined the direction of economic development in Ghana, Guinea, and Mali. The Soviet government did not push for the establishment of a fully planned communist system in West Africa. Conscious that even relatively limited investments would shape the economic future of Ghana, Guinea, and Mali, Soviet advisers found a third way between communism and capitalism, which focused on state institutions as vehicles of modernization but left ample space for functioning markets. In the ongoing debate on the role of the national bourgeoisie and the prospects of so-cialism in Africa and the Third World, Soviet assistance to Ghana, Guinea, and Mali put the stress on building a form of capitalism that was dominated by the state. As Potekhin put it, "call it as you like, state capitalism or simply state sec-tor, but this is state property."[141]

The Soviet leadership was not particularly concerned by the prominent role that bourgeois leaders like Nkrumah, Sékou Touré, and Keïta had in the pur-suit of modernization in Ghana, Guinea, and Mali. It did not even matter that the socialist world did not have a monopoly on economic cooperation. Address-ing criticism from MID officials who lamented that there were still Western economic interests in Ghana, Guinea, and Mali, Degtiar' (the deputy head of GKES) responded that "Lenin did not prevent the Soviet Union from granting concessions."[142] What mattered was that the reins of modernization were firmly in the hands of the local governments, and little space was left to international private capital. As for the bourgeoisie, Degtiar' believed that in "twenty-thirty years, when in the economic competition we will have defeated the United States of America, the international situation will change, and the African bourgeoise will not get enough time from history to form itself as a class."[143]

The Soviet approach to development in West Africa resembled closely an import-substitution industrialization strategy (ISI), similar to what a number of Third World countries—such as Brazil, India, South Korea, and Taiwan—had adopted in the past, adopted at the same time, or would adopt years later, with varying degrees of success. Focusing on agriculture and light industry, then transferring resources to heavy industry later, as the USSR planned to do in West Africa, mirrored the approach taken by the Japanese colonial administration and then by the Kuomintang in Taiwan between 1870 to 1960, by Brazil in the 1930s and by South Korea in the 1960s. Robert Wade has shown how agricultural re-form, mechanization, and investment in light industry lay the foundation for Taiwan's industrialization in future decades. The first development plan, from 1953 to 1956, "assigned most of its resources to agriculture, fertilizers, and tex-tiles."[144] Similarly, the first decade of Korea's push for import-substitution de-velopment was "dominated by labor-intensive, light consumer goods, and by the 1970s, by a push toward heavy industry."[145] Likewise, during the 1930s, Brazil boosted basic industrial production aimed at the domestic market—consumer goods such as "textiles, shoes, clothing, and foodstuffs"—and only after World War II it pushed to transfer resources from agriculture to industry.[146] On the contrary, independent India's development strategy focused immediately on heavy industrialization, and provided comparatively limited investment in ag-riculture during the Nehru era.[147] Therefore, the Soviet approach to development in West Africa resembled more closely the choices made by right-wing, statist governments—like the KMT in Taiwan, Brazil's during the Estado Novo period, and Park Chung-hee's South Korea—than those of a country that was directly inspired by the USSR, such as Nehru's India.

Close cooperation between the USSR and its partners in West Africa was also squarely in the tradition of import substitution. In the Soviet government's vision of development for West Africa, full economic self-sufficiency was never a goal. The Soviet advisers were conscious that Ghana, Guinea, and Mali could acquire advanced technology and expertise in key areas only from abroad, and therefore cooperation with the socialist bloc would remain essential for the success of their economic development strategies even in the longer term. Once again, the crucial role of foreign capital, technology, and expertise mirrored what happened or would happen in other countries that chose import substitution. India, where "foreign investors were by and large discouraged, mainly because they might have threatened hard-won national sovereignty," was rather exceptional.[148] Contrary to India, foreign aid and investment—particularly American and Japanese— played a pivotal role in East Asia. In Taiwan, "over the 1950s economic aid equaled about 6% of GNP and nearly 40% of gross investment." Most US aid to Taiwan, "38 percent, went to finance imports of intermediate goods (mainly cotton, yam, ores, metals, and fertilizer); 30 percent went for consumer goods (mainly food); another 19 percent went for capital goods (machinery and tools)."[149] Likewise, South Korea benefited greatly from American largesse first and later from the interest of Japanese investors in financing and sharing technology with Korean businesses. This was a crucial component of the Korean economic miracle in the 1960s, to the point that "Japanese business and government assumed proportionally larger roles in Korea's economic decision-making" and "the Koreans could not build or operate new plants without Japanese approval and cooperation."[150] In the same way, in post-1945 Brazil the government went to great lengths to attract foreign capital and technology to develop new branches of the economy. As Tobias Rupprecht showed, the administrations of Juscelino Kubitschek, Jânio Quadros, and João Goulart were especially interested in the Soviet Union as a potential economic partner. Following the military coup in 1964, Brazil changed direction, but resources for import substitution still came from abroad. Nearly 80 percent of capital inflow came from the United States, whose government also pushed the International Monetary Fund and the World Bank to grant Brazil loans.[151]

In Ghana, Guinea, and Mali the Soviet Union aimed to do the same. While the Soviet government discouraged investment from the capitalist world, it judged the inflow of capital—both physical and human—from the socialist world as necessary to support development in West Africa. The USSR, through loans, trade, and advisers, planned to play in West Africa a role similar to that of American money, Japanese technology, and foreign investment in Brazil and in East

Asia. Given the relatively small size of Ghana, Guinea, and Mali, this appeared feasible.

Generous public spending and strong state control over finance and the money supply, as the USSR recommended in West Africa, were also stalwarts of import substitutions strategies, both past and future. In his classic study of the "Japanese miracle," Chalmers Johnson noted how the Bank of Japan since the 1950s was "essentially an operating arm of the Ministry of Finance." Budget deficits and generally high inflation rates contributed to fueling Japan's growth until the 1970s.[152] In South Korea after the war, the central bank was modeled on its Japanese equivalent. Moreover, the government nationalized all existing banks and created new credit institutions to finance development with public money. As a consequence, "the South Korean state did not follow a program of austerity. It took in large amounts, and it spent even more—investing in wise, long-term projects—making up the difference by borrowing." Likewise, "deficit financing was the order of the day" in Brazil at least until 1964, and India nationalized all its banks in 1969, during Indira Gandhi's rule, adopting a similar policy with regard to government spending.[153]

Leaving aside the relative wisdom of Soviet-financed investments in Ghana, Guinea and Mali, which will be discussed in the next chapter, budget deficits and inflation in West Africa could be sustained as long as the USSR was willing to provide loans and to accept local currencies and local products in exchange for basic goods and services. As the next chapter will show, once the Soviet Union ceased to act as de facto lender of last resort, the system collapsed.

The trade policy followed by the governments of Ghana, Guinea, and Mali in conjunction with the Soviet Union was also inspired by the same principles as other states that opted for import substitution. Protection from excessive reliance on goods and commodities that had to be purchased from Europe was a core aim of the development strategy in West Africa. The same can be said of virtually all countries in the ISI framework: Brazil, India, Taiwan, and South Korea, among others, all imposed restrictions on imports with the aim of stimulating domestic production and protecting local industry from foreign competition. At the same time, they tried to foster export sectors to enter the global market from a position of relative strength. As Wade has argued in the case of Taiwan, this required treating different branches of the economy differently, with a mix of subsidies to produce in export areas, and tariffs and other barriers to imports in areas where the government aimed to develop local industry.[154] Unlike East Asia, Ghana, Guinea, and Mali after independence did not have the resources to develop high value-added industries for export (from cars to semiconductors) in a short time. Yet, their "traditional production," as Soviet advisers referred to cocoa, coffee, peanuts, and tropical fruit, did have an international market. Here, the most obvious comparison with a classic ISI country is with Brazil, where different governments continued to support the production and international sale of coffee "well past the Second World War" and despite the declining terms of trade.[155]

In the Soviet plan for West Africa, most of this produce would be exchanged for technology and expertise from the socialist world. Whatever was left could be sold to the West. As productivity increased in West Africa thanks to Soviet investments—as the governments in Accra, Bamako, Conakry, and Moscow expected—Ghana, Guinea, and Mali would be able to sell more and more of their traditional produce on the international market and, in due course, even develop new export sectors. Sanchez-Sibony explored how the Soviet leadership looked at the global market as an opportunity for the USSR's export commodities, and indeed often as the only way to obtain crucial technology from abroad. When participating in the management of foreign, nonsocialist economies, the Soviet leadership took a similar approach. It saw the possibility for Ghana, Guinea, and Mali to sell on the international market as a necessary step in their own search for development and modernization.[156]

The Soviet Man's Burden

Soviet involvement in Ghana, Guinea, and Mali was extensive, comparable in size and scope to what the colonial powers did before independence. Was the Soviet Union simply replacing Britain and France as a new colonial power in West Africa? The colonial overtones of Soviet discourse were unmistakable. During meetings, official visits, and general addresses, Khrushchev, Mikoian, and other Soviet leaders constantly presented the Soviet Union as a "developed" society, and thus implicitly understood to be superior to those of their West African allies. Scholars and analysts in Moscow repeated the same points, depicting Ghana, Guinea, and Mali as premodern societies, stuck in the fifteenth century and abandoned to their destiny by the former European rulers. On the contrary, the USSR was described as benevolent and generous, and therefore ready to share its knowledge and experience, guiding its new friends toward modernity they could not otherwise reach on their own. These are tropes of all forms of colonialism, both paleo and neo. The Soviet leadership itself appeared somewhat conscious of the risk of being perceived as just another colonial power and tried their best to differentiate their actions from those of the Europeans that had preceded them in West Africa. The results bordered on the farcical. In 1962, while on an official visit to Guinea, Mikoian spent a few minutes chatting with some Guinean builders working on Soviet-sponsored projects in Conakry. A Radio

Moscow correspondent thus reported the exchange: "[Mikoian:] How is the work going? [Workers:] Very well! [Mikoian:] How are the relations with the Soviet specialists? [Workers:] Perfect! [Mikoian:] Are they like the colonizers? [Workers:] No! No!"[157]

Besides discourse, Soviet practice offered a similar picture. Soviet trade was downright colonial. High value-added products left the Soviet Union for Africa, while raw materials were received from Ghana, Guinea, and Mali (often purchased at artificially high prices, as France had long done with its African colonies). Moreover, Soviet specialists took the jobs that had been traditionally occupied by colonial officials. Following the signing of the 1959 agreements, specialists from the USSR and from the rest of the Soviet bloc began to arrive in Guinea to occupy key positions as advisers and experts in government administration, industry, agriculture, media, and defense. As of December 1961, there were about 1,200 Soviet-bloc specialists and technicians in Guinea. In addition to the approximately 500 Soviet specialists working in industry, agriculture, infrastructure, and study missions, the USSR fielded forty-five teachers working in the Ministry of Education, twenty-five advisers in the Ministry of Public Works, fourteen specialists helping to manage the Conakry port, fifteen technicians in the Société Nationale d'Electricité, thirty-five pilots working for Air Guinée, who flew Soviet Iliushin 14s and 18s, five helicopter pilots flying the presidential vehicles, and five Soviet security officers working with the presidential office.[158] Education was a sector where Soviet assistance was particularly welcome. The Conakry government aimed to boost literacy in the country by increasing the number of Guinean children who went to school. In 1960, a dozen Soviet teachers were posted to Guinea to help train local teachers both in primary schools and lycées. Thanks also to Soviet assistance, between 1958 and 1961 the total number of Guinean children in primary school rose from 40,000 to 125,000. Moreover, the government scaled back religious education considerably, which caused resentment among both Catholics and Muslims in the country.[159]

Cooperation with the USSR had a profound impact on Guinea's society. A Soviet youth delegation invited to attend the PDG's fifth congress in October 1959 reported that cooperatives and collective farms were spreading, that the organization of the PDG was explicitly modeled on that of a Soviet-sponsored communist party, and that the "remains of colonialism are being successfully removed."[160] The remains of colonialism were the tribal chiefs, the traditional institution the French colonizers had worked with to keep control over local affairs. The Guinean government was replacing them with local administrators, often Soviet-trained, who represented the authority of the central state in each of the country's districts.[161] The Soviet delegates noticed with pleasure that PDG

FIGURE 4.3.   Soviet boxing coach V. Konchenko holds a training session in the Conakry stadium, built with financial and technical assistance from the Soviet Union. June 1966. Credit: Sputnik.

members and government officials such as the new administrators showed a considerable degree of interest in the ideas and principles of Marxism. The USSR was indisputably the new hegemon in Guinea. In the words of a PDG officer to the First Secretary of the Soviet embassy in Conakry, "we are glad of the fact that your country [the USSR] now occupies the most prominent place in the economic life of Guinea."[162]

Something comparable happened in Ghana, on a lesser scale. Besides the indispensable engineers and technicians, Soviet doctors and nurses went to work in Ghanaian hospitals, Soviet science professors taught Ghanaian teachers-in-training, and Soviet football teams toured Ghana playing friendly games with local clubs.[163] Moreover, Soviet academics gave public lectures in Accra, the Soviet embassy organized screenings of documentaries and photography exhibitions about life in the USSR, and CPP officials requested copies of the works of Marx, Engels, and Lenin (and, somewhat surprisingly, of Khrushchev too) to fill the Party library shelves.[164] The USSR entered the world of news and reporting too. Until 1960, the only alternative to Ghanaian radio and newspapers, which relied on briefs from Reuters, was the BBC. In November 1960, TASS, the Soviet press agency, was allowed to open an office in Accra. Moscow could finally give its own version of world affairs, transmit news from the USSR, and discuss the problems of world Communism. In the end, by mid-1963, the Soviet embassy in Accra printed and distributed 900 copies per day of its daily news bulletin, the largest circulation in Africa.[165]

In Mali, Keïta intended to organize both the US-RDA and his government like their equivalents in the Soviet Union. In 1962, he wrote to Mikoian with a list of questions on "state work," and to Ponomarev with a similar list on "party work." He wanted information on very basic aspects of Soviet political life, such as how many people there were in the Central Committee and the Supreme Soviet, how often they met, and whether all regions had representatives in them.[166] Besides high politics, Mali wanted to follow the Soviet example in other areas too. The Bamako government asked for information on the Soviet approach to such disparate topics as how to grant taxi licenses in the cities or how to manage the teaching of the Russian language as opposed to other languages in the USSR. They regarded Bambara, the country's lingua franca, as performing the same role in Mali.[167] Moreover, following the 1961 agreement, Soviet-Malian cooperation expanded to the training of Malian professional and technical cadres. The negotiators agreed that "the Soviet party will elaborate and send to the Republic of Mali the study plans, the programs, the textbooks, the essentials for school, the films, etc. as well as the equipment for ateliers, workshops and labs; the Soviet Union will also send for this same purpose its advisers, foremen, instructors and teachers."[168] Soviet specialists trained their Malian counterparts in virtually everything—from engineers to school teachers, and from nurses to air traffic controllers.[169] As in Guinea and Ghana, Soviet involvement in Mali touched on nearly all aspects of society.

At the same time, many West Africans traveled to the Soviet Union to attend training courses, pursue higher education, and take part in conferences and workshops. Shortly after the signing of the bilateral agreements, there were about 80 Guinean students on scholarships in the socialist bloc (of which about half were in the USSR), with an additional forty scheduled to leave in the near future. At the same time, there were about seventy Guinean students in the West and in Senegal. In 1962, the Ghanaian government proposed that 150 students from Ghana attend institutes of higher education and technical schools in the USSR, in accordance with the cultural agreement signed in 1960. In 1961, there were 20 students from Mali in the Soviet Union, but 31 more would be commencing their studies in the following academic year. The Ideology Commission of the TsK recommended admitting more in the near future, broadening the scope of Soviet education for African students, and introducing longer courses.[170]

The experiences of African students in the USSR were multifaceted. In many cases, they were negative. Many students from West Africa complained about the constant surveillance they faced while living in the Soviet Union, the lack of amenities, and few opportunities to socialize with Soviet people. Episodes of racism, including violence, toward African students were common in the Soviet cities where they resided. Julie Hessler has explored the circumstances surrounding the racially motivated murder of a Ghanaian medical student, Eduard Asare-Addo, in 1963. The murder led to a large-scale demonstration on Red Square in Moscow by African students, who lamented the structural racism of Soviet society and the constant abuse to which they were subjected while in the USSR. Nana Osei-Opare uncovered many more episodes of racial discrimination and gratuitous violence against Ghanaian students and diplomats in the Soviet Union. Anika Walke revealed how the mistreatment of African students in the USSR reflected the racist ideas that already existed in Soviet society. Sean Guillory analyzed the cultural clash between Soviet citizens and African students, who were more likely to resist the oppressive values of the Soviet Union. Maxim Matusevich showed how African students in the USSR tended to be much more worldly and cosmopolitan than their Soviet hosts, challenging the prejudice of who was supposed to modernize whom. Finally, Ophélie Rillon and Tatiana Smirnova have looked at Malian women who studied in the Soviet Union, highlighting the many dimensions of their experience, which involved racism and discrimination but also excitement and emotional attachment.[171]

The findings of this impressive new literature may need a few qualifications for this specific chronological, geographical, and political context. First, the number of African—and even more so West African—students in the USSR was always low. There were about 4,000 students from various parts of sub-Saharan Africa in the Soviet Union in the late 1960s. This number pales when compared to what happened in the West at the same time. More than 30,000 students from the developing world were enrolled in US universities and colleges during the 1960s, a significant proportion of whom came from Africa. European countries were even more popular destinations to study for young Africans. More than twice as many Africans studied in Britain than in the USSR and Eastern Europe combined. Figures were comparable in France, and even West Germany had more African students than the Soviet Union in the early 1960s. The experience of Africans studying in the West was not necessarily always positive, for racism in Britain, France, and the United States was not unheard of at the time. In 1961, the US National Security Council reported to the Kennedy administration that "many foreign students already have become embittered by their experiences in this country," advocating better resources and more effort in this field. Moreover, the social background of African students in the USSR was a complex issue. African visitors to the Soviet Union did not necessarily come from disadvantaged backgrounds. Going abroad was a privilege in West Africa in the 1960s, and the opportunity to study in a foreign country (including the USSR) was often reserved for the children of the political, economic, military, and cultural elite. Both Soviet officials and French observers described Guinean and Malian students in Moscow in the early 1960s as privileged and belonging to the families of "dignitaries" (which did not shield them from racist abuse). Some of the West African students in the USSR were used to a relatively high standard of living at home, and some had already experienced life in London, New York, or Paris. The notoriously shabby dorms in Soviet universities were unlikely to make a positive impression on them. Racism shattered their remaining hopes about life in the Soviet Union.[172]

For other West Africans, studying in the USSR was a more transformative experience. Souleymane Cissé, one of Mali's most famous film directors, received a scholarship to study cinema and photography in Moscow. His attitude toward the Soviet Union is unemotional. "Accepting one of those scholarships was a decision of the government and not mine."[173] Nonetheless, Cissé values the education he received in the USSR. "The masters who trained me never inculcated a system in me," he told an interviewer in 2020. "We are not immune to influences, but above all I learned to make films. Our teachers were engaged: if we did not understand something in class, they came to our place to continue. I admired this a lot."[174]

Like Ousmane Sembène, another great West African director trained in the USSR, Cissé was interested in exploring the impact of colonialism on African society. Their radical politics made the Soviet Union and its art attractive to them. Likewise, the poet Atukwei Okai spent years at the Maxim Gor'kii Literary Institute in Moscow during the 1960s. He remembers discovering Soviet poetry as a young man in Ghana and marveling that "Russian poetry was made for the people." Despite the difficulty of learning Russian, he "opted for Moscow" when scholarships became available in 1961. Atukwei remembers his time in Moscow fondly. Echoing Rodney a few years earlier, he was impressed by the efforts of the Soviet state to make culture accessible: "They demolished all barriers to self-enlightenment because they understand, or understood, that the development of the individual is equal to the development of the society. So they made books very cheap. A book that would cost ten dollars here, there it would cost five cents. Incredible!"[175]

Whether positive or negative, the experience of being a student in the Soviet Union was peripheral in Ghana, Guinea, and Mali. The number of West African students in the USSR was always low compared to the West, and it did not increase in the second half of the 1960s.

In sum, Soviet engagement with Ghana, Guinea, and Mali had more than an echo of colonialism in it. The discourse that surrounded cooperation, the asymmetry of exchanges at all levels, the patronizing attitudes of Soviet specialists who worked with West Africans, and the racism of Soviet society all pointed to a relationship dominated by prejudice and discrimination. Nevertheless, seeing Soviet involvement in West Africa uniquely as a neocolonial project may not be entirely accurate. The most obvious complication is that the Soviet Union did not gain much from its engagement. Ghana, Guinea, and Mali were small countries deprived of precious natural resources. The commodities the USSR imported from them—mainly agricultural products and some raw materials—could all have been acquired elsewhere, often at more convenient conditions. Gains, of course, do not need to be material to motivate exploitation. The hope to use Ghana, Guinea, and Mali as potential showcases of socialist modernity for the rest of the Third World to see and ponder played a prime role in the Soviet decision to invest there. However, the kind of expansion the Soviet leadership had in mind was different from that practiced by Western powers in Africa, Asia, and Latin America during the heyday of colonialism, or by the Soviet Union itself in Eastern Europe. The point was not to replicate the same ideas and structures of power and production that existed at home, as one could say France did in Algeria and the USSR in Poland, but to create new ones that prioritized maximizing material output over the formation of a political consciousness. A much more thorough investigation would be needed to explore Soviet colonialism in the Third World during the Cold War. For the purpose of this book, the evidence suggests that the top Soviet leadership was interested in Ghana, Guinea, and Mali primarily for the potential to establish there a model of development that they presented as an alternative to capitalism. All other considerations, from extracting resources to constructing a new system of values in West Africa, were secondary. For this reason, mixing and matching elements from different intellectual traditions was inevitable. According to the Soviet vision for West Africa, the revolution could wait; economic growth could not.

In 1961, Sékou Touré became the first African statesman to be awarded the Lenin Peace Prize, the "Soviet Nobel." The following year the prize went to Nkrumah, and Modibo Keïta was awarded it in 1963. Ostensibly given to prominent individuals for furthering the cause of international peace, the Lenin prize was frequently bestowed on prominent foreign political and cultural figures who enjoyed Moscow's favor. Radical Third World leaders were among the most common winners, including Ahmed Ben Bella, Fidel Castro, and Sukarno. Many of them were not communists. Sékou Touré, Nkrumah, and Keïta certainly were not. Rewarding non-communists was indicative of the Soviet approach to West Africa at the time, and it applied to development as much as to high politics.

What the Soviet Union offered Ghana, Guinea, and Mali was not communism. Rather than a universalistic vision of the world, Moscow tried to advance in West Africa a simple model of development based on its own experience but mitigated by many surviving elements of a standard market economy. It was more NEP than Five-Year Plan. More than anything else, the Soviet plan for West Africa resembled the kind of import-substitution growth models pioneered by several Third World countries since the 1930s, and that would rise to prominence again during the late 1960s and 1970s. In West Africa, the stress was on limiting, and eventually ending entirely, dependency on Western imports for basic goods and commodities. This could only be achieved by kick-starting industrialization, with the goal of producing domestically basics such as processed food, clothes, and household equipment. Industrialization, even just of the most basic kind, required infrastructure. Energy to power production was essential, just like roads, ports, and railways to distribute products. Building infrastructure, in its turn, necessitated capital, technology, and expertise that could only come from abroad. None of the above could succeed without a modern, mechanized agriculture that guaranteed food security for the population and enough raw commodities for industrial processing.

By extending loans, knowledge, guidance, and materials, the USSR promised to have a solution for all these issues. The Soviet solution differed from the Western one not in terms of techniques and goals, which largely overlapped, but in vision and method. The West promoted a vision of development that relied on private foreign investment to provide the capital and on individual entrepreneurship to use it. The Soviet ambition was instead demonstrating that Third World states could achieve the same goals detaching themselves from exploitative trade with the West, replacing foreign investment with so-called fraternal trade and loans from the socialist world. Third World governments could use them to pursue an agenda dictated by a plan elaborated in conjunction with the Soviet Union. This approach places the USSR squarely in the tradition of dependency theory and import substitution industrialization. Indeed, Soviet development assistance to West Africa represented one of the first attempts to initiate an import-substitution development strategy in a newly independent country in the postwar era.

In short, the West consistently prioritized the market as a vehicle for economic modernization. The Soviet Union believed in the state, even if it was bourgeois-nationalist and not communist. The shared vision between the Soviet government and its partners in Ghana, Guinea, and Mali appeared unshakeable. This honeymoon, alas, was not to last forever.

THINGS FALL APART

"First it was Ghana and Guinea"—sang E.T. Mensah, Ghana's King of Highlife—"Later Ghana Guinea Mali; Soon it will be all Africa." Mensah, one of West Africa's most influential musicians, wrote the song "Ghana-Guinea-Mali" in the early 1960s to celebrate the formation of the Union of African States. Ghana and Guinea had formed a political union in 1958, and Mali joined it in 1961. Sharing a similar political outlook, Nkrumah, Sékou Touré, and Keïta hoped that the union would become the basis for a future federation of all independent African states. Pursuing ambitious development strategies was an integral part of this project, and cooperation with the USSR offered some of the means to achieve it. Mensah's song reflected the optimism prevalent in West Africa at the time.[1]

In the Soviet Union, however, the mood was changing:

> Requests to provide economic aid pour in from African countries like from a cornucopia. The volume of our economic aid is increasing like an avalanche. And what will happen in two-three years? We plan our economy, including our economic relations and our aid, but do we know what kind of needs the African countries will have next year, in five years' time? We do not know. Often, we receive from them requests that are completely absurd. When you ask [them] why you need such a huge hydroelectric power station, what are you going to do with the electricity, they reply: "we will light up houses." It turns out that the country would be able to use only one tenth of that energy, but the construction of such a power station remains in the plan nonetheless.[2]

Igor' Kolosovskii, the author of this tirade, was the deputy head of the Department of African Countries at MID. Speaking at the end of the yearly town hall meeting of the Institute of Africa, Kolosovskii did not mince his words. He complained at length about the lack of preparedness he saw in African bureaucracies, about Soviet aid that he believed disappeared in Africa as in a bottomless pit, and about African leaders whom he found arrogant and impossible to please. According to Kolosovskii, they complained about the price of Soviet products for their countries, but then squandered their hard currency reserves on "French wine, Dutch and German beer, American cigarettes."[3]

Kolosovskii may have been especially grumpy, even by the standards of Soviet diplomacy, but he was not the only one to see problems and complain about the USSR's engagement in West Africa. A few months after Kolosovskii's lamentations, P.N. Tret'iakov, a young postdoctoral researcher in economics at the Institute of Africa, wrote a long report on Soviet aid to Mali following a period of field research in West Africa. The report, which Potekhin forwarded to MID, contained a strong indictment of Moscow's current policy. Tret'iakov lauded the Soviet effort to strengthen the role of the state in the Malian economy and praised the Bamako government's attempt to differentiate production and reduce dependency on imports. However, he denounced the USSR's involvement in projects whose immediate utility "raised questions," such as large infrastructure projects. Moreover, Soviet advisers were often left out of areas where their help would be crucial, such as the organization of agricultural cooperatives. Tret'iakov concluded that "all this indicates that until the signing of the government agreement between the USSR and Mali proper economic studies had not been conducted, and at the time [of their signing] particularly appropriate ways to solve this or that economic problem were not suggested to the Malian leadership."[4]

Such sharp criticism of Soviet policy and such a negative outlook on Third World allies were unusual in Khrushchev's Soviet Union. What had changed the previous atmosphere of optimism and confidence in the Soviet model of economic aid? Several factors challenged the idea that the noncapitalist model of development could be expanded in Africa and elsewhere, and that Moscow had found in Ghana, Guinea, and Mali three ideal allies. The Soviet resolve to invest in Africa suffered a significant blow after 1961. On the one hand, the old-fashioned Cold War, as seen in the evolution and tragic conclusion of the Congo crisis, revealed all the limits of Soviet power in the Third World. On the other, the Soviet economy began to lose the great dynamism of the second half of the 1950s. A resurgent West abroad, especially after a new administration entered office in Washington, and declining growth rates at home made the Soviet leadership reconsider the opportunity of investing lavishly in places like Ghana, Guinea, and Mali. Moreover, things on the ground looked less promising than they had only a few years earlier. The cost of economic cooperation in West Africa kept growing, together with expectations, while the initial estimates of local resources and capabilities proved unrealistic. As the governments in Moscow, Accra, Conakry, and Bamako shifted the blame onto each other for spiraling costs, abandoned construction sites, and bureaucratic chaos, the West African states faced financial crises. Cutting plans, expenditure, and eventually ambition was the solution adopted by all sides. The consequences were dire. By the time of Khrushchev's fall from power in late 1964, very little was left of the Soviet dream of creating thriving noncapitalist states in West Africa. This chapter investigates why and how things fell apart between the USSR and Ghana, Guinea, and Mali, exploring both structural and contingent factors.

Unhappy Degrowth

The 1950s were a decade of economic optimism in the Soviet Union. The USSR's economy grew at high rates, postwar reconstruction was completed, and living standards increased significantly. Khrushchev was captured by the enthusiasm of the times, to the point that he made promises that could not be kept. Khrushchev insisted that statistics that "proved" that the USSR would overtake the United States in many branches of production by the early 1980s be included in the new CPSU program, which was presented at the Twenty-second party congress in October 1961. In his speech at the same congress, Khrushchev famously confirmed that communism, the final stage of development of Soviet society, would be achieved by 1980.[5]

The reality of the Soviet economy at the time was far less exciting. The USSR kept growing in the early 1960s, but at rates lower than the recent past, whatever set of numbers one chooses to believe (from an average of about 5 percent per year in the 1950s to one of about 2 percent per year in the 1960s). Soviet growth was still respectable, but the economy was beginning to lose most of the dynamism of the 1950s. The USSR's agriculture, whose modernity the West African leaders admired, was a particularly sore point. Following a couple of encouraging harvests in the late 1950s and early 1960s, in 1963 the Soviet Union experienced an especially bad year for agricultural production. The contribution of the Virgin Lands—Khrushchev's pet project—was particularly disappointing. A combination of poor weather conditions, questionable techniques, the usual illogical system of incentives and disincentives to produce, and unrealistic expectations at the top forced the USSR to import grain from abroad to feed the population. It was a humiliation for the Soviet Union and one that continued to the very end as Soviet agriculture never quite managed to produce enough even in coming decades.[6]

Imports were not limited to agriculture alone. It was in this period that several key branches of Soviet industry became reliant on Western advanced technology and machinery. By facilitating exchanges with the outside world, the Khrushchev leadership made it possible to obtain better equipment than what could be produced in the USSR or obtained from Eastern Europe. Although this had obvious benefits for the Soviet economy, it also signaled the abandonment of the ambition to develop native technology that was comparable to what was made in the West. The USSR thus became an importer of advanced technology and an exporter of raw materials (primarily oil and gas), especially from the early 1970s on. This was the very economic structure that Soviet advisers were in theory attempting to reverse in West Africa.[7]

The changes and reforms championed by Khrushchev also produced underwhelming results. One of Khrushchev's most ambitious plans was to transfer a good deal of economic decision-making from the central apparatus to multiple regional bodies. Introduced in 1957, the *sovnarkhozy* (*sovety narodnogo khoziaistva*) were regional councils that coordinated all aspects of the economy (bar anything that had to do with the military) in a specific region. The idea was to obtain a more holistic approach to production and distribution in which a single body managed the economy as a whole in a regional unit, instead of branch ministries in Moscow that dealt with a single industry or economic sector for the whole country. The reform was not popular. The Moscow apparatus resisted what it regarded as a loss of power, and individual bureaucrats dreaded having to leave the capital to settle in the provinces. Moreover, the immense and powerful Soviet military-industrial complex was determined not to make even the smallest concession to Khrushchev's regionalist plan. As a consequence, the *sovnarkhoz* reform brought more confusion than innovation. Khrushchev's response to these difficulties was to double down on it. In 1962, he proposed that the huge CPSU apparatus be divided into two separate branches—one to manage industry and the other agriculture. Given the predominance of the Communist party in all areas of life in the USSR, virtually any organization in the country would have needed splitting up in two. It was not Khrushchev's brightest idea. His Presidium colleagues put a brave face on it, but many were already wandering whether the First Secretary had overstayed his welcome at the top of Soviet politics.[8]

Despite structural problems and haphazard attempts at reform, in the 1960s Soviet citizens "never had it so good." In purely material terms, they were better off than at any other point in the USSR's history. Housing was poor in absolute terms but better than in previous decades. The availability of consumer goods was nowhere near the West but better than in the prewar era. Soviet public services were inefficient and patchy but better than they had been under Stalin. This moderate but noticeable improvement in living standards had some negative consequences too. People in the USSR had more money, but no way to spend it. As incomes slowly grew, Soviet citizens became more used to the possibility of buying goods for consumption. The economy, however, did not produce enough as producers had no incentives to respond to increased demand, and planners were seldom able to predict increases or decreases in either. In the Soviet planned system, the result was the "shortage economy," in which goods were rarely available and long lines and black markets to acquire them were a daily reality in the USSR. Some Soviet economists, partly influenced by the bourgeois economics of the West, advocated a radical measure to improve the situation: inflation— the textbook consequence of excess demand in a market system. After some hesitation, the Soviet leadership authorized a generalized increase in the price of primary goods in June 1962. The results were far from encouraging. Soviet workers were enraged, and multiple demonstrations to protest the price hikes broke out throughout the Soviet Union. In Novocherkassk, the Soviet army fired on the protesters, killing more than twenty. The increases remained in place, but further experiments with prices were put on hold.[9]

The worsening of the USSR's economic prospects in the 1960s did not mean that the system was close to collapse. There were structural problems and new challenges, but the Soviet economy still functioned and even grew. It would have been unthinkable for the USSR to continue to grow at the same breakneck rates of the years of forced industrialization or of post-war reconstruction. By the early 1960s, the Soviet Union had become a middle income economy, with suitably moderate growth rates. From an economic point of view, becoming a middle income society was no small achievement. However, the dream of catching up and overtaking the West was dead in all but the most optimistic official rhetoric. In this climate, the idea of pouring resources into the Third World to build development appeared to many in the Soviet leadership like an extravaganza that the USSR could not afford. Several international crises added to Khrushchev's woes.

Vulgar Display of Power

At the dawn of the 1960s, politics in Africa seemed to be moving in a very promising direction from the Soviet point of view.[10] Seventeen African territories gained independence in 1960 alone, which led journalists and UN officials to dub it "the year of Africa." The governments of these new states embraced anticolonialism, at least in principle, and many of them harbored progressive ideas for the future. The USSR approved, and Ghana, Guinea, and Mali continued to be the best Soviet allies on the continent. As the grip of European colonialism on Africa decreased, and Ghana, Guinea, and Mali continued to follow their radical path, there were reasons to believe that the Soviet Union's presence on the continent was destined to increase.

The Congo crisis shattered this illusion. Initially, Congo's independence seemed to fit the pattern. In the summer of 1960, Patrice Lumumba emerged as the leader of newly independent Congo. Although not a communist, Lumumba was a radical with strong anti-colonial convictions and a certain anti-Western attitude, in similar fashion to Nkrumah, Sékou Touré, and Keïta. Like Ghana, Guinea, and Mali, Congo was eager to cut dependency links to Western Europe and detach itself from the former colonial power—Belgium. Contrary to Ghana, Guinea, and Mali, Congo was a large country (the second largest in Africa), with a population that equaled that of the three West African states combined (15 million in 1960). Moreover, Congo was rich in natural resources, including the uranium that had been used for the Manhattan Project. Gaining an ally of Congo's size and importance, as well as denying the West access to precious resources, would have been the consecration of Khrushchev's new policy of engagement in Africa.

Following the transfer of power from Belgium to the new Congolese government headed by Lumumba and Joseph Kasavubu in late June 1960, the USSR moved swiftly. A Soviet delegation visited Léopoldville, as the Congolese capital was known at the time, establishing diplomatic relations and promising economic aid and technical cooperation. Before any concrete step could be taken, however, the situation in Congo worsened. Following a mutiny of the Congolese army, the southern province of Katanga, where Western mineral interests were especially strong, seceded itself from the rest of the country, under the leadership of Moïse Tshombe and with the support of Belgian troops and foreign mercenaries. The central Congolese government, unable to recapture Katanga on its own, appealed to the United Nations for help. The UN set up an operation, which quickly became embroiled in controversies with Lumumba and other African leaders (including Nkrumah and Sékou Touré) over the mission mandate, the role of UN troops, Western interference, and reluctance to involve newly independent African countries in the operation. The Soviet government took Lumumba's side, promising support and clashing with both the UN apparatus and the Western powers on multiple occasions.

By the end of July, Lumumba had become fed up with the UN and, anxious to reestablish sovereignty over Katanga, decided to ask the Soviet Union for direct military support. This was when the headaches began in Moscow. Despite Khrushchev's characteristic boastfulness, the USSR had no practical means to assist its ally in Congo. The Soviet armed forces had at their disposal a limited number of long-range aircraft, no bases abroad in useful locations, and not even a real blue-water navy. Mounting a large-scale operation of any kind in support of Lumumba was impossible. The most the USSR could do, overcoming great logistical difficulties, was rerouting a few airplanes destined for the UN mission to Lumumba, enabling his troops to be transported to the conflict areas. Even this, however, did not last long. In early September 1960, UN forces in Congo, acting in coordination with the US government, took control of all airports in the country, preventing Soviet airplanes from landing. At the same time, Lumumba was ousted first briefly by Kasavubu and then once and for all by Joseph Mobutu, a staunch Western supporter, who proceeded to cut diplomatic relations with Moscow and expel all socialist bloc personnel from Congo. Lumumba was first put under house arrest and later transferred in unclear circumstances to the Katanga separatists, who murdered him in January 1961. The USSR may have had an attractive model of development to offer its allies in the Third World, but when it came to the projection of military power, it lagged behind its Western competitors.

Thus, the first major Cold War crisis in sub-Saharan Africa ended in complete defeat for the USSR and its allies. Not only was Congo now off-limits for the entire socialist bloc, but the circumstances of its loss had repercussions for Soviet overall policy in the Third World. In the context of Africa, as soon as the Soviet Union tried to extend its political and economic influence on a large, strategically significant newly independent country, the Western reaction had been powerful and devastating. It was one thing to compete with the West in terms of models of economic development, where the USSR may have had an edge; it was another altogether to compete militarily, where both sides knew Moscow stood no chance.

The implications of the failure in Congo were not lost on the Soviet leadership. Khrushchev and the others in the Presidium maintained a public face of disdain for what they regarded as an obvious manifestation of Western imperialism and disproportionate influence on the UN, and officially retained confidence in the USSR as a vehicle for the political and economic liberation of the peoples of Africa, Asia, and Latin America. However, in more private conversations, Khrushchev often referred to Congo as an open wound. When in 1964 Madeira Keïta met with the Soviet leader in Moscow and asked for more support from the USSR for Mali, Congo was the first obstacle that Khrushchev mentioned. "Every people—said Khrushchev—must build with patience. We saw the things that the imperialists and their lackeys did in Congo-Léopoldville."[11]

Moreover, at the middle level of Soviet bureaucracy pessimism about the quality of independence achieved by Third World countries and skepticism about the Soviet role in it began to seep through. Kolosovskii was among the first ones to openly admit that there was a serious problem. "As the example of Congo shows— he argued at the Institute of Africa—there will be many attempts to take political independence away in all ways." According to Kolosovskiii, the United States, Britain, France, Belgium, and Portugal were going to use every possible means, including military ones, to make sure that former colonies stayed on a capitalist path to defend the positions of their "monopolies."[12] The KGB produced similar assessments. In March 1963, Vladimir Semichastnyi, the KGB chairman, reported to the Presidium about growing US activities in the developing world. Soviet intelligence was particularly concerned by the Kennedy administration's new aggressive strategy for the Third World, which combined increased military resources with a novel approach to development. Soviet intelligence reported about the significant progress made by the "main adversary" (the United States in KGB parlance) in recent years in developing flexible military resources, such as special forces and "partisans" (defined as local "saboteurs" able to act without being detected), ready to be mobilized in the Third World to tilt the balance in favor of the United States, as had happened in Congo. The implication was that any new Soviet ally in the Third World was at risk of being toppled by Western power.[13]

Like most intelligence and security agencies in the world, the KGB had a strong penchant for paranoia. Semichastnyi was not completely wrong, though. The Kennedy administration, which entered office in January 1961, brought a different approach to US involvement in the Third World. The new president was more outward-looking than his predecessor and, as Philip Muehelenbeck has written, "Kennedy's interest in Africa far surpassed that of any other American Cold War president."[14] He advocated engagement, including the provision of economic aid, which increased significantly during his tenure in Washington. Kennedy was determined to challenge the Soviet Union's positions in Ghana, Guinea, and Mali, and America had abundant means to do so. Crucially, the US government was now willing to court African leaders even when this meant going against the interests of its European allies. Kennedy's involvement in the Third World was not just about economic aid and Peace Corps volunteers either. He famously paid increased attention to American special forces units and covert operations groups, which soon became a hallmark of US presence in the Third World, from Southeast Asia to Latin America.

The USSR now faced a much more proactive main adversary. Did the Soviet Union have the drive, resources, and ability to respond to this challenge? The Congo crisis provided some negative early indicators. The sum of other factors led to a negative answer.

Our Man in Conakry

Congo was not the only event to shake the fragile Cold War order during the early 1960s. Other parallel international crises tested the Soviet leadership to the limit of their capacities. Khrushchev's push to force the West to come to the negotiating table about the situation in Germany resulted in the erection of the Berlin Wall in 1961 and little more. The Soviet decision to install nuclear missiles in Cuba in 1962 produced a prolonged standoff with the US government, and eventually an agreement to dismantle them. Meanwhile, the brotherhood between the USSR and China disappeared. Mao disapproved of Khrushchev's domestic and foreign policies, and by 1962 the Sino-Soviet split was too obvious to hide. In none of these cases the Soviet Union emerged as an obvious loser; however, the USSR hardly improved its international standing. Whereas the turmoil in Eastern Europe and the Middle East in 1956 had arguably helped to consolidate Khrushchev's position in the Kremlin, these new set of crises left him personally more isolated at home, and the Soviet Union in a more precarious international situation.[15]

West Africa was not spared by the turbulence of the 1960s either. With the Congo crisis, the Cold War in its most basic manifestation came to Africa. Earlier on, newly independent African states were careful to stress their neutrality in the bipolar conflict, and most of them at least flirted with the idea of nonalignment. Now, the situation in Congo forced them to pick a side. Ghana, Guinea, and Mali predictably supported Lumumba and the socialist bloc against the UN apparatus and the Western powers. Together with left-leaning Egypt, Libya, Morocco, and the Front de Libération Nationale government in Algeria, the three West African states formed the "Casablanca group," a loose association whose aim was to promote political integration in Africa. On the other side, the French-speaking Communauté with Ethiopia, Liberia, Nigeria, Sierra Leone, Somalia, Togo, Tunisia, and Mobutu's Congo formed the "Monrovia group," an even looser grouping that rejected their adversaries' pan-Africanism and their calls for deep integration. The Casablanca countries were generally friendly with the USSR and the socialist bloc; the Monrovia states tended to side with the West. The relationship between the USSR and its allies in Africa was complex. Contrasts and incidents were common.

In February 1961, Leonid Brezhnev, at the time chairman of the Supreme Soviet, visited Guinea as part of a wider tour of Africa. Brezhnev's profile was on the ascendance in the Kremlin, and he was the highest-ranking Soviet official to have ever visited an African state. On the surface, the visit was a great success. Brezhnev was received with all honors by the Guinean government, and he made sure to show he was greatly enjoying his stay. The French embassy in Conakry reported that:

> The PDG deployed all its talents as organizer of mass demonstrations. For twelve kilometers on both sides of the road [from the airport to Conakry], besides the soldiers dressed in uniform and presenting arms

every fifty meters, Guinean men and women and innumerable children were amassed. The women and the children, in colorful dresses, waved little Soviet and Guinean flags, together with portraits of the visitor; here and there, Ghanaian and Malian flags could also be seen. Groups of women, and occasionally mixed, folk dancers performed accompanied by tam-tams and large drums.[16]

Some details, however, suggested there was tension lurking beneath the facade of cordiality. As was customary, Brezhnev and Sékou Touré exchanged congratulatory speeches in Conakry. Their tone was rather different. The Guinean president spoke at length about the importance of Soviet aid and expressed the hope that development assistance from the USSR would continue and increase over time, whereas Brezhnev made few references to bilateral economic cooperation in his speech. He focused much more on the perils of Western imperialism, of which the Congo crisis was the most obvious but not unique manifestation, and praised Guinea for its support in the battle against colonialism. Brezhnev's assessment of Guinea's economic performance was cautious. The Soviet leader reminded his hosts that Guinea had been independent only for a short time, and that what had been done were only the very first steps toward modernization. Brezhnev even reminded Sékou Touré that the USSR was "a huge country with a population of several millions" and "many internal tasks" still to complete, but nonetheless it used part of its resources to help Guinea, a small newly independent state.[17]

Brezhnev's words contrasted sharply with the usual Soviet boastfulness about the breathtaking pace of socialist modernization in the Third World, especially considering that just a couple of months earlier Khrushchev had addressed the UN General Assembly presenting the USSR as the only trustworthy friend of "young nations," promising assistance with no strings attached and regardless of political interest.[18] Brezhnev's attitude signaled a more sober assessment of Guinea's importance for the Soviet Union and growing pessimism about the effectiveness of Soviet development programs. From Moscow's point of view, resources seemed never to be enough. Despite the large Soviet assistance program, the Guinean government demanded on multiple occasions new loans and additional Soviet purchases of Guinean goods. Following the currency reform of 1960, Sékou Touré solicited Soviet ambassador Solod to intercede with Moscow to relieve the difficult situation in Guinea. The Soviet Union agreed to buy an additional 500 tons of coffee and then, in September 1960, agreed to concede Guinea a new loan, of 86 million rubles, on top of the existing credit.[19] At the time of Brezhnev's visit in early 1961, Sékou Touré again asked for additional Soviet purchases of Guinean goods and for a new loan. Brezhnev responded that he understood Guinea's problem, but that the Soviet government would need to examine Sékou Touré's requests before anything concrete could be promised, and this would take some time.[20]

On his return to Moscow, Brezhnev spoke of Guinea in favorable terms, but it was evident that patience in the Kremlin was running out.[21] A series of disagreements between Moscow and the Guinean president on the best uses of Soviet economic aid over the course of 1960–61 changed the way in which Sékou Touré was perceived by the Soviet government.[22] In the summer of 1960, the Soviet embassy in Conakry reported to Moscow allegations that Sékou Touré and his associates were quietly watering down the socialist dimension of the three-year development plan. A few months later, the Soviet Ministry of Foreign Affairs described Sékou Touré as a staunch anti-imperialist but also as a volatile and unreliable leader. In August 1961, GKES cited Guinea as a particularly bad example of economic mismanagement in a long report to the CPSU Central Committee on aid to Africa.[23]

Sékou Touré was not a naive politician, and he quickly realized that Soviet assistance may become less forthcoming than it had been. Thus, the PDG government began to explore the possibility of receiving aid from the United States and France.[24] As a consequence, relations with the USSR worsened even more. The situation reached the point of no return in December 1961, when ambassador Solod was suddenly declared persona non grata in Guinea and urged to leave the country. Solod was accused of being part of an ill-defined plot to oust Sékou Touré, which involved schoolteachers, Marxist-Leninist reading groups, and French and Senegalese saboteurs.[25]

The accusations against Solod appeared preposterous. "Had I organized it [the plot], it would have succeeded," Solod told the French ambassador to Guinea, Jean-Marie Pons, shortly after the first allegations against him emerged. On December 18, the Guinean ambassador to Moscow, Alpha Diallo, met with both Gromyko and Khrushchev to explain the situation. Diallo told Gromyko that in Guinea there was a widespread conspiracy, led by left-leaning schoolteachers and civil servants, who criticized the government and planned to overthrow it. Many of these supposed conspirators were arrested, and the PDG government claimed to have found among their seized possessions documents that were "not favorable" to the ambassadors of the Soviet bloc countries. Solod was upset by the allegations, which led to a heated exchange with Sékou Touré. Gromyko pushed the Guinean ambassador to reveal more about Solod's alleged role in the plot, but Diallo refused, saying that he "prefers not to talk about small things (*melkie fakty*) right now." When Gromyko asked if the Conakry government really was in possession of documents that could implicate any of the Eastern European ambassadors, Diallo remained silent.[26]

Khrushchev was less diplomatic. He told Diallo that he did not understand why Sékou Touré had taken such a step, which risked compromising Soviet-Guinean relations, and that he was sure the Guinean government had no compromising material on Solod or anyone else. Diallo resorted to a time-honored tactic in the Soviet Union: blaming the West. He claimed that the Western powers were on the offensive everywhere in Africa and must certainly have to do with the plot to destroy the Guinean revolution. Khrushchev quipped that after the 1917 revolution, "Russia was attacked by the British, the French, the German, the Poles, the Americans, the Japanese, whereas no one has attacked Guinea with weapons."[27]

Despite the harsh tones, both sides wished to mend fences and move on. Both Sékou Touré in writing and Diallo in person expressed the wish to receive a Soviet delegation in Guinea to discuss the future, and both insisted that the Guinean government had nothing against the Soviet Union as a whole, but only a problem with Solod individually. The Soviet response was equally conciliatory. Khrushchev announced that Mikoian would visit Guinea in early 1962 and that Dmitrii Degtiar' would be the new ambassador to Conakry. Neither side conceived the incident with Solod as the end of the partnership that had existed since Guinea's independence. When Khrushchev jokingly asked Diallo if he had "come to declare war" to the Soviet Union, the Guinean ambassador responded that "if there will be war, then Guinea and the USSR will be on the same side."[28]

Solod's expulsion was the product of economic malaise in Guinea. The PDG government certainly wanted to signal to French and American observers that Guinea was ready to modify the course of its foreign policy and open space for the West. However, it was the sorry state of Soviet-Guinean economic cooperation that motivated Sékou Touré to send an even stronger signal to the USSR. The Quai d'Orsay had little illusions in this respect: "Sékou Touré has seized the opportunity he had not to distance himself from the Soviet Union, but to send Moscow a warning with the aim to obtain a change in its attitude vis-à-vis Guinea. If he has, in the process, affirmed Guinea's right to choose its path to socialism, this warning aimed certainly to obtain an increase in the volume of Soviet aid."[29]

When pressed by Gromyko, Diallo admitted that his government resented Solod because he "criticizes Guinea's policy and tells everyone that the Guineans are lazy and do not want to work."[30] Conakry had much to complain about the way Soviet aid was organized, not to mention the patronizing ways of Soviet officials. At the same time, GKES and MID were extremely critical of how the Guinean government approached Soviet aid. Both sides, however, knew that for the PDG government to continue its policy Soviet aid would still be essential, as Diallo had told Khrushchev multiple times, and that cutting aid now would mean the end of whatever had been achieved since 1958. The choice of the new ambassador confirmed the centrality of economic aid in Soviet-Guinean relations. Degtiar' had been instrumental in the definition and application of the idea of "noncapitalist development" and in the running of Soviet aid programs in West Africa. His appointment showed that the Soviet government was ready to try its best to rescue its relationship with Sékou Touré and the PDG. If Degtiar' could not fix Soviet-Guinean economic cooperation, then no one else could.

Guinea's difficult domestic situation complicated cooperation with the Soviet Union. The same was true in Ghana and Mali too. In Ghana, Nkrumah was deeply shaken by the course and the outcome of the Congo crisis. He looked at Lumumba as a new ally and also as somewhat of a mentee. Ghana carved a prime role for itself during the crisis, contributing troops to the peacekeeping mission and taking Lumumba's side in all the debates at the UN. Nkrumah's open ambition was to make Congo, one of the largest independent sub-Saharan African countries, part of his project of an African union. The conclusion of the crisis and Lumumba's tragic death shocked and scared the Ghanaian president in multiple ways. Above all, the Congo crisis changed Nkrumah's view of the West. He had always been suspicious of the European colonial powers but, despite the negative experience with the Akosombo dam, he retained an overall positive image of the United States, as the first nation to break free from empire and a country with a large, if oppressed, population of African descent. The Congo crisis showed Nkrumah that the US government was ready to ignore its anti-imperial rhetoric and take the side of the colonizers, if this helped keep the USSR at bay. Nkrumah was upset by the coup that removed Lumumba from power and horrified by his subsequent murder. Like Khrushchev, Nkrumah was convinced that the Europeans would not have dared or even been capable of mounting an anti-Lumumba operation or supporting the Katanga separatists on their own, and that therefore the United States must have given at the very least its implicit consent, if not open support. First, this made Nkrumah suspicious of Western, including American, interference in Africa. Second, it made him worried that what happened to Lumumba may happen to him too.[31]

Imagining a coup in Ghana was not too far-fetched, for the domestic situation was far from stable. In late 1961, a wave of strikes and demonstrations against Ghana's new budget, which raised taxes and cut benefits, rocked the country. Opposition to Nkrumah came from the trade unions and from the ranks of the CPP itself, under Minister of Information Tawia Adamafio's leadership. In August 1962, Nkrumah suffered the first attempt on his life. A hand grenade, allegedly hidden in a flower bouquet held by a schoolgirl, exploded near Nkrumah while he was visiting Kulungugu, a town right at the border with Upper Volta (Burkina Faso). The Ghanaian president was only lightly injured, but a few people died in the blast, including the schoolgirl. About a month later, in September 1962, another bomb exploded, this time at Flagstaff House in Accra, the presidential palace. A third grenade attempt was made in 1964, while earlier on the same year a policeman on guard at Flagstaff House had opened fire on Nkrumah, narrowly missing him. During these years, a few more bombs not directly aimed at Nkrumah went off in various locations in Accra, and threatening messages were issued from mysterious opposition groups in Togo.[32]

Nkrumah reacted with severity. Using the special powers granted to him by the 1960 constitution, Nkrumah imprisoned Adamafio and Ako Adjei (previously Minister of the Interior), both accused of being behind the assassination attempts. Gbedemah was expelled from the CPP and later exiled, while Botsio—previously disgraced—was rehabilitated. Moreover, the government strengthened already existing repressive measures, such as the law that allowed "preventive incarceration," and several hundred opposition members (or presumed so) were arrested. In 1964, Ghana was officially declared a "one-party state." Following the assassination attempts, Nkrumah became increasingly paranoid about the possibility of a Western-supported coup. The CPP official organs accused the British government of being behind the unrest in 1961, and Nkrumah saw the CIA plotting in many African countries. In February 1964, Nkrumah took issue with President Lyndon Johnson, complaining of alleged CIA interference in Ghana and renewing his pledge to socialism rather than capitalism.[33]

Christopher Andrew and Vasilii Mitrokhin have argued that the KGB was instrumental in feeding Nkrumah with false information about Western plots and CIA conspiracies.[34] From the actual Mitrokhin papers, it seems that the KGB did have a number of informers and agents in Ghana, including in the security services, able to spread misinformation and at the same time provide Moscow with intelligence on Western activities in the country. However, it also appears that information about Western covert operations in Ghana reached Nkrumah first through a disgruntled US military intelligence officer.[35] What is for sure is that, following the second attempt on his life, Nkrumah wrote to Khrushchev requesting Soviet assistance with his personal security. He was sent "Mr. Svertchov," most likely a KGB operative from the Ninth Directorate (the Protection Service).[36]

Besides the role of Soviet and Western intelligence, Soviet observers were generally pleased with the turn things were taking in Ghana. After the Congo crisis, the Ghanaian government often took the side of the Soviet Union in international disputes. From Berlin to Cuba, Accra issued statements that condemned the Western policy and supported the USSR. When Nkrumah learned that Brezhnev was going to visit Africa in early 1961, he made sure that the Soviet leader stopped in Ghana too. Nkrumah personally instructed his ministers to arrange the nicest possible stay for Brezhnev, despite the little time left to organize an official visit.[37] A few months later, in the summer of 1961, Nkrumah took a long trip to the Soviet Union. Like other visitors from Africa before him, the Ghanaian president visited Moscow and Leningrad, chatted with Khrushchev and Brezhnev in the Kremlin, toured the Bratsk power station, and was introduced to the secrets of irrigation in Uzbekistan. Nkrumah showed great enthusiasm during the visits, and always praised his hosts and the achievements of the USSR. In a partial break with the past, this time Nkrumah had no reservations in identifying the Soviet Union as the model to follow, as the archetype Ghana strived to imitate.[38] In Ghana, Nkrumah's government reshuffle, which followed the show trials of Adamafio and Adjei, excluded a number of anti-Soviet elements in favor of more left-leaning CPP high officials, such as Kojo Botsio and Krobo Edusei, improving Moscow's chances of finding interested partners in Accra. Moreover, the Soviet embassy reported that Nkrumah was working hard to curb British influence in the country. The purges that followed the assassination attempts hit Ghana's police and army, and most British officers, including the army's commanding general, were discharged. Most worrying for British analysts, Nkrumah now openly talked about full nationalization of the cocoa industry.[39]

FIGURE 5.1. Kwame Nkrumah, left, and Leonid Brezhnev, right, reviewing guards of honor before the Ghanaian president's departure from the USSR at Vnukovo airport in Moscow. July 1961. Credit: Sputnik.

Despite these positive signals, relations between Ghana and the Soviet Union did not enter a new phase. The Soviet leadership remained skeptical about Nkrumah and his designs for Ghana and Africa. Brezhnev's report following his trip to Ghana was on the whole lukewarm. Like most of the Kremlin leadership, he found Nkrumah's talk of "African socialism" or, even worse, of "Nkrumahism" deeply problematic. Nkrumahism, in particular, was in the Soviet view an ill-defined philosophy that mixed a strong interest in collectivism with the traditional pan-Africanism of the Ghanaian president. Ghana, according to Moscow, was still far from real "scientific socialism," and with few chances of ever reaching it, if it continued with the "personality cult" of its president. As the next sections will show, Nkrumah became more and more radical, and more interested in cooperation with the USSR. However, the Soviet government became less and less responsive to his requests. The future of Soviet-Ghanaian cooperation was in jeopardy.[40]

The plot against Sékou Touré in Guinea was largely a product of his own scheming. Violent opposition against Nkrumah's rule in Ghana, followed by waves of repression, was real enough. In Mali, Keïta's government perhaps faced an even bigger challenge to its authority. In 1962–63, part of the Tuareg population of Northern Mali rose in rebellion against the Bamako government in what has since become known as the Alfellaga ("the rebellion" in Tamasheq). Materially poorer than the rest of the country and historically populated by nomadic Tuaregs, the North of Mali's relationship with the South was always fractious. The Tuareg clans tended to regard Mali's independent government as no better, and possibly even worse, than the French colonial administration. Keïta's determination to modernize the North of the country was especially contested. In Gregory Mann's words, the Keïta administration "understood the object of government to be not only the economy, but society itself."[41] This drive to reinforce central political control and introduce new economic structures in the North, which Baz Lecocq has compared to a *mission civilisatrice*, frequently clashed with Tuareg customs, traditions, and preexisting political arrangements. Many Tuaregs resented being governed by black Malians, whom they traditionally regarded as their inferiors and even as slaves. Moreover, the patronizing attitude of Malian officials toward the Tuaregs, and their often heavy-handed approach, soon alienated a significant portion of the local population.[42]

Over the course of 1962, a series of incidents involving Tuaregs and Malian officials and policemen caused tension in the North. The first episodes of violence happened in this context. The response of the central government was to send a large number of troops to the North, which escalated the conflict. By early 1963, there was a real armed struggle between the Malian army and a couple hundred of Tuareg fighters. The scale and aims of the rebellion are an object of debate. The

Tuaregs, who were outnumbered and outgunned by the government forces, did not appear to have had a wholly coordinated military strategy. They mostly carried out raids and ambushes against government posts and army detachments. Some of them, however, did aspire to detach their territory from Mali, possibly with the help of Algeria and France. The Bamako authorities regarded the Tuareg rebels as a threat to Mali's unity and were determined to repress the revolt once and for all. Despite their numerical and technological advantages, it took the Malian army about a year and a half to end the rebellion. Repression was harsh, and it included forcibly resettling the civilian population in concentration camps. Many Tuaregs were executed, and many more suffered abuses at the hands of the government forces. The Bamako government declared victory in the summer of 1964. In the North, the memory of the Alfellaga and its repression lived on and fueled future Tuareg rebellions against the central government.[43]

The Soviet government was not directly involved in the insurrection and its repression. MID reported that the Malian armed forces were struggling to bring the situation in the North back under control. The government's fiscal policy, which had increased taxation, contributed to the disturbances. Keïta's government appeared weaker and less popular than immediately following independence. Like Ghana and Guinea, Mali too proved to be a risky investment for the Soviet Union.[44]

The international conjuncture, the economic slowdown in the USSR, and the political situation in West Africa all contributed to the downfall of Soviet ambitions in Ghana, Guinea, and Mali. The difficulty of managing the aid programs on the ground was no less determinant. The following sections will examine the issues encountered, the proposed solutions, and the final outcomes.

The Elephants in the Room

Nothing has captured the attention of contemporary observers, historians, and memorialists more than the so-called white elephants that the USSR financed in West Africa—monumental projects that required a large amount of resources while producing little to no economic benefit. The most celebrated episode is no doubt that of the snowplows. In the most established version of the story, the USSR sent Guinea a boatload of snowplows, which lay unused in the capital city's docks. In other versions of the same story, the snowplows ended up in Ghana. It makes little difference. Both Ghana and Guinea—generations of acute analysts have pointed out—have a tropical climate. There is no snow there, and therefore no need for snowplows. The fact that the Soviet Union sent completely useless snow equipment to West Africa is taken as proof that Soviet advisers did not understand Africa. This is sometimes contrasted to the expertise of the Americans and especially the Europeans, whose resourcefulness and experience as colonial masters supposedly equipped them with great knowledge of West Africa and its lack of snow.[45]

Like most good stories, the one about the snowplows is apocryphal. The original source seems to have been a British reporter, who saw the snowplows in Conakry and told William Attwood, the US ambassador, about them. Attwood dismissed the story. He thought they were brush cutters, not snowplows. Other Western observers also knew the snowplow story to be false, already at the time.[46] No one cared. Like most good stories, the one about the snowplows of West Africa was too good not to be true and has been repeated countless times in books, articles, and conference papers. It will no doubt continue to be told for generations to come.

Yet there is no need to make stories up to find traces of Soviet incompetence and West African wastefulness. Mazov presented many such examples.[47] Everywhere in West Africa the USSR financed and supervised the construction of buildings whose scale defied logic. In Guinea, the PDG government asked for state buildings to be added to the list of objectives to be realized with Soviet help. These included a brand new building for the National Assembly, new premises for a few ministries, two large hotels for international visitors to be built in Conakry, and a large presidential residence for Sékou Touré.[48] Soviet-sponsored building projects always tended toward the grand, often with little consideration for costs and benefits. In all three countries the USSR was building polytechnic institutes. Each one was expected to have no fewer than 300 students; on their premises, Soviet engineers and technicians planned to build large swimming pools, gyms, dormitories, labs, and workshops. In Accra, Conakry, and Bamako there were going to be Soviet-built stadiums, all with a capacity of 25,000 spectators—extravagantly large when compared to the size of the cities (the population of Conakry at the time of independence was less than 80,000 people). Soviet advisers questioned the utility of some of the infrastructure projects they were helping to realize: "In cases such as when we build an airport or a road from the airport, as in Guinea, that, of course, is also aid, and this is highly valued by the people of these countries, but from the point of view of the economic development of these countries this is not particularly effective aid, which could help these countries to proceed on the path to socialism."[49]

These kind of projects were the most obvious source of tension. Virtually all Soviet agencies involved in Guinea expressed perplexity about some of the construction projects in which they were involved, particularly the stadiums and hotels. However, the PDG government asked to prioritize these objectives. Ismaël Touré justified his government's request claiming that finishing the hotel "would help to build other facilities, since this hotel could provide housing for all arriving specialists."[50] Moreover, Touré insisted that modern air-conditioners be installed in each room, because they were "seen as progress," even though the design of the hotels was based on natural ventilation and ceiling fans to contain expenses.[51]

Hotels, palaces, and stadiums consumed resources, caused headaches to all parties involved, and generated delays. The scale of the projects was difficult to manage. In Conakry, 1,700 builders were supposed to work on the stadium, but only 1,000 were actually employed. The situation at the nearby building site for the polytechnic was worse: of the 1,600 workers that were judged necessary, only 800 could be found. The Guinean government argued that it could not afford to increase the total wages it paid for these projects. The Soviet government had no intention of covering extra expenses.[52] In Bamako, the USSR sponsored the construction of a large "higher school of administration" and an even larger agricultural college. In neither case did the Malian government have the necessary number of teachers to staff them.[53] Everywhere, most prestige projects took much longer than expected to be completed. Many were abandoned, often leaving construction halfway. Others were eventually completed but remained empty or unused—the fate that eventually befell Guinea's luxury hotels.[54]

The West African governments often requested white elephants for reasons of prestige. The Soviet government, however, just as often proposed questionable projects even when they should have known better. In particular, the extensive geological surveys and explorations looking for oil and precious metals in the remotest corners of West Africa proved especially costly and distinctly unproductive. In Mali, both the Soviet experts and the Bamako government showed considerable enthusiasm for the prospect of exploiting the underground riches in the north of the country—supposedly oil, gold, and diamonds. Mali's development plan foresaw an investment of more than a billion CFA francs to develop the mining and extraction sector "to make Mali a state worthy of modern Africa."[55] The Soviet Union acted as both financial sponsor and provider of personnel and equipment for the surveys and geological works. The Bamako government hoped for rich deposits and oilfields, whose yields would be the easiest way to prop up Mali's finances and gain new resources to invest in development. Counterintuitively, the Soviet government had little interest in Mali's mineral wealth. Anything that (allegedly) could be extracted from West Africa's subsurface was already present in large quantities in the USSR—a gigantic country with remarkable mineral wealth. However, Moscow was more than happy to encourage and support geological work for the Soviet leadership felt much more comfortable investing in a country that exported oil and precious metals rather than peanuts. This was, after all, what the Soviet Union itself did.

Despite the enthusiasm, since the early stages the geological surveys run into problems, both logistical and financial. The first group of Soviet geologists sent to Mali died in a plane crash in the north of the country in May 1961. When new groups arrived and began to work, new difficulties emerged: the harsh terrain required prolonged and expensive preparatory work, and carrying equipment around presented numerous challenges. Soviet specialists needed to remain in Mali longer than expected, and costs levitated. Neither Bamako nor Moscow were able or willing to cover the extra expenses. When Keïta asked Khrushchev for extra funds, all the Soviet government offered was to use part of the commercial loan that Moscow had already granted Mali, which was supposed to allow Mali to purchase basic goods and commodities from the USSR, to pay for Soviet specialists instead.[56]

What was more, the preliminary surveys did not produce the results that Moscow and Bamako hoped for. In some cases, no mineral wealth could be found. In others, extracting oil or precious metals would have been too expensive to guarantee any returns. In October 1961, Mamadou Aw (the Malian minister of public works) asked the Soviet government to review contracts for geological exploration. He hoped that the USSR would be willing to cover the costs of the surveys in case no oil was found. Without a precious commodity to sell, the Malian government would not have been able to pay for the surveys. Nevertheless, A.I. Alikhanov, from GKES, insisted that the exploration works go ahead as planned.[57] It took a few more months for both sides to realize that the geological works were mostly just a waste of time and resources, and to agree that they should be reduced significantly. Aw admitted that the contracts on geological surveys were signed "without taking into account the real capabilities of the country and the requirements of the five-year plan." In 1962, Mikoian and Keïta agreed to "cut the resources for oil surveys by half, so that ten million rubles can be allocated to agriculture."[58] A couple of months later, while reviewing and revising the objectives of the five-year development plan, the Malian government put an end to any hope of reversing the country's fortunes through mineral wealth. "Mineral prospecting, which we had wanted systematic and exhaustive at the outset, must no longer preserve these two epithets."[59] In a foolish move by both governments, the single largest chunk of the Soviet loan to Mali had been originally destined for geological works. By the time ideas changed, only part of it could be salvaged and rerouted to other uses.

Things were no different in Ghana and Guinea. Given that the extraction of bauxite was in Western hands, the USSR committed 13 million rubles to assist Sékou Touré's government in looking for gold and diamonds (roughly 10 percent of the initial Soviet loan to Guinea). Despite the usual difficulties that Soviet personnel encountered, the head of the Soviet mission believed that minerals

FIGURE 5.2. Modibo Keïta, left, and chairperson of the Supreme Soviet of the Uzbek SSR Yadgar Nasriddinova, right, at Tashkent airport. October 1962. Credit: Sputnik.

would have provided Guinea with a prime source of income through export.[60] Soon, however, the full extent of the disaster of mineral prospecting in Guinea became clear. As of April 1961, there were sixty-four Soviet geologists at work in the country, together with 450 Guineans. None of them had the proper equipment, which was still in the Soviet Union. There were only four translators, meaning that most Soviet-Guinean groups worked together without being able to understand each other.[61] Despite GKES's best efforts, little could be done. The main problem was that Guinea lacked the basic infrastructure necessary to supply Soviet and local personnel with the equipment they needed. Port facilities were overwhelmed; there were few roads and virtually no railways. Transporting machines and delicate instruments to some of the most remote areas of the country, where geologists tended to work, proved nearly impossible.[62] In a conversation with US ambassador Attwood, Degtiar' revealed that results in the joint Soviet-Guinean search for diamonds were "very modest." Attwood quipped that "here, as always, the Guineans have overstated their potential."[63]

Guinea's goals were certainly very ambitious. In a conversation with Skachkov in late 1964, Sékou Touré still believed that Guinea could produce up to 500,000 carats of diamonds a year (a relatively small amount). Skachkov objected that this rate was absolutely impossible given the actual level of resources that Soviet geologists estimated to exist. The Guinean president would hear none of it—production had to go ahead. By this point, the Soviet-supervised exploitation of Guinea's mineral wealth had reached a stalemate. Guinea did not have the resources to proceed, and Moscow had lost hope in the country's subsoil.[64]

In Ghana, cooperation with the USSR to exploit mineral wealth started with an ambitious program that included a general geological survey of the country, and mineral and hydrogeological prospecting to assess resources and their possible use. The total cost was expected to be close to 2.5 million Ghanaian pounds. Already at this stage there were some perplexities. Reviewing the Soviet project, the Ghanaian Geological Survey Department noted that "there is no working plan, and no clue as to how the team will be organized or how the work will be done."[65] The Soviet geological team, made up of nearly 150 people and operating mostly out of Tamale to survey the north of the country, faced fierce resistance from its local counterpart. The Ghanaian geologists resented that Soviet specialists were meddling in their area of competence and did not hesitate to make their displeasure known to the government.

> Sir, the Geological Survey of Ghana has a tradition to uphold, a reputation to maintain and a duty to perform. This duty is being performed with the strictest economy and great efficiency. We require more money and personnel to expand our future activities threefold. . . . The Surveys work will of greatly impaired [sic] if the Soviet team, for the next three years, is allowed to hop about all over the country checking the work of the rightful local geological Survey. Two cooks in one kitchen have many problems, but to ask them to cook in the same pot at the same time brings chaos.[66]

Besides hurt feelings and competition for scarce resources between Ghana's Geological Survey Department and the Soviet geologists, there were legitimate concerns about the work of the Soviet mission. First, Northern Ghana was a harsh, difficult terrain that presented numerous topographical, climatic, and logistical challenges. Completing a full survey in three years, as the initial plan stipulated, appeared very optimistic. Northern Ghana's long rainy season—from April to October—meant that the Soviet geologists could expect to work only six months each year. Second, the Accra government asked the Soviet team to assess the mineral resources present in the Volta basin, which were believed to be substantial. However, this was the area that would soon be flooded by the construction of the dam on the Volta, making geological exploration considerably more difficult unless the work was completed before flooding. In both areas, the key to success was starting the work as early as possible.[67]

This proved impossible. As in Mali and Guinea, supplying Soviet geologists in Ghana with equipment turned out to be a real nightmare. Everything had to be transported from the Soviet Union to the port of Takoradi, and from there to the north and to the Volta region. However, the usual logistical problems, plus bureaucratic chaos, and possibly nefarious interference from some government departments, meant that nearly one month after signing the contract for geological exploration most of the equipment was stuck in Takoradi. Meanwhile, the facilities to house the Soviet specialists and their families in Tamale were still at the planning stage. The head of the Soviet team complained that: "Though two months are left prior to the rainy season in the northern part of Ghana, when the field work is impossible to be carried out, the Ghanaian side has not yet practically settled a single question without the settling of which the beginning of the field work is possible."[68]

The conclusions were damning. "This means that a large group of Soviet specialists, as a matter of fact, will have no work to do. The time of completion of all kinds of geological work in the Republic of Ghana, under contract No. 393, will be postponed as well."[69] The Soviet side questioned the choice of Tamale as a base, because of its relatively remote location, and blamed the Ghanaian Geological Survey Department for trying to keep the Soviet specialists away from the south of the country. There was one thing on which Soviet and Ghanaian geologists agreed: both blamed the Ministry of Industry for delays, incompetence, and unnecessary interference in their plans. By early 1963, the Accra government realized that the initial funds allocated were "wholly inadequate to meet the expenses in connection with the geological survey work being undertaken by the Soviet Geological Team in this country."[70] As elsewhere, neither the USSR nor the local government was willing or able to commit more resources to the project. Geological cooperation continued with more limited objectives until it was canceled in 1966, following the change of government in Accra.

Too Big Not to Fail

The most obviously extravagant projects and the geological surveys could be cut or reduced, once the USSR and its allies agreed that they were not particularly useful. Reducing waste in other fields was more difficult, for the tendency to gigantism affected many more development projects in West Africa. The story of rice production in Guinea, one of the most important projects sponsored by the Soviet Union, is particularly illustrative in this respect. The Soviet-Guinean cooperation agreement stipulated that the USSR would provide the Conakry government with a loan and technical expertise to develop rice farms on a large area, judged fundamental for Guinea's food security. In March 1960, a group of seven specialists from the Soviet Ministry of Agriculture traveled to Guinea to carry out the preliminary surveys. They identified the valley of the Fié River (a tributary of the Niger), approximately 100 kilometers north of the regional capital Kankan, as a promising area. The Soviet specialists proposed the construction of two dams of about 15–19 meters each. One would be built on the Fié, the other one on the smaller Ni (a tributary of the Fié). Together, they would create an artificial lake whose water could be used for irrigation through a system of canals to be built in the region. The estimated cost for the whole project was 13.5 million (new) rubles. The part of the Soviet credit destined to the development of rice farms was initially only 4.5 million (new) rubles. To cover the remaining amount, the two governments agreed that Guinea would contract a new loan and, thanks to what the Guinean government estimated the production of rice in Fié would be, pay back the expenses in rice in about fifteen to twenty years. Moscow and Conakry fretted to sign the contract in December 1960, and a new group of Soviet experts traveled to the Haute Guinée region to begin the works. This is when problems began. "Topographic difficulties" (the initial studies had underestimated how hilly and densely forested the Guinean Highlands were) meant that building a tall dam on the Fié turned out to be extremely complicated due to the lack of a sufficient area that could be flooded. The dam that had been initially proposed would have required a water reservoir of about 5,000 hectares, whereas only about 800 were available. Even though the second dam was unaffected by the problem, the actual total area that could be used for rice cultivation was about 4,500 hectares rather than 7,000 as initially believed. The Soviet specialists concluded that building a tall dam on the Fié made little sense, since it would be very expensive, technically complex, and add only a very limited additional surface that could be used for rice. Therefore, they proposed to build a medium dam on the Ni, as originally established, but only a small dam on the Fié (about five meters tall), which would greatly contain the costs. The proposed project was submitted for approval to the Guinean government in August 1961.[71]

Sékou Touré was very displeased with the Soviet proposal. On August 19, he wrote to Khrushchev complaining that his government had been informed only at the last minute about the change of plans. "The project that was presented on one hand does not correspond to the request of the Guinean side, and on the other does not address our hope about the building of a complex of facilities, which could be expanded in the future." Sékou Touré explained that the development of the Fié valley was a long-held dream of the PDG government, which saw rice cultivation as only the first step in a long process that would lead to the birth of a hydroelectric power station and eventually industrial facilities in the area. Without a big dam, this was not going to be possible. Moreover, he lamented the fact that the timeframe for the repayment of the Soviet loan was too short.[72]

Aside from technical questions, it seemed that financing the project was the main problem. About a week after Sékou Touré's letter to Khrushchev, Sory Barry, Guinea's Minister of Agriculture, made the same point to A.V. Parshin, the attaché for economic affairs at the Soviet embassy. Barry said that, despite initial estimates, Guinea did not have the resources to pay the loan back in the time proposed by Moscow and could not afford the Fié project under these conditions. Parshin objected that the timeframe for repayment was already longer than usual (sixteen years instead of twelve), that the Soviet government had already conceded Guinea special loans, and that presumably it would be willing to negotiate an extension on this occasion too. However, this was not judged sufficient by the Guinean government. Sékou Touré decided to abort the Fié project altogether and asked to use the Soviet credit for different purposes, such as purchasing agricultural machines. As for the Soviet specialists who had been working on the Fié project, Barry "did not know" how and where they could be employed now. About a month after the Fié project was canceled, Solod was expelled.[73]

Throughout the exchange, it was evident how the Soviet side was not entirely sure what had gone wrong. Parshin kept asking whether the problem was technical or financial, and Khrushchev insisted that his specialists had proposed to downsize the dam only because they were looking for the most economical (*ekonomichkii*) way of completing the project, and they had no intention of offending Sékou Touré. The real problem, which the Soviet leadership struggled to understand, was that Guinea could not pay the loans back, even at the relatively favorable conditions the USSR had offered. In Fié, as in other cases, the Soviet government had jumped into a project with an excessively optimistic outlook. There was no way Guinea could produce enough rice to pay the loan back in a time that was even remotely compatible with the timeframe both governments had agreed upon. As the example of Fié shows, the initial Soviet studies were rushed and tended to underestimate costs and technical problems. On the other side, the Guinean government tended to overestimate the country's productive capacity and its financial resources. What is more, coordination on the ground between Soviet officials and their Guinean counterparts was poor, and the leadership on both sides were impulsive and inconsistent.

It is therefore not surprising that many other projects followed the Fié pattern. The most illustrious victim was the proposed Konkouré dam and hydroelectric complex, another of the flagship projects in Guinea's development plan. During his visit in early 1961, Brezhnev reassured the Guinean government on the Soviet commitment to the Konkouré project, which was meant to provide Guinea with much-needed electricity and at the same time develop the aluminum sector thanks to a smelter to be built on the same site. Following Brezhnev's visit no more concrete steps had been undertaken, besides a preliminary estimate of the costs (which Moscow believed to be high).[74] The question of the Konkouré project was raised regularly during bilateral meetings. In 1962, following Solod's expulsion, a high-level Soviet delegation formed by officials from the CPSU, GKES, and MVT accompanied Mikoian to Guinea to conduct talks with their PDG counterparts. Keïta N'Famara, Guinea's Minister of Trade, seized the occasion of one such meeting to ask, "what stage the study of the Konkouré question is now." A few months later, Ismaël Touré repeated the same question to Degtiar', the new ambassador. In both cases, the Soviet answer was evasive and non-committal: the project was being studied in Moscow.[75]

In fact, the fate of the Konkouré project was already sealed. As in Fié, the problem was how to finance it. The dam alone was expected to cost about 300 million rubles. The Guinean government was unable to muster such a sum, and the USSR's Eastern European satellites showed little enthusiasm for the project, meaning that Moscow would have had to foot the bill on its own. The (optimistic) solution that was being studied was that Guinea would pay the Soviet Union back over time using the revenues from the sale of aluminum on the international market. In November 1962, the Soviet Ministry of Foreign Trade put this idea to rest. The MVT's research department reported that selling Guinean aluminum was a delusion. Even if a functioning smelter could be built in a reasonably short amount of time, the domestic market was tiny, and competition was too stiff for Guinea's aluminum to break into the international market. Several leading producers in Norway and Japan were already planning to increase production in the following years, leaving very little space for potential competitors. According to the MVT's assessment, despite investment and ambitious plans, Guinea would continue to export only agricultural commodities for the foreseeable future, making it impossible to rely on trade revenues to finance development.[76]

In Fié, as in Konkouré, and in many other cases in West Africa, the only way for the development projects to go ahead was for the Soviet government to accept relatively high expenses with little to no chance of getting at least part of the investment back. This was precisely what the Guinean government hoped for, even after Solod's expulsion. Speaking to the Soviet delegation in early 1962, Minister of Cooperatives Keïta N'Famara explained that "out of necessity we were forced to turn to our friends so that they make some sacrifices." Even though N'Famara "knows and understands" that raw materials such as iron ore and bauxite, with which the Guinean government proposed to repay the Soviet credits, were "of no value" to the USSR, he still asked Moscow to accept them. Without Soviet credits, not only there was no chance to pursue the development plan, but even purchasing basic goods and commodities would be impossible. In this case, the situation in Guinea would become "hard, really hard." According to N'Famara, the economic survival of Guinea itself was at stake.[77]

Nevertheless, the Soviet government showed limited availability to come to its ally's rescue. The Konkouré project, for example, was abandoned. In the summer of 1964, just a few months before Khrushchev's fall from power, N'Famara (now minister of economic cooperation) once again reminded Semën Skachkov (the chairman of GKES) of the Soviet commitment to finance the dam project. Skachkov's reply was curt: the Konkouré project required "very substantial investments." No more was heard of it. In the end, it would be the Italian multinational Impregilo to build a large dam on the river Konkouré, but only thirty-five years later, in 1999.[78]

Such fiascos were not limited to Guinea alone. In Ghana, the much-vaunted plan to turn the town of Tema into a bustling port city with modern facilities for the fishing industry run into similar problems. The Tema project was one of the first ones that the Soviet government agreed to contribute to, and Soviet advisers had been working on it since late 1960. As of late 1963, the building of residential blocs and the realization of a number of fishing factories in Tema had reached a stall. The estimates provided by the Soviet experts did not satisfy the Ghanaian cabinet, which complained that the financial situation was unclear and the costs excessive. The Accra government lamented that in nearly two years the Soviet side had not been able to produce a concrete plan for Tema, including architectural drawings of the project and a proposed timeframe. The only certainty was that the Soviet equipment and machinery required at the design stage of the project were already quite expensive—more than half a million pounds.[79]

As usual, it was not clear whether Ghana could afford the Tema project, and the Soviet government was hesitant to increase its level of commitment. GKES estimated that expenditure for the share of the cost of the Volta dam and Tema project that the Ghanaian government had agreed to cover would total about 70 million pounds. This was all Ghana could afford for at least five-six years, meaning that if both went ahead no other development project could be financed. Although the Ghanaian Ministry of Finance was predictably concerned about the cost of the development plan, the USSR showed no willingness to increase its own share of the expenses to help Ghana.[80] Naturally, the project had to be scaled down. The only part of the original Tema project to survive more or less untouched was the establishment of fisheries in Tema with Soviet financial and technical assistance, and the training of Ghanaian fishing personnel in the USSR (but only 70 Ghanaian officers, instead of 180 as initially planned).[81]

After the coup that removed Nkrumah from power in 1966, the Soviet contribution to the Tema project was canceled. Successive Ghanaian governments looked at the private sector to attract investment in the area. Tema, nowadays part of the Greater Accra area, is still in many ways an ongoing project. The passenger railway line to connect central Accra with Tema, one of the ideas explored in Nkrumah's early plan, ran its first train in October 2010.

Plowshares into Debt Shares

Similar to industry and infrastructure, agriculture suffered from comparable problems. Gigantism was among the biggest issues. In Ghana, the Soviet Union had agreed in 1961 to assist the CPP government in setting up three very large state farms to cultivate rice and corn. A team of experts was sent to finalize a program. In early 1962, the Ghanaian cabinet discussed the results of the Soviet fact-finding mission. The Soviet proposal was to realize the two rice farms, of respectively 19,000 and 29,000 acres, in Adidome and Afife, not far from the delta of the Volta in the southeast of the country. The corn farm (10,000 acres) would be located in the Ashanti region, 100 kilometers north of Kumasi. The total investment for the realization of the farms was estimated at 2.5 million Ghanaian pounds, including machinery, equipment, and training for the farmers, but excluding running costs.[82] The Accra government judged the costs excessive, especially given that the Soviet plan did not include provisions for the "organization, establishment, and management of the farms." After lengthy negotiations, the Soviet side proposed that a number of experts from the USSR (initially 69, then reduced to 59) could assist with the running of the farms. Even if Moscow accepted halving the salaries of its experts, the total cost would still be close to 3 million pounds.[83] Besides the cost, the Ghanaian Ministry of Agriculture insisted that the Soviet specialists would need to be completely in charge of the farms for at least the first three years, and possibly longer, since managerial expertise in Ghana was limited. However, V. P. Karamyshev, the head of the Soviet agricultural team in Ghana, was adamant that his specialists would only be able to train their Ghanaian counterparts, but they would under no circumstances assume full responsibility for the management of the state farms.[84] After a year and a half during which the Soviet agricultural team in Ghana did little more than attending meetings, the two parties agreed that in early 1963 sowing in the two rice farms could begin, on a much reduced surface compared to the initial hopes (700 acres in Adidome and 500 in Afife).[85] Ghana could not afford the extremely large state farms that had been planned originally, and needed to reduce costs drastically. The USSR had no intention of committing its specialists to the management of Ghanaian agriculture for an indefinite time, especially since it appeared unlikely that the Accra government would be able to pay for them. Hence, agricultural modernization—one of the main objectives of Soviet-Ghanaian cooperation since Benediktov's very first visit in 1957—was scaled down to negligible levels.

As of late 1964, an official from the Soviet Ministry of Agriculture admitted that "the results are not what they could be" in the state farms. To illustrate the situation, he cited the fact that a shorthorn cow in the USSR weighed on average 500 kilograms; in Ghana, they weighed less than 500 pounds (225 kilograms). The Soviet Ministry of Agriculture blamed the "weak technical and material base" for the poor results in agriculture, meaning that the Ghanaian workers were poorly trained, and the Accra government had committed insufficient resources to the sector. There was a chronic shortage of specialized personnel, including engineers, agronomists, irrigation experts and zoo technicians. Despite this, Nkrumah considered firing the director of the state farms programs—one of the few Ghanaian officials who had gained some experience in the field. Negotiations between the Soviet and Ghanaian government on agricultural cooperation continued until 1966, with little effect on the disappointing results on the ground.[86]

In Mali and Guinea, agricultural cooperation with the USSR suffered from the same disease. The Office du Niger, the second-largest recipient of Soviet aid in the country, struggled to fulfill its mission. By mid-1962 it was evident that the resources initially committed were not going to be enough. In the spring of 1962, the Bamako government prepared an interim report on the state of the development plan eight months after its launch. The situation of agriculture was not satisfactory: "The establishment and start-up of the new structures have not yet made it possible to tackle all the technical problems required to achieve the agricultural production objectives foreseen for the end of the Plan and which must come from an increase in yields more than cultivated surfaces."[87]

Lack of resources was the most pressing problem. Mamadou Aw, the minister of public works, reported to the Malian cabinet that the Office du Niger needed an extra 40 million rubles for agricultural modernization. However, before considering a new loan, the Soviet government expected Mali to use first the funds it already had available, which amounted to only 24 million rubles.[88] The prognosis was dire. For the three remaining years of the development plan, "the increase in agricultural and livestock production to the maximum extent that is humanly possible remains objective number one; if it is not achieved, it will be the end of the Plan."[89] Plagued by lack of specialized personnel and constant underfunding, Mali's agriculture never managed to reach the productivity goals Keïta's government hoped for. By the end of 1964, it was clear in Moscow that the plan had failed.[90]

Things in Guinea followed the same pattern. Sékou Touré's development plan stipulated in 1959 that five hundred new cooperative farms would be created in three years. By the summer of 1961, 170 cooperative farms were operative, employing 43,000 people throughout the country. However, only fifteen out of the thirty "modernization centers" envisaged in the plan, which were supposed to supply cooperative farms with equipment, could be created. Land was still cultivated using "traditional" techniques, with an obvious detrimental impact on agricultural productivity in Guinea. Moreover, no modernization center had the necessary equipment to assist farmers with cattle raising, which saw no significant improvement in the first three years of the plan. The situation was no better as far as state farms were concerned. Of the six projected peanut farms, not even one existed as of late 1961. The Guinean government did manage to create five state farms to produce bananas, pineapples, and palm products. However, they all lacked technical equipment and qualified personnel, meaning that most of the work was done "by hand." In conclusion, lack of trained personnel, difficulties in providing farms with machines and equipment and, last but not least, the fiasco with dam construction and rice production meant that by the end of 1964 the PDG government was still discussing how to follow up on the agricultural development plan approved four years earlier. Meanwhile, in Moscow, the Soviet agency that coordinated the provision of specialized training in West Africa complained that neither the Guinean nor the Malian government had specified how many training cadres they required in the polytechnic schools and agricultural colleges that the USSR had helped to build. The shortage of trained personnel remained severe. Agricultural production remained insufficient.[91]

The Blame Game

Agricultural and industrial schemes took much longer than expected to be completed, costs rose considerably above initial estimates, and many building projects had to be downsized or abandoned. The blame game between Moscow and the West African capitals thus began. Soviet agencies blamed their counterparts in Ghana, Guinea, and Mali for poor results on the ground. In June 1961, GKES prepared a report to the Central Committee on the state of Soviet economic help to West Africa, highlighting the problems encountered. Although the governments of Ghana, Guinea, and Mali had begun to move in the right direction in their development strategies, cooperation with the USSR achieved relatively little. GKES believed that the problem was the nature of the agreements signed, which often gave the West African states the last word on where to channel the resources that came from the Soviet Union. Although Soviet specialists were invited to study the economic situation of the countries and formulate suggestions, their recommendations were not always taken into account. Soviet funds and expertise were instead often directed toward the realization of projects with high visibility but little economic utility. The example of Guinea was cited as particularly bad in this respect.[92]

The Soviet Ministry of Foreign Affairs was even harsher. Looking at the implementation of Guinea's development plan, the Soviet embassy in Conakry reported that most objectives in agriculture and industry had not been realized, and delays were going to be significant. Available funds were not sufficient. The initial estimates of the Guinean government proved wrong, and costs turned out to be much higher. A large proportion of the Soviet credits had to be used to pay for the working force and the materials, whereas Guinea's own funds had initially been expected to be enough to cover them. The concluding passages of the report contained a real indictment of Guinea's leadership.

> A significant part of the resources allocated for the realization of the three-year development plan turned out to have been squandered. A large misappropriation of state resources also took place. . . . In connection to this, in the opinion of the embassy, it would be desirable to send a Soviet economic delegation to Guinea with the aim of inspecting the progress in the realization of the objectives in the three-year plan to be realized with Soviet help, and of establishing the priority of their construction from the point of view of a more rational use of Soviet equipment and building machinery, of a possible reduction in their deliveries in order to use part of the Soviet credits to finance the internal expenses of the Guinean side.[93]

French observers were equally unimpressed with the Guinean government. In explaining the tension between Sékou Touré and Moscow that followed Solod's expulsion in late 1961, the French ambassador to Conakry Jean-Louis Pons reminded his superiors in Paris that Soviet investments in Guinea proved "unproductive" but that the projects "have been chosen and decided by the Guinean government itself in relation to its own political preferences." Pons had no doubt as to who was to blame. "The moment often comes for governments and individuals alike to try to shift onto others the blame of mistakes that they themselves have made, once the evidence of them begins to surface."[94]

In turn, government officials and local planners in West Africa had plenty to complain about Soviet aid. In much-maligned Guinea, relations between local workers and Soviet engineers in building sites around the country were often difficult, with mutual accusations of incompetence and even brawls between them. Moreover, delays with the delivery of Soviet equipment, materials, and personnel were a daily occurrence. Ismaël Touré, Ibrahim Barry, the minister of planning, and Keïta N'Famara, the minister of trade, regularly complained about missing materials and specialists from the USSR who never showed up in Guinea. In the end, MVT and GKES had to admit that the Soviet side had frequently committed mistakes in this respect. Once Soviet equipment got to West Africa, its quality was often questioned. The government of Ghana, in particular, complained about machines and vehicles that were ill-suited for the tropical climate and broke down too easily. The Soviet side rejected most accusations, in turn blaming Ghanaian workers for mishandling the equipment and using it for inappropriate tasks, which damaged it (such as attempting to start engines with sealed carburetors, smashing stones with drills meant for wood, overloading cranes and winches). However, a representative of the Soviet embassy in Accra had "to admit that there really were deliveries of individual vehicles with suboptimal paint and an insufficient protective coating, which caused premature corrosion. . . . Also, there was premature wear of the valves of car engines as a result of using high-octane gasoline" (Soviet engines were designed for lower-quality fuel). The Soviet trade organizations were also often superficial in their arrangements. In July 1961, Alpha Diallo, the Guinean minister of foreign affairs, complained to the Soviet embassy that tons of bananas and pineapples were rotting in the Conakry port because the Soviet ships that were supposed to pick them up had insufficient capacity (800 tons instead of 1,000).[95]

These were by no means isolated incidents. The situation in Ghana and Mali was just the same. In Ghana, one of the new state farms needed corn seeds to begin sowing in the spring of 1963. However, the seeds, sent from the USSR, had been stuck for a month in the port of Tema, and the majority went rotten. It was unclear who was responsible for delivering them to the farm. Mali, a landlocked country, depended on the Abidjan port in Côte d'Ivoire for its exports. However, lack of storage in the port and lack of capacity in Soviet ships caused a large proportion of Mali's export commodities destined to the USSR (mostly peanuts) to be abandoned and rot. Deliveries of Soviet goods were in an even worse state. In August 1961, the Soviet embassy in Bamako warned Moscow that "the lack of reserves of foodstuff and other basic goods in the country are caused, essentially, by the delays in the deliveries of Soviet goods." As the previous chapter has shown, countries like Guinea, Mali and, to a lesser extent, Ghana could hardly survive without Soviet assistance. Delays caused scarcity, even of essentials.[96]

There were also cultural differences that made negotiations between Soviet and West African officials often complicated. For instance, the Soviet trade organizations were used to thinking in terms of quantities, whereas the Ghanaian trade officials habitually thought in terms of prices. This gave rise to many surreal exchanges between the two sides in which they seemed to be speaking mutually unintelligible languages. In early 1962, the Ghanaian government announced that it was ready to step up trade with the USSR and purchase much larger quantities of Soviet foodstuff and construction materials, such as cement and concrete. Ghana's Ministry of Trade asked for the prices of these items. The MVT responded that it would be impossible to specify a price without knowing the exact quantity of a good Ghana intended to buy. The Ghanaians replied that they could not decide how much they wanted of something without knowing how much it would cost. This continued for about a month, until the Soviet side agreed to provide "average prices" based on current market rates.[97]

In other cases, incompetence and superficiality on both sides conjured up intricate problems that appeared impossible to solve. For example, the completion of a footwear factory in Kindia was delayed because apparently neither the Guinean government nor the Soviet specialists had realized that to function the factory would need electricity. To supply the area with electricity, it was necessary to build an extension to the existing line, which required both time and money. Predictably, neither side was especially happy to take on the additional costs and tried to shift the responsibility for the extension onto each other. Likewise, the construction of a preserve factory in Mamou was delayed by the difficulty of supplying the building site with materials from the Conakry port. Guinea's network of roads left much to be desired. The country had 32,000 kilometers of roads but only 200 had been refurbished with asphalt as of 1964, which meant that reaching even relatively major towns could be a real challenge, especially during the rainy season. The situation in the more remote N'Zérékoré, where the USSR was sponsoring a wood processing factory, was even worse. There were 1,100 tons of equipment and materials stuck in the Conakry port for there was no way of delivering them to southeastern Guinea. Neither the Guinean planners nor the Soviet specialists who assisted them seemed to have taken this problem into account when choosing where to build. The result was, once again, the need for more time and more money.[98]

It was in places like Kindia and N'Zérékoré that the complexity of development was revealed to the Soviet specialists involved in its pursuit in West Africa. Without basic infrastructure, including energy and transport, it was impossible to realize even the simplest of productive enterprises. However, without essential goods and commodities it was impossible to build said infrastructure. Either importing these goods and commodities or producing them in loco required that very same basic infrastructure that was missing. The USSR found itself in a vicious circle that was impossible to break without the expenditure of considerable resources and the acceptance of a much longer timeframe than initially imagined.

Nothing showed the intricacy of modernization like the large transport infrastructure projects that the USSR attempted to realize in Guinea and Mali. Mali, landlocked and isolated, desperately needed easy access to a port from which the goods and commodities it needed could be imported. Guinea, whose road and rail network was in dire conditions, was in great need of investment in the transport sector. The most natural solution seemed to be creating a fast and effective connection between the two countries, so that a modernized Conakry port could serve Mali as well, and at the same time Guinea's roads and railways would receive much-needed refurbishment. Reality, alas, proved much more complicated.

The West African and Soviet specialists who worked on Guinea and Mali's development plans focused on two projects that would address both countries' viability and transport problems. First, the Soviet Union would sponsor and supervise the construction of a railway line to link Bamako with Kankan, in Guinea, and then connect this new line to the old Kankan to Conakry railway (built by the French in colonial times), which needed to be repaired. The Guinean and Malian government would split their share of expenses equally. Second, the Soviet government agreed to look into the possibility of improving the navigability of the River Niger in Mali, which provided a way to reach the north of the country from Bamako but was subject to significant seasonal variation in the level of water.

The beginnings were promising. The refurbishment of the existing Guinean section of the railway (from Conakry to the town of Kouroussa, about ninety kilometers from Kankan) was practically completed by mid-1962, despite a significant delay and an increase in the projected cost of about 15 percent. The Soviet government agreed to cover a larger share of the expenses for the first section of the railway given that in February 1962 the Guinean government announced it did not have the means to pay. The construction of the new section, which should have linked Guinea and Mali together, turned out to be even more complex. Besides technical and topographical difficulties, funding proved to be the most serious hindrance. The Guinean government did not have the resources to pay for the new section of the railway but would have liked the works to go ahead, as long as the USSR footed most of the bill. The Mali government was equally ambivalent about the project. Aw, the minister of public works, requested to the GKES representatives that Mali pay its share only for the part of the railway that crossed its own territory, and that Guinea pay for the rest (the railway would mainly traverse Guinean territory, with only the final 100 kilometers or so in Mali). The Soviet government made it clear that it was not willing to shoulder the cost of the railway by itself. It was Brezhnev himself, during his visit to Guinea in 1961, to tell Sékou Touré that the USSR intended to honor its commitment to refurbish the Conakry-Kankan railway, but it would not be going further as the only sponsor.[99]

As a result of the financial impasse, all work on the railway was interrupted by the end of 1962. It never resumed. In November 1963, reviewing the sorry state of Soviet-Guinean economic cooperation, the Soviet embassy in Conakry reported that work on the country transport infrastructure, including the railway, had stopped completely. Meanwhile, a large amount of equipment destined to the northeastern section of the railway had either "become worthless" due to wear and tear or disappeared altogether.[100] In mid-1964, when Soviet-Guinean cooperation had all but ended, Sékou Touré presented a new seven-year development plan, in which investment in transport infrastructure was supposed to be one of the key priorities. However, the Soviet Ministry of Foreign Affairs, reviewing the plan, concluded that Guinea still did not have the resources to invest, and no foreign government thus far had stepped in to offer financial and technical assistance despite Conakry's requests.[101] Not much changed for the following fifty years. As of March 2019, the Guinean and Malian governments were still holding meetings in the hope of realizing the section of the railway between Kankan and Bamako that would link the two countries, possibly with Chinese funding.[102]

The failure to connect the Conakry port with Mali via rail spelled the end of the Niger project too. Following the signing of the Mali-USSR agreement in 1961, several groups of Soviet specialists traveled to West Africa to assess the possibility of improving the navigability of the river. They came up with some preliminary suggestions, which were submitted to the Malian government for further study in 1962. It was all useless. As Tret'iakov—a junior economist at the Institute of Africa—explained in a study he produced after a research trip to Mali, the idea of using the Niger as a transport artery seemed good on paper but did not take into account several basic problems. The project was predicated on the assumption that agricultural products from the northeast of Mali would be sent upstream to Bamako, while import products would be sent downstream from the capital toward the north of the country.[103] However, this was the wrong assumption because trade routes in Mali tended to bypass Bamako almost entirely. Since the dissolution of the Mali Federation, when Dakar was the main port, the main trade route went south toward the port of Abidjan in Côte d'Ivoire via Ségou or Bla and Sikasso. According to Tret'iakov, the volume of goods transported along this route had increased tenfold since 1961. Bamako was too poorly connected to other countries and to the rest of Mali to represent a useful transport hub for goods and commodities. As long as the capital was not connected to the Conakry port in an effective way, the main direction of trade in Mali would remain North-South rather than East-West.[104]

Moreover, even if the Bamako-Conakry railway existed, problems would still remain. The Conakry port was simply too small to manage the handling of goods and commodities for two countries. Tret'iakov estimated that the total capacity of the Conakry port, even allowing for the proposed Soviet-sponsored refurbishment, would be no more than 20,000 tons per year, which would be just about sufficient for Guinea alone. There was plenty of evidence that Tret'iakov was right. Sékou Touré himself revealed to the Soviet ambassador that in 1960 almost 120,000 tons of goods were amassed in the Conakry port. Guinea's entire fleet of railway coaches, plus 2,000–3,000 transport trucks (which Guinea did not have), would have been necessary to move everything out of the port. Lack of storage in the port, especially refrigerators, meant that perishables were easily wasted. In 1961 alone, 2 billion Guinean francs worth of food were lost due to the poor quality of the storage and transport infrastructure.[105]

The project to improve navigability on the Niger and link Mali to the sea remained in the list of objectives for Soviet-Malian cooperation until 1964, even though no progress was ever made following the initial study. Improving transport infrastructure in Mali, and more broadly in West Africa, was considered a key priority in the heyday of Soviet engagement in the region. By the mid-1960s, the idea had completely escaped from the mind of the Soviet leadership, and not only metaphorically as Madeira Keïta discovered the hard way. When visiting Moscow in August 1964 to discuss the state of Soviet-Malian economic cooperation, the first question that Khrushchev asked him was whether Mali had access to the sea. It must have been a particularly disheartening moment.[106]

The Worth of Peanuts

By the mid-1960s, the majority of Soviet-sponsored development projects in Ghana, Guinea, and Mali had run into a combination of political, financial, and technical problems. Most were interrupted; many would never be completed. Bilateral trade was in no better shape. The barter trade agreements, which on paper allowed the West African states to exchange their relatively inexpensive commodities with Soviet machinery and technology, proved a burden for state coffers on both sides. As had happened with the aid programs, the initial assumptions governing trade turned out to be wrong. Estimates of productive capacity and assessments of needs were wide of the mark, leading to costly delays and a staggering level of waste. As a consequence, both Soviet and West African finances had to undergo adjustment, which proved difficult and painful in Ghana, Guinea, and Mali. However, no degree of economic inefficiency or technical difficulty could kill off bilateral trade between the USSR and West Africa. As in other areas, what ended it was the Soviet government's lack of political will to sustain additional costs.

Mali is perhaps the best example to illustrate the issues with Soviet-West African trade. As the previous chapter has shown, Mali's economy had long been dominated by the production and sale of a single agricultural commodity: peanuts. For little under a century France bought the entire stock of Mali's peanuts, usually paying a price that was significantly above the market rate. Revenues from selling peanuts were used to purchase from French producers the goods and commodities that Mali needed. Following independence and the signing of the comprehensive agreement with the USSR, Moscow offered Mali a trade deal to overcome dependency on France. The Soviet Union replaced the colonial power as the main buyer of peanuts and the supplier of those necessary goods that could not be produced in Mali. Rather than selling its peanuts to France, Mali could exchange them with Soviet technology and machinery. The treaty that the Moscow and Bamako governments signed in early 1961 was a barter agreement. Mali did not dispose of hard currency resources, and the USSR was anxious not to deplete its own currency reserves, especially to buy a commodity that had little market value. Barter seemed to make perfect sense for both.[107]

Officials from the Soviet Ministry of Foreign Trade established together with the SOMIEX the value of peanuts. This was expressed in both rubles and Malian francs, but in practical terms it meant how many tons of peanuts could be exchanged with how many Soviet tractors, cars, barrels of oil, and so on. Peanuts could also be used to pay for part of the building projects and the geological surveys that were undertaken at the same time by Soviet specialists in the context of the cooperation agreement. The arrangement was generally favorable to Mali. As France had done before, the Soviet Union valued Malian peanuts about 20 percent above the market price.[108]

The barter agreement initially functioned relatively well. In 1961, the USSR bought 20,000 tons of Mali's peanuts, more or less 40 percent of the total stock. The Soviet government paid for 40 percent of Mali's peanuts in hard currency, as a

FIGURE 5.3. The Soviet commercial and industrial exhibition central pavilion in Bamako. September 1964. Credit: Sputnik.

"favor" to Keïta's government, and exchanged the remaining quantity with Soviet goods and services, including industrial machines, vehicles of various kind, gasoline and other oil products, cement, and sugar. The barter system could be intricate to navigate for both the MVT and SOMIEX, and delays and logistical problems were common. For example, much-needed Soviet sugar reached Mali with a considerable delay, meaning that for a few months there was no sugar at all in the country. Moreover, only half of the expected quantity of peanuts could be sent to the USSR by the end of 1961. Soviet cargo ships could not carry the whole amount in one trip, and the Abidjan port, which the USSR and Mali were forced to use, did not have sufficient storage. Nonetheless, despite these problems, the Soviet embassy reported that 75 percent of the commercial exchanges for 1961 had taken place in accordance with the initial plan. Bilateral trade was essential for Mali as it provided a way to obtain the goods it needed without the need for hard currency.[109]

This relatively manageable state of affairs did not last long. Already in 1962, SOMIEX, which Keïta had called "an essential tool for our independence," struggled to keep up with the increasing volume of trade with the USSR and the socialist bloc. As the Soviet embassy reported, there were only three people who had any specific training in trade and commerce in the whole organization. SOMIEX's small staff could hardly process the paperwork necessary to guarantee smooth exchanges. The Soviet trade organizations, which managed the sale and provisions of specific categories of products, complained that their Malian counterparts rarely knew what they wanted to buy and in what quantities. Moreover, transport was a nightmare. The Soviet organizations wanted to sell "Free on Board" (FOB), while the Mali government insisted on "Cost, Insurance and Freight" (CIF).[110] Given the state of Mali's roads, railways, and storage facilities, neither side wanted to accept the significant risk of damage or loss during transport.[111]

These were still theoretically solvable problems, but something else threatened the very base of Soviet-Malian trade. About a year after the signing of the trade agreement, it became apparent that Mali did not produce enough peanuts. The Soviet advisers from GKES and MVT lamented that the Malian government had overestimated the country's productive capacity. Even valuing peanuts above market price, as the Soviet Ministry of Trade did, what was available was not enough to cover the exchanges that had been agreed upon with the USSR. The fact that the Mali government needed peanuts to pay for prestige projects and geological surveys—both expensive enterprises—made the problem even more severe. In the short run, this was not an insurmountable obstacle. The Soviet economy did not have an especially pressing need for peanuts, which Moscow bought largely to relieve Mali from the need to use hard currency to buy equipment. Therefore, the Soviet side continued to deliver goods and commodities even without receiving a corresponding amount of peanuts by the end of the year (meaning that the "clearing accounts" did not, in fact, clear). Mali thus accumulated debt vis-à-vis the Soviet Union.[112]

After about a year and a half, both sides realized that Mali would never be able to settle this debt. As in many other cases, the initial estimates of future production were too optimistic. Mali's development plan stipulated that the country's export resources would increase by 70 percent by 1965. This was impossible. Arable land was limited, funds were scarce, and a large part of agricultural production was needed to feed the population. In addition, the prices of the agricultural commodities Mali hoped to export had been decreasing sharply since the late 1950s. As far as trade with the USSR was concerned, agriculture in Mali grew too slowly to provide enough commodities to be exchanged with relatively pricey Soviet machines and technology, even after cutting or downsizing unnecessary projects. The only solution was to increase the worth of peanuts artificially, so that fewer Malian peanuts could pay for more Soviet tractors or barrels of oil. SOMIEX and various members of the Bamako government, including Modibo Keïta himself, proposed this on multiple occasions, asking the Soviet Union to value their peanuts more than 20 percent above the current market rate and at the same time to offer *"prix de faveur"* for Soviet industrial goods. The Soviet government, despite promises to look into the matter and assurances of eternal friendship and fraternal solidarity, never agreed. Essentially, Moscow insisted that Mali settle at least part of its debt, even though it knew that the West African country would never be able to. Negotiations between the two sides continued for years, without achieving much, as Soviet deliveries of goods and services dwindled. After 1968, when Modibo Keïta's government was overthrown in a military coup, the new executive "defaulted" on the USSR—Mali's debt would never be settled, neither using peanuts nor money, and the two countries stopped whatever little commercial exchanges they had at that point.[113]

Before analyzing the reasons that led to the collapse of Soviet-Malian trade, it is worth exploring Soviet trade with Guinea, which suffered from similar problems. The premises were the same as in Mali. Barter trade with the socialist world was supposed to provide goods and services that Guinea needed without resorting to transactions in hard currency. Contrary to Mali, Guinea did not have a single traditional export commodity, for its mineral resources were still underexploited following independence. With the partial exception of bauxite and iron ore, whose production was largely in Western hands, Guinea exported only fruit and some coffee. As in Mali, the Conakry government expected the USSR and other socialist countries to value Guinean products above current market rates. The Ministry of the Economy explained that France used to buy Guinean bananas paying 30–40 percent more than the average world price and hoped that the Soviet Union would do the same. This, in the Guinean view, was based on the "Marxist theory" of "equal exchange."[114]

As in Mali, for the first few years following the signing of the trade agreement in 1959, barter trade between the USSR and Guinea functioned relatively well, despite the numerous logistical problems that both sides encountered. The usual structural problems lurked ahead, though. Similar to Mali, Guinea's export resources were limited and did not grow at the expected rate: minerals were expensive to extract and faced a saturated market, the price of coffee was declining, and the country produced too little tropical fruit. Guinean cooperative banana farms were expected to cultivate 400 acres of land, but they could only manage twenty due to shortages of qualified personnel and equipment. As a result, the Guinean export organization, CGCE, was unable to deliver to the USSR the quantities of commodities stipulated in the plan. Therefore, the Guinean government accumulated debt to the Soviet Union—eight million dollars in unfulfilled trade exchanges alone in 1964, excluding loans. To reduce this debt, Guinea could not export more for it was unable to produce more. The Conakry government tried to explore the possibility of persuading the USSR to increase the valuation of its exports but to no avail. The view in Moscow was that Guinea's bananas were already overpriced enough. The Soviet Ministry of Foreign Trade refused to consider unbalanced trade (it insisted that clearing accounts had to clear) and threatened to stop deliveries of Soviet goods to Guinea if at least part of the debt was not settled. The PDG government was desperate for options, and it advanced a paradoxical solution. Keïta N'Famara, the minister of trade, proposed that the Soviet Union import not only fruit and coffee but bauxite and iron ore too. The problem was that the Soviet Union was a net exporter of both materials, meaning that the USSR was not only able to produce enough to satisfy its domestic requirements, but also to sell some on the international market. Hence, the Soviet Union had no need for Guinea's bauxite and iron ore. The Guinean representatives insisted on this solution for nearly two years until, after much back-and-forth between the two governments, in January 1964 Moscow agreed to accept 200,000 tons of bauxite as payment for some of its exports. The bauxite never materialized.[115]

By the spring of 1964, Guinea's commercial debt toward the USSR had crossed the threshold of ten million dollars. "Given the economic situation of the country," the Guinean trade attaché in Moscow told the MVT representatives in May 1964, "the Guinean Republic cannot extinguish a debt of 10.6 million US dollars either this year or in the future." This moment signaled the end of Soviet-Guinean trade as a tool for economic development. Commercial relations between the two countries continued but on a much smaller scale. Soviet exports, only a couple of years earlier the prime source of machinery and technology in Guinea, were reduced to a trickle.[116]

Why was the Soviet Union so rigid in its management of trade with Guinea and Mali? Insisting on the repayment of trade debt in the face of the obvious difficulties that the USSR's West African allies experienced was not a particularly productive strategy. The trade system collapsed, and the Soviet Union recouped only a minimal part of its losses. One possible explanation is that the USSR's rigidity with regard to trade agreements derived from the Soviet economy's own rigidity. As officials from MVT told their West African counterparts on numerous occasions, the Soviet Union planned its economy. Fulfilling the plan depended on pre-established exchanges of goods and commodities at given times, both domestically and in terms of foreign trade. Importing fewer peanuts than expected from Mali or less fruit from Guinea meant that some productive branches of the Soviet economy received fewer raw materials than they expected according to the plan. This caused their output to be inferior to planned, which in turn caused problems to other branches of the Soviet economy—other factories or shops—that depended on this output for further processing or distribution. Therefore, a seemingly trivial issue such as fewer peanuts or pineapples reverberated across the Soviet economy, creating headaches for local planners and putting some factories at risk of penalties for insufficient production. The Soviet Ministry of Trade claimed to be sympathetic to the Guinean and Malian officials who tried to negotiate more manageable exchanges for their countries but argued that Gosplan and Gosbank would never allow radical changes to what had been agreed and inserted in the central plan.[117]

Though indicative of certain problems with the Soviet economy when dealing with international exchanges, the focus on the rigidity of central planning offers only a partial explanation of the problems with trade in West Africa. Certainly, the MVT representatives who conducted negotiations were aware of the problems with the plan and had no incentive to come to Guinea or Mali's rescue by lobbying on their behalf with Gosplan and Gosbank. These organizations, when they were involved in negotiations on international trade, showed even less inclination to make concessions that would complicate their work. However, this did not mean that changes could not be made. The reality of the plan was much less rigid than what was routinely described to the Guineans and the Malians. Changes and adjustments to the plan had to be made on a daily basis, simply as a consequence of the economic and technical problems, the poor estimates, and the unavoidable contingencies that affected the Soviet economy. International trade was no exception. When altering quantities or prices was necessary, it could be done. What was necessary was political will from the top. For example, despite numerous declarations from the Soviet Ministry of Foreign Trade that the USSR would never accept bauxite from Guinea because it had no need for it, the Soviet government, in the end, did accept some bauxite as payment. Importing bauxite from Guinea was not easy for the Soviet trade organizations: it required reneging on a previous deal to buy the material from Greece, let alone the fact that Guinean bauxite never arrived in the required quantity. However, the exchange happened because the Guineans successfully lobbied with Khrushchev himself, who persuaded the MVT to go ahead.[118]

Commercial viability never motivated Soviet trade policy toward Africa during the Khrushchev era. As long as the Soviet government believed that investing in Guinea and other newly independent Third World states was furthering the cause of state-led development in Africa and Asia, then it was willing to incur losses and override its own skeptical bureaucracy. By the time the USSR agreed to buy bauxite from Guinea, however, this was more of an isolated token gesture than a global strategy. As the Soviet belief in the noncapitalist model of development encountered mounting challenges, Moscow's willingness to lose money and find solutions to make things work became much less strong. Bauxite could be purchased once but not regularly. Buying and selling disregarding world prices was no longer appealing in Moscow. "I no longer believe"— Khrushchev told Madeira Keïta in August 1964—"that it is possible to sell to the Third World below the world prices." Skachkov, the head of GKES, was even blunter. "The USSR and the socialist countries cannot support the moral and material needs of Third World states." By the summer of 1964, only a few months before Khrushchev's fall from power, it was clear how the Soviet Union had lost interest in the establishment of a state-led development model in the Third World, which had previously guided Moscow's involvement in West Africa. This is what killed trade with Guinea and Mali—politics, not technicalities.[119]

The Cocoa Connection

Soviet trade with Ghana presented similarities with commercial exchanges with Guinea and Mali, but also a few crucial differences. Like Mali, Ghana specialized in the production and sale of a specific commodity—cocoa beans—to the colonial power (Britain). Unlike Mali's peanuts, after independence Ghana's cocoa beans were still considered important by British businesses. Although the same could be said about Guinea's bauxite and iron ore, the production and sale of cocoa in Ghana were already well established, whereas in Guinea mineral extraction was still to be developed. This meant that the British businesses that had long operated in Ghana aimed to maintain their commercial arrangements more or less unaltered in the postindependence era and actively resisted Soviet attempts to break into the cocoa market. This was why the Soviet Union encountered more difficulties in Ghana than in Guinea or Mali to establish itself as an alternative to trading with the former colonial masters. Ghana's transformation into a republic in the summer of 1960, and Nkrumah's push to bring trade under government control, favored the growth of commercial relations with the USSR, but structural problems remained.

The main issue that plagued Soviet-Ghanaian trade was sorting out payments. During the negotiations that led to the 1961 trade agreement, Gosbank insisted that bilateral trade should be organized with the usual clearing accounts and that the USSR had to minimize the use of hard currency resources. The Accra government found it difficult to accommodate Soviet preferences. The Cocoa Marketing Company had little interest in guaranteeing to the Soviet government a stable long-term price for Ghana's cocoa beans, which would have greatly simplified barter trade. The company's insistence on negotiating prices each time made planning barter trade virtually impossible: neither the Ghanaian nor the Soviet government could know in advance exactly how many tons of cocoa beans would equal the value of a Soviet tractor or the salary of a Soviet agronomist working in Ghana. The company quoted a price for cocoa on a weekly basis, and the Soviet trade organizations could decide whether to buy at that price. Soviet officials routinely complained that the Cocoa Marketing Company proposed to the USSR prices much less convenient than those it offered buyers in London—210 pounds per ton to the Soviet agency Prodintorg as opposed to 186 pounds per ton on the London market in January 1962. The reason was simple: The Cocoa Marketing company offered a discount only to the buyers that maintained "a large apparatus" in Ghana and that acted as "consultants and agents" for the company—these were the traditional British businesses that had been involved in the cocoa trade for over a century. Prodintorg, despite being a relatively large buyer, could not hope to obtain the same favorable conditions and to have the same influence on the cocoa trade.[120]

Not everyone in the CPP government in Accra was happy with this state of affairs. The officials closer to Nkrumah believed that selling cocoa beans at a fluctuating price was too much of a risk, given that cocoa was Ghana's prime export resource and that its price had been declining (in 1964 it was at its lowest since 1948). The idea of establishing a fixed price for five-six years was obviously attractive to the Ghana government, which could shield itself from further decreases in the price of its main export commodity and guarantee itself an influx of much-needed foreign capital. The only potential commercial partners that would consider such an arrangement were the socialist countries, in the context of the usual barter agreements—agreeing on a fixed price higher than the declining market price made little sense for anyone else. In December 1964 Amoako-Atta, Ghana's minister of finances, approached the MVT with the proposal to base the sale of Ghana's cocoa beans to the USSR on fixed prices, as the Soviet trade organizations had been requesting for years. Amoako-Atta explained that the government wanted to maximize revenues from the cocoa trade, but that "Western companies oppose this attempt" and that "the countries of the socialist camp could provide invaluable help in the solution of this problem." He anticipated that trade would be reformed in Ghana, and he promised new and better conditions for the Soviet organizations. Despite Amoako-Atta's best efforts, it was too late. By that time, Khrushchev had already been deposed, and the Soviet government was focused on reducing its external commitments rather than trying to revive an old project of cooperation. The reply from the MVT was noncommittal—Moscow would review Ghana's proposal and prepare an official response in due course. In the end, the coup that removed Nkrumah from power in 1966 ended any chance of a revival in Soviet-Ghanaian trade. As of early 1967, the new government was still deciding what to do with the debt the previous administration had accumulated toward the USSR.[121]

From the Soviet point of view, the cocoa trade in Ghana was impenetrable because of the power and influence that the West, especially Britain, maintained in the country after independence. Disruptive British influence was not limited to the cocoa sector alone. Even after July 1960, there were still numerous British officials and advisers who worked in the Ghanaian state apparatus. They tended to resist trade with the socialist world. For example, in March 1961 the Soviet embassy in Accra reported that the head of the technical department of the Ghanaian Army, responsible for procurement, was a certain Nicholson—a British colonel. Nicholson opposed the sale of Soviet-made GAZ-69s (a Jeep-like four-wheel-drive vehicle) to the Ghanaian Army and argued that Land Rovers should be purchased instead. The MVT did not fail to stress that the fact that a British officer deciding what the Ghanaian Army could or could not buy made their task a lot more difficult. Something similar happened in the aviation sector. In 1961, the government of Ghana had purchased eight Iliushin-18 airplanes from the Soviet Union for Ghana Airways. In late 1962, Ghana's Ministry of Finances announced that it did not approve the release of the budget to man the Soviet aircraft, including payment of the Soviet specialists who were supposed to help with the maintenance of the Il-18s. The Soviet airplanes were grounded indefinitely. The government would now buy some second-hand Britannia aircraft from the British Overseas Airways Corporation (BOAC, a progenitor to British Airways).[122]

This was indicative of the confusion that reigned in the organization of Ghana's trade, which reflected the tension in the country between supporters of state-led development and others who preferred a market-focused approach and looser relations with the socialist bloc. In Ghana there were multiple organizations that dealt with foreign trade, often with unclear remits and overlapping responsibilities. In theory, the Ghanaian National Trading Corporation (GNTC), established in 1961, was supposed to manage all trade with foreign countries, including the USSR. The GNTC was a government agency created to bring Ghana's trade under state control in accordance with Nkrumah's views. In practice, however, the Corporation operated in competition with other agencies and corporations, including pre-existing ones such as the Cocoa Marketing Company, that managed commercial exchanges in specific areas. While the GNTC was generally in favor of trade with the socialist countries, its competitors tended not to be. The Soviet trade organizations were often caught in the crossfire of turf wars between different agencies and government ministries. For example, in the summer of 1962 the Soviet Ministry of Foreign Trade tried to find out what exactly the newly established Ghanaian Purchasing Commission was, who was in charge of it, and what its exact tasks were. The reply was baffling. Ababio, the representative of the commission, responded that his organization was under state control, but not total like a ministry. It operated in conjunction with the Planning Commission to determine the needs of the Ghanaian government and buy "this or that" good. Whether processing the purchases of Soviet goods and commodities for the Accra government was the responsibility of the National Trading Corporation or of the Purchasing Commission was not always easy to determine. Delays and unfulfilled contracts were the unavoidable consequence of bureaucratic confusion. For example, in January 1963, neither the Ministry of Agriculture nor the

Purchasing Commission seemed to know which one of them had to approve the purchase of Soviet tractors for Ghana's state farms.[123]

As in Guinea and Mali, logistical problems and poor organization on both sides delayed deliveries of goods and payments. Predictably Ghana blamed the USSR, and vice versa. The problem with payments and mounting debt did not affect the Soviet Union alone. In late 1962, the Bank of Ghana organized a meeting with the representatives of all socialist countries which traded with Ghana, including the USSR, the People's Republic of China, and Yugoslavia. In a rare display of socialist solidarity, the Soviet, Chinese, and Yugoslav officials all accused the Ghanaian organizations of sabotaging trade with the socialist world due to incompetence and malevolence. Although the socialist countries bought large quantities of cocoa, the Ghanaian trade organizations delayed their corresponding purchases of Chinese, Soviet, and Yugoslav goods. This created an "artificial" debt on the side of the socialist countries, which some of the Ghanaian organizations argued should be settled in hard currency. The Chinese representative blamed the National Trading Corporation for this trick. An Englishman—Sir Patrick Fitzgerald—had become the head of the GNTC and, in the Chinese and Soviet view, he pushed for the purchase of Western rather than socialist products. The Ghanaians rejected the accusations and argued that British citizens who worked for the government simply followed instructions and operated with Ghana's best interests in mind.[124]

The role of British citizens in Ghana was complicated. Fitzgerald, appointed to head the GNTC, was the former general manager of the Ghana branch of the United Africa Company (UAC)—one of the most well-known and reviled symbols of British imperialism in Africa. In the mid-1960s, the UAC still owned and managed a large number of shops in Ghana. In a meeting with B.A. Borisov, the Soviet trade representative, Fitzgerald explained that he was not uninterested in buying household products from the Soviet Union, but he had to take into account the "conservative" tastes of Ghanaian consumers. He argued that local buyers would not like new products, such as Soviet flour or Czechoslovak shoes, and that it was preferable to stick to the traditional suppliers. Fitzgerald recognized that being able to buy flour or shoes using local commodities rather than hard currency would be beneficial for the Ghanaian state, but he could not convince local consumers to buy these "new" products. The UAC shops certainly did not like Soviet stuff. A couple of years earlier, the Soviet embassy had reported that they did not want Soviet tomato paste because the tag on the can was green, whereas Ghanaian consumers were used to a yellow tag.[125]

The initial Soviet diagnosis in Ghana—that it was impossible to compete with entrenched Western positions in the country—proved correct. Despite various attempts by the MVT to establish the USSR as a trade partner, and Nkrumah's desire to nationalize trade, commercial exchanges with the West remained much larger in volume. Moreover, Western businesses and officials enjoyed better conditions and more extensive influence in the country. The MVT reported that, by the end of 1963, one-third of Ghana's external trade was with Britain, 20 percent with the European Economic Area, and 10 percent with the United States. The volume of the entire socialist world's trade with Ghana was less than 8 percent. It equaled that of Japan alone—a country that had no previous history of trade with West Africa and had never made a deliberate effort to break into the region's market. As in Guinea and Mali, the root of failure in Ghana was politics, both domestic and international. Ghana was a complex polity where trade was contested between different groups with diverging ideas and agendas. At the same time, British businesses resisted Soviet penetration. The combined effect eventually squeezed the Soviet Union out of Ghana.[126]

The Moscow Consensus

The costs of ambitious development strategies, complex monetary reforms, and the disappointing results of trade with the Soviet Union had significant repercussions on the finances of Ghana, Guinea, and Mali. Revenues could not keep up with the level of expenditure, the balance of trade was always negative, and the West African states accumulated debt, both internal and external. Moreover, a marked increase in the money supply, plus the continuous reliance on pricey imports, contributed to high inflation rates in all countries. The governments of Ghana, Guinea, and Mali reacted to their worsening finances by slashing state expenditure and raising taxes (austerity) and by lowering salaries to reduce imports and boost exports (structural adjustment). These measures, traditionally associated with neoliberal economics, found an unusual supporter: the USSR. This was yet another sign that, by the mid-1960s, the Soviet leadership had all but given up on the dream to establish a state-led model of development in the Third World.[127]

In 1966, the US-RDA government in Bamako conducted a thorough review of Mali's five-year development plan. The results were not encouraging.

> The conquest of independence and the execution of the Plan have caused excessive expenses in relation to revenues due to military expenses, sovereignty expenses, expansion of the Civil Service, creation of factories whose cost has been in part covered by internal resources.
>
> To cover these new expenses, due to the lack of normal revenues, the Central Bank has incessantly printed new money.

Moreover, the State Societies and Enterprises that were created have encountered some difficulties due in part to the lack of experience of their managers and the insolvency of the State, which could not pay for the goods and services that it requested.

The resulting deficit was largely financed by advances from the Bank of the Republic of Mali that were rarely repaid, resulting in a new creation of money without counterpart. Since 1962, the money supply, that is to say the whole range of means of payment, has increased by 300%.[128]

The needs of development and Mali's quantitative easing, which gave the state apparatus more money to spend, resulted in an increase of imports, which in turn caused a mounting deficit in the balance of payments. "Thus, our hard currency reserves were exhausted, rendering us incapable of ensuring the normal procurement for the functioning of the state services, the commercial companies and the population. Shortages began, and with them rising prices and speculation."[129]

The overall picture was very similar in Guinea and Ghana. Since independence in 1958, Guinea's expenditure to maintain its state apparatus had grown twofold. Administration, the military, and education each accounted for about 20 percent of the yearly state budget. The country's foreign debt, mostly to socialist countries through loans and trade imbalances, reached 160 million dollars in 1964. This was more than three times Guinea's yearly state budget. As the Soviet Ministry of Foreign Trade concluded, "the use of credits and the actual amount of payments to clear off the foreign debt in 1963–65 will be significantly higher than estimated." Ghana's state finances were in no better shape. The extent of the country's fiscal woes was clear, at least since 1962. The government needed to start repaying the loans that financed its development plan. However, growing administrative costs and the declining price of cocoa caused lower-than-expected revenues. "This deficit, as a rule, is covered by way of reducing foreign assets, mainly Ghana's currency reserves."[130]

To stop the hemorrhage of hard currency from state coffers and grant the governments the means to pay back some of the debts they had accumulated, West African and Soviet economists agreed on a solution that could have been taken straight from a macroeconomics textbook: cut imports and boost exports. While this was an obvious component of any import-substitution development strategy, hoping to improve the trade balance in West Africa was wishful thinking on the part of the local governments and an outright absurdity coming from Soviet advisers. Ghana, Guinea, and Mali could not survive without importing most of what their populations needed because these basic goods and commodities could not be produced locally. In 1964, Ghana's three largest categories of

imports were still foodstuff, "finite products" (any household product), and "vehicles and transport equipment" (anything from bicycles to trucks). Guinea and
Mali were even more reliant on imports, especially from the Soviet Union itself—
the same country that now refused to offer *prix de faveur* for its products and
insisted on the repayment of its credits. Moreover, Ghana, Guinea, and Mali's
possibilities to increase their exports were limited. The commodities they produced faced saturated markets and their prices had been declining for years.
Given that the socialist bloc was no longer willing to buy at artificially inflated
prices, prospects were dire.[131]

Since improving the trade balance was essentially impossible, the West African governments tried to reduce domestic expenditure and boost tax revenues.
The previous sections have shown how the Accra, Conakry, and Bamako governments reduced their commitments for the development plans and canceled
projects—all cuts in government spending. They also decided to increase taxes
and cut wages. In 1962, the CPP government in Ghana introduced a series of
harsh fiscal measures. Import taxes were increased, especially for those goods
that could be "made in Ghana." Excise duties on the sale of alcohol, the regis-
tration of vehicles, and the issuance of driving licenses also rose. More important, the government passed new laws that reduced the tax-free allowance on
salaries and decreased the minimum wage, including for government jobs. These
were measures that Lewis had advocated already in 1958. Guinea and Mali introduced similar policies to discourage imports, reduce government spending,
and boost tax revenues. The USSR approved. Soviet analysts praised the "progressive nature" of the tax reforms in West Africa, which in their view affected
only the richest citizens and targeted Western businesses that exported to Ghana,
Guinea, and Mali.[132]

What the Soviet advisers believed may have been valid in theory, but the reality on the ground was more complicated. In a context of widespread poverty,
scarcity of basic goods, and rampant inflation, decreasing salaries and increasing taxes further squeezed the buying power of citizens. As a result, according
to the French embassy in Guinea, "the state shops are frequently closed, and the
shop windows are empty." Scarcity caused tension between the populations and
the governments, including waves of strikes and demonstrations, often resulting in clashes with the armed forces. Moreover, even from a strictly financial
point of view, the contractionary fiscal policy pursued by the West African governments produced disappointing results. It was difficult to increase tax revenues in economic systems in which there was not that much wealth to tax. At the
end of the 1962 fiscal year, the first under the new taxation regime, the Ghanaian
government expected to collect eleven million pounds in tax revenues. In fact, it
obtained seven. In 1963, the Mali government expected a revenue of 9.8 billion

francs but got only five. Looking at the poor results of tax collection in Ghana, Guinea, and Mali, Soviet analysts blamed high levels of poverty in the population, bureaucratic confusion, porous borders that facilitated smuggling and elusion, and the ability of Western companies to dodge taxation through legal loopholes.[133]

As the deficits kept growing and loan repayments became more difficult every year, the governments of Ghana, Guinea, and Mali resorted to even more desperate measures. Guinea partly re-opened its market to foreign businesses in the hope of attracting investment. Starting in 1963, the PDG government allowed the formation of mixed companies, which involved local and foreign partners. The Bamako government restored the convertibility of the Malian franc with the CFA and the French franc, following two devaluations in 1963 and in 1967, returning to the franc zone after a five-year experiment with monetary independence. In 1965, the Ghanaian government introduced the cedi, the new national currency, which was pegged to the British pound but at a lower exchange rate compared to the old Ghanaian pound. The cedi needed to be devaluated in 1966 and then again in 1967, following the coup against Nkrumah. All talk of leaving the British pound zone waned.[134]

In late 1963, both Guinea and Mali joined the International Monetary Fund and the World Bank. All three governments explored the possibility of receiving loans and financial aid from them (Ghana had been a member of both organizations since 1957). These openings to foreign capital and international finance were possibly even less successful than other measures. Western investors and international organizations were either uninterested in West Africa or proposed draconian conditions.[135] By this point, the Soviet Union was no longer an option. In November 1964, the Accra government wrote to Moscow asking whether the USSR would be willing to contribute to Ghana's National Investment Bank, a recently created institute with the aim to revive development projects. The Soviet response left no doubt as to the new priorities in the Kremlin: the Soviet government could not contribute capital to the new bank because the USSR did not meddle in the internal affairs of other countries.[136]

In May 1962, Modibo Keïta became the third West African leader to tour the USSR, after Sékou Touré and Nkrumah. Relations between the Soviet Union and Mali were good, and Keïta was treated like a guest of honor. Everything went smoothly until the Malian president exchanged congratulatory speeches with Khrushchev in Moscow. The first secretary could not help lecturing his guest on the great achievements of the Soviet Union. Khrushchev then launched himself in a tirade that clearly referred to the problems Soviet-Malian cooperation was encountering. Constructing socialism was a complex task: "It would be wrong to present the thing in such a way that it is enough to proclaim the slogan 'we are for socialism!'—and then lie down under the shade of a tree and wait for everything to happen by itself. Instead, the building of socialism requires a lot of energy, persistence, work from the people."[137]

Keïta did not react to Khrushchev's racist provocation, but its meaning was not lost. The barb was symptomatic of a generalized malaise in Soviet-West African relations. The previous chapter showed how the pursuit of modernization and development in Ghana, Guinea, and Mali was not possible without the Soviet Union's expertise and funds. This chapter has examined what happened once the Soviet willingness to invest disappeared. As the ambitious development strategies became unsustainable, little remained of the initial enthusiasm and optimism. It was the reduced Soviet commitment to Ghana, Guinea, and Mali that ravaged their economies and brought them close to collapse.

There were multiple causes behind the USSR's decision to stop its engagement with West Africa. First, the Soviet economy did not perform as well in the 1960s as it had in the previous decade. Declining growth rates and disappointing harvests made the Soviet leadership wary of investing in the Third World. Second, the Cold War entered a new phase. A new US leadership emerged, seemingly more willing to challenge Soviet advances in the Third World using both financial and military means. Successive crises in Europe, the Caribbean, and Asia made the USSR more insecure globally and Khrushchev less confident of his leadership at home. The Congo crisis demonstrated the limits of Soviet power in Africa. Moreover, development in Ghana, Guinea, and Mali revealed itself as a much more complex and expensive enterprise than anyone in Moscow had anticipated. Projects required more and more time and money, budgets were smaller and smaller, and local partners appeared unreliable. The Soviet leadership chose disengagement and disinvestment, with the devastating consequences analyzed above. The following chapter will explore the long-term consequences of the withdrawal from West Africa and the end of the socialist or noncapitalist model of development in West Africa.

THE END OF THE AFFAIR

Khrushchev celebrated his seventieth birthday on April 15, 1964. By then, he was an insecure, almost unstable, leader. The slow decline of the USSR's economy, the ongoing quarrel with China, and the international crises of the past couple of years had taken their toll on the First Secretary. He appeared less prone to take decisions based on his intuition, he was more and more alienated from his colleagues in the Presidium, and he openly talked about retirement. His family was worried about his physical and mental state. This was a far cry from the Khrushchev of the late 1950s—a boisterous leader ready to take the Soviet Union into uncharted territory. Change was in the air.

The evolution of Soviet involvement in West Africa mirrored the personal parable of the first secretary of the CPSU. The failings and frustrations examined in the previous chapter led to a slow but steady decline in Soviet interest in the region. As Ghana, Guinea, and Mali explored alternative approaches to modernization, the noncapitalist model of development, once the guiding principle behind both Soviet and West African efforts, receded into the past. The new Soviet leadership that replaced Khrushchev at the end of 1964, and both the old and new West African leaders of the second half of the 1960s, reverted to more traditional ways of managing the economy and international relations. This chapter analyzes the withdrawal of the USSR from West Africa, the end of the affair between the Soviet Union and Ghana, Guinea, and Mali, and its implications in the short term.

Go West

By the end of 1963, in Ghana, Guinea, and Mali the results of cooperation with the USSR were unimpressive. If the idea of focusing on state investment and planning was generally appreciated, progress on the ground appeared limited. The political space for economic development in West Africa was always contested. The Soviet approach was dominant, but Ghana, Guinea, and Mali's attitude to economic cooperation had been to look for sponsors anywhere and accept aid from all possible sources. Thus, looking for Western help to integrate or replace Soviet aid was a natural move for the West African governments. The problem was that neither the United States nor Western Europe proved particularly interested in matching the Soviet effort.

Ghana was the most divided. Forever caught in between the temptation of socialism and the pressure that came from London and Washington, the CPP government had maintained working relationships, albeit complicated, with both sides of the Cold War divide. Different officials pushed for different solutions, and Nkrumah's ability and willingness to mediate was limited. Following the 1960 constitutional referendum, the Congo crisis, and the purges of 1961–1962, Ghana seemingly moved closer to the socialist bloc, ridding itself in the process of a large number of British soldiers, officials, and advisers—"an ugly lurch to the left" in Walt Rostow's words. However, the US government was conscious that the key Volta project was in Western hands, that British influence in the country was far from vanquished, and that Ghana's difficult economic situation made everyone in Accra less picky about where assistance came from. The American ambassador to Ghana, William Mahoney, told Kennedy that Nkrumah's "Marxist bark is worse than his bite," and he believed the US government "must learn to live with him."[1]

Live with him they did, at least for a while, but there was no chance that the US government would replace the Soviet Union as aid donor on the same scale. Besides the Volta project, a significant part of which was financed through private operators, there was little more the Kennedy and especially Johnson administrations were willing to do. Economic cooperation remained in the remit of the private sector. Between 1963 and 1965, some Western firms (including British and US ones) committed to supplying credits for the building of factories in Ghana. The total amount, however, was far inferior to the sums the USSR was willing to invest (the United States gave Ghana less than 10 million dollars in aid in total). Moreover, these were individual projects. There was no coherent overall strategy for the economic modernization of Ghana that came from the West. Western priorities in Ghana were making sure that Nkrumah did not veer too much toward the left, and defending existing business interests and developing new ones. As one of Johnson's aides put it, "US policy continues to be the encouragement of private investment and technical assistance in Ghana for its further development."[2] The Western world insisted on the primacy of market over state, something Nkrumah and others in his government regarded with suspicion. There was no way the West could replace the Soviet Union in Ghana. This was not so much because Soviet aid was larger, but rather because the USSR and the West approached economic cooperation differently. As long as Nkrumah was in charge, the inspiration for the development model that Ghana wished to follow remained statist rather than market-driven, something with which the West had little desire to engage.[3]

The same was true in Guinea and Mali, where Soviet influence was even stronger. Since 1961–1962, both governments had tried to rekindle their relationship with France and to obtain economic and technical assistance from the United States. Even more than in Ghana, the results were disappointing. If the US government was hesitant and careful in Ghana, it showed minimal interest in Guinea and Mali. Sékou Touré had done everything possible to show the Americans that he was a reliable potential new ally. In October 1962, about a year after Solod's expulsion in late 1961, the Conakry government refused to authorize Soviet aircraft en route to Cuba to make a refueling stop at the Conakry airport—refurbished with Soviet money—citing Guinea's need to maintain its policy of neutrality. This decision greatly angered Khrushchev. The following year he took his revenge on Sékou Touré, refusing a Guinean request for basic military supplies. "We turned to them with such great hopes. He [Sékou Touré] did not appreciate it so much and behaves arrogantly," Khrushchev blurted to his Presidium colleagues.[4]

However, despite Sékou Touré's openings and the State Department's opinion that the US government should provide aid to Guinea, the Kennedy administration remained lukewarm at the prospect. The costs of helping Sékou Touré's government with large infrastructure projects were judged too high. When Moussa Diakité, the governor of the bank of Guinea and the head of a delegation that visited Washington in the spring of 1962, proposed that the US help Guinea with its balance of payments, Kennedy responded that "the US also had its balance of payments problems." As of 1963, Guinea and Mali received less than 10 million dollars in US aid. There were few chances to go past this threshold in the near future.[5] Robert W. Komer, an influential member of Johnson's National Security Council (NSC), believed that: "Soapy Williams and our country teams all tend to see the African problem too much in terms of US aid. We are already investing about $145 million in economic aid and MAP and $150 million in food. I don't see us going up very fast. Nor do I think we'd buy much. The new African countries are mostly in such a primitive state of development, and are so hipped on internecine quarrels that I doubt whether even a massive US investment now would show a commensurate result."[6]

In 1965, the United States spent on the whole of Africa an amount comparable to what the Soviet Union had invested in Ghana, Guinea, and Mali alone (230 million dollars as of 1964, excluding military aid, according to the CIA). The Johnson administration seemed even more disillusioned than the Kremlin leadership about the prospects of development in Africa. The private sector was equally unresponsive. William Attwood, about to leave his post as American ambassador to Conakry, told Degtiar' in August 1963 that US "capitalists" were wary of political instability in Guinea and reluctant to commit resources despite Sékou Touré's guarantees for foreign investors. The message that the Guineans and Malians representatives received from Washington and from Wall Street was that they had to look for help elsewhere.[7]

Since American assistance was not forthcoming, the Conakry and Bamako governments turned to France, the old colonial master. Although generally willing to recover some of the ground it had lost in former French West Africa, Paris was neither able nor willing to provide aid or re-establish trade on a scale similar to the colonial era. Despite the PDG government's efforts, the sums that France gave Guinea were limited. As of late 1963, the two governments were still discussing a 3.5 million francs loan and trying to solve the issue of the pensions of Guinean veterans who had fought in World War II with the French armed forces. The total Guinea received from all OECD countries combined in 1963 was about 23 million US dollars, less than half the amount provided by the USSR alone. There were no signs of a change of plans for Guinea in Paris or elsewhere.[8]

Mali, whose relationship with France had never suffered the same break as Guinea, was luckier. MID reported that France gave the Bamako government about 40 million rubles in 1962–1963, and a further 20 million came from the European Development Fund. The volume of capitalist aid remained inferior to socialist assistance. Moreover, Madeira Keïta explained to his hosts in Moscow in August 1964 that Mali "cannot refuse" Western aid out of necessity, but "we in Mali have opted freely and irreversibly for the socialist path of social, economic and cultural development." Madeira invited his Soviet allies, "very friendly, but honestly," to do more for Mali and countries like Mali. "The Union Soudanaise-RDA and the popular masses of Mali are convinced of the triumph of socialism. Only, they want this to happen as rapidly as possible, in order to block the way for the implantation of capitalism in the Third World." Even in the face of obvious Soviet disengagement from West Africa, part of the Malian leadership still harbored more trust in the socialist world than in the West. Looking at the scale of economic aid, this was not illogical. As in Guinea, the West was even less interested in Mali than the USSR and its allies.[9]

Seeking assistance from international organizations proved equally frustrating for Ghana, Guinea, and Mali. Joining the International Monetary Fund (IMF) and the World Bank was far from a panacea for the US-RDA government in Mali. Jean-Marie Koné, the minister of the plan, explained to his colleagues in the Bamako cabinet that "our subscription to the Fund is especially weak." Mali could access no more than 13 million dollars in IMF "special withdrawing rights," clearly not enough to solve the country's balance of payment crisis. Dealing with the World Bank was even harder. Koné and the other ministers were hopeful that the bank's new president—the American George Woods, a former investment banker—would be more receptive to the needs of Third World countries and less constrained by an orthodox view of economics and finance. This, unfortunately for Mali, was true only in part. When a Malian delegation visited the IBRD headquarters in Washington in September 1963, Woods lectured them about the importance of private investors in developing countries. He exhorted them not to close the doors to private capital, a crucial resource in his view, but a policy that ran contrary to the choices the Mali government had made. Moreover, the World Bank showed little support for Mali's development. The Bamako government proposed that the bank offer Mali a loan to complete the Bamako-Koulikoro railway and to build the dam at Gouina, in both cases replacing or complementing Soviet aid. Koné reported that the reaction from the bank was "distinctly unfavorable." Quite simply, "they estimate that the project is way too expensive for the expected result." In 1966, the bank did provide a 9 million US dollars loan to cover part of the railway project (less than sixty kilometers), which took eight years to be completed. The rest of the work took much longer. The full railway became operative only in 2003. The Gouina dam project was approved in 2013 and is still in construction. If there was one thing on which the Soviet leadership and Western financial institutions agreed, it was that development projects in Mali were just too expensive.[10]

The outcomes of engagement with the IMF and the World Bank were similar in Ghana and Guinea. Already in 1962, the head of Guinea's Central Bank complained with Degtiar' that the procedures to join the two financial institutions were "long and complicated." He also appeared surprised that Guinea was expected to make a significant payment to be able to join the IMF. According to the Quai d'Orsay, the US State Department was "shocked by the naivety and ignorance manifested by the Guinean negotiators" in their dealings with the West. Guinea had to wait until the end of the 1960s for the World Bank to get involved in the building of infrastructure for bauxite mining.[11]

The World Bank was active in Ghana since the approval of the Volta project and continued to finance small-scale projects in infrastructure throughout the 1960s. In late 1965, the Accra government explored the possibility of receiving more significant aid, and representatives from both the IMF and the World Bank traveled to Ghana. They recommended cutting government spending and privatizing state-run farms and industries to reassure foreign investors. Nkrumah refused, and the door to further aid from the international financial institutions was closed. It was only after Nkrumah's overthrow in 1966 that the fund and the bank returned to Ghana.[12]

The classic Cold War narratives of a zero-sum game or of the tail wagging the dog run into a number of problems in West Africa. It is true that development was the object of a contest between the socialist and the capitalist world, but the modalities in which said contest was conducted were very different. When the USSR reduced its commitment to Ghana, Guinea, and Mali, the West did not step it up. What was important for Moscow was not necessarily equally important for London, Paris, or Washington. Therefore, the ability of the Accra, Bamako, and Conakry governments to play West against East, as in a classic Cold War move, was limited. Most development projects from which the USSR withdrew in West Africa did not find new sponsors and were either abandoned or took decades to complete. Besides strategic, economic, and contingency factors, which all played a role, it was ideological differences between socialism and capitalism that determined this outcome. The Soviet Union, at least as long as Khrushchev was in control, believed in the possibility of development through state investment, which was broadly compatible with the desires and aspirations of the leaderships in Ghana, Guinea, and Mali. The capitalist world—be it the United States, British, and French governments or the IMF and the World Bank—believed instead in fostering domestic private capital and developing through investment from foreign private businesses. Cold War competition in West Africa was between two alternative visions of society and production, one founded on the state and the other on the market. Therefore, what the Soviet Union had dropped, the West would not pick up—ideologically more than financially or strategically.

China Syndrome

The USSR did not face competition from the capitalist West alone in West Africa. Cold War historiography has highlighted the extent and success of the People's Republic of China's efforts to establish itself as a leading political and economic force in the Third World. China was certainly a formidable presence, to the point that Gregg Brazinsky wrote that "when it came to crafting policy toward the Third World, Americans sometimes viewed Beijing as an even greater threat than Moscow."[13]

Following the Sino-Soviet split in the early 1960s, China and the Soviet Union became competitors, especially in the Third World.[14] The Chinese line was harsh but clear. Imperialism could be shaken off only through violent revolution, and the noncapitalist model of development would not lead to socialism. Beijing was skeptical of nationalist bourgeois leaders in the Third World and openly suspicious of Soviet aid. Mao's mantra at the time was "to develop using one's own forces," therefore rejecting the need for foreign aid. In more abstract terms, Chinese propaganda attacked both the West and the USSR for being "white," imperialist powers bent on gaining new territories to exploit in Africa, Asia, and Latin America. China was instead presented as the only socialist state with a credible revolutionary agenda, which had managed to escape its past as a colony and create a new society by itself.[15]

From this point of view, Chinese efforts had considerable success. It was difficult to deny China's painful colonial past and its long and bloody revolutionary war against imperialist powers. What was more, both the United States and the Soviet Union were on shaky grounds when posing as champions of liberation movements and newly independent states, given their history of meddling in other countries' affairs and their frequent engaging in colonial practices. Students, trainees, and visiting officials from the Third World often encountered chauvinism and patronizing attitudes in the Soviet Union as in the capitalist West. Likewise, Soviet and Western personnel often displayed racism when working with African, Asian, and Latin American colleagues. Moreover, Chinese denunciations of the Soviet search for disarmament and detente found interested listeners among national liberation movements from Algeria to Southeast Asia, whose armed struggles the USSR supported only half-heartedly.[16]

In this context, West Africa offered a complex picture. The leaders of Ghana, Guinea, and Mali understood Chinese critiques of the USSR and the West and appreciated the assistance that came from Beijing. Partly contradicting its no foreign aid policy, the PRC did provide significant financial and technical assistance to the Accra, Conakry, and Bamako governments. China could not compete with the Soviet Union in terms of the volume of aid it provided. However, the symbolism was powerful. During Guinea's difficult early days as an independent country, the PRC was among the first to take action, organizing much-appreciated deliveries of rice to help relieve the food crisis the French embargo had provoked. The Chinese government gave aid free of charge, which compared favorably to the interest rates that both Soviet and Western loans carried. Moreover, Chinese specialists and advisers were often praised by their West African hosts for their professionalism, work ethic, and lack of pretentiousness, especially when compared to some of their colleagues from other countries. Looking at

Guinea, the OECD reported that "the personnel sent by the Soviet Union and by China was of excellent quality, while the same could not always be said of the personnel sent by the countries of Eastern Europe."[17]

By 1963, the PRC was an established donor country in West Africa. Beijing had negotiated interest-free credits of about 20 million rubles with both Guinea and Mali, and it supervised development projects, including a cigarette factory in Guinea, a cotton factory in Ghana and one in Mali, and rice farms in all three countries. In total, the PRC fielded more than 2,500 specialists working in sub-Saharan Africa in 1965, from only 55 in 1960, reflecting the growth in importance of the African continent in Beijing's foreign policy.[18]

Despite these successes, China's appeal in West Africa remained limited. Nkrumah, Sékou Touré, and Keïta were the leaders of established postindependence governments and not liberation movements. Beijing's dogmatism and endless promotion of the revolutionary cause were more likely to unnerve them than to generate support. Although many in West Africa admired Mao and his thinking—in Guinea and Mali more than in Ghana—few were ready to apply his ideas in practice. The war between China and India in late 1962 shook the PRC's status with the nonaligned world. Moreover, China's blasé attitude toward nuclear war worried the West African leaders, who spent considerable effort protesting the French nuclear tests in the Sahara and promoting the cause of a denuclearized Africa. The French embassy in Conakry explained that, while Sékou Touré was sympathetic toward the PRC, "Guinea, like the majority of African countries, is wrestling with difficulties of all kind, first among them the consequences of colonialism and underdevelopment; therefore, the Guinean government does not feel immediately concerned about nuclear issues."[19]

Mao's calls for armed struggle and revolutionary warfare fell on deaf ears in West Africa. Ghana, Guinea, and Mali had all gained independence peacefully, and their leaders had no desire to see their revolutionary credibility questioned or diminished by the Chinese government. Even more so, they did not want to see rebels at home emboldened by Beijing's revolutionary rhetoric. Moreover, the tendency of Chinese delegates at congresses and meetings to judge other countries' policies and other peoples' revolutions did not win them many friends. The delegation from the Soviet Solidarity Committee with Africa and Asia that attended the 1961 international solidarity conference in Conakry reported tension between the Chinese members and several African delegations. In particular, the Chinese delegation insisted that no aid should be accepted from Western countries ("we don't need dirty money!") and that Antoine Gizenga, the Congolese leader who briefly continued the struggle against Mobutu after Lumumba's death, was "like Tito's Yugoslavia," "a dog of the imperialists." At a time in which the Congo crisis was in its most dramatic phase and several of the newly

independent countries in Africa were anxious to secure external funds for development, Chinese intransigence seemed to many participants out of place.[20]

West African governments looked at the Sino-Soviet split with puzzlement.
The reasons for the split remained obscure and difficult to understand for most
foreign policy specialists in Ghana, Guinea, and Mali. Its consequences were
judged nefarious for the anti-imperialist cause. In Guinea and in Mali, many in
the PDG and the US-RDA may have been disappointed with the USSR and in-
clined to side with more radical China, but both governments remained silent on
the matter and did not pick a side. In Ghana, Nkrumah commissioned the Bureau
of African Affairs, which often acted like an in-house think-tank for the Accra
government, to prepare a detailed report on the Sino-Soviet split, its causes and
consequences. The Bureau examined speeches and declarations by Soviet and
Chinese leaders, articles and denunciations that had appeared in both countries'
press, and it reflected on what Ghanaian diplomats and officials had observed in
meetings with both sides. The conclusion was that the split had less to do with
"doctrinal differences" and more with "great power rivalry" through "the pursuit
of influence and prestige" worldwide. From Ghana's point of view, the Accra government certainly did not have any incentive to pick a side and alienate the other.
However—the report added—"that does not preclude Ghana from forming an
opinion on the principal points of difference raised." The verdict was damning for
Beijing's positions, which were judged too risky. The only concession to Chinese
ideas was the potential necessity to liberate parts of Africa using "non-peaceful
means," but only if a peaceful solution was not possible. Otherwise, "any world
war could throw us back on our program of development as well as in our attainment of African Unity. . . . The Soviet view has therefore more appeal to Africa."
Hence, Ghana should "support the Russian view of peaceful coexistence."[21]

Grand strategy and the global Cold War mattered, but something else made
China's position in West Africa complicated: The PRC did not have a model to
export. In the early 1960s, the USSR promoted a vision of development based
on state investment and collective enterprise. The West also advanced the idea
of development but based on private investment and market competition. What
did China stand for? Part of the literature argues that the PRC did have a specific approach to modernization and economic development, separate from the
Soviet Union's. According to this view, while the USSR focused on rapid industrialization and the development of heavy industry—traditional Soviet priorities under Stalin—China stressed the importance of agrarian reform and
agricultural modernization. However, in the case of West Africa at least, this is
a misconception. As chapter 4 has shown, agriculture was a primary preoccupation for the USSR, from the beginning of its engagement with Ghana, Guinea,
and Mali. This was natural, given Khrushchev's desire to break with Stalin's

economic policies and his own obsession with agricultural modernization at home and abroad. In fact, the governments in Accra, Conakry, and Bamako were much more interested in heavy industry than the Kremlin leadership. What was then the difference between a Soviet-sponsored collective farm and a Chinese-sponsored collective farm?

Like the Soviet Union, China believed in state investment and central planning; unlike the Soviet Union, China's means to spread this model abroad were limited in the 1960s. The country had only just emerged from the Great Leap Forward, whose results were unlikely to inspire Third World governments to adopt similar policies. Mao's idea that Third World countries had to develop counting primarily on their own forces because aid created dependency was a strong rhetorical device with which it was difficult to disagree. Nonetheless, this was unlikely to encounter the favor of leaders like Nkrumah, Sékou Touré, and Keïta, whose ambitious modernization strategies required considerable resources from abroad. In terms of aid, which was what mattered the most in 1960s Ghana, Guinea, and Mali, China could not yet match the Soviet Union. The CIA estimated that between 1954 and 1966, the USSR provided approximately 900 million US dollars in economic aid to African countries. China could manage only about 350.[22]

There was also a substantial qualitative difference in the type of projects the PRC was able to sponsor in the early 1960s. The Accra government recorded that in 1962 China was sponsoring five projects in Ghana. Besides the provision of handicrafts and medicines, the PRC financed the construction of a soap factory, a pencil factory, and a plywood factory. Initial Ghanaian requests to Beijing included thirty storage silos, twenty between collective and state farms, and fourteen polytechnic institutes. The fate of these projects was indeterminate.[23] A few years later, the Quai d'Orsay recorded that in 1965, supposedly at the peak of Sino-Soviet competition for Africa, the only Chinese visitors for the year in Guinea and Mali were a 48-strong folklore troupe. Over the same period, Ghana hosted only a small team of Chinese geographers. This was not nearly enough to fill in for declining Soviet engagement. While some Chinese ideas were met with favor in West African capitals, the quality and quantity of China's development work were unlikely to turn the table in its favor.[24]

As in the case of the West, competition between the Soviet Union and China in West Africa was not a simple binary. Despite its best efforts, Beijing could not replace Moscow as main donor and political inspiration in Ghana, Guinea, and Mali because it lacked the means to provide aid on the same scale and because its ideological outlook was different from Moscow's. Ultimately, neither Chinese aid nor its ideology proved a good match for the aspirations of the West African governments.

Coups, Coups, Coups

In May 1964, Khrushchev made his first and only visit to Africa. He traveled to Egypt to meet Nasser and take part in the inauguration of the Aswan Dam, the most important development project financed by Moscow and the best-known symbol of Soviet engagement in the Third World. The trip was a mixed bag. Nasser and Khrushchev enjoyed each other's company, Ahmed Ben Bella traveled from Algeria to join them, and Egyptian hospitality impressed the Soviet leader. Nevertheless, Khrushchev was often in a bad mood. His antics puzzled and annoyed his hosts, and his outlandish behavior and quickness to take offense embarrassed the colleagues and family members who traveled with him.[25]

By the time he came back to Moscow, Khrushchev's days in power were numbered. He was irritable, old, and frail, and his colleagues in the Presidium had tired of his unpredictability and arbitrariness. In 1964, the Soviet Union seemed to be in a worse position than it had been in 1954, at the beginning of Khrushchev's tenure in power. Many officials at all levels of the CPSU and the Soviet state believed the first secretary was to blame. Khrushchev's increasingly unhinged personality did not help his popularity in Moscow. Even the most loyal among his colleagues and collaborators believed that the USSR needed change at the top.

In October 1964, while Khrushchev was on holiday in Abkhazia, the long-planned coup against him unfolded. The first secretary was called back to Moscow for a special Presidium meeting, during which all members subjected him to a barrage of political and personal criticism. In the best Soviet tradition, the charge against Khrushchev was led by the very people he had helped to climb to the top of Soviet politics—Brezhnev, Aleksei Kosygin, Nikolai Podgornyi, Aleksandr Shelepin, and many more. Conscious of his blunders and certain of having alienated every single one of his colleagues, Khrushchev had neither the will nor the means to fight back. The Presidium's unanimous decision was that Khrushchev had to step down and retire, officially on account of ill health. Brezhnev was nominated party secretary and Kosygin premier of the USSR. A new era thus began.[26]

There was seemingly no love lost between Khrushchev and his allies in West Africa. A few days after the official announcement of their "promotion," both Brezhnev and Kosygin received warm congratulations from Accra, Bamako, and Conakry. No mention was made of Khrushchev. The former first secretary lived the rest of his life as a pensioner in a dacha on the outskirts of Moscow, tending to his garden, entertaining the occasional guest, and dictating his memoirs. Recollections of Africa were bittersweet. The issue of Soviet engagement with newly independent countries in Africa was "a difficult question to answer," Khrushchev told the tape-recorder on which he recorded his memoirs. He praised Sékou

Touré for having brought Guinea away from France and closer to socialism. However, he still resented him for having somewhat changed his course, and still remembered bitterly the Guinean government's refusal to let Soviet aircraft refuel in Conakry during the days of the Cuban crisis. "In short, the events in Guinea were not a source of satisfaction for us," Khrushchev summed up. Nkrumah was an even more difficult figure to assess. The former Soviet leader appreciated Nkrumah's intelligence and erudition, but also blamed him for his excessive caution in taking the socialist path. Khrushchev remained convinced that Ghana's over-reliance on Britain and British officials jeopardized Nkrumah's plans, and eventually lost him his power. Keïta came off better than either of his allies in Khrushchev's recollections. He fondly remembered the Malian leader's impressive physique and his sharp political intelligence. According to Khrushchev, Keïta was also the only one who had had the courage and the conviction to embark on the road to "scientific socialism" without hesitation.[27]

In his memoirs, Khrushchev stated that despite the setbacks the Soviet Union had suffered under his tenure, he still believed that socialism would triumph in Africa. The new Soviet leadership that replaced Khrushchev in Moscow did not share the former First Secretary's optimism. Brezhnev and Kosygin were far less interested in the Third World than Khrushchev had been, at least at the beginning of their time in power. Others in the Presidium (which would again be called Politburo after 1966), who had been on Khrushchev's side in his push to open up relations with countries in Africa, Asia, and Latin America, either changed their minds or preferred to keep their opinions for themselves in the face of the new leadership. In November 1964, Brezhnev addressed the Presidium in his new role as first secretary on the topic of relations with the Third World. He did not mention economic aid at all.[28]

It was the shape of things to come. In the second half of the 1960s, the Soviet government signed fewer economic or technical cooperation agreements with Third World states, and none with Ghana, Guinea, and Mali. Soviet trade with Guinea and Mali was reduced to negligible levels. The USSR continued to trade with Ghana—buying cocoa and selling oil, minerals, and tractors—but the exchanges followed a commercial logic. Moscow purchased more cocoa beans when the price was relatively low, and fewer when the price increased at the end of the 1960s. Gone was the idea of trade as a pillar of the noncapitalist model of development in West Africa.[29]

West Africa changed too. Nkrumah's government in Ghana did not survive much longer than Khrushchev's. On February 21, 1966, Nkrumah left Ghana for China, on his way to meet with Ho Chi Minh in North Vietnam. A few days later, a group of army and police officers who had long resented Nkrumah and the CPP seized the opportunity for which they had been hoping for a while. They instructed their soldiers and policemen to capture strategic locations in Accra and arrest prominent ministers who were loyal to Nkrumah. Few had the resources to resist, given that most of the armed forces sided with the plotters. Nkrumah was officially deposed on February 24, 1966, after nearly a decade in power. Initially, Ghana was run by the National Liberation Council—a group of officers with ill-defined responsibilities. The CPP and all its satellite organizations, including trade unions, women's leagues, and the young pioneers, were disbanded and outlawed. Diplomatic representatives, advisers, and technicians from the Soviet bloc were ordered to leave Ghana, while the new government suspended its own diplomatic representation in the socialist world. After Nkrumah, Ghana was no longer a contested polity. Komer called the new government in Accra "almost pathetically pro-Western."[30]

The genealogy of the coup in Ghana has always been a matter of controversy. Nkrumah had no doubt that the action against him and his party was inspired by the United States, of which he had become more and more critical since the Congo crisis and Lumumba's tragic death. "In Ghana—Nkrumah wrote—the embassies of the United States, Britain, and West Germany were all implicated in the plot to overthrow my government." According to him, it was not difficult for them to find willing "quislings" among the armed forces. "Approximately one-sixth of Ghana's officer corps were trained at Sandhurst, though for some years we had been sending an increasing number to train in the Soviet Union and in other socialist countries. It is significant that not one of the officers trained in the Soviet Union took part in the February rising."[31]

The Soviet government was uncharacteristically cagey about the coup in Ghana. In late February 1966, it was a Soviet plane that flew Nkrumah back to Africa from China. However, Soviet support for its ally was limited at best. Moscow officially condemned the coup and did not recognize the new government. *Pravda* covered the coup in relative detail and gave ample space to Nkrumah's and Sékou Touré's indictment of the new government as a puppet of the imperialists. However, the Soviet government rarely brought the matter up again after the first couple of months. This choice, which contrasted sharply with previous Soviet stances on "imperialist crimes" in Congo and Southern Africa, was yet another sign that in the early Brezhnev years the way the USSR approached Africa had changed.[32] Natalia Telepneva looked at the plans that Czechoslovak and Soviet intelligence made to explore the possibility of organizing a "counter-coup" to reinstall Nkrumah to power. The operation was quickly aborted.[33]

Over the years, the 1966 coup has generated numerous allegations and conspiracy theories, usually involving the United States, Britain, and a few retired intelligence officers eager to share stories from their days in the CIA or MI6.[34] The available evidence is ample, but inconclusive. Nkrumah had never been popular among Ghana's armed forces and police, which generally favored close relations with the West rather than flirting with the USSR. Moreover, some of the CPP's economic policies were genuinely unpopular and caused widespread resentment against the government. The British and US governments also never particularly liked Nkrumah, especially following his "lurch to the left" in the years between the Congo crisis and the coup. Declassified American documents show that the US embassy in Accra maintained close contacts with army officers who disliked Nkrumah and openly discussed the possibility of a coup. In his report to Johnson immediately after the coup, Komer called it a "fortuitous windfall." A few months earlier, however, he had written to his boss at the NSC, McGeorge Bundy, informing him that "we may have a pro-Western coup in Ghana soon. . . . The plotters are keeping us briefed, and State thinks we're more on the inside than the British." Komer maintained that the United States was not formally involved in the coup preparations. However, the State Department's position was that "US pressure, if appropriately applied, could induce a chain reaction eventually leading to Nkrumah's downfall. Chances of success would be greatly enhanced if the British could be induced to act in concert with us."[35]

Whether or not they were behind the coup, the American and British governments were more than happy to see Nkrumah removed from power. However, this did not mean that they were ready to step up economic assistance to the new government in Accra. Komer was clear: "I am not arguing for lavish gifts to these regimes—indeed, giving them a little only whets their appetites, and enables us to use the prospect of more as leverage."[36] The officers who now run Ghana inaugurated a new course in economics and expected aid from abroad. The IMF, which Nkrumah had snubbed, was invited back in. As a result of IMF recommendations, most of the large state-run development projects in agriculture and industry were abandoned, and most state assets were privatized and ended up in the hands of foreign multinational corporations. Despite the new government's zeal, the IMF was unable to provide significant financial relief. Faced with growing foreign debt, lower cocoa prices, and lack of external funds, the National Security Council resorted to currency devaluation. Living standards in Ghana did not improve. In 1969, the generals handed over power to a civilian government led by Kofi Busia, an old enemy of Nkrumah from the defunct United Party. Busia returned from his exile at St Antony's College, Oxford, to successfully contest the first post-Nkrumah elections in Ghana. The USSR recognized Busia's government and reestablished diplomatic relations with Ghana. However, neither government was interested in rekindling the close relationship of the Nkrumah days. Ghana faced the usual problems. Following a series of coups and electoral upheavals during the 1970s and 1980s, and despite the involvement of the IMF, the World Bank, and the US government, Ghana's economy continued to struggle. It faced mounting debt, rampant inflation, and low cocoa prices until the dawn of the twenty-first century.[37]

Following the coup that ousted him, Nkrumah took refuge in Guinea. Sékou Touré offered him asylum and the position of honorary vice president. Not unlike Khrushchev, Nkrumah was shut off from political life in his country, which he would not see again for the rest of his life. He continued to write on international politics, pan-Africanism, and imperialism. In the first few years of his exile, Nkrumah frequently issued declarations condemning the military junta in Accra and denouncing their policies. In later years, his writings focused less on Ghana and more on the problems of apartheid and decolonization in Southern Africa. His political stance slid even more toward the left. As a political exile, Nkrumah embraced socialism with no reservations. He argued that liberation for the oppressed peoples of the world, from Southeast Asia to Rhodesia to the American south, could come only through a socialist revolution. Nkrumah remained a popular figure in the Soviet Union, occasionally celebrated in official rhetoric as a hero of African independence. Nonetheless, his more radical writings were never translated in the USSR.[38]

A couple of years after the coup in Ghana, something similar happened in Mali. Like Ghana, Mali was going through a difficult period in the mid-1960s. The aftermath of the Tuareg rebellion in the North, plus a generalized economic malaise following currency devaluation and austerity measures, made Modibo Keïta's government vulnerable to popular discontent. In 1966, the US-RDA government dissolved parliament and suspended the constitution in an attempt to weather the storm through repression. However, the government lost the support of part of the armed forces, which had never shared Keïta's resolve to build socialism in Mali. On November 19, 1968, a group of army officers, headed by Moussa Traoré, ordered their troops to encircle Bamako and capture Keïta, who was forcibly deposed and arrested. The officers run Mali as a collective for a couple of months. In 1969, the Comité Militaire de Libération Nationale ceded power to Traoré himself, who instituted a harsh military regime that lasted until 1991, when a new coup deposed him. Keïta, together with other prominent members of the US-RDA, remained imprisoned in an internment camp in Kidal, in the North of the country.[39]

The soldiers in Mali behaved like the soldiers in Ghana. They stopped Keïta's ailing program of socialist-inspired development and expelled all Soviet and socialist-bloc personnel from Mali. Besides formal protests, there was nothing the Soviet government could or would do. Likewise, neither the Johnson nor the Nixon administrations seemed too preoccupied with Mali. Thus, Mali slid out of the focus of both superpowers, at least until the mid-1970s, when the Bamako government was hungry for Soviet weapons. Meanwhile, Mali re-entered the

French orbit. Since the late 1960s, France has remained Mali's largest aid donor and main trade partner.[40]

Sékou Touré's regime in Guinea was the only one to survive the end of the 1960s. The PDG government maintained a somewhat schizophrenic foreign policy, alternating moments of rapprochement and tumultuous ruptures with the USSR, the United States, and China. Despite relative economic isolation, growing indebtedness, and a generally poor economic performance, Guinea not only survived but became directly involved in the liberation struggle in West Africa, offering assistance in the fight against the Portuguese in Guinea-Bissau. In 1970, a group of soldiers from Guinea-Bissau loyal to Portugal launched an operation against Conakry, hoping to overthrow Sékou Touré. Guinean forces managed to repel the attack, and the PDG government inaugurated a long period of repression against plotters. Careful not to alienate the armed forces and ready to launch successive waves of repression against real and imagined enemies, Sékou Touré remained in power until the mid-1980s. Shortly after his death, Lansana Conté, an army officer, took power following a coup in 1985. The PDG and all its satellite organizations were outlawed and disbanded. Most surviving members of Sékou Touré's government, including Béavogui and Ismaël Touré, were arrested and executed. The last remains of Guinea's radical orientation died with them. However, the profound changes of the long Sékou Touré era continue to shape life in the country today. Mike McGovern argued that the socialism pursued by the PDG government, despite its repressive violence, managed to create a new Guinean identity that still holds the country together, helping it escape conflict and civil war in the face of difficult economic conditions.[41]

Nkrumah and Keïta were not the only radical African leaders to be overthrown in coups in those years, and Sékou Touré was not the only one to change his country's political outlook multiple times. As Jean Allman wrote, if the birth of the independent African nation-state inaugurated the "global sixties" as an era of hope and political experimentation, a succession of coups—often supported by the West—closed it and ushered in the consolidation of the US empire founded on neoliberalism. Lumumba was the first to go, followed a few years later by Ben Bella in Algeria, Nkrumah in Ghana, and Keïta in Mali. But radicals were on the retreat everywhere: in 1964, the Brazilian army deposed Goulart and installed a military regime. The same year, Nehru died. Sukarno was removed from power by a group of army generals in 1966. In 1970, a heart attack took Nasser's life. By that point, the United States had tried to oust Castro at least a couple of times, and a bloody war had been raging in Vietnam for almost a decade. An entire generation of radical anti-imperialist leaders, in Africa and elsewhere, had been wiped out by the end of the 1960s.[42]

The Soviet Union remained with very few friends in the Third World. After Khrushchev's own fall from power in 1964, it mattered less. Confidence in the mixed economic model the USSR had been selling the Third World was shattered. The new Soviet leadership took refuge in more traditional ways of engaging the rest of the world.

Development's Little Helpers

Change did not happen only at the top. In the second half of the 1960s, virtually the entire apparatus that had inspired, guided, and carried out the USSR's vision of exporting development to West Africa underwent profound changes. Degtiar', perhaps the person that more than anyone else had embodied the Soviet project in West Africa, left his post of ambassador to Guinea in December 1964. He returned to GKES, where he resumed his old job as deputy head of the organization. He retired shortly thereafter, in 1969. Degtiar' was replaced in Conakry by Aleksei L. Voronin, a career diplomat who had served in Iran and Turkey beforehand. He was an experienced functionary of MID, but his background was in Middle Eastern affairs, and he did not have any particular experience in economic matters. Extensive economic cooperation between the Soviet Union and Guinea was a thing of the past.[43]

With Khrushchev gone, the coups in Ghana and Mali, and a change of course in Guinea, the Institute of Africa in Moscow found itself short of work. Up to that point, the institute's record had been far from satisfactory. Created in late 1959 together with other specialized and area studies institutions, its official purpose was to develop expertise about Africa and guide Soviet policy toward a new region of interest. Despite the initial enthusiasm and the frequent grand declarations of intents, the institute struggled with limited funding and poor coordination with other agencies that dealt with Africa. Between 1959 and 1964, the institute repeatedly complained about its meager budget, which made it impossible to receive and translate literature from Africa, let alone organize fieldwork and research trips for fellows. Building expertise when only a tiny minority of professors, researchers, and doctoral students could travel to Africa proved nearly impossible. The Institute of Africa's publication record suffered. At the time of foundation, the institute was supposed to produce a dozen major books by 1962–1963. Despite a workforce that expanded to 130 in 1962, by the summer of 1964 only one book had been published (on "forms of colonialism" in Africa). The edited volume on the "path to development" of newly independent African states, which was considered the first task of the institute in 1959, had not even been started. In June 1964, the institute's faculty estimated the book would be completed by the end of 1966, rather optimistically. Given these premises, it is not surprising that that the world of Soviet policymaking took relatively little notice of the institute's work. The occasional joint conferences organized with representatives of MID, GKES, and other agencies tended to deteriorate in a barrage of mutual accusations of not taking each other's work seriously.[44]

Shortly before Khrushchev's fall from power, the Institute of Africa took another blow. In September 1964, Potekhin stepped down as director of the institute because of health problems. He died a few days later. Like Degtiar', Potekhin had embodied the USSR's push to establish itself as a reliable political and economic partner for the leaderships of postcolonial Africa. One of the relatively few Soviet scholars who had been able to spend time in Africa, Potekhin was considered a pioneer of African studies in the USSR. Although not a specialist in economic matters, he had firmly supported the provision of aid and technical expertise to Ghana, Guinea, and Mali. Potekhin maintained that the kind of development the most radical African countries were building was different from simple capitalism, and that the Soviet Union had the duty to support it. As the director of the Institute of Africa, his was the only voice to which the Kremlin leadership, MID and GKES paid some serious attention.[45]

Potekhin was replaced by Vasilii G. Solodovnikov, who was parachuted in from the Soviet delegation to the United Nations in New York. Not an Africanist by training, Solodovnikov's background was in foreign trade. He, too, was convinced of the necessity to engage with postcolonial Africa and in time became an influential figure in the USSR, especially with regard to the fight against apartheid in Southern Africa. However, at the beginning of his tenure as director of the Institute of Africa, Solodovnikov made it clear that "our state and party relations with a series of African countries have become different from what they were in 1959." The USSR should still provide assistance to newly independent African countries, but this time paying attention to their internal conditions. Solodovnikov warned against "adventurism" and critiqued "bourgeois" ideas about development. In his view, research at the Institute of Africa should focus on economics and economic planning but at the same time take into consideration questions of class, ideology, and social problems. It was a return to tradition and the shape of things to come.[46]

Outside of the Soviet Union, the experts and advisers that had participated in the search for development in West Africa in the first decade or so after independence continued their careers with mixed results. After his disappointing experience in Ghana, Arthur Lewis returned to the Caribbean to take up the position of vice-chancellor of the University College of the West Indies in 1959. In 1963, he was appointed professor of political economy at the Woodrow Wilson School of Public and International Affairs of Princeton University, where he remained until his death in 1991. At Princeton, Lewis scaled down his commitment to advising and consulting for Third World governments, focusing mostly on teaching and research. In 1965, he published a book inspired by his experience in Ghana, titled *Politics in West Africa*. In it, Lewis criticized the trend in West Africa for forming systems with strong governments or even one-party states. Reinstating his conviction that Western-style democratic institutions and market mechanisms were the key to economic success, he also lamented the lack of experience and the political naivety of young radical officials in the CPP and other West African political organizations.[47] In 1979, Lewis was awarded the Nobel memorial prize for economics, in recognition of his pioneering work in the field of development economics. His basic intuition—that surplus labor needs to move from subsistence agriculture into manufacturing for economic growth to happen—continues to inspire development economists today.[48]

Charles Bettelheim—the prominent French Marxist economist who advised the Guinean government—received accolades of a different kind. Bettelheim's Center for the Study of Modes of Industrialization at the EHESS was a leading institution for radical Third World governments looking for ideas and inspiration. Bettelheim personally worked with a number of them, most notably in Cuba when Ernesto "Che" Guevara took charge of the country's economy. In Paris, Bettelheim was a well-known participant in the debates of the French left at the time, taking the side of Louis Althusser, a personal friend of his. After 1968, when a new generation of radicals began to challenge the ways of the French left, Bettelheim found himself more isolated. At the same time, many of the experiments with economic radicalism in the Third World he had supported failed, and postcolonial governments looked increasingly at traditional economic remedies. Bettelheim took (intellectual) refuge in China in the decade of the Cultural Revolution. However, when China too embarked on a different path after 1976, his uncompromising Marxist approach to the economy made Bettelheim unpopular, even among old friends and acquaintances. He remained committed to his view of Marxism until his death in 2006.[49]

Coda

Khrushchev died in September 1971, at the age of seventy-seven. He was the first Soviet leader not to be buried in the Kremlin wall, where his predecessors lay, but in Moscow's Novodevich'e Cemetery. Nkrumah died six months later, in April 1972. He was in Bucharest to receive treatment for prostate cancer. He was sixty-three. Nkrumah's body was initially sent to Guinea, where he had been an exile since his overthrow, before the new Ghanaian government agreed to bury him in his native Nkroful. In 1992, Nkrumah's remains were transferred to a mausoleum in Accra. It was built on the site where he had declared Ghana independent from the British empire thirty-five years prior. Keïta remained a prisoner in Kidal until early 1977, when he was transferred back to Bamako, possibly in preparation for his release. He died in May 1977, at the age of sixty-two, in circumstances that remain unclear. A monument commemorating Keïta was inaugurated in Bamako in the summer of 1999. Sékou Touré lived until March 1984, when he succumbed to complications while undergoing heart surgery in Cleveland, Ohio, also at the age of sixty-two. His body was buried in the Grand Mosque in Conakry, built in 1982 using funds from Saudi Arabia, where it remains to this day.

The tribulations of all leaders involved in the Soviet project in West Africa, in some cases even decades after their death, show how complex the legacy of socialist development was, and to a certain extent still is. Soon after the termination of Soviet extensive engagement in Ghana, Guinea, and Mali, it seemed that a similar experience was unlikely to be ever repeated. The official indictment of Khrushchev, published in *Pravda* a few days after his resignation in October 1964, did not explicitly mention West Africa, or even the Third World in general. The wording of the editorial, however, could have been easily used to attack the former first secretary's line of conduct in Ghana, Guinea, and Mali: "harebrained scheming, half-baked conclusions and hasty decisions and actions divorced from reality, bragging and bluster."[50] In the mid-1950s, the Soviet leadership had accepted with enthusiasm the challenge of exporting a model of development and contributing to building a new society in West Africa. In the mid-1960s, it gave up. Hope turned into disappointment as the costs of cooperation with Ghana, Guinea, and Mali continued to grow and results on the ground failed to materialize. The new leaders who replaced Khrushchev at the end of 1964 were determined not to make what, from their point of view, had been major mistakes. For the first few years of the Brezhnev/Kosygin ticket, the days of extensive engagement with the Third World seemed past.

Staying out of Africa proved impossible for Brezhnev as it had been for Khrushchev. Even West Africa was not completely written off the map after 1964. A return to extensive economic cooperation was out of the question, but commercial exchanges were still possible. As explained above, the USSR continued to buy cocoa from Ghana. Furthermore, in late 1969 the Soviet government extended a loan to Guinea to develop the bauxite resources in Débélé, located halfway between Conakry and Kindia. The project included the realization of the necessary infrastructure, including a rail link to the capital, and specified that the facilities would remain under Guinean control after completion. The loan was large—100 million US dollars, one of the largest that the USSR ever conceded to a Third World country. The government of Guinea would pay the loan back using the bauxite extracted from the Débélé site. The project was completed in 1973, and the first shipload of Débélé bauxite was sent in early 1974 from Conakry to Zaporozh'e in then-Soviet Ukraine to be transformed into aluminum.[51]

On the surface, the Débélé project seemed a continuation—indeed an intensification, given the scale—of the previous Soviet engagement in Guinea. A large loan to develop mining infrastructure, to be paid back using a local resource, and maintaining Guinean ownership of the plant. However, the Débélé project took shape in a different context and responded to different necessities. Developing a new site for bauxite mining was a stand-alone project and not part of a coordinated effort to modernize Guinea's economy. The Soviet government was no longer involved in the drafting of a development plan or in the identification of priorities for Sékou Touré's government. The USSR was simply a commercial partner necessary to Guinea to exploit its natural resources, just like what US, French, and Canadian companies were already doing in other bauxite sites such as Fria and Boké.

Moreover, the Soviet decision to finance a new mine in Guinea followed a precise commercial logic. In the post–World World II era, global demand for aluminum had been continually growing and reached its peak in the second half of the 1960s. The Soviet Union, thanks to its huge hydroelectric capacity, was well placed to boost its production and aimed to become the single largest producer of aluminum in the world. Although the USSR had significant bauxite reserves, its quality was not especially high, making the production of aluminum relatively expensive. To respond to increased demand and improve the overall aluminum production process, since the late 1960s the Soviet government imported significant amounts of high-quality bauxite from Yugoslavia, Greece, Turkey, and Guinea, which has the largest reserves of bauxite in the world. It was in this context that the decision was made to invest in bauxite extraction in Débélé. The possibility for the Soviet Union to help the development of Guinea's mining industry, in exchange for bauxite, had been raised multiple times by Sékou Touré in the 1960s. However, the Khrushchev leadership shunned the project and advised its Guinean allies to focus on agriculture first. Under Brezhnev, this decision was reversed following a change in commercial interests. The Débélé site is to this day managed and partly owned by RUSAL, the Russian aluminum company.[52]

Besides commercial exchanges, Moscow's interest in liberation movements in central and southern Africa continued, and in some cases deepened, during the Brezhnev era. As Solodovnikov implied when taking office at the Institute of Africa, one of the USSR's mistakes during the 1950s and 1960s had been to rely too much on bourgeois leaders. Therefore, since the second half of the 1960s, the Soviet agencies and departments that dealt with Africa began to focus more on leaders and movements that claimed Marxist sympathies. In what was then still the Portuguese empire, the Movimento Popular de Libertação de Angola, the Frente de Libertação de Moçambique (FRELIMO) and the Partido Africano da Independência da Guiné e Cabo Verde all matched this description. Led by Marxist-inspired intellectuals, they aimed to free their territories from imperial domination resorting to all means necessary, including violence. Nkrumah, Sékou Touré, and Keïta were heads of government interested in experimenting with state socialism. Leaders like Agostinho Neto, Samora Machel, and Amílcar Cabral were revolutionaries whose first priority was liberation from Portuguese domination. They were far less hesitant than their West African predecessors to define themselves as Marxists or even Marxist-Leninists.[53]

For about a decade, the USSR provided technical expertise, propaganda advice, and in some cases military training and equipment to liberation movements in southern Africa. While this was a far less extensive engagement than economic aid and technical cooperation to Ghana, Guinea, and Mali during the 1950s and 1960s, it tied the Soviet Union to the region and opened the door for a grand return to the African continent in the second half of the 1970s. Since 1975, the Soviet government was directly involved in the Angolan civil war and its aftermath, in the continuation of the struggle against apartheid in Southern Africa, and from the mid-1970s on in sustaining Ethiopia following the revolution that overthrew Haile Selassie. In all these instances, the military dimension was paramount. The USSR provided weapons, equipment, tactical advice, and occasionally commanding officers and troops to support an ally at war against enemies usually sponsored by the West and/or China. Development still played an important role, but a secondary one compared with the previous engagement in West Africa. In Angola and Ethiopia, the Soviet Union stayed in the country following a successful military campaign, assisting the local government with the construction of socialism in the newly liberated or secured territory. This, however, resembles much more a case of "mission creep," as analysts call it. The Soviet priority was ensuring the survival of a new ally, which tended to require the provision of economic aid and technical expertise on a large scale. In Mozambique, where Soviet military engagement was less driven by the military, the development dimension may have been more pronounced from the beginning. However, whether the Soviet leadership regarded its engagement with Angola, Ethiopia, Mozambique, and eventually Afghanistan as the dawn of a new model of development in the Third World is a question that historians are still exploring.[54]

In West Africa, the Soviet Union was not pushed out by superior Western aid or by more serious Chinese commitments. The USSR failed to establish a model of development in the region because of its own inability to bear the costs of modernization—political as well as economic costs. What appeared promising in 1955 became onerous in 1965. The intensification of the Cold War, the USSR's generally poor economic performance at home, and the rising costs of cooperation abroad dented the Soviet leadership's resolve to continue investing in Ghana, Guinea, and Mali. Coups in Moscow and in West Africa ended meaningful cooperation and nearly cut off the Soviet Union from Africa completely.

However, not all was lost. State capitalism, and the wish to construct an alternative to capitalist development in the Third World, did not end with the termination of the Soviet project in Ghana, Guinea, and Mali. It even survived the Soviet Union.

CONCLUSION

Wandering around West Africa today, one would struggle to find traces of past Soviet presence. The shape and size of a few public buildings in capital cities may suggest a certain affinity with Soviet aesthetics. Wandering farther, one may encounter crumbling collective farms half-reclaimed by the forest, railway tracks whose gauge fits no European train, rusty tractors made in Cheliabinsk or Volgograd. A visitor to most university departments in Legon, Conakry, or Bamako would encounter elderly professors whose doctorate was awarded by Moscow or Leningrad State University, or perhaps by Novosibirsk State Technical University.

These are meager remains. They pale in comparison to the Aswan Dam, the Bhilai steel plant, the streets clogged with Ladas of Addis Ababa, the Soviet-style residential *mikroraiony* of Hanoi, and the gems (or monsters, depending on one's point of view) of Soviet modernism in Havana. And yet, the relatively few and scattered traces of Soviet involvement in Ghana, Guinea, and Mali hide a story of engagement as deep and complex as anywhere else in the Third World. The Soviet attempt to export a model of modernization in West Africa run deeper and wider than elsewhere. Nowhere else had Soviet economists, planners, agronomists, engineers such open access to the very creation of a development strategy. GKES specialists and trade experts shaped all stages of conceptualizing and pursuing development. They participated in the identification of priorities, the drafting of yearly plans, the estimation of necessary human and material resources, their costing, the construction and supervision of development projects, and—more often than not—their subsequent dismissal in the most economical way possible.

Despite its lack of tangible results, the history of the Soviet search for development in the Third World had West Africa at its center. The gargantuan projects the USSR pursued in India and Egypt, among others, were much bigger than anything Moscow ever considered realizing in West Africa. However, they tended to be one-off enterprises rather than part of a coherent overall development strategy elaborated by local governments in conjunction with the Soviet Union from the very beginning. For the USSR, the pursuit of development in West Africa was not simply a matter of financing and building. Rather, the first dimension of Soviet engagement in Ghana, Guinea, and Mali was intellectual. How to solve the problem of development? What solutions would be appropriate to tackle the many issues that newly independent countries faced? The answer the Soviet Union proposed was ambitious, even though it was not particularly original. Rather than sponsoring an impossible search for communism, Soviet planners and advisers recommended a hybrid model centered on the establishment of an expansive state sector as the engine of modernization. Although the Soviet answer to the development question was the same everywhere, it was only in West Africa that the USSR could shape the entirety of a modernization strategy, at least outside of the socialist world.

This was possible because of special circumstances. Ghana, Guinea, and Mali emerged from decades of colonial domination with the strong will to seek rapid modernization. Western assistance—whether from the former colonial powers or from the United States—proved either unavailable or disappointing. The appeal of the Soviet Union peaked right at that time. A decade of fast economic growth, widely publicized technological exploits, and Khrushchev's new policy of openness toward the post-colonial world made the USSR the obvious model at which to look. Whereas Western governments dragged their feet or proposed ideas and models that always privileged the market and the private sector, the USSR offered to put the state at the center of West Africa's search for modernization. This was the vision that the radical leaderships of Ghana, Guinea, and Mali were looking for. For a while, this looked like a match made in heaven.

Things became complicated soon. The Soviet Union was not simply asked to realize one or more construction projects, but to inspire, finance, and supervise an entire development strategy from beginning to end. Soviet specialists worked together with Ghanaian, Guinean and Malian politicians, economists, and technicians on every aspect of economic life. The pursuit of development, as imagined in Moscow, Accra, Conakry, and Bamako meant that everything was connected. Creating local light industry that would reduce a country's need to import basic goods from Europe required not just designing and building a plant. Construction work needed bricks, cement, and energy, which themselves needed to be first produced and then transported to the building site. Transportation needed basic infrastructure—roads, railways, power plants—and vehicles—trucks, jeeps, railcars, wires. Those needed to be imported, and thus the local government needed a reliable trade network that allowed them to procure industrial goods and materials in exchange for commodities and agricultural products. Once construction work began, builders, engineers, and translators needed to be supplied, fed, and paid. Local governments needed control over money and banking to be able to finance their development strategies. The Soviet Union helped draft the plans, build the roads, survey the soil, move workers and materials, exchange goods and services internationally, manage the money supply, and create new credit institutions. The search for development in West Africa came to equal the pursuit of an independent economic life in its totality.

The colonial overtones of the Soviet project in Ghana, Guinea, and Mali were obvious. Even though many of the development projects sponsored by the USSR were never completed, such a profound engagement with the economies and societies of Ghana, Guinea, and Mali had happened only during the colonial era. The Soviet Union effectively replaced Britain and France as a provider of capital, financier, and supervisor of development projects, and—for some at least—the main source of political inspiration. Of course, Soviet officials always maintained that they had been asked to provide assistance by the local governments. In their view, the plans they came up with cut old dependency links and pushed newly independent countries toward having an independent economy too. Whether this was enough to distinguish Soviet engagement from other, contemporary forms of neocolonialism is beyond the scope of this book.

What is clear was that the complexity of development in West Africa was too much for the Soviet Union. At multiple stages along the way, things went wrong. Estimates proved inaccurate, costs too high, exchanges too complicated, the soil too treacherous, and the people too quarrelsome. Crucially, the Soviet and the West African governments' visions of development, which had seemed so close at the beginning, began to diverge. People in Accra, Conakry, and Bamako were concerned about results. In Moscow, they worried about keeping costs down. Already before Khrushchev's fall from power, Soviet engagement in Ghana, Guinea, and Mali had become an exercise in damage control. What had started as an ambitious program to assist new states' transition from the colonial era into modernity became a petty argument about who was going to pay for what.

As a consequence, Soviet involvement in West Africa is usually described as an unmitigated disaster. Was it? Would approaches different from the Soviet one have been more effective? More than fifty years after the end of Soviet engagement, Ghana, Guinea, and Mali still struggle with some of the same problems. Over the years, a wide variety of recipes and counter-recipes have been tried by a succession of West African governments and international organizations. Fiscal conservatism, devaluation, and structural adjustment have produced mixed results, just like public spending and state investment did in the 1960s. Today, the governments in Accra, Conakry, and Bamako are still pursuing some of the same development projects that the USSR helped to conceptualize some six decades ago. Some have been completed only in the 2000s and 2010s.

Regardless of its relative success or failure, Soviet engagement in West Africa remains a prime example of the USSR's approach to economic development abroad.

Everything in Its Right Place: The USSR, West Africa, and Import Substitution

The conditions in which Ghana, Guinea, and Mali found themselves after independence were harsh. The vignette of African economies and societies stuck in the fifteenth century due to colonial exploitation was a classic of Soviet propaganda. It was far from reality in the vibrant societies of West Africa at the dawn of independence, but the new governments of Ghana, Guinea, and Mali undeniably faced severe challenges. The more cautious Soviet diagnosis of the problem identified the need to break traditional links of dependency on the former colonial masters as the heart of the matter. This required boosting agricultural productivity to guarantee what development experts today call food security, creating local light industry to produce at home what usually was imported from abroad, and building modern infrastructure to supply energy, provide connections, and distribute goods and commodities.

The Soviet vision corresponded with the ambition of the new governments in Accra, Conakry, and Bamako. All three believed in the need for rapid modernization, and all three were radical enough to reject the advice that came from the West. The architecture of the Soviet/West African search for modernity had much in common with the basic tenets of import substitution development strategies. In broad terms, these were an activist state that identified the sectors to be developed and provided conspicuous investment, and a coordinated effort aimed at decreasing imports and boosting exports. Import-substitution has a long tradition in the political economy of development. Outside of Europe, Japan from the Meiji restoration of the 1870s to the 1980s, South Korea and Taiwan since the 1950s, India from independence until the late 1970s, and Brazil and Mexico in the 1960s and 1970s can all be said to have employed policies not dissimilar from those recommended by the USSR in West Africa.

It is in this tradition that Soviet engagement in Ghana, Guinea, and Mali should be placed historically and understood historiographically. Just as much as the Cold War, socialist internationalism, or the need to join the global econ-omy, it was its idea of development that guided the USSR's entry into West Af-rica and determined its exit a few years later. The Soviet vision of modernization for Ghana, Guinea, and Mali was founded on the belief that dependency needed to be overcome and that state investment offered the best chance of success. How-ever, to be successful, import-substitution often needed support from abroad. This was clear both to the Soviet leadership and to the governments in West Af-rica. Self-sufficiency was impossible for relatively small countries like Ghana, Guinea, and Mali. For a time, the USSR aspired to be for West Africa what Japan and the United States were for South Korea during the 1950s and 1960s: lender of capital, provider of technology, and source of inspiration. However, Ja-pan and the United States invested in South Korea because of the Korean War first, and then simply looking for profit. The Soviet Union invested in West Af-rica due to a strong belief in the relevance of the model of development it of-fered. Once confidence in this model began to be questioned in Moscow, the willingness to invest in Ghana, Guinea, and Mali quickly disappeared.

The absence of profit as motivation partly sets the Soviet model apart. Atul Kohli, one of the most prominent scholars of state-directed development, has written that: "State intervention in rapid industrializers was often characterized by market-reinforcing behavior, understood in the sense of supporting profit-ability for private investors. . . . The state versus market mind-set thus is simply not very helpful for understanding how the interaction of states and markets has served to produce a range of economic outcomes."[1]

Kohli argued that in successful states that pursued an import-substitution agenda, such as South Korea and to a lesser extent Brazil and India, state inter-vention fostered favorable conditions for private investors and created new mar-kets altogether. This was clearly not the case in West Africa. The Soviet strategy for Ghana, Guinea, and Mali was based on state-directed investment that let markets survive and even thrive to an extent, but favored state ownership and collective enterprise. In the galaxy of import-substitution, the coordinated Soviet-West African effort occupied a decidedly leftist, *dirigiste* position.

Once again, this was not new or exceptional. Ghana, Guinea, and Mali were certainly not the first newly independent countries that aspired to build a strong state. At the same time, Soviet experts and advisers were not the first to believe that keeping markets in check would be the best strategy to modernize, and they would not be the last. Countries like South Korea, but also Brazil and India, had already undergone at least some degree of industrialization by the mid-twentieth century. They could think about the ratio between state and market in the do-mestic economy and their relationship to the global economy from a position of relative strength. Things were different in Ghana, Guinea, and Mali. The absence of industry and the pressing need for basic infrastructure did not leave much room for maneuver: the alternative was either channeling state investment and relying on favorable credit from the socialist world, or having to accept dependence on private foreign capital, usually from the former colonial powers. As the second option was politically unacceptable, the governments of Ghana, Guinea, and Mali settled for a model of development that stressed state over market even more strongly than in other contexts that experimented with import-substitution. The Soviet Union supported this form of state capitalism.

It was precisely confidence in this hybrid development model that motivated the USSR's engagement in Ghana, Guinea, and Mali. The idea that the Soviet Union built economic relations with the Third World to become more integrated into the global capitalist economy certainly makes sense, given the weaknesses of the Soviet system. This book provides ample evidence in this sense: Soviet trade organizations were clearly conscious of the USSR's need to obtain resources from abroad and did not believe that autarky could be possible—for the USSR, and even less so for its allies in West Africa. International trade was a necessity.

However, until about 1964, the argument that the USSR aimed to use trade with former colonies in West Africa to increase its commercial exchanges with the capitalist world is difficult to sustain. Looking at Soviet exchanges with Ghana, Guinea, and Mali, it becomes clear that there was not much of an international market in the region in the first place. Imperial trade was still prominent. Colonial-era businesses dominated the economies of Ghana, Guinea, and Mali, largely thanks to links of convenience and sometimes patronage with the local governments. These were closed networks, which London and Paris intended on keeping isolated from external interference, whether capitalist or socialist. In the early Khrushchev era, the USSR tried to disrupt these links. The Soviet government entered in direct competition with former colonial businesses and their political backers. The case of Ghana is indicative. No attempt was made on the part of the Soviet Union to become integrated into the existing cocoa trade, or even just to adapt to its rules. The goal was to replace it entirely with barter agreements. The Soviet decision to trade with Ghana (and with Guinea and Mali) aimed to reduce the influx of private capital from the West, thus opening the way for state investment in cooperation with the socialist world. Soviet attitudes changed in the second half of the 1960s, and the USSR's exchanges with West Africa easily fit the search for international economic integration (and, why not, profit) in this second phase.

Before then, profitability was a minor consideration in Soviet-West African exchanges. The agricultural commodities and raw materials Ghana, Guinea, and Mali could offer were of virtually no value to the Soviet economy. Everything that was in West Africa's sub-soil could be found in the Soviet Union as well, and most products from West Africa could be obtained elsewhere, often at better prices. The case of trade with Mali is illustrative: the peanuts Moscow bought were neither particularly in demand nor relatively cheap. However, they served the double purpose of allowing Mali to acquire from the USSR the goods and commodities it needed, while at the same time cutting Mali's existing links to France. Trade was therefore unambiguously subordinated to the overall development strategy. This development strategy was itself subordinated to the Soviet vision of the Cold War during the Khrushchev era. Establishing an alternative model of development in the Third World became a key objective for the USSR in open competition with the Western world. Even though it was an economic Cold War, rather than military or diplomatic, competition between the West and the socialist world was still at its core.

Eye of the Beholder: Soviet/Socialist/ Noncapitalist Development

An economic Cold War may have been, but what exactly was the difference between the two sides? The approach to modernization and economic development that the USSR aimed to export to Ghana, Guinea, and Mali had little to do with communism. The most striking element is the balance between agriculture and industry that the Soviet Union regarded as appropriate for West Africa. The Soviet way to manage the economy is usually assumed to focus on central planning and a strict preference for heavy industrialization, at home as well as abroad. In the case of West Africa, this is a misconception. From the early stages of the USSR's engagement in Ghana, Guinea, and Mali, Soviet leaders, advisers, and technicians focused squarely on agriculture as the principal sector to modernize. The expansion of light industry to reduce imports from Europe was an important element, too, but pushing for the development of heavy industry was never in the Soviet plan. If anything, the USSR resisted pressure from the local governments to focus more on industrialization. To use a simple metaphor, when interacting with the Soviet Union the governments of Ghana, Guinea, and Mali expected a Stalinist five-year plan but were given NEP instead.

Is this enough to conclude that the Soviet approach was just the same as the Western one? There were certainly many similarities. Both Cold War sides believed in the necessity to improve infrastructure, modernize agricultural production, and eventually develop industry in Ghana, Guinea, and Mali. Many of the projects the USSR sponsored and supervised in all three countries derived from ideas that the old colonial governments had initially studied. In some cases, the Soviet Union and the West bid to realize the exact same thing—for example, the Soviet government would have been happy to take over the construction of the Volta River dam in Ghana had the West given up on it. More broadly, both the Soviet Union and the West tended to analyze the necessities and challenges of development in West Africa through the prevalent approaches of the time: relatively large-scale projects, relatively high levels of state intervention in the economy, and a relatively loose monetary policy. They both followed high modernist approaches to society and production.

And yet, concluding that the Soviet and the Western vision of development in West Africa was the same is an oversimplification. Surely, the USSR and the West shared some assumptions and many ideas. However, what they had in common was much more superficial than what they disagreed upon. Here, the devil is not in the details but in the bigger picture. There was nothing inherently socialist or capitalist in the way a dam was to be built, rice cultivated, or fish caught. There were, however, crucial differences between how the socialist world and the West imagined that a dam could be financed, a farm be administered, or a new fishing community be organized.

First, the USSR and the West had two completely different understandings of the extent the state should participate in the economic life of Ghana, Guinea, and Mali. This was obvious from the way Soviet, as opposed to Western, advisers discussed development with West African interlocutors. American and European advisers extolled the virtues of the private sector and of traditional exports. Their Soviet counterparts stressed the need to channel state investment and to seek shelter from predatory foreign companies. This was more than rhetoric. The Western conception of modernization in West Africa was that state investment was an inescapable necessity, but it was private capital that the governments of Ghana, Guinea, and Mali should strive to attract. The Soviet vision was the opposite. While markets were tolerated, it was the state that needed to shoulder the lion's share of investment and supervision for modernization. Both were hybrid systems, which mixed and matched elements of different traditions. Nonetheless, the Soviet approach was unabashedly state-centric, whereas the Western vision remained focused on the market.

This was no trivial difference, as the governments of Ghana, Guinea, and Mali understood. Their choice of approach was based on a precise vision. They appreciated the Soviet project because it promised to build modern and strong states, an ambition they all shared after independence. At the same time, they were also aware that the Western approach guaranteed the convenience of remaining part of the international economic networks of which Ghana, Guinea, and Mali had been part for decades. Classic Cold War narratives would have Third World countries play one side against the other to obtain more resources to pursue homogenous modernization projects. Looking more in detail at Soviet engagement in West Africa reveals this idea as inaccurate and superficial. There certainly was a competition between East and West. However, this was based on different approaches, diverging ideas, and opposite promises.

Besides the basic difference between a state-centered and a market-centered approach to development, there were other factors that separated the Soviet view from the Western one. Their notion of ownership was certainly not the same. Once completed, Soviet development projects, not just in West Africa, were property of the local government. The Soviet Union offered loans and expertise to realize the project, but the local government remained in control and was free to use whatever was built in collaboration with the USSR in the way it preferred. Arrangements with the West tended to be different. The case of the Volta River project in Ghana shows that the US government, its European allies, and also international organizations had strong ideas about how projects should not only be constructed but managed as well. The dominant role of private businesses in the Volta project was designed to last well after the completion of the dam and the aluminum smelter that Western capital financed.

Though the Volta case was an especially controversial one, the general Western approach always had openness to private investors at its heart. This was consistent with the broad belief that development in Ghana, Guinea, and Mali should be sought through market mechanisms rather than state supervision. The Western vision was founded on the construction of a business-friendly economic environment in West Africa, which managed to attract foreign capital with the promise of significant profit. The Soviet vision was that of a strong state sector acting as the prime engine of economic development, which tolerated for-profit private operators but did not need them to finance growth. The most obvious example of this difference is the management of public finances. The West recommended strong, independent central banks, able to print money but also to limit inflation and guarantee attractive interest rates for foreign investors. The USSR insisted that monetary policy should be under the total and absolute control of the local governments in West Africa. The needs of development trumped those of financial stability. In Ghana, Guinea, and Mali, the USSR maintained a strictly political understanding of money; the West had a more purely financial one.

Similarly, the USSR and its Western competitors had very different ideas about the management and organization of the projects they sponsored after completion. Tools and techniques were the same—a dam is a dam, and a tractor is a tractor—but who controlled them and how was a matter of debate at the core of the competition for development in West Africa. In line with its traditions, the Soviet Union favored state ownership of the means of production in Ghana, Guinea, and Mali. Large infrastructure projects, in particular, were meant to remain in the hands of the local governments. Industry and, above all, agriculture allowed for more flexibility. Farms and factories were not necessarily built to become the property of the West African governments. On the contrary, with the exception of a few large-scale projects, the expectation was that they would be run by cooperatives. The cooperative model, which the Soviet Union supported in West Africa, was based on the idea of a group of citizens who pooled resources to manage production collectively. A fishing cooperative or a small-scale collective farm had access to state capital and state supervision, including Soviet equipment and experts, but were left free to determine their level of production, set the prices, and choose techniques.

This was far from the collectivization of Soviet agriculture and the strict central planning of Soviet industry. At the same time, it also differed from the Western model, which remained focused on individual as opposed to collective entrepreneurship. Once again, this was no trivial difference. When governments in West Africa chose the Soviet approach, they did so knowing that statism and collectivism, and not communism, would play a major role in their country's economy. The politicians in Accra, Bamako, and Conakry who supported the USSR believed that collectivism would help the construction of a strong society and ultimately of a strong state. Those who opposed the Soviet Union were suspicious of the idea of a strong state and argued in favor of the Western mantra of the individual's search for profit. This was the essence of the contest for development in West Africa.

What was the place of the Soviet Union in this contest? Despite the many similarities with the ideas and policies of its Western rivals, the USSR built a specific position for itself in Ghana, Guinea, and Mali. The Soviet philosophy of development put the state before the market and the collective before the individual. This was a precise political choice that corresponded to deeply held beliefs in Moscow and equally deeply held ambitions in Accra, Bamako, and Conakry. The search for development and modernization was a political project before an economic enterprise or a technical challenge.

Where exactly did this political project sit on the communism-capitalism spectrum? This is a more difficult question to answer. In no small part, this depended (and still depends) on the eye of the beholder. The Soviet academics, politicians, and advisers involved with Ghana, Guinea, and Mali during the Khrushchev era were sure that what they were building in West Africa was not communism. What exactly it was remained a matter of debate, but the key thing was that the development they were pursuing was noncapitalist. That was enough for them.

West African leaders were just as comfortable with this indeterminacy. Their political and economic vision was neither capitalist nor communist but could be socialist or simply specifically African. African socialism was perhaps their preferred term of reference for their project, which frequently irked their Soviet colleagues. Samir Amin believed in it instead. In 1965, shortly after his stint working in Mali's Ministry of Planning ended, Amin argued that the socialist option of Ghana, Guinea, and Mali was still the best bet to pursue development, despite its many problems and the pitfalls of foreign aid from the Soviet bloc. The series of coups in the late 1960s put an end to this experiment in West Africa, but Amin remained a believer in socialist development to the end of his days.[2]

Western beholders harbored the least doubts. CIA agents, US ambassadors, European businessmen, and their local clients often referred to Ghana, Guinea, and Mali as communist with little hesitation. Their rigid view of the Cold War allowed no indeterminacy. This was an enemy to fight. Others in the US, Europe, and the rest of West Africa disagreed, but tended to play along for the sake of capitalist unity.

The historians of today are even less certain of what development, and specifically Soviet-style development in the Third World, was than Soviet advisers, African politicians, or CIA agents. Historians are fond of breaking binaries. This book breaks a few simplistic Cold War binaries and complicates economic determinism. At the same time, it also shows that in the political economy of development some binaries are very resistant, even with a considerable degree of nuance: state versus market, collective versus individual, ultimately Soviet versus Western.

Notes

INTRODUCTION

1. Otchet o rabote delegatsii na Konferentsii narodov Afriki v Akkre, December 25, 1958, in Gosudartstvennyi Arkhiv Rossiiskoi Federatsii (State Archive of the Russian Federation, henceforth GARF), f. R9540, op. 2, d. 9, ll. 12–13.

2. Joseph Morgan Hodge, "Writing the History of Development (Part 2: Longer, Deeper, Wider)," *Humanity: An International Journal of Human Rights, Humanitarianism, and Development* 7, no. 1 (2016): 158–159; David Engerman, *The Price of Aid: The Economic Cold War in India* (Cambridge, MA: Harvard University Press, 2018); Artemy Kalinovsky, *Laboratory of Socialist Development: Cold War Politics and Decolonization in Soviet Tajikistan* (Ithaca, NY: Cornell University Press, 2018); Timothy Nunan, *Humanitarian Invasion: Global Development in Cold War Afghanistan* (New York: Cambridge University Press, 2015).

3. Anthropological literature on all aspects of development in theory and practice is incredibly vast. Good starting points for critical perspectives are Arturo Escobar, *Encountering Development: The Making and Unmaking of the Third World* (Princeton, NJ: Princeton University Press, 1995); Uma Kothari, *A Radical History of Development Studies: Individuals, Institutions and Ideologies* (London: Zed Books, 2005); Jan Nederveen Pieterse, *Development Theory: Deconstructions/Reconstructions* (London: Sage, 2010). For an overview of the historiography on development, see Joseph Morgan Hodge, "Writing the History of Development (Part 1: The First Wave)," *Humanity: An International Journal of Human Rights, Humanitarianism, and Development* 6, no. 3 (2015): 429–463; Hodge, "Writing the History of Development (Part 2: Longer, Deeper, Wider)," 125–174. See also Stephen Macekura and Erez Manela, eds., *The Development Century: A Global History* (New York: Cambridge University Press, 2018).

4. Khrushchev quoted in Susan E. Reid, "Cold War in the Kitchen: Gender and the De-Stalinization of Consumer Taste in the Soviet Union under Khrushchev," *Slavic Review* 61, no. 2 (2002): 221.

5. Kwame Nkrumah, "Broadcast to the Nation, 24 December 1957," in Kwame Nkrumah, *Axioms of Kwame Nkrumah* (London: Panaf Books, 1969), 51.

6. Fodéba Keïta, February 1959, quoted in Ministère de la France d'Outre-Mer, Bureau d'Etudes d'Outre-Mer, Transmission de renseignements, March 13, 1959, "Activités diplomatiques guinéen," in Archives Nationals (Pierrefitte-sur-Seine, Paris, henceforth AN), Fonds Foccart, 5/AG/F/555.

7. Discours de Modibo Keïta, September 10, 1962, in Archives Nationales du Mali, Bureau Politique National, Union Soudanaise, Rassemblement Démocratique Africain (Hamdallaye, Bamako, henceforth ANM), Fond du Bureau Politique National, US-RDA (henceforth, BPN USRDA), Carton 3e, Dossier 5: Congres de l'US-RDA.

8. Georgii Mirskii, "Razvivaiushchiesia strany," in *Bol'shaia Sovetskaia Entsiklopediia*, ed. Aleksandr Prokhorov et al. (Moscow: Izdatel'stvo "Sovetskaia Entsiklopediia," 1975), 21:408–409.

9. Emanuel Joseph Sieyés, a prominent essayist in the wake of the French Revolution, famously wrote: "What is the Third Estate? Everything. What has hitherto been in the

political order? Nothing. What does it demand? To become something." See Emmanuel Joseph Sieyès, *What Is the Third Estate?* (London: Pall Mall, 1963).

10. Hannah Arendt, "On Violence," in Hannah Arendt, *Crises of the Republic* (New York: Harvest, 1972), 123; Vijay Prashad, *The Darker Nations: A People's History of the Third World* (New York: New Press, 2007), xv.

11. Robert Legvold, *Soviet Policy in West Africa* (Cambridge, MA: Harvard University Press, 1970).

12. Sergei Mazov, *A Distant Front in the Cold War: The USSR in West Africa and the Congo, 1956–1964* (Stanford, CA: Stanford University Press, 2010), 256.

13. For geoideological, see Nigel Gould-Davis, "Rethinking the Role of Ideology in International Politics During the Cold War," *Journal of Cold War Studies* 1, no. 1 (1999), 90–109.

14. O. Arne Westad, *The Global Cold War: Third World Interventions and the Making of Our Times* (New York: Cambridge University Press, 2005), 396.

15. David Engerman, "Ideology and the Origins of the Cold War, 1917–1962," in *The Cambridge History of the Cold War*, vol. 1: *Origins*, ed. Melvyn Leffler et al. (New York: Cambridge University Press, 2010), 20–43.

16. Oscar Sanchez-Sibony, *Red Globalization: The Political Economy of the Soviet Cold War from Stalin to Khrushchev* (New York: Cambridge University Press, 2014).

17. For an overview focused on Africa, see Rostislav Ul'ianovskii, *Nekapitalisticheskii put' razvitiia stran Afriki* (Moscow: Nauka, 1967).

18. Walter Johnson, "On Agency," *Journal of Social History* 37, no. 1 (Autumn 2003), 113–124.

19. W. Scott Thompson, *Ghana's Foreign Policy, 1957–1966: Diplomacy, Ideology and the State* (Princeton, NJ: Princeton University Press, [1969] 2015).

20. Jeffrey Ahlman, *Living with Nkrumahism: Nation, State, and Pan-Africanism in Ghana* (Athens: Ohio University Press, 2017); Harcourt Fuller, *Building the Ghanaian Nation State: Kwame Nkrumah's Symbolic Nationalism* (London: Palgrave, 2014); Frank Gerits, "'When the Bull Elephants Fight': Nkrumah, the Non-Aligned Movement and Pan-Africanism as an Interventionist Ideology," *International History Review* 37, no. 5 (2015): 951–969; Jennifer Hart, *Ghana on the Go: African Mobility in the Age of Motor Transportation* (Bloomington: Indiana University Press, 2016); Stephan Miescher, "Building the City of the Future: Visions and Experiences of Modernity in Ghana's Akosombo Township," *Journal of African History* 53, no. 3 (2012): 367–390; Abena Dove Osseo-Asare, *Atomic Junction: Nuclear Power in Africa after Independence* (New York: Cambridge University Press, 2019).

21. Nana Osei-Opare, "Uneasy Comrades: Postcolonial Statecraft, Race, and Citizenship, Ghana-Soviet Relations, 1957–1966," *Journal of West African History* 5, no. 2 (2019): 85–111.

22. Robyn d'Avignon, "Primitive Techniques: From 'Customary' to 'Artisanal' Mining in French West Africa," *Journal of African History* 59, no. 2 (2018): 179–197; Gregory Mann, *From Empires to NGOs in the West African Sahel: The Road to Nongovernmentality* (New York: Cambridge University Press, 2015); Ophélie Rillon, "Corps rebelles: La mode des jeunes urbains dans les années 1960–1970 au Mali," *Genèses* 4, no. 81 (2010): 64–83; Laura Ann Twagira, "Robot Farmers and Cosmopolitan Workers: Technological Masculinity and Agricultural Development in the French Soudan (Mali), 1945–68," *Gender & History* 26, no. 3 (2014): 459–477; Monica Van Beusekom, *Negotiating Development: African Farmers and Colonial Experts at the Office du Niger, 1920–1960* (Portsmouth, NH: Heinemann, 2002).

23. Elizabeth Schmidt, *Cold War and Decolonization in Guinea, 1946–1958* (Athens: Ohio University Press, 2007).

24. André Lewin, *Ahmed Sékou Touré (1922–1984), Président de la Guinée*, 8 vols. (Paris: L'Harmattan, 2009–2011).

25. Mike McGovern, *Unmasking the State: Making Guinea Modern* (Chicago: University of Chicago Press, 2012); Mike McGovern, *A Socialist Peace? Explaining the Absence of War in an African Country* (Chicago: University of Chicago Press, 2017).

26. Sanchez-Sibony offers an insightful overview of the struggle to measure the Soviet economy: Sanchez-Sibony, *Red Globalization*, 12–21. Modern quantitative studies of the Soviet economy tend to focus on the early years, on the impact of Stalinism, and on the USSR's collapse. See, among others, Robert Allen, *Farm to Factory: A Reinterpretation of the Soviet Industrial Revolution* (Princeton, NJ: Princeton University Press, 2003); Mark Harrison, *Accounting for War. Soviet Production, Employment and the Defense Burden, 1940–1945* (Cambridge: Cambridge University Press, 1996); Henry S. Rowen and Charles Wolf, eds., *The Impoverished Superpower: Perestroika and the Soviet Military Burden* (San Francisco: Institute for Contemporary Studies Press, 1990).

27. Angus Maddison, *The World Economy*, vol. 1: *A Millennial Perspective*; vol. 2: *Historical Statistics* (Paris: OECD, 2004).

28. On Soviet cultural diplomacy and transnational cultural exchanges, see, among others, Rachel Applebaum, "The Rise of Russian in the Cold War: How Three Worlds Made a World Language," *Kritika: Explorations in Russian and Eurasian History* 21, no. 2 (2020): 347–370; Michael David-Fox, *Showcasing the Great Experiment: Cultural Diplomacy and Western Visitors to the Soviet Union* (New York: Oxford University Press, 2012); Rossen Djagalov, *From Internationalism to Postcolonialism: Literature and Cinema between the Second and the Third Worlds* (Montreal: McGill-Queen's University Press, 2020); Anne E. Gorsuch and Diane P. Koenker, eds., *The Socialist Sixties: Crossing Borders in the Second World* (Bloomington: Indiana University Press, 2013); Hanna Jansen, "Internationalizing the Thaw: Soviet Orientalists and the Contested Politics of Spiritual Solidarity in Asia, 1954–1959," in *Alternative Globalizations: Eastern Europe and the Postcolonial World*, ed. James Mark et al. (Bloomington: Indiana University Press, 2020), 209–228; Masha Kirasirova, "Sons of Muslims in Moscow: Soviet Central Asian Mediators to the Foreign East," *Ab Imperio* 4 (2011): 106–132; Maxim Matusevich, "Harlem Globetrotters: African-American Travelers in Stalin's Russia," in *The Harlem Renaissance Revisited: Politics, Art, Letters*, ed. Jeffrey Ogbar (Baltimore, MD: Johns Hopkins University Press, 2010), 211–244; Tobias Rupprecht, *Soviet Internationalism after Stalin: Interaction and Exchange between the USSR and Latin America during the Cold War* (Cambridge: Cambridge University Press, 2015); Jennifer Wilson, "Queer Harlem, Queer Tashkent: Langston Hughes's 'Boy Dancers of Uzbekistan,'" *Slavic Review* 76, no. 3 (2017): 637–646. Literature on African students in the USSR is discussed in chapter 4.

29. On gender and development in Africa, see, among others, Priya Lal, *African Socialism in Postcolonial Tanzania* (New York: Cambridge University Press, 2015), 78–128; Lahra Smith, *Ethnicity, Gender, and National Identity in Ethiopia* (New York: Cambridge University Press, 2013), 169–191. For literature on gender in the USSR during the Khrushchev era, see chapter 1.

30. V.P. Shumilina, *Deiatel'nost' KPSS po razvitiiu obshchestvenno-politicheskoi aktivonosti zhenshchiny: Opyt KPSS v reshenii zhenskogo voprosa* (Moscow: Mysl', 1981), 200–219.

31. Tat'iana Zonova, "Gendernyi faktor v politike i diplomatii," *Mezdunarodnye protsessy: Zhurnal teorii mezdunarodnykh otnoshenii i mirovoi politiki* 2 (2010): 94–100.

32. Ivan I. Potekhin, "Otchet instituta Afriki akademii nauk SSSR za 1961 god," January 1961, in Arkhiv Rossisskoi Akademii Nauk, Moscow, Russia (henceforth, ARAN), fond 2010, opis' 1, delo 12, listy 1–21.

33. On the United States, see "Top Women Appointments in the Eisenhower Administrations (1953–1959), 1959," Dwight Eisenhower Presidential Library, https://eisenhower

.archives.gov/research/online_documents/women_in_the_1950s/Top_Women_Appoint
ments.pdf; "Women in the United States Congress, 1959," Dwight Eisenhower Presidential
Library, https://eisenhower.archives.gov/research/online_documents/women_in_the_1950s
/Women_in_US_Congress.pdf; "Women in the Foreign Service, 1959," Dwight Eisenhower
Presidential Library, https://eisenhower.archives.gov/research/online_documents/women
_in_the_1950s/Women_in_Foreign_Service.pdf; "The Department Addresses Inequality,"
US Department of State, Office of the Historian, https://history.state.gov/departmenthistory
/short-history/inequality. On the UK, see Richard Kelly, *Women Members of Parliament*,
Briefing Paper No. 06652 (London: House of Commons Library, 2019), 4–6; Steve Brown-
ing, *Women in Parliament and Government*, Briefing Paper No. 01250 (London: House of
Commons Library, 2019), 4–8; Foreign and Commonwealth Office, *Women and the Foreign
Office: A History*, History Notes 20 (London: Foreign Office, 2018), 18–26. On France, see
Assemblée Nationale, *Les Gouvernements et les Assemblées Parlamentaires sous la Ve République* (Paris: Assemblée Nationale, 2004), 11–24; Yves Denéchère, "La place et le rôle des
femmes dans la politique étrangère de la France contemporaine," *Vingtième Siècle. Revue
d'histoire* 78 (2003): 89–98.

34. Christine Varga-Harris, "Between National Tradition and Western Modernization: *Soviet Woman* and Representations of Socialist Gender Equality as a 'Third Way'
for Developing Countries, 1956–1964," *Slavic Review* 78, no. 3 (2019): 758–781.

35. On gender issues in Ghana, Guinea, and Mali, see Ahlman, *Living with Nkruma-
hism*, 148–175; Ophélie Rillon, "Sexualité juvénile sous contrôle dans les écoles secon-
daires maliennes (1960–1970)," *Clio. Femmes, Genre, Histoire* 2, no. 42 (2015), 77–97;
Naaborko Sackeyfio-Lenoch, "Women's International Alliances in an Emergent Ghana,"
Journal of West African History 4, no. 1 (2018): 27–56; Elizabeth Schmidt, *Mobilizing the
Masses: Gender, Ethnicity, and Class in the Nationalist Movement in Guinea, 1939–1958*
(Portsmouth, NH: Heinemann, 2005); Twagira, "Robot Farmers and Cosmopolitan
Workers," 459–477.

1. A FAREWELL TO ARMS

1. Henri Cartier-Bresson, *The People of Moscow* (London: Thames and Hudson, 1955).

2. Walter Rodney, *Walter Rodney Speaks: The Making of an African Intellectual* (Trenton, NJ: Africa World Press, 1990), 17.

3. Lev Trotskii, *History of the Russian Revolution* (Chicago: Haymarket Books, [1932]
2008), 23.

4. See, for example, Vladimir Lenin, *The Development of Capitalism in Russia* (Moscow: Freedom Press, [1899] 1974); Vladimir Lenin, *Imperialism: The Highest Stage of Capitalism* (Moscow: Progress, [1916] 1982), 70–79.

5. Stalin, "On Soviet Industrialization," Speech to Industrial Managers, February 1931,
in Iosif Stalin, *Problems of Leninism* (Moscow: Foreign Languages Publishing House,
1953), 454.

6. Alec Nove, *An Economic History of the USSR, 1917–1991* (London: Penguin, 1992), 1.

7. See, for example, Andrei Markevich and Mark Harrison, "Great War, Civil War,
and Recovery: Russia's National Income, 1913 to 1918," *Journal of Economic History* 71,
no. 3, (2011): 672–703; Andrei Markevich and Ekaterina Zhuravskaia, "The Economic
Effects of the Abolition of Serfdom: Evidence from the Russian Empire," *American Economic Review* 108, no. 4–5 (2018), 1074–1117. The journal *Slavic Review* has dedicated a
special issue to the debate surrounding the uses and misuses of statistics and quantification in Russian history: Alessandro Stanziani, "European Statistics, Russian Numbers
and Social Dynamics, 1861–1914," *Slavic Review* 76, no. 1 (2017): 1–23; Yanni Kotsonis,
"Read Zamiatin, but Not to Correct His Math," *Slavic Review* 76, no. 1 (2017): 24–29;
Steven Nafziger, "Quantification and the Economic History of Imperial Russia," *Slavic*

Review 76, no. 1 (2017): 30-36; Mikhail Avrekh, "On the Uses of Russian Statistics: A Response to Alessandro Stanziani's 'European Statistics, Russian Numbers and Social Dynamics, 1861-1914,'" *Slavic Review* 76, no. 1 (2017): 37-44; Andrei Markevich and Ekaterina Zhuravskaia, "Quantitative Approach to the Russian Past: A Comment on 'European Statistics, Russian Numbers and Social Dynamics, 1861-1914,'" *Slavic Review* 76, no. 1 (2017): 45-52.

8. R.W. Davies has explored the development of the Soviet economy in the 1930s in a monumental, seven-volume history: R.W. Davies, *The Industrialization of Soviet Russia*, vols. 1-3, 1929-1930 (Cambridge, MA: Harvard University Press, 1980-89); R.W. Davies, *The Industrialization of Soviet Russia*, vols. 4-7, 1931-1939 (London: Palgrave Macmillan, 1996-2018). For a more compact overview, see R.W. Davies, *Soviet Economic Development from Lenin to Khrushchev* (Cambridge: Cambridge University Press, 1998). On the strictly economic dimension of Stalinism, see Robert Allen, *Farm to Factory: A Reinterpretation of the Soviet Industrial Revolution* (Princeton, NJ: Princeton University Press, 2003); A. Cheremukhin et al., "Was Stalin Necessary for Russia's Economic Development?," NBER Working Paper No. 19425, September 2013. The literature on Stalinism as a political, economic, social, and cultural phenomenon is immense. The books that perhaps more than any others have driven the debate on Stalinism are Sheila Fitzpatrick, *Stalin's Peasants: Resistance and Survival in the Russian Village after Collectivization* (New York: Oxford University Press, 1994); Sheila Fitzpatrick, *Everyday Stalinism: Ordinary Life in Extraordinary Times: Soviet Russia in the 1930s* (New York: Oxford University Press, 1999); Stephen Kotkin, *Magnetic Mountain: Stalinism as a Civilization* (Berkeley: University of California Press, 1995); Terry Martin, *The Affirmative Action Empire: Nations and Nationalism in the Soviet Union, 1923-1939* (Ithaca, NY: Cornell University Press, 2001).

9. Angus Maddison, *The World Economy*, vol 2: *Historical Statistics* (Paris: OECD, 2006), 466-467, 478-479.

10. Walter Rodney, *How Europe Underdeveloped Africa* (Washington, DC: Howard University Press, [1972] 1982), 11.

11. Padmore, quoted in Leslie James, *George Padmore and Decolonization from Below: Pan-Africanism, the Cold War, and the End of Empire* (London: Palgrave Macmillan, 2015), 108. For more on Padmore's view of the USSR, see George Padmore, *How Russia Transformed Her Colonial Empire: A Challenge to the Imperialist Powers* (London: Dobson, 1946); Theo Williams, "George Padmore and the Soviet Model of the British Commonwealth," *Modern Intellectual History* 16, no. 2 (2019): 531-559.

12. Sheila Fitzpatrick, *On Stalin's Team: The Years of Living Dangerously in Soviet Politics* (Princeton, NJ: Princeton University Press, 2015), 225-254; Constantine Pleshakov and Vladislav Zubok, *Inside the Kremlin's Cold War. From Stalin to Khrushchev* (Cambridge, MA: Harvard University Press, 1997), 78-109, 142-164.

13. Pleshakov and Zubok, *Inside the Kremlin's Cold War*, 162-163. For a thorough exploration of Khrushchev's life and times, see William Taubman, *Khrushchev: The Man and His Era* (New York: W.W. Norton, 2003).

14. For more details on the Anti-Party coup, see Fitzpatrick, *On Stalin's Team*, 255-268; Pleshakov and Zubok, *Inside the Kremlin's Cold War*, 191, 197; Vladislav Zubok, *A Failed Empire: The Soviet Union in the Cold War from Stalin to Gorbachev* (Chapel Hill: University of North Carolina Press, 2007), 119-120. See also N.V. Kovaleva, ed., *Molotov, Malenkov, Kaganovich. 1957: Stenogramma iiun'skogo plenuma TsK KPSS i drugie dokumenty* (Moscow: ROSSPEN, 1998).

15. Aleksandr Fursenko and Timothy Naftali, *Khrushchev's Cold War: The Inside Story of an American Adversary* (New York: W.W. Norton, 2007), 22-25; Zubok, *A Failed Empire*, 101-105.

16. The existing literature on the Twentieth Congress, de-Stalinization, and the Thaw is extensive. For the main political aspects, see Taubman, *Khrushchev*, 270–299; Zubok, *A Failed Empire*, 112–119. See also Melanie Ilic and Jeremy Smith, eds., *Soviet State and Society under Khrushchev* (London: Routledge, 2009). For more specific analyses of culture and society, see Miriam Dobson, *Khrushchev's Cold Summer: Gulag Returnees, Crime, and the Fate of Reform after Stalin* (Ithaca, NY: Cornell University Press, 2009); Eleonory Gilburd, *To See Paris and Die: The Soviet Lives of Western Culture* (Cambridge, MA: Harvard University Press, 2018); Eleonory Gilburd and Denis Kozlov, eds., *The Thaw: Soviet Society and Culture during the 1950s and 1960s* (Toronto: University of Toronto Press, 2013); Polly Jones, *Myth, Memory, Trauma: Rethinking the Stalinist Past in the Soviet Union, 1953–70* (New Haven, CT: Yale University Press, 2014). For everyday life, see Christine Varga-Harris, *Stories of House and Home: Soviet Apartment Life during the Khrushchev Years* (Ithaca, NY: Cornell University Press, 2015); Donald J. Raleigh, *Soviet Baby Boomers: An Oral History of Russia's Cold War Generation* (New York: Oxford University Press, 2011). For an overview of intellectual life in the USSR in the wake of the Twentieth Congress, see Vladislav Zubok, *Zhivago's Children: The Last Russian Intelligentsia* (Cambridge, MA: Belknap, 2009).

17. Pleshakov and Zubok, *Inside the Kremlin's Cold War*, 184; Margot Light, *The Soviet Theory of International Relations* (Brighton: Wheatsheaf, 1988), 47; Nikita Khrushchev, "On Peaceful Coexistence," *Foreign Affairs* 38, no. 1 (1959): 1–18.

18. Nikita Khrushchev, *Khrushchev Remembers* (Boston, MA: Little, Brown, 1971), 512.

19. Reports and statements of Soviet foreign policy: notes on "USSR, Communism and the Cold War," in TNA, FO371/116652 NS1021/38.

20. Khrushchev, quoted in Fursenko and Naftali, *Khrushchev's Cold War*, 57; Pleshakov and Zubok, *Inside the Kremlin's Cold War*, 172.

21. Khrushchev, *Khrushchev Remembers*, 507.

22. Pleshakov and Zubok, *Inside the Kremlin's Cold War*, 185.

23. Pleshakov and Zubok, *Inside the Kremlin's Cold War*, 206–209.

24. Philip Hanson, *The Rise and Fall of the Soviet Economy. An Economic History of the USSR from 1945* (London: Routledge, 2014), 9–47. For figures, see Maddison, *The World Economy*, 2:476–479.

25. Khrushchev in "Transcript of a Meeting of the Party group of the USSR Supreme Soviet, 8 February 1955," Cold War International History Project, Digital Archive, https://digitalarchive.wilsoncenter.org/document/113336.

26. Hanson, *The Rise and Fall of the Soviet Economy*, 52–57.

27. Aaron Hale-Dorrell, *Corn Crusade: Khrushchev's Farming Revolution in the Post-Stalin Soviet Union* (New York: Oxford University Press, 2018).

28. Martin McCauley, *Khrushchev and the Development of Soviet Agriculture: Virgin Land Program, 1953–1964* (London: Palgrave, 1976).

29. For more context on the rise of consumption, improving living standards and "everyday" technology in Khrushchev's USSR, see Kristy Ironside, "Khrushchev's Cash-and-Goods Lotteries and the Turn to Positive Incentives," *Soviet and Post-Soviet Review* 41, no. 3 (2014): 296–323; Susan Reid, "Who Will Beat Whom? Soviet Popular Reception of the American National Exhibition in Moscow, 1959," *Kritika: Explorations in Russian and Eurasian History* 9, no. 4 (2008): 855–904; Susan Reid, "The Khrushchev Kitchen: Domesticating the Scientific-Technological Revolution," *Journal of Contemporary History* 49, no. 2 (2005): 289–316; Mark Smith, *Property of Communists: The Urban Housing Program from Stalin to Khrushchev* (DeKalb: Northern Illinois Press, 2010).

30. For a complete overview of the Soviet space program, see Asif Siddiqi, *Sputnik and the Soviet Space Challenge* (Gainesville: University of Florida Press, 2003) and Asif Siddiqi, *The Soviet Space Race with Apollo* (Gainesville: University of Florida Press, 2003).

31. Yanek Mieczkowski, *Eisenhower's Sputnik Moment: The Race for Space and World Prestige* (Ithaca, NY: Cornell University Press, 2013), 11–26. For *Sputnik*-related hysteria in the UK, see Nicholas Barnett, "'Russia Wins Space Race': The British Press and the Sputnik Moment, 1957," *Media History* 19, no. 2 (2013): 182–195.

32. Tobias Rupprecht, *Soviet Internationalism after Stalin: Interaction and Exchange between the USSR and Latin America during the Cold War* (Cambridge: Cambridge University Press, 2015), 43.

33. *Rhodesian Herald*, quoted in Thembisa Waetjen, "Sputnik from Below: Space Age Science and Public Culture in Cold War Southern Africa," *Interventions: International Journal of Postcolonial Studies* 18, no. 5 (2016): 693.

34. Geormbeeyi Adali-Mortty, "Education for the People," in *Ghana: One Year Old. A First Independence Anniversary Review*, ed. Moses Danquah (Accra: Guinea Press, 1958), 19; Posol SSSR v Gane M.D. Sytenko—General'nomu direktoru TASS N.G. Pal'gunovu, November 27, 1959, in *Rossiia i Afrika: Dokumenty i Materialy XVIII v.–1960 g.*, vol. 2: *1918–1960*, ed. Apollon Davidson and Sergei Mazov (Moscow: IVI RAN, 1999), 201–202.

35. Evgenii Evtushenko, *Bratsk Station and Other New Poems* (New York: Anchor Books, 1967), 1–13.

36. The Bratsk project has so far generated more interest among literary writers than historians. Besides the Evtushenko poem, Valentin Rasputin wrote a famous novel exploring the displacement of people on the site of the project: Valentin Rasputin, *Farewell to Matyora* (Evanston, IL: Northwestern University Press, [1976] 1991). For historical assessment and technical information, see Janet Hartley, *Siberia: A History of the People* (New Haven, CT: Yale University Press, 2014), 220; Vladimir Nikoforov, "Razvitie toplinivno-energeticheskogo kompleksa Vostochnoi Sibiri v 1950–1980-kh gg.: Na materialakh Krasnoiarskogo kraia, Buriatskoi ASSR i Irkutskoi oblasti" (PhD diss., Buryat National University, 2011).

37. Artemy Kalinovsky, *Laboratory of Socialist Development: Cold War Politics and Decolonization in Soviet Tajikistan* (Ithaca, NY: Cornell University Press, 2018), 117–143.

38. Rapport de Mameuteu Coulibaly (Député), Délégation USRDA en URSS, Juillet-Aout 1964, in ANM, BPN USRDA, carton 87, dossier 296: Délégation de l'US RDA en Union Soviétique, 1964.

39. Jerry F. Hough and Merle Fainsod, *How the Soviet Union is Governed* (Cambridge, MA: Harvard University Press, 1979), 455–479.

40. For more information on Mikoian, see Anastas Mikoian, *Tak bylo: Razmyshleniia o minuvshem* (Moscow: Vagrius, 1999); M.Iu. Pavlov, *Anastas Mikoian: Politicheskii portret na fone sovetskoi epokhi* (Moscow: Mezhdunarodnye otnosheniia, 2010).

41. Elizabeth Teague, "The Foreign Departments of the Central Committee of the CPSU," Supplement to *Radio Liberty Research Bulletin*, October 27, 1980, 14. See also Mark Kramer, "The Role of the CPSU International Department in Soviet Foreign Relations and National Security Policy," *Soviet Studies*, 42, no. 3 (1990); Robert W. Kitrinos, "International Department of the CPSU," *Problems of Communism* 33, no. 5 (1984).

42. Ned Temko, "Soviet Insiders: How Powers Flows in Moscow," in *The Soviet Policy in the Modern Era*, ed. Erik Hoffmann and Robbin Laird (New York: Aldine de Gruyter, 1984), 181.

43. Karen Brutents, *Tridtsat' let na Staroi ploshchadi* (Moscow: Mezhdunarodnye otnosheniia, 1998), 130–196.

44. David Engerman, *The Price of Aid: The Economic Cold War in India* (Cambridge, MA: Harvard University Press, 2018), 84; Sovet Ministrov SSSR, Postanovlenie 27 marta 1959 g., No. 336, "Ob utverzhdenii polozheniia o gosudarstvennom komitete soveta ministrov SSSR po vneshnim ekonomicheskim sviaziam i struktury komiteta," in in Rossiiskii Gosudarstvennyi Arkhiv Ekonomiki, Moscow, Russia, f. 645, op. 1, d. 28.

45. "Skachkov, Semën Andreevich," in *Gosudarstvennaia vlast' SSSR. Vysshie organy vlasti i upravleniia i ikh rukovoditeli, 1923–1991 gg.*, ed. V.I. Ivkin (Moscow: ROSSPEN, 1999), 525–526; "Degtiar', Dmitrii Danilovich," in *Diplomaticheskii Slovar'*, ed. Andrei Gromyko et al. (Moscow: Nauka, 1985), 1:285.

46. "Patolichev, Nikolai Stepanovich," in Ivkin, *Gosudarstvennaia vlast' SSSR*, 463.

47. Nikita Khrushchev in "Transcript of a CC CPSU Plenum, Evening," June 28, 1957, Cold War International History Project, Digital Archive, http://digitalarchive.wilsoncenter .org/document/111990.

48. Shepilov quoted in Feliks Chuev, *Kaganovich. Shepilov* (Moscow: Izdatel'stvo "Olma-Press," 2001), 347.

49. Andrei Gromyko, *Memoirs* (New York: Doubleday, 1989), 263–265.

50. Anatolii Dobrynin, *In Confidence: Moscow's Ambassador to Six Cold War Presidents* (New York: Random House, 1995), 404–405.

51. For more discussion of Potekhin's trip to Ghana, see chapter 3. For more information on his life and career, see V. Datsyshen, "Osnovatel' Instituta Afriki—Urozhenets Azii," *Aziia i Afrika Segodnia* 8 (2004): 40–44.

52. Plan nauchno-issledovatel'skogo instituta Afriki AN SSSR na 1960 g., December 1959, in Arkhiv Rossiiskoi Akademii Nauk, Moscow, Russian Federation, f. 2010, op. 1, d. 1, l. 1–3.

53. For more information on the Youth Festival, see Gilburd, *To See Paris and Die*, 55–102; Pia Koivunen, "The 1957 Moscow Youth Festival. Propagating a New, Peaceful Image of the Soviet Union," in *Soviet State and Society under Nikita Khrushchev*, ed. Melanie Ilič and Jeremy Smith (London: Routledge, 2008), 46–65; Kristin Roth-Ey, "'Loose Girls' on the Loose? Sex, Propaganda and the 1957 Youth Festival," in *Women in the Khrushchev Era*, ed. Melanie Ilič, Susan Reid, and Lynne Atwood (London: Palgrave, 2004), 75–95.

54. Godfrey Meynell, "What Have I Done for You?," *Time and Tide*, August 31, 1957, 1072.

2. BRAVE NEW WORLD

1. Karl Marx in *New-York Daily Tribune*, June 25, 1853, in Karl Marx and Frederick Engels, *Collected Works*, vol. 12: *1853–1854* (New York: International Publishers, 1975), 126.

2. Karl Marx in *New-York Daily Tribune*, June 25, 1853, 126, 131.

3. Karl Marx in *New-York Daily Tribune*, June 25, 1853, 132

4. Karl Marx, *Capital* (London: Penguin, 1976), 1:873–942; Ernest Mandel, *Marxist Economic Theory* (New York: Monthly Review Press, 1968), 95–131; G.A. Cohen, *Karl Marx's Theory of History: A Defense* (Oxford: Oxford University Press, 1978), 175–215.

5. Vladimir Lenin, *Imperialism, The Highest Stage of Capitalism* (Moscow: Progress, [1916] 1982).

6. Vladimir Lenin, "Doklad komissii po natsional'nomu kolonial'nomu voprosam," July 26, 1920, in Vladimir Lenin, *Polnoe Sobranie Sochinenii*, vol. 41: *Mai–Noiabr' 1920* (Moscow: Izdatel'stvo Politicheskoi Literatury, 1981), 243–244.

7. Lenin, "Doklad komissii po natsional'nomu kolonial'nomu voprosam," 244–245.

8. Trotskii in "Anti-Imperialist Struggle Is Key to Liberation, Trotskii Tells Mateo Fossa," *Socialist Appeal*, November 5, 1938, 3.

9. For Soviet and Comintern policy toward the external world in this period, see Jonathan Haslam, "Comintern and Soviet Foreign Policy, 1919–1941," in *Cambridge History of Russia*, vol. 3: *The Twentieth Century*, ed. Ronald Suny (New York: Cambridge University Press, 2006), 636–661. For more context on communism in Shanghai, see Stephen Smith, *A Road is Made: Communism in Shanghai, 1920–1927* (Honolulu: University of Hawaii Press, 2000).

10. O. Arne Westad, *The Global Cold War: Third World Interventions and the Making of Our Times* (New York: Cambridge University Press), 54.

11. The "two camps" theory was officially formulated by Andrei Zhdanov, a leading Politburo member, during the conference that rebooted the Comintern as Cominform in September 1947.

12. Margot Light, *The Soviet Theory of International Relations* (Brighton: Wheatsheaf, 1988), 99–106.

13. Kennan quoted in C. Grove Haines, ed., *The Threat of Soviet Imperialism* (Baltimore: Johns Hopkins University Press, 1954), 14.

14. Haines, *The Threat of Soviet Imperialism*, 14–15.

15. "USSR, Communism and the Cold War," 1955, in TNA, FO371/116654 NS1021/75.

16. Maevskii cited in Guy Laron, "Cutting the Gordian Knot: The Egyptian Quest for Arms and the Czechoslovak Arms Deal," *Cold War International History Project Working Paper* 55 (Washington, DC: Woodrow Wilson International Center for Scholars, 2007), 18.

17. Khrushchev cited in Alvin Rubinstein, *Moscow's Third World Strategy* (Princeton, NJ: Princeton University Press, 1988), 20–21.

18. Trends of Communist Policy: papers for discussion at monthly meetings of Russia Committee, 1954, in TNA, FO371/111683 NS1022/12.

19. Reports on and statements of Soviet foreign policy, 1955, in TNA, FO371/116654 NS1021/67. The French paper was forwarded to the British Foreign Office, whose Northern Department thought it "well balanced."

20. For more information on Bandung, its origins and its legacy, see Cindy Ewing, "The Colombo Powers: Crafting Diplomacy in the Third World and Launching Afro-Asia at Bandung," *Cold War History* 19, no. 1 (2019): 1–19; Christopher Lee, ed., *Making a World after Empire: The Bandung Moment and Its Political Afterlives* (Athens: Ohio University Press, 2010); Robert Vitalis, "The Midnight Ride of Kwame Nkrumah and Other Fables of Bandung (Ban-doong)," *Humanity: An International Journal of Human Rights, Humanitarianism, and Development* 4, no. 2 (Summer 2013): 261–288.

21. Reports on and statements of Soviet foreign policy, 1955, in TNA, FO371/116650 NS1021/12.

22. Dipesh Chakrabarty, "The Legacies of Bandung: Decolonization and the Politics of Culture," in Lee, *Making a World after Empire*, 50.

23. Roy Allison, *The Soviet Union and the Strategy of Non-Alignment in the Third World* (Cambridge: Cambridge University Press, 1988), 29–31.

24. Vojtech Mastny, "The Soviet Union's Partnership with India," *Journal of Cold War Studies* 12, no. 3 (2010): 54–55.

25. Laron, "Cutting the Gordian knot," 1.

26. Laron, "Cutting the Gordian knot," 16–19.

27. Telegramma iz Kaira . . . ot 12 noiabria 1955, November 16, 1955, in *Prezidium TsK KPSS 1954–1964*, ed. Aleksandr Fursenko (Moscow: ROSSPEN, 2004), 1:63.

28. Reports on and statements of Soviet foreign policy, 1955, in TNA, FO371/116655, NS1021/90.

29. Reports on and statements of Soviet foreign policy, 1955, in TNA, NS1021/90 and NS1021/91.

30. Foreign Office, Northern Department (Soviet Union), "Leadership," 1955, in TNA, FO371/122776 NS1017/2.

31. Doklad tt. Khrushcheva i Bulganina o poezdke v Indiiu, Birmu i Afganistan, 22 December 1955, in *Preszdium TsK KPSS 1954–1964*, 1:72–75; Nikita Khrushchev, *Memoirs of Nikita Khrushchev*, vol. 3: *Statesman, 1953–1964* (University Park: Pennsylvania State University Press, 2007), 726–750.

32. Engerman, *The Price of Aid: The Economic Cold War in India* (Cambridge, MA: Harvard University Press, 2018), 89–190.

33. Doklad tt. Khrushcheva i Bulganina o poezdke v Indiiu, Birmu i Afganistan, 22 December 1955, in *Prezidium TsK KPSS 1954–1964*, vol. 1:74.

34. Telegramma tt. Khrushcheva i Bulganina o voprosakh okazaniia pomoshchi Afganistanu, 16 December 1955, in *Prezidium TsK KPSS 1954–1964*, 2:72.

35. Telegram from the Embassy in India to the Department of State, November 25, 1955, in US Department of State, *Foreign Relations of the United States (FRUS), 1955–1957*, vol. 8: *South Asia* (Washington, DC: United States Government Printing Office, 1987), 298.

36. Paul McGarr, *The Cold War in South Asia: Britain, the United States and the Indian Subcontinent, 1945–1965* (Cambridge: Cambridge University Press, 2013), 121.

37. Foreign Office, Northern Department (Soviet Union), "Foreign Policy," 1956, in TNA, FO371/122782 NS1021/13.

38. Douglas Little, "The Cold War in the Middle East: Suez Crisis to Camp David Accords," in *Cambridge History of the Cold War*, vol. 2: *Crises and Détente*, ed. Melvyn P. Leffler and O. Arne Westad (New York: Cambridge University Press, 2010), 307–308.

39. Fursenko and Naftali, *Khrushchev's Cold War*, 132–137; Little, "The Cold War in the Middle East," 309–312.

40. Proekt ukazanii sovetskoi delegatsii na konferentsii po voprosu o Suetskom kanale, August 11, 1956, in *Prezidium Tsk KPSS 1954–1964*, 1:156.

41. Ob okazanii pomoshchii Egiptu, November 5, 1956, in *Prezidium Tsk KPSS 1954–1964*, vol. 1, 203.

42. The experiences of West African visitors to the USSR during the Khrushchev era will be discussed in chapter 4.

43. Apollon Davidson and Irina Filatova, *The Hidden Thread: Russia and South Africa in the Soviet Era* (Johannesburg: Jonathan Ball, 2013); Robert Edgar, *The Making of an African Communist: Edwin Thabo Mofutsanyana and the Communist Party of South Africa, 1927–1939* (Pretoria: Unisa Press, 2005); Maxim Matusevich, *No Easy Row for a Russian How: Ideology and Pragmatism in Nigerian-Soviet Relations, 1960–1991* (Trenton, NJ: Africa World Press, 2003), 11–56; Meredith Roman, *Opposing Jim Crow: African Americans and the Soviet Indictment of US Racism* (Lincoln: University of Nebraska Press, 2012); Holger Weiss, "Between Moscow and the African Atlantic: The Comintern Network of Negro Workers," *Monde(s)* 10, no. 2 (2016): 89–108; Nikolai Zakharov, *Race and Racism in Russia* (London: Palgrave, 2015), 34–45.

44. Jeffrey Byrne, *Mecca of Revolution: Algeria, Decolonization, and the Third World Order* (New York: Oxford University Press, 2016), 54–63.

45. Dmitrii Ol'derogge and Ivan Potekhin, *Narody Afriki* (Moscow: Izdatel'stvo Akademii Nauk SSSR, 1954).

46. Soviet Union activity in Africa and Afghanistan, 1955, in TNA, FO371/116668, NS1041/5, and NS1041/6.

47. Memorandum of a Conversation Between the Ambassador in Liberia (Jones) and President Tubman, Monrovia, January 5, 1956, in *FRUS, 1955–1957*, vol. 28: *Africa*, 389, 391.

48. Telegram from the Embassy in Liberia to the Department of State, January 9, 1956, in *FRUS, 1955–57*, XVIII, 393.

49. Westad, *The Global Cold War*, 71.

50. David Engerman, "The Romance of Economic Development and New Histories of the Cold War," *Diplomatic History* 28, no. 1 (2004): 31.

51. Foreign Office, Northern Department (Soviet Union, "Foreign Policy," 1956, in TNA, FO371/122782 NS1021/15.

52. Westad, *The Global Cold War*, 69.

53. Deborah A. Kaple, "Soviet Advisors in China in the 1950s," in *Brothers in Arms: The Rise and Fall of the Sino-Soviet Alliance, 1945–1963*, ed. O. Arne Westad (Stanford, CA: Stanford University Press, 1998), 119.

54. Westad, *The Global Cold War*, 69.

55. Modest Rubinshtein, "A Non-Capitalist Path for Developing Countries (1)," *New Times*, July 5, 1956, 3–6; Modest Rubinshtein, "A Non-Capitalist Path for Developing Countries (2)," *New Times*, August 2, 1956, 6–9. For a discussion of the importance of Rubinshtein's ideas, see David Engerman, "Learning from the East. Soviet Experts and India in the Era of Competitive Coexistence," *Comparative Studies of South Asia, Africa and the Middle East* 33, no. 2 (2013): 232–233.

56. Spravka, October 28, 1958, in RGANI, fond 5, op. 30, d. 273, l. 40.

57. Spravka, October 28, 1958, in RGANI, fond 5, op. 30, d. 273, l. 67.

58. RGANI, f. 5, op. 35, d. 79, l. 1, 31.

59. RGANI, f. 5, op. 35, d. 79, l. 79, 107, 137, 139.

60. For a more detailed discussion of this aspect, see Alessandro Iandolo, "De-Stalinizing Growth: Decolonization and the Development of Development Economics in the Soviet Union," in *The Development Century: A Global History*, ed. Stephen J. Macekura and Erez Manela (New York: Cambridge University Press, 2018), 197–219.

61. Rostislav Ul'ianovskii, *Nekotorye voprosy za ekonomicheskuiu nezavisimost' v nesotsialisticheskikh stranakh* (Moscow: Akademiia Nauk SSSR, 1960).

62. Iaroslav Vasil'kov and Marina Sorokina, *Liudi i sud'by. Biobibliograficheskii slovar' vostokovedov—zhertv politicheskogo terrora v sovetskii period (1917–1991)* (St Petersburg: Peterburgskoe Vostokovedenie, 2003), 382–383. The 1935 order to arrest Ul'ianovskii was authorized by Khrushchev, who at the time was Moscow's party boss.

63. Boris Ponomarev, "O gusudarstve natsional'noi demokratii," *Kommunist* 8 (1960): 43–47.

64. Nikita Khrushchev, "For New Victories for the World Communist Movement," *World Marxist Review* 4, no. 1 (1961): 2–27.

65. Khrushchev, "For New Victories for the World Communist Movement," 20.

66. RGANI, f. 5, op. 30, d. 273, l. 112–115.

67. RGANI, f. 4, op. 4, d. 469, l. 73–75; Sergei Mazov, *Politika SSSR v Zapadnoi Afrike, 1956–1964: Neizvestnye stranitsy kholodnoi voiny* (Moscow: Nauka, 2008), 16.

68. J.H.A. Watson to N.D. Watson, May 27, 1958, in UKNA, FO371/131187; and "The Communist Drive into Africa," July 1958, in UKNA, FO371/131188.

69. See chapter 1 for more discussion.

70. RGANI, fond 5, op. 30, d. 273, l. 44–46, 112–115, 121–126, 177–184.

71. Central Intelligence Agency, *Communist Aid Activities in Non-Communist Less Developed Countries, 1979 and 1954–79* (Washington, DC: CIA, 1980), 7.

72. Nikita Khrushchev, "Otchetnyi doklad tsentral'nogo komiteta kommunisticheskoi partii Sovetskogo Soiuza XX s"ezdu partii," February 14, 1956, in TsK KPSS, *XX S"ezd Kommunisticheskoi Partii Sovetskogo Soiuza. Stenograficheskii otchet* (Moscow: Gosudarstvennoe Izdatel'stvo Politicheskoi Literatury, 1956), 1:25.

73. Telegramma iz Kaira . . . ot 12 noiabria 1955, November 16, 1955, in *Prezidium TsK KPSS, 1954–1964*, 1:63.

74. Elizabeth Valkenier, *The Soviet Union and the Third World: An Economic Bind* (New York: Praeger, 1983), 8.

75. Ministère des Affaires Étrangères, "Revue Synthétique de l'Actualité Internationale, semaine du 23 au 30 octobre 1960, document n. 6: l'URSS et les pays sous-développés," November 1960, in ANM, BPN USRDA, Carton 84, Dossier 283: Ministère des Affaires Étrangères Mali, 1960–1968.

76. National Intelligence Estimate, November 1, 1955, in US Department of State, *FRUS*, 1955–1957, vol, 19: *National Security Policy*, 133.

77. Foreign Office, Northern Department (Soviet Union), "USSR, Communism and the Cold War," 1955, in TNA, FO371/116655, NS1021/76.

78. Foreign Office, Northern Department (Soviet Union), "USSR, Communism and the Cold War," 1955, in TNA, FO371/116655, NS1021/89.

79. Direction des Affaires Économiques et Financières, "Esquisse d'une politique nouvelle d'aide aux pays sous-développés," April 13, 1956, in Ministère des Affaires Étrangères, *Documents Diplomatiques Français (DDF)*, 1956, vol. 1: *1er Janvier–30 Juin* (Paris: Imprimerie Nationale, 1988), 586–587; M. Dejean to M. Pinay (French foreign minister), January 17, 1956, in *DDF*, 1956, 2:50.

80. Chapter 4 will explore these more in detail.

3. FIRST CONTACT

1. Raymond Scupin, *Cultural Anthropology. A Global Perspective* (London: Pearson, 2016), 2.

2. Karen Brutents, *Tridtsat' let na Staroi ploshchadi* (Moscow: Mezhdunarodnye otnosheniia, 1998), 197.

3. Brutents, *Tridtsat' let na Staroi ploshchadi*, 198.

4. For context, see Toby Green, *A Fistful of Shells: West Africa from the Rise of the Slave Trade to the Age of Revolution* (London: Allen Lane, 2019); J.F. Ade Ajayi and B.O. Oloruntimehin, "West Africa in the Anti-Slave Trade Era," in *Cambridge History of Africa*, vol. 5: *From c.1790 to c.1870*, ed. John Flint (Cambridge: Cambridge University Press, 1977), 200–221; Yves Peterson and Yvonne Brett, "Western Africa, 1870–1886," in *Cambridge History of Africa*, vol. 6: *From 1870 to 1905*, ed. Roland Oliver and G.N. Sanderson (Cambridge: Cambridge University Press, 1985), 208–256; J.D. Hargreaves, "Western Africa, 1886–1905," in *Cambridge History of Africa*, 6:257–297.

5. Hargreaves, "Western Africa, 1886–1905," 6:280–288.

6. Gareth Austin, "Vent for Surplus or Productivity Breakthrough? The Ghanaian Cocoa Take-off, c.1890–1936," *Economic History Review* 67, no. 4 (2014): 1035–1064; A.G Hopkins, *An Economic History of West Africa* (London: Routledge, 2020), 173–217.

7. Frederik Cooper, *Decolonization and African Society: The Labor Question in French and British Africa* (New York: Cambridge University Press, 1996); D.C. Dorward, "British West Africa and Liberia," in *Cambridge History of Africa*, vol. 7: *From 1905 to 1940*, ed. A.D. Roberts (Cambridge: Cambridge University Press, 1986), 399–459; Michael Crowder, "The Second World War: Prelude to Decolonisation in Africa," in *Cambridge History of Africa*, vol. 8: *From c.1940 to c.1975*, ed. Michael Crowder (Cambridge: Cambridge University Press, 1984), 8–51; David Williams, "English-Speaking West Africa," in *Cambridge History of Africa*, 8:331–382.

8. Basil Davidson, *Black Star: A View of the Life and Times of Kwame Nkrumah* (Oxford: James Currey, 2007); June Milne, *Kwame Nkrumah: A Biography* (London: Panaf, 2000); Marika Sherwood, *Kwame Nkrumah and the Dawn of the Cold War: The West African National Secretariat, 1945–48* (London: Pluto Press, 2019).

9. Jeffrey Ahlman, *Living with Nkrumahism: Nation, State, and Pan-Africanism in Ghana* (Athens: Ohio University Press, 2017), 78–83; Frederik Cooper, *Africa since 1940: The Past of the Present* (New York: Cambridge University Press, 2002), 49–53.

10. Ahlman, *Living with Nkrumahism*, 49–60; Angus Maddison, *The World Economy*, vol. 2: *Historical Statistics* (Paris: OECD, 2004), 598–604.

11. Kwame Nkrumah, *I Speak of Freedom* (London: Panaf, 1973), 107.

12. For a thorough discussion of Nkrumah's political economy in theory and practice, see Ahlman, *Living with Nkrumahism*, 115–147.

13. Robert Legvold, *Soviet Policy in West Africa* (Cambridge, MA: Harvard University Press, 1970), 46; Sergei Mazov, *A Distant Front in the Cold War: The USSR in West Africa and the Congo, 1956–1964* (Stanford, CA: Stanford University Press, 2010), 46.

14. Memorandum from the Assistant Secretary of State for Congressional Relations (Hill) to the Vice President, February 18, 1957, in *FRUS, 1955–1957*, 28:372–375.

15. Benediktov had been an important figure in Soviet agriculture since the late 1930s. He did not approve of some of Khrushchev's schemes and methods to boost productivity. The two eventually fell out, and Benediktov was sent to Delhi as Soviet ambassador to India in 1959. See "Benediktov, Ivan Aleksandrovich," in *Gosudarstvennaia vlast' SSSR. Vysshie organy vlasti i upravleniia i ikh rukovoditeli, 1923–1991 gg.*, ed. V.I. Ivkin (Moscow: ROSSPEN, 1999), 219–220.

16. Spravka, July 1957, in AVP RF, f. 573, op. 1, p. 1, d. 3, l. 9; Memorandum for Cabinet Meeting, January 14, 1958, in Public Records and Archive Administration, Accra, Ghana (henceforth, PRAAD), ADM/13/2/44.

17. U.K. High Commission in Ghana, Fortnightly Report for the Period 6th–20th March—Part II, 26 March 1957, in TNA, FO371/125294; Memorandum from the Assistant Secretary of State for Congressional Relations (Hill) to the Vice President, February 18, 1957, in *FRUS, 1955–1957*, XVIII, 373.

18. U.K. High Commission in Ghana, Fortnightly Report for the Period 6th–20th March—Part II, 26 March 1957, in TNA, FO371/125294.

19. AVP RF, f. 573, op. 1, p. 1, d. 3, l. 9–14.

20. AVP RF, f. 573, op. 2, p. 1, d. 3, l. 1–10; Cabinet meeting, January 14, 1958, in PRAAD, ADM/13/1/27; Memorandum for Cabinet Meeting, January 14, 1958, in PRAAD, ADM/12/2/44.

21. AVP RF, f. 573, op. 1, p. 1, d. 4, l. 1–5.

22. M.E. Allen to H.F.T. Smith, June 25, 1958, in TNA, FO371/131187; J.R.A. Bottomley to J.H. Ellis, August 22, 1958, in TNA, FO371/131188.

23. AVP RF, f. 573, op. 2, p. 1, d. 3, l. 1–10; Cabinet meeting, January 14, 1958, in PRAAD, ADM/13/1/27; Memorandum for Cabinet Meeting, January 14, 1958, in PRAAD, ADM/12/2/44.

24. Memorandum of Conversation, July 24, 1958, in US Department of State, in *FRUS, 1958–1960*, vol. 14: *Africa*, 647–652.

25. Telegram from the Embassy in Ghana to the Department of State, August 13, 1958, in *FRUS, 1958–1960*, XIV, 652.

26. Cabinet Meeting, January 14, 1958, in PRAAD, ADM/13/1/27; Memorandum for Cabinet Meeting, January 14, 1958, in PRAAD, ADM/13/2/44.

27. Memorandum of a Conversation, Accra, March 4, 1957, in *FRUS, 1955–1956*, 28:378.

28. Telegram from the Embassy in Ghana to the Department of State, November 6, 1957, in *FRUS, 1955–1957*, 28:382.

29. Telegram from the Embassy in Ghana to the Department of State, November 6, 1957, in *FRUS, 1955–1957*, 28:383.

30. M.E. Allen to P. Hayman, March 25, 1958, in TNA, FO371/135273.

31. From Foreign Office to Khartoum, February 28, 1958, in TNA, FO371/131187; Memorandum for Cabinet Meeting, January 14, 1958, in PRAAD, ADM/13/2/44.

32. Potekhin's visit to Ghana caused a degree of distress in London and Washington. See L.J.D. Wakely to M.E. Allen, November 22, 1957, in TNA, FO371/125303; and Telegram From the Embassy in Ghana to the Department of State, December 4, 1957, in *FRUS, 1955–1957*, 28:387–838. Ghanaian authorities immediately decided to keep an eye on Pothekhin, suspecting political reasons behind the visit. See Cabinet Meeting, August 30,

1957, in PRAAD, ADM/13/1/26; and Memorandum for Cabinet Meeting, August 30, 1957, in PRAAD, ADM/13/2/40.

33. Informatsiia zamestitelia direktora Instituta etnografii I.I. Potekhina o vstrechakh s ganskimi politikami vo vremia ego prebyvaniia v Gane v oktiabre–dekabre 1957 g., January 31, 1958, in *Rossiia i Afrika: Dokumenty i materialy XVIII v.–1960 g.*, vol. 2: *1918–1960*, ed. Apollon Davidson and Sergei Mazov (Moscow: IVI RAN, 1999), 198–199.

34. Informatsiia zamestitelia direktora Instituta etnografii I.I. Potekhina, in *Rossiia i Afrika*, 2:198–199.

35. AVP RF, f. 573, op. 2, p. 1, d. 6, l. 2–29.

36. Informatsiia o sovetsko-ganskikh otnosheniiakh iz obzornoi spravki po Gane, podgotovlennoi attashe posol'stva SSSR v Londone N.A. Makarovym, June 11, 1958, in *Rossiia i Afrika*, 2:200–201.

37. Informatsiia zamestitelia direktora Instituta etnografii I.I. Potekhina, in *Rossiia i Afrika*, 2:199.

38. For more information on Padmore, see chapter 1.

39. Otchet o rabote delegatsii na Konferentsii narodov Afriki v Akkre, December 25, 1958, in Gosudarstvennyi Arkhiv Rossiiskoi Federatsii, Moscow, Russia (henceforth, GARF), f. r9540, op. 2, d. 9, l. 19–20.

40. Otchet o rabote delegatsii na Konferentsii narodov Afriki v Akkre, l. 2–20.

41. Nana Osei-Opare, "Uneasy Comrades: Postcolonial Statecraft, Race, and Citizenship, Ghana-Soviet Relations, 1957–1966," *Journal of West African History* 5, no. 2 (2019): 85–111.

42. AVP RF, f. 573, op. 2, p. 1, d. 6, l. 2–29.

43. Informatsiia o sovetsko-ganskikh otnosheniiakh iz obzornoi spravki po Gane, podgotovlennoi attashe posol'stva SSSR v Londone N.A. Makarovym, June 11, 1958, in Davidson and Mazov, *Rossiia i Afrika*, 2:201.

44. Ministerstvo Vneshnei Torgovli SSSR, *Vneshniaia torgovlia SSSR za 1957 god* (Moscow: Vneshtorgizdat, 1958), 149; Ministerstvo Vneshnei Torgovli SSSR, *Vneshniaia torgovlia SSSR za 1959–1963 gody* (Moscow: Vneshtorgnzdat, 1965), 430–433.

45. Informatsiia o sovetsko-ganskikh otnosheniiakh iz obzornoi spravki po Gane, podgotovlennoi attashe posol'stva SSSR v Londone N.A. Makarovym, in *Rossiia i Afrika*, 2:200–201.

46. Spravka o sisteme prodazh kakao-bobov Zolotogo Berega, February 1957, in Rossiiskii Gosudarstvennyi Arkhiv Ekonomiki, Moscow, Russia (henceforth, RGAE), f. 413, op. 13, d. 7992, l. 2.

47. Sarah Stockwell, *The Business of Decolonization: British Business Strategies in the Gold Coast* (Oxford: Oxford University Press, 2000), 37–66.

48. Minutes of the 89th special board meeting held in the offices of the Board, Accra, 12 January 1956, in TNA, CO1029/173; Cocoa Marketing Board Development Fund, 7 February 1956, in TNA, CO1029/173.

49. For a detailed discussion of British imperial practices in the cocoa trade, see Jan-Georg Deutsch, *Educating the Middlemen: A Political and Economic History of Statutory Cocoa Marketing in Nigeria, 1936–1947* (Berlin: Verlag das Arabische Buch, 1995).

50. Cabinet Meeting, June 9, 1959, in PRAAD, ADM/13/1/28.

51. For more on Tansley, the UAC, and the Cocoa Board, see David Meredith, "The Colonial Office, British Business Interests and the Reform of Cocoa Marketing in West Africa, 1937–1945," *Journal of African History* 29, no. 2 (1988): 285–300; David K. Fieldhouse, *Merchant Capital and Economic Decolonization: The United Africa Company, 1929–1987* (Oxford: Clarendon Press, 1994).

52. Kwame Nkrumah, *Ghana: The Autobiography of Kwame Nkrumah* (Edinbirgh: T. Nelson, 1957), x.

53. H.F.T. Smith to L.T. Tomes, April 4, 1957, in TNA, FO371/125292.

54. W. Scott Thompson, *Ghana's Foreign Policy, 1957–1966: Diplomacy, Ideology and the State* (Princeton, NJ: Princeton University Press, [1969] 2015), 17–18. Gbedemah's celebrity in the West derived mostly from being denied the possibility to consume an orange juice inside a chain restaurant in Delaware during a visit to the United States in late 1957. Eisenhower personally apologized to Gbedemah and invited him for breakfast at the White House. America's racism did not reduce Gbedemah's resolve to receive economic aid from Washington. See Telegram from the Department of State to the Embassy in Ghana, October 9, 1957, in *FRUS*, 1955–1957, 28:378–379.

55. Memorandum of a Conversation, Accra, March 4, 1957, in *FRUS*, 1955–1957, 28:374–378.

56. Memorandum of Conversation, July 24, 1958, in *FRUS*, 1958–1969, 14:647–652.

57. Telegram From the Embassy in Ghana to the Department of State, 6 November 1957, in *FRUS*, 1955–1957, 28:383.

58. Informatsiia o sovetsko-ganskikh otnosheniiakh iz obzornoi spravki po Gane, podgotovlennoi attashe posol'stva SSSR v Londone N.A. Makarovym, in *Rossiia and Afrika*, 2200. On the politics and legacy of the Akosombo project, see Stephan Miescher, "'Nkrumah's Baby': The Akosombo Dam and the Dream of Development in Ghana," *Water History* 6, no. 4 (2014): 341–366; Dzodzi Tsikata, *Living in the Shadow of the Large Dams: Long Term Responses of Downstream and Lakeside Communities of Ghana's Volta River Project* (Leiden: Brill, 2006).

59. Robert Tignor, *W. Arthur Lewis and the Birth of Development Economics* (Princeton, NJ: Princeton University Press, 2006), 6–108. Lewis was knighted in 1963, and he received the Nobel Prize for Economics in 1979. His most famous contribution to development economics is W. Arthur Lewis, "Economic Development with Unlimited Supplies of Labour," *Manchester School of Economic and Social Studies* 22 (1954): 139–191. For a more general overview of Lewis' ideas, see W. Arthur Lewis, *The Theory of Economic Growth* (London: Allen & Unwin, 1955).

60. Cabinet Meeting, June 27, 1958, in PRAAD, ADM/13/1/27.

61. Cabinet Meeting, June 27, 1958, in PRAAD, ADM/13/1/27.

62. Informatsiya zamestitelia direktora Instituta etnografii I.I. Potekhina o vstrechakh s ganskimi politikami vo vremia ego prebyvaniia v Gane v oktiabre-dekabre 1957 g., 31 ianvaria 1958 g., in *Rossiia i Afrika*, 2:198–199.

63. Cabinet Meeting, June 27, 1958, in PRAAD, ADM/13/1/27.

64. Establishment of Soviet Embassy in Accra, May 5, 1959, in TNA, CAB179/6, JIC(59)69; Apollon Davidson, Sergei Mazov, and Georgii Tsypkin, *SSSR i Afrika, 1918–1960: Dokumentirovannaia istoriia vzaimootnoshenii* (Moscow: IVI RAN, 2002), 176.

65. Foreign Embassies C.E. Section Special Branch, May 27, 1959, in PRAAD, SC/BAA/317.

66. Orestov's report is attached to: Maevskii to MID, May 1959, in AVP RF, f. 573, op. 3, p. 2, d. 5, l. 2.

67. Franz Fanon, *The Wretched of the Earth* (New York: Grove Press, [1961] 2004), 67. For more on Fanon in Ghana, see Jeffrey Ahlman, "The Algerian Question in Nkrumah's Ghana, 1958–1960: Debating 'Violence' and 'Nonviolence' in African Decolonization," *Africa Today* 57, no. 2 (2010): 66–84.

68. Maevskii to MID, May 1959, in AVP RF, f. 573, op. 3, p. 2, d. 5, l. 2–41.

69. Agenda for Cabinet Meeting, April 14, 1959, in PRAAD, ADM/13/2/59; Cabinet Meeting, April 14, 1959, in PRAAD, ADM/13/1/28.

70. Davidson, Mazov, and Tsypkin, *SSSR i Afrika*, 176–177.

71. Obmen notami mezhdu predstavitelem Ministerstva vneshnei torgovli SSSR i Ministrom torgovli i promyshlennosti Gany, June 10, 1959, in RGAE, f. 413, op. 13, d. 8471, l. 4.

72. Ministerstvo Vneshnei Torgovli SSSR, *Vneshniaia Torgovlia SSSR za 1959–1963 gody* (Moscow: Vneshtorgnzdat, 1965), 430–433; Davidson, Mazov, and Tsypkin, *SSSR i Afrika*, 177; O sostoianii torgovykh otnoshenii mezhdy SSSR i Ganoi, November 27, 1959, in *Rossiia i Afrika*, 2:203–205.

73. Michael A. Gomez, *African Dominion: A New History of Empire in Early and Medieval West Africa* (Princeton, NJ: Princeton University Press, 2018); Toby Green, *A Fistful of Shells: West Africa from the Rise of the Slave Trade to the Age of Revolution* (London: Allen Lane, 2019); Ade Ajayi and Oloruntimehin, "West Africa in the Anti-Slave Trade Era," 200–221; Peterson and Brett, "Western Africa, 1870–1886," 208–256; Hargreaves, "Western Africa, 1886–1905," 257–297.

74. Catherine Coquery-Vidrovitch, Elizabeth Edwards, and Andrew Roberts, "French Black Africa," in *Cambridge History of Africa*, vol. 7: *From 1905 to 1940*, ed. A.D. Roberts (Cambridge: Cambridge University Press, 1986), 329–398.

75. See, for example, Pierre Herbart, *Le Chancre du Niger* (Paris: Gallimard, 1939). André Gide wrote the introduction. On the Office du Niger, see Monica Van Beusekom, *Negotiating Development: African Farmers and Colonial Experts at the Office du Niger, 1920–1960* (Portsmouth, NH: Heinemann, 2002).

76. The Free French regime was arguably even worse, for resources from French West Africa were needed for the final Allied offensive against Nazi Germany. See Cooper, *Decolonization and African Society*, 73–109, 141–166.

77. Frederik Cooper, *Citizenship between Empire and Nation: Remaking France and French Africa, 1945–1960* (Princeton, NJ: Princeton University Press, 2014), 26–213; Gregory Mann, *Native Sons: West African Veterans and France in the Twentieth Century* (Durham, NC: Duke University Press, 2006), 108–145.

78. Schmidt, *Cold War and Decolonization in Guinea*, 8–67. On Sékou Touré's biography in this period, see André Lewin, *Ahmed Sékou Touré, Président de la Guinée*, vol. 1: *1922–février 1955* and vol. 2: *1956–1958* (Paris: L'Harmattan, 2009).

79. For biographical information, see Seydou Camara, "Une grande figure de l'histoire du Mali: Modibo Keïta, 1915–1977," *Mande Studies* 5 (2003): 10–12.

80. Cooper, *Africa since 1940*, 76–81.

81. In West Africa, the percentages of votes in favor of the new constitution ranged from 75 percent in Niger to 99.99 percent in Côte d'Ivoire. See Cooper, *Citizenship between Empire and Nation*, 310–324.

82. Cooper, *Citizenship between Empire and Nation*, 333–349.

83. Schmidt, *Cold War and Decolonization in Guinea*, 157–169.

84. Schmidt, *Cold War and Decolonization in Guinea*, 170–178.

85. Telegramma predsedatelia Prezidiuma Verkhovnovo Soveta SSSR Prezidentu Gvinei Seku Ture, October 4, 1958, in Ministerstvo Inostrannykh Del SSSR, *SSSR i strany Afriki, 1946–1962 gg. Dokumenty i materialy*, vol. 1: *1946 g.–Sentiabr' 1960 g.* (Moscow: Gosudarstvennoe Izdatel'stvo Politicheskoi Literatury, 1963), 382–383.

86. Ministère de la France d'Outre-Mer, Direction des Affaires Politiques, "Note pour Monsieur le Ministre," September 27, 1958, in Archives du Ministère des Affaires Étrangères, La Courneuve, Paris, France (henceforth, MAE), Guinée 1953–1959, vol. 7; J-M. Couve de Murville (Minister of Foreign Affairs) to Frech diplomatic representatives abroad, October 11, 1958, in Ministère des Affaires Étrangères, *Documents Diplomatiques Français (DDF)*, 1958, vol. 2: *1er juillet–31 décembre* (Paris: Imprimerie Nationale, 1993), 496–498; Telegram from the Embassy in France to the Department of State, October 15, 1958; Telegram from the Department of State to the Consulate General at Dakar, October 17, 1958; Alphand to Couve de Murville, October 20, 1958, in *DDF*, 1958, 2:554–555; Alphand to Couve de Murville, October 24, 1958, in *DDF*, 1958, 2:571–573; Memoran-

dum from Secretary of State Dulles to President Eisenhower, October 31, 1958, in *FRUS*, 1958–1960, 14:672–674, 679–680.

87. Zapiska o neobkhodimosti ustanovleniia diplomaticheskikh otnoshenii mezhdu SSSR i Gvineiskoi Respublikoi, October 3, 1958; O meropriiatiiakh po ustanovleniiu kontaktov s pravitel'stvom Gvineiskoi Respubliki, November 8, 1958, in *Rossiia i Afrika*, 2:216–217.

88. E. Kisselev to MID, July 19, 1958 in AVP RF, f. 573, op. 2, p. 1, d. 3, l. 1–4; M. Sytenko to MID, December 15, 1958, in AVP RF, f. 573, op. 2, p. 1, d. 3, l. 9–10; O meropriiatiiakh po ustanovleniiu kontaktov s pravitel'stvom Gvineiskoi Respubliki, November 8, 1958, in *Rossiia i Afrika*, 2:216–217.

89. Iz otcheta o poezdke v Gvineiskuiu Respubliku dlia peregovorov c gvineiskim rukovodstvom o perspektivakh sovetsko-gvineiskikh otnoshenii, December 20,1958, in *Rossiia i Afrika*, 2:218.

90. Iz otcheta o poezdke v Gvineiskuiu Respubliku, 2:219–220.

91. Iz otcheta o poezdke v Gvineiskuiu Respubliku, 2:220–221.

92. Iz otcheta o poezdke v Gvineiskuiu Respubliku, 2:221–222.

93. Boubacar Diallo Telli, a law graduate who rose to a high rank in the French colonial administration in West Africa, traveled to the United States in late 1958 to present Guinea's request to join the UN. He was later appointed Guinea's ambassador to the United States, even though Guinea could not yet afford to open a real embassy in Washington. He met with officials from the State Department several times pleading for good will and aid. See Memorandum of Conversation, December 1, 1958; Memorandum of Conversation, April 24, 1959, in *FRUS*, 1958–1960, 14:85–87.

94. Davidson, Mazov, and Tsypkin, *SSSR i Afrika*, 205.

95. Guinea, April 7, 1959, in TNA, CAB179/6, JIC(59)65; Ministère de la France d'Outre-Mer, Bureau d'Etudes d'Outre-Mer, "Arrivée d'artmement et de matériel militaire tchèque," April 13, 1959, in AN, Fonds Foccart, AG/5(F)/555; Ministère de la France d'Outre-Mer, Bureau d'Etudes d'Outre-Mer, "Transmission de renseignements," April 27, 1959, in AN, Fonds Foccart, AG/5(F)/555; Direction d'Afrique-Levant, "Fourniture d'armes tchecoslovaques à la Guinée," April 11, 1959, in MAE, Guinée 1958–1959, vol. 3.

96. Pribytie v Konakri posla SSSR v Gvineiskoi Respublike P.I. Gerasimova i vruchenie im veritel'nykh gramot prezidentu Seku Ture, May 12, 1959, in *Rossiia i Afrika*, 2:222–224; Rech' prezidenta Seku Ture, proiznesennaia po sluchaiu vrucheniia veritel'nykh gramot Poslom Sovetskogo Soiuza 20 aprelia 1959 goda, in AVP RF, f. 575, op. 2, p. 1, d. 6, l. 10; "Nomination d'un Ambassadeur de l'URSS en Guinée," March 11, 1959, in MAE, Guinée 1958–1959, vol. 2.

97. Conté was a medical doctor who had exercised his profession in Dakar, Senegal, before becoming active in the PDG following the referendum. See "Nomination des représentants diplomatiques guinéens," September 4, 1959, in MAE, Guinée 1958–1959, vol. 2.

98. Davidon, Mazov, and Tsypkin, *SSSR i Afrika*, 206–207.

99. Spravka, May 1959, in AVP RF, f. 0575, op. 1, p. 1, d. 2, l. 19.

100. O vnutripoliticheskom i ekonomicheskom polozhenii Federatsii Mali (spravka), February 18, 1961, in AVP RF, f. 0607, op. 1-a, p. 1-a, d. 9, l. 2–12.

101. A. Gromyko (Foreign Minister, USSR) to TsK KPSS, June 17, 1960, in AVP RF, f. 0607, op. 1-a, p. 1-a, d. 6, l. 1–2.

102. Davidson, Mazov, and Tsypkin, *SSSR i Afrika*, 223.

103. Telegramma predsedatelia Soveta Ministrov SSSR N.S. Khrushcheva predsedateliu Soveta Ministrov Federatsii Mali Modibo Keita, June 20, 1960, in Ministerstvo Inostrannykh Del SSSR, *SSSR i Strany Afriki, 1946–1962 gg. Dokumenty i Materialy* (Moscow: Gosudarstvennoe Izdatel'stvo Politicheskoi Literatury, 1963), 2:547–548.

104. V. Kuznetsov (First Deputy Minister, MID) to TsK KPSS, October 1, 1960, in AVP RF, f. 0607, op. 1-a, p. 1-a, d. 9, l. 5.

105. O vnutripoliticheskom i ekonomicheskom polozhenii Federatsii Mali (spravka), February 1961, in AVP RF, f. 0607, op. 1-a, p. 1-a, d. 9, l. 10–11.

106. O vnutripoliticheskom i ekonomicheskom polozhenii Federatsii Mali, l. 35.

107. Telegramma predsedatelia Soveta Ministrov SSSR N.S. Khrushcheva predsedateliu pravitel'stva Mali Modibo Keita, October 8, 1960, in SSSR i strany Afriki, 1946-1962 gg., 2:36–37.

108. Couve de Mourville to French diplomatic representatives abroad, September 9, 1960, in Ministère des Affaires Étrangères, in DDF, 1960, vol. 2: 1er juillet-31 décembre (Paris: Imprimerie Nationale, 1996), 302-303; Direction d'Afrique-Levant, "Entretiens franco-britanniques sur l'Afrique (Londres, 13-14 decembre 1960)," December 26, 1960, in DDF, 1960, 2:797-804.

109. Memorandum from Acting Secretary of State Dillon to President Eisenhower, September 23, 1960, in FRUS, 1958-1960, 14:226.

110. Memorandum of a Conference with President Eisenhower, November 1, 1960, in FRUS, 1958-1960, 14:236-239.

111. Davidson, Mazov, and Tsypkin, SSSR i Afrika, 228-230.

112. SDECE, "Penetration Sovietique en Afrique—L'Etat-Major du P.C. de l'U.R.S.S. pour fomenter ou entretenir les révoltes sur tout le Continent africain," November 5, 1959, in Archives Nationales, Pierrefitte-sur-Seine, Paris, France (henceforth, AN), Fonds "Foccart," AG/5(F)/329.

4. THE HEART OF THE MATTER

1. "Gerasimov, Pavel Ivanovich," in Diplomaticheskii Slovar', ed. Andrei Gromyko et al. (Moscow: Nauka, 1985), 1:254.

2. "L'action soviétique pour établir en Guinée un centre de propagande et d'agitation communiste sur l'Afrique Occidentale," Extrait d'un rapport du Service de Renseignement d'Allemagne Fédérale, April 29, 1959, in MAE, Guinée 1953–1959, vol. 7.

3. On Mukhitdinov, Central Asia, and decolonization, see Artemy Kalinovsky, "Not Some British Colony in Africa: The Politics of Decolonization and Modernization in Soviet Central Asia, 1955-1964," Ab Imperio 2 (2013): 191–222.

4. Angus Maddison, The World Economy, vol 2: Historical Statistics (Paris: OECD, 2006), 474-475, 487-488, 540, 542, 583.

5. Maddison, The World Economy, 487, 584-585.

6. Apollon Davidson, Sergei Mazov, and Georgii Tsypkin, SSSR i Afrika, 1918-1960: Dokumentirovannaia istoriia vzaimootnoshenii (Moscow: IVI RAN, 2002), 205.

7. Ministère de la France d'Outre-Mer, Bureau d'Etudes d'Outre-Mer, Transmission de renseignements, "Signature d'accords commerciaux entre l'U.R.S.S. et la Guinée," February 15, 1959, in AN, Fonds Foccart, 5/AG/F/555; Davidson, Mazov, and Tsypkin, SSSR i Afrika, 205-206.

8. Soglashenie o tovarooborote i platezhakh mezhdu SSSR i Gvineem 13 February 1959, in Ministerstvo Inostrannykh Del SSSR, SSSR i Strany Afriki, 1946-1962 gg. Dokumenty i Materialy, vol. 1: 1946 g.-Sentiabr' 1960 g. (Moscow: Gosudarstvennoe Izdatel'stvo Politicheskoi Literatury, 1963), 421-424.

9. Annex II to Review of Current Intelligence Review, February 24, 1959, in TNA, CAB179/6.

10. For more details on the opening of the Soviet embassy, see chapter 3.

11. Vypiska iz zapisi o vstreche Pravitel'stvennykh delegatsii Sovetskogo Soiuza i Gvineiskoi Respubliki, August 17, 1959, in GARF, f. r5446, op. 120, d. 1736, l. 1; Dejean to Paris, August 20, 1959, in MAE, Guinée 1958–1959, Vol. 20; Informatsiia dlia TsK KPSS

o prebyvanii v SSSR pravitel'stvennoi delegatsii Gvinei s 17 po 21 avgusta 1959 g., August 21, 1959, in Davidson and Mazov, *Rossiia i Afrika*, 2:226–229.

12. Informatsiia dlia TsK KPSS . . . , in *Rossiia i Afrika: Dokumenty i Materialy XVIII v.–1960 g.*, vol. 2: *1918–1960*, ed. Apollon Davidson and Sergei Mazov (Moscow: IVI RAN, 1999), 226–227.

13. Direction Afrique-Levant, Note "Guinée-URSS," September 7, 1959, in MAE, Guinée 1958–1959, vol. 20.

14. Soglashenie mezhdu SSSR i Gvineei ob ekonomicheskom i tekhnicheskom sotrud-nichestve, August 24, 1959, in *SSSR i strany Afriki*, 1:460–461.

15. P. Reilly (British Ambassador to Moscow) to Selwyn Lloyd (Foreign Minister), December 1, 1959, in TNA, FO371/138825.

16. Soobshchenie ob obede v Gagre, dannom Predsedatelem Soveta Ministry SSSR N. S. Khrushchevym v chest' Prezidenta i Predsedatelia pravitel'stva Gvinei Seku Ture, November 25, 1959, in *SSSR i strany Afriki*, 1:488–490; Rech' pervogo zamestitelia Predse-datelia Soveta Ministrov SSSR F. R. Kozlova v Kremle na mitinge druzhby mezhdu narodami SSSR i Gvinei, November 26, 1959, in *SSSR i strany Afriki*, 1:490–502.

17. Zapis' besedy predsedatelia prezidiuma verkhovnogo soveta SSSR K.E. Voro-shilova s prezidentom i predsedatelem pravistel'stva gvineiskoi respubliki Seku Ture, November 23, 1959, in AVP RF, f. 575, op. 2, p. 1, d. 6, l. 16.

18. Spravka o vruchenii 3 marta 1960 goda veritel'nykh gramot Poslom SSSR v Gvi-neiskoi Respublike D.S. Solodom Prezidentu Seku Ture, in AVP RF, f. 575, op. 3, p. 2, d. 12, l. 13–14; R. Duvauchelle (French Embassy in Guinea) to Paris, "Présentation des lettres de créance de M. Solod," March 11, 1960, in MAE, Guinée 1960–1965, vol. 35.

19. Spravka pechati, January 1960, in AVP RF, f. 573, op. 4, p. 5, d. 16, l. 1–7, 12–15.

20. W.A. Lewis cited in Robert Tignor, *W. Arthur Lewis and the Birth of Development Economics* (Princeton, NJ: Princeton University Press, 2006), 170.

21. W.A. Lewis, "Aspects of Development" (speech), 1958, in Rare Books and Special Collections, Seeley G. Mudd Library, Princeton University, Princeton, NJ, United States (henceforth, RBSC), W. Arthur Lewis Papers (MC092), box 20, folder 4; W.A. Lewis, "Second Development Plan" (note), July 7, 1959, in RBSC, W. Arthur Lewis Papers (MC092), box 21, folder 7.

22. Cabinet Meeting, June 27, 1958, in PRAAD, ADM/13/1/27.

23. Sytenko to MID, October 4, 1959, in AVP RF, f. 573, op. 3, p. 2, d. 3, l. 1–16. On Padmore's last years in Ghana, see Leslie James, *George Padmore and Decolonization from Below: Pan-Africanism, the Cold War, and the End of Empire* (London: Palgrave Mac-millan, 2015), 164–190.

24. Fifty-four percent of Ghanaian voters took part in the referendum, and 88.47 percent of them voted for the republic. Ghana remained a member of the Common-wealth. Nkrumah received 89 percent of the votes in the presidential elections. See Egon Schwelb, "The Republican Constitution of Ghana," *American Journal of Comparative Law* 9, no. 4 (1960): 634–656.

25. Spravka, April 30, 1960, in RGANI, f. 5, op. 30, d. 336, l. 96–107.

26. N. Gavrilov, "K voprosu ob ekonomicheskoi politike nezavismykh stran Afriki i k razvitiiu ikh svizsei s Sovetskim Soiuzom," June 30, 1961, in Arkhiv Rossiiskoi Aka-demii Nauk, Moscow, Russia (henceforth, ARAN), f. 2010, op. 1, d. 16, l. 90–91; Sytenko to MID, January 1961, in AVP RF, f. 573, op. 4, p. 6, d. 28, l. 1–10.

27. Frank Gerits and Gerardo Serra, "The Politics of Socialist Education in Ghana: The Kwame Nkrumah Ideological Institute, 1961-6," *Journal of African History* 6, no. 3 (2019): 407–428.

28. Cabinet Meeting, August 16, 1960, in PRAAD, ADM/13/1/29; Meeting of the Fi-nance Committee, October 6, 1961, in Cadbury's Archives, Bournville, Birmingham,

United Kingdom (henceforth, CB), 101/003612; Meeting of the Finance Committee, February 16, 1962, in CB, 101/003612; Meeting of the Finance Committee, April 5, 1963, in CB, 101/003612; Meeting of the Finance Committee, May 15, 1964, in CB, 101/003612.

29. MID to TsK KPSS, March 22, 1960, in AVP RF, f. 573, op. 4, p. 4, d. 12, l. 26–31.

30. Telegram from the Embassy in Ghana to Department of State, September 5, 1960, in *FRUS*, 1958–1960, 14:660–661.

31. Memorandum of a conversation, September 22, 1960, in *FRUS*, 1958–1960, 14:661.

32. For more context on the Ghana-VALCO agreement and its consequences, see Stephanie Decker, "Corporate Political Activity in Less Developed Countries: The Volta River Project in Ghana, 1958–66," *Business History* 53, no. 7 (2011): 993–1017; Rod Sims, "The Volta Aluminium Company Agreements in Ghana," in *Developing with Foreign Investment*, ed. Vincent Cable and Bishnodat Persaud (London: Routledge, 1987), 178–190.

33. Telegram from the Embassy in Ghana to the Department of State, October 7, 1960, in *FRUS*, 1958–1960, 14:666.

34. Thomas Noer, "The New Frontier and African Neutralism: Kennedy, Nkrumah, and the Volta River Project," *Diplomatic History* 8, no. 1 (1984): 62.

35. Telegram from the Embassy in Ghana to the Department of State, October 25, 1960, in *FRUS*, 1958–1960, 14:669.

36. Davidson, Mazov, and Tsypkin, *SSSR i Afrika*, 180.

37. Informatsiia o prebyvanii parlamentskoi delegatsii Gany v Moskve 5–6 maya 1960 g., May 26, 1960, in *Rossiia i Afrika*, 2:209–210.

38. I. Kolosovskii (African department, MID) to TsK, 30 April 1960, in RGANI, f. 5, op. 30, d. 336, l. 32–39, 56–57; Spravka, May 1960, in AVP RF, f. 573, op. 4, p. 4, d. 15, l. 5–17; Davidson, Mazov and Tsypkin, *SSSR i Afrika*, 182.

39. K. Nkrumah to N.S. Khrushchev, June 3, 1960, in AVP RF, f. 573, op. 4, p. 5, d. 21, l. 1–3; Davidson, Mazov, and Tsypkin, *SSSR i Afrika*, 182.

40. A.W. Snelling, "Ghana: Relations with the Soviet Union," August 18, 1960, in TNA, FO371/146801.

41. Spravka, May 1960, in AVP RF, f. 573, op. 4, p. 4, d. 15, l. 20–21.

42. Agreement for Economic and Technical Cooperation between the Republic of Ghana and the Union of Soviet Socialist Republics, August 4, 1960, in PRAAD, MFA/4/83; Cabinet Memorandum, August 30, 1960, in PRAAD, ADM/13/2/74; Cabinet Meeting, November 1, 1960, in PRAAD, ADM/13/1/29.

43. Long Term Payments Agreement between the Republic of Ghana and the Union of Soviet Socialist Republics, November 4, 1961, in PRAAD, MFA/4/153; Dolgosrochnoe torgovoe soglashenie mezhdu SSSR i Ganoi, November 4, 1961, in *SSSR i strany Afriki*, 2:443–448; Ministerstvo Vneshnei Torgovli SSSR, *Vneshniaia Torgovlia SSSR za 1959–1963 gody* (Moscow: Vneshtorgnzdat, 1965), 432–433.

44. Sytenko to MID, December 1960, in AVPRF, f. 573, op. 4, p. 5, d. 18, l. 3–5.

45. On January 1, 1961, the Soviet Union introduced a new ruble, which was worth ten old rubles. Its international exchange rate, however, was altered differently. Before 1961, one US dollar was worth four old rubles; after 1961, one US dollar was exchanged with 0.90 ruble (90 kopecks). Therefore, the total amount granted to Mali was in line with the previous loans to Guinea and Ghana (approximately 160 million old rubles).

46. Respublika Mali (kratkaia spravka), December 25, 1961, in AVP RF, f. 0607, op. 2, p. 3, d. 7, l. 16–17; Accord sur la coopération économique et technique entre la République du Mali et l'Union des Républiques Soviétiques Socialistes [*sic*], 1961, in ANM, BPN USRDA, carton 45, dossier 117.

47. *Vneshniaia Torgovlia SSSR za 1959–1963 gody*, 438–439; National Intelligence Estimate, "Guinea and Mali as Examples of African Radicalism," July 11, 1962, in *FRUS*,

1961–1963, vol. 21: *Africa*, 320–322; "Memorandum from the President's Special Assistant (Dungan) to President Kennedy," March 6, 1963, in *FRUS*, 21:329–330.

48. Discours de Modibo Keïta, 10 septembre 1962, in ANM, BPN USRDA, carton 3e, dossier 5 "Congres de l'USRDA, 10–12 septembre 1962."

49. P. Bouzou, Ambassade de la République du Mali en URSS, "Le XXIIeme Congres du Parti Communiste de l'URSS et la nouvelle étape de l'économie soviétique," October 1961, in ANM, BPN USRDA, carton 8, dossier 17: "XXII Congres du Parti Communiste de l'URSS, 1961–1967"; Ambassade de la République di Mali en URSS, "La direction de l'économie en URSS," 1962, in ANM, BPN USRDA, carton 8, dossier 17: XXII Congres du Parti Communiste de l'URSS, 1961–1967.

50. Rapport de Mameuteu Coulibaly (Député), Délégation USRDA en URSS, Juillet-Aout 1964, in ANM, BPN USRDA, carton 87, dossier 296: Délégation de l'US RDA en Union Soviétique, 1964.

51. Organisation de coopération et de développement économiques, "La situation économique de la Guinée et les résultats de l'aide extérieure," March 16, 1965, in MAE, Guinée 1960–1965, vol. 62.

52. All figures in 1990 international US dollars. Such broad comparisons are indicative only. Comparing wealth across vast spatial and temporal distances makes little sense beyond providing some very rough terms of reference to grasp differences and similarities. For historical data, see Maddison, *The World Economy*, 2:473, 486–487, 600–601. The conversion to 1990 dollars assumes an inflation rate of 5 percent.

53. Stenogramma zasedania uchenogo soveta instituta Afriki AN SSSR 4 maya 1960 g., in ARAN, f. 2010, op. 1, d. 4, l. 3–7.

54. Ekonomika Gvinei (kratkii obzor), January 26, 1961, in RGAE, f. 365, op. 2, d. 218, l. 9; Otchet o nauchnoi komandirovke mladshego nauchnogo sotrudnika Instituta Afriki AN SSSR Kupriianova P.I. v Ganu, 1962, in ARAN, f. 2010, op. 1, d. 20, l. 31–34; Respublika Mali (kratkaia spravka), December 25, 1961, in AVP RF, f. 0607, op. 2, p. 3, d. 7, l. 17–18; Stenogramma sovmesntogo zasedaniia uchenykh sovetov Instituta Afriki i instituta geografii Akademii nauk SSSR 23-go maia 1961 goda, in ARAN, f. 2010, op. 1, d. 15, l. 41–42.

55. Respublika Mali (kratkaia spravka), December 25, 1961, in AVP RF, f. 0607, op. 2, p. 3, d. 7, l. 17–19; Gvineiskaia Respublika (kratkaia spravka), February 25, 1959, in AVP RF, f. 575, op. 2, p. 1, d. 8, l. 1–6.

56. Dejean to Paris, "Déclaration de M. Sékou Touré," August 24, 1959, in MAE, Guinée 1958–1959, vol. 20.

57. Soglashenie o tavorooborote i platezhakh mezhdu Soiuzom Sovetskikh Sotsialisticheskikh Respublik i Gvineiskoi Respublikoi, February 13, 1959, in RGAE, f. 413, op. 13, d. 8472, l. 2–7; Torgovoe sglashenie mezhdu Soiuzom Sovetskikh Sotsialisticheskikh Respublik i Respublikoi Ganoi, August 4, 1960, in RGAE, f. 413, op. 13, d. 8710, l. 2–9; Torgovoe soglashenie mezhdu Soiuzom Sovetskikh Sotsialisticheskikh Respublik i Respublikoi Mali, October 25, 1960, in RGAE, f. 413, op. 13, d. 8717, l. 8–15.

58. J.P. Hadengue, Note à l'attention de Monsieur le President de la République, le President de la Communauté, "Le commerce extérieure de la Guinée," September 19, 1962, in AN, Fonds Foccart, 5/AG/F/1640.

59. Memorandum o besede c ministrom promyshlennosti Gany g-nom Krobo Eduseem, sootoiavsheisia 15 ianvaria 1962 g., in RGAE, f. 413, op. 13, d. 9448, l. 3–5; Zapis' besedy torgovogo sovetnika v Gane t. Myshkova V.N. s General'nym direktorom "Gana Kokou Marketing Bord" g-nom Dodu, sostoiavsheisia 15 fevralia 1961 g., in RGAE, f. 413, op. 13, d. 9046, l. 2; K. Nazarkin (Gosbank) to K.K. Bakhtov (MVT), November 5, 1961, in RGAE, f. 413, op. 13, d. 8472, l. 8–10.

60. Ministère de la France d'Outre-Mer, Note de Renseignement, December 18, 1958, "Organisation du commerce guinéen," in AN, Fonds Foccart, 5/AG/F/555.

61. Procès verbal de réunion du bureau politique national de l'union soudanaise R.D.A., July 27, 1961, in ANM, BPN USRDA, carton 23, dossier 55: Les Sociétés et Entreprises d'Etat.

62. Ministère de la France d'Outre-Mer, Bureau d'Etudes d'Outre-Mer, "La République de Guinée en avril 1959," June 4, 1959, in AN, Fonds Foccart, AG/5(F)/555.

63. Discours de Modibo Keïta, September 10, 1962, in ANM, BPN USRDA, carton 3e, dossier 5: Congres de l'USRDA, September 10–12, 1962.

64. Procès verbal de réunion du bureau politique national de l'union soudanaise R.D.A., July 27, 1961, in ANM, BPN USRDA, carton 23, dossier 55: Les Sociétés et Entreprises d'Etat.

65. Le Mali et la Zone Franc, January 15, 1960, in ANM, BPN USRDA, carton 129, dossier 481: Le Mali et la Zone Franc.

66. Ministère de la France d'Outre-Mer, Bureau d'Etudes d'Outre-Mer, Transmission de renseignements, "Situation économique en Guinée," February 9, 1959, in AN, Fonds Foccart, 5/AG/F/555.

67. Appendix to the Trade Agreement between the Republic of Ghana and the USSR of 4th August 1960, in PRAAD, RG 7/1/1968; Liste "A" des produits pour l'exportation de l'U.R.S.S. vers la République de Guinée, in AN, Fonds Foccart, 5/AG/F/555; Dejean to Couve de Murville, "Accord commercial entre l'URSS et la Guinee," February 19, 1959, in MAE, Guinée 1958–1959, vol. 20.

68. V.S. Baskiniy (kandidat ekonomiki, Institute of Africa), "Effektivnost' ekonomicheskogo sotrudnichestva SSSR so stranami Afriki," June 20, 1963, in ARAN, f. 2010, op. 1, d. 37, l. 15–16.

69. Priem Predsedatelem Soveta Ministrov SSSR N.S. Khrushchevym Prezidenta i Predsedatelia Pravitel'stva Gvineiskoi Respubliki Seku Ture, November 23, 1959, in GARF, f. r5446, op. 120, d. 1736, l. 8.

70. GKES to Khrushchev, September 7, 1959, in RGANI, f. 5, op. 30, d. 305, l. 116–120.

71. Baskinyi, "Effektivnost' ekonomicheskogo sotrudnichestva SSSR so stranami Afriki," June 20, 1963, in ARAN, f. 2010, op. 1, d. 37, l. 18.

72. Spravka ob obiazatel'stvakh Sovetskogo Soiuza po Sovetsko-Gvineiskomu soglasheniiu i khode ikh vypolneniia, May 1960, in AVP RF, f. 575, op. 3, p. 3, d. 19, l. 28; Zapis' besedy sovetnika Parshina AV c ministrom plana Gvineiskoi Respubliki Keita N Famara, March 21, 1960, in RGAE, f. 365, op. 2, d. 221, l. 29.

73. Jeffrey Ahlman, Living with Nkrumahism: Nation, State, and Pan-Africanism in Ghana (Athens: Ohio University Press, 2017), 62.

74. Ministère de la France d'Outre-Mer, Bureau d'Etudes d'Outre-Mer, Transmission de renseignements, March 13, 1959, "Activités diplomatiques guinéen," in AN, Fonds Foccart, 5/AG/F/555.

75. Jacques Foccart to Prime Minister, November 6, 1959, in AN, Fonds Foccart, 5/AG/F/555.

76. Zapisy konferentsii AN o stranakh Azii i Afriki, October 31, 1958, in RGANI, f. 5, op. 35, d. 79, l. 52–71.

77. Frederik Cooper, Africa since 1940: The Past of the Present (New York: Cambridge University Press, 2002), 92.

78. François Denord and Xavier Zunigo, "'Révolutionnairement vôtre.' Économie marxiste, militantisme intellectuel et expertise politique chez Charles Bettelheim," Actes de la recherche en science sociales 3, no. 158 (2005): 8–29; Ministère de la France d'Outre-Mer, Bureau d'Etudes d'Outre-Mer, "La République de Guinée en avril 1959," June 4, 1959, in AN, Fonds Foccart, AG/5(F)/555.

79. Cheick Oumar Diarrah, *Le Mali de Modibo Keïta* (Paris: L'Harmattan, 1986), 62; Samir Amin, *Trois expériences africaines de développement: Le Mali, la Guinée et le Ghana* (Paris: Presses Universitaires de France, 1965), 80–130.

80. Jean Bénard, "Note sur les mesures immédiates de sauvegarde et de décolonisation de l'économie soudanaise," September 21, 1960, in ANM, BPN USRDA, carton 136, dossier 533: "Organisation monétaire en R. du Mali."

81. A copy of the three-year plan was sent to Paris from Jean-Yves Eichenberger, the CEO of Bauxites du Midi, a French company that had operated in Guinea since the 1920s. See Eichenberger to Foccart, March 8, 1960, "Plan Triennal," Chapitres I&II, in AN, Fonds Foccart, 5/AG/F/555.

82. Stenogramma zasedania uchenogo soveta instituta Afriki AN SSSR 4 maya 1960 g., in ARAN, f. 2010, op. 1, d. 4, l. 13–14; Ministère du Plan et de l'Economie Rural, "Dossier Plan," 1962, in ANM, USRDA(BPN)/CMLN/UDPM, Article 01: Plan Quinquennal de développement économique et social de la République du Mali, 1962–1963.

83. "Plan Triennal," Chapitre III, in AN, Fonds Foccart, 5/AG/F/555; Ambassade de France en Guinée, "La conférence de Kankan et le plan triennal," April 1960, in MAE, Guinée 1960–1965, Vol. 61; Ambassade de France en Guinée, Plan triennal, Annexe 1, "Mécanisation de l'agriculture," 18 May 1960, in MAE, Guinée 1960–1965, Vol. 61.

84. Stenogramma sovmesntogo zasedaniia uchenykh sovetov Instituta Afriki i instituta geografii Akademii nauk SSSR 23-go maia 1961 goda, in ARAN, f. 2010, op. 1, d. 15, l. 40–42; Spravka ob obiazatel'stvakh Sovetskogo Soiuza po Sovetsko-Gvineiskomu soglasheniiu i khode ikh vypolneniia, May 1960, in AVP RF, f. 575, op. 3, p. 3, d. 19, l. 29–31; Zapis' besedy Mikoiana s Nkruma v g. Akkra, January 14, 1962, in RGAE, f. 365, op. 2, d. 338, l. 179–181; "Plan Triennal," Chapitre III&IV, in AN, Fonds Foccart, 5/AG /F/555.

85. Beseda s poslom Respubliki Mali v SSSR Mamadu Fadila Keita, August 4, 1962, in GARF, f. r5446, op. 120, d. 1687, l. 20–26.

86. Otchet o nauchnoi komandirovke mladshego nauchnogo sotrudnika Instituta Afriki AN SSSR Kupriianova P.I. v Ganu, 1962, in ARAN, f. 2010, op. 1, d. 17, l. 38–42.

87. W. Arthur Lewis, "The Agricultural Development Corporation" (report), June 24, 1958, in RBSC, W. Arthur Lewis Papers (MC092), Box 20, Folder 7.

88. Intervention du Docteur Kouyaté, Ministre du Développement, Chef de la Délégation de la République du Mali au colloque sur les politiques de développement et les voies africaines du socialisme, 2 au 8 décembre 1962, Dakar, in ANM, BPN USRDA, carton 86, dossier 290, "Rapports de missions à l'extérieur du Mali, 1962–1968."

89. Zapis' besedy s ministrom sel'skogo, vodnogo i lesnogo khoziaistva Salakh Niare, February 15, 1961, in AVP RF, f. 607, op. 2, p. 1, d. 4, l. 8–9.

90. Otsenka, ekonomicheskogo polozheniia respubliki Mali i nekotorye voprosy sovetsko-maliiskogo ekonomicheskogo sotrudnichestva, January 17, 1962, in AVP RF, f. 0607, op. 3, p. 5, d. 12, l. 61; Respublika Mali (kratkaia spravka), December 25, 1961, in AVP RF, f. 0607, op. 1, p. 3, d. 7, l. 20–21.

91. Plan Triennal, Chapitre IV, in AN, Fonds Foccart, 5/AG/F/555; Ob agrarnykh otnosheniiakh v Gvineskoi Respublike (kratkaia spravka), August 1960, in AVP RF, f. 575, op. 3, p. 3, d. 23, l. 111–120; Zapis' besedy s Ministrom obshchestvennykh rabot i zhilishchnogo stroitel'stva Respubliki Mali Mamadu Avom ot 13 marta 1961 goda, in AVP RF, f. 607, op. 2, p. 1, d. 4, l. 27–28; Ambassade de France en Guinée, "La conférence de Kankan et le plan triennal," April 1960, in MAE, Guinée 1960–1965, Vol. 61.

92. Sékou Touré to Khrushchev, July 19, 1960, in AVP RF, f. 575, op. 3, p. 3, d. 18, l. 2–5; Ambassade de France en Guinée, Bordereau d'envoi, "Ephéméride politique septembre 1960," October 6, 1960, in AN, Fonds Foccart, 5/AG/F/1637.

93. Vypiska iz zapisi besedy N.S. Khrushchev s prezidentom i predsedatelem pravitel'stva Gvineiskoi respubliki Seku Ture, September 7, 1960, in GARF, f. r5446, op. 120, d. 1736, l. 22–25.

94. Zapis' besedy Skachkov s poslom gvineiskoi respubliki Biro Bubakar Barri, October 16, 1962, in RGAE, f. 365, op. 2, d. 339, l. 84; Spravka ob uchastii Sovetskogo Soiuza v osyshchestvlenii stroitel'stva kompleksa sooruzhenii, namechaemykh na reke Konkure v Gvineiskoi Respublike, March–April 1961, in RGAE, f. 365, op. 2, d. 300, l. 13–22.

95. Spravka ob uchastii Sovetskogo Soiuza v osyshchestvlenii stroitel'stva kompleksa sooruzhenii, namechaemykh na reke Konkure v Gvineiskoi Respublike, March–April 1961, in RGAE, f. 365, op. 2, d. 300, l. 13–22.

96. P. Grushin (MID) to N.M. Smelov (GKES), October 25, 1962, in RGAE, f. 365, op. 2, d. 354, l. 108; Letter to the commercial counselor, embassy of the USSR in Ghana from the Development Commission [in English], September 26, 1960, in RGAE, f. 365, op. 2, d. 238, l. 7; Spravka o khode vypolneniia obiazatel'stv SSSR po okazaniiu tekhnicheskogo sodeistviia Respublike Gane v stroitel'stve predpriiatii i provedenii otdek'nykh rabot po soglasheniiu ot 4 avgusta 1960 g. i protokolu k nemu ot 23 dekabria 1960 g., in GARF, f. R5446, op. 120, d. 1727, l. 74–78; Zapis' besedy s Ministrom obshchestvennykh rabot i zhilishchnogo stroitel'stva Respubliki Mali Mamadu Avom ot 13 marta 1961 goda, l. 27–28.

97. "Frankreichs Zeit in Afrika ist Abgelaufen," *Der Spiegel*, January 28, 1959, 46.

98. Ministère de la France d'Outre-Mer, Bureau d'Etudes d'Outre-Mer, Transmission de renseignements, March 13, 1959, "Activités diplomatiques guinéen," in AN, Fonds Foccart, 5/AG/F/555.

99. Ekonomika i vneshniaia torgovlia Gvineiskoi Respubliki (kratkaia spravka), November 30, 1962, in RGAE, f. 413, op. 13, d. 9450, l. 2–3; Khruschev to Sékou Touré, August 30, 1960, in GARF, f. R5446, f. 120, op. 120, d. 1736, l. 20–21.

100. Plan Triennal, Chapitre III&V, in AN, Fonds Foccart, 5/AG/F/555.

101. Spravka ob obiazatel'stvakh Sovetskogo Soiuza po Sovetsko-Gvineiskomu soglasheniiu i khode ikh vypolneniia, May 1960, in AVP RF, f. 575, op. 3, p. 3, d. 19, l. 29–31.

102. Modibo Keïta to Khrushchev, December 13, 1960, in AVP RF, f. 0607, op. 2, p. 3, d. 7, l. 5–8; Spravka ob innostrannoi pomoshchi Respublike Mali, December 1962, in AVP RF, f. 0607, op. 3, p. 5, d. 12, l. 43–48.

103. Rapport d'activité économique du Ministère du Commerce au cours de l'année 1959/1960, in ANM, BPN USRDA, carton 29, dossier 63: Conseil des Ministres II, 1961.

104. Zapis' besedy s Ministrom obshchestvennykh rabot i zhilishchnogo stroitel'stva Respubliki Mali Mamadu Avom ot 13 marta 1961 goda, in AVP RF, f. 607, op. 2, p. 1, d. 4, l. 27–28; Soglasitel'nyi protokol mezhdu Gvineiskoi respublikoi i respublikoi Mali ot 5 maia 1961 goda (perevod c frantsuzskogo), in RGAE, f. 365, op. 2, d. 293, l. 11; Effektivnost' ekonomicheskogo sotrudnichestva SSSR so stranami Afriki, June 20, 1963, in ARAN, f. 2010, op. 1, d. 37, l. 20.

105. Zapis' besedy Arkhipova s N Famara Keita, February 22, 1962, in RGAE, f. 365, op. 2, d. 339, l. 50–52; Doklad o sostoianii rabot po rekonstruktsii aerodroma Konakri na 15 iiunia 1961 goda, in RGAE, f. 365, op. 2, d. 298, l. 155; Predlozheniia po uskoreniiu okazaniia tekhnicheskogo sodeistviia Sovetskogo Soiuza v stroitel'stve i rekonstruktsii riada ob"ektov Gvineiskoi Respubliki, September 18, 1960, in AVP RF, f. 575, op. 3, p. 3, d. 19, l. 54–55; Spravka ob obiazatel'stvakh Sovetskogo Soiuza po Sovetsko-Gvineiskomu soglasheniiu i khode ikh vypolneniia, May 1960, in AVP RF, f. 575, op. 3, p. 3, d. 19, l. 29–31.

106. On automobile modernization in Ghana, see Jennifer Hart, *Ghana on the Go: African Mobility in the Age of Motor Transportation* (Bloomington: Indiana University Press, 2016), 113–116.

107. Vystuplenia pered rabochimi-stroiteliami zhilogo kompleksa v gorode Tema, January 12, 1962, in GARF, f. R5446, f. 120, d. 1725, l. 21.

108. Census Office of Ghana, *1960 Population Census of Ghana*, vol. 1: *The Gazetteer. Alphabetical List of Localities with Number of Population and Houses* (Accra: Census Office, 1962), 368. On Soviet and socialist housing projects in Ghana, see Łukas Stanek, *Architecture in Global Socialism: Eastern Europe, West Africa, and the Middle East in the Cold War* (Princeton, NJ: Princeton University Press, 2020), 35–96.

109. P.E.I. Preko (Ministry of Public Works) to M.I. Malakov (GKES), October 23, 1962, in RGAE, f. 365, op. 2, d. 352, l. 12–13; K. Aomoa-Awuah (Minter of Industry) to Sudoimport, November 30, 1962, in RGAE, f. 365, op. 2, d. 408, l. 4; Zapis' besedy chlena GKES Sheviakov GN c poslom Elliotom, January 18, 1961, in RGAE, f. 365, op. 2, d. 277, l. 3; V. Myshkov (SovEmb Accra) to Skachkov (GKES), February 10, 1960, in RGAE, f. 365, op. 2, d. 238, l. 2–3; Cabinet Memorandum, August 30, 1960, in PRAAD, ADM/13/2/74; Cabinet Meeting, 1 November 1960, in PRAAD, ADM/13/1/29; Contract No. 8406, 25 October 1963, in PRAAD, MFA 4/172.

110. P. Siraud to Ministère des Affaires Etrangères, "Plan triennal," February 27, 1960, in MAE, Guinée 1960–1965, vol. 61; Beseda Timofeeva s nachal'nikom arkhitekturno-stroitel'nogo upravleniia gor. Konakri Konde, January 5, 1962, in RGAE, f. 365, op. 2, d. 339, l. 7–9.

111. Zapis' besedy s predstaviteliami Ganskoi storony ot 8 ianvaria 1962 g., in RGAE, f. 365, op. 2, d. 338, l. 200–202; Spravka ob obiazatel'atvakh Sovetskogo Soiuza po Sovetsko-Gvineiskomu soglasheniiu i khode ikh vypolneniia, in AVP RF, f. 575, op. 3, p. 3, d. 19, l. 29–30; Ministère des Travaux Public, des Mines, de l'Habitat et des Recherches Scientifiques, "Note sur le programme de prospection minière du plan quinquennal," 1961, in ANM, BPN USRDA, carton 29, dossier 63: Conseil des Ministres II, 1961; Skachkov to TsK KPSS, 4 November 1961, in AVP RF, f. 0607, op. 2, p. 3, d. 7, l. 10–12; Gromyko to TsK KPSS, 22 April 1961, in AVP RF, f. 0607, op. 2, p. 3, d. 7, l. 21.

112. J.P. Hadengue, "Note à l'attention de Monsieur le Secrétaire General," September 13, 1960, in AN, Fonds Foccart, 5/AG/F/1640; Spravka ob obiazatel'stvakh Sovetskogo Soiuza po Sovetsko-Gvineiskomu soglasheniiu i khode ikh vypolneniia, May 1960, in AVP RF, f. 575, op. 3, p. 3, d. 19, l. 29–31; K.K. Apeadu (Development Secretariat) to C.M.O. Mate (Ministry of Education and Welfare), May 2, 1961, in PRAAD, RG 3/4/50; Ministry of Industry to the Principal Secretary, Ministry of Education, September 8, 1962, in PRAAD, RG 3/4/50.

113. Spravka ob okazanii tekhnicheskogo sodeistviya Gvineiskoi Respublike v stroitel'stve promyshlennykh predpriyatii i drugikh ob"ektov, March 24, 1961, in AVP RF, f. 575, op. 4, p. 4, d. 19, l. 2–11; Stenogramma zasedaniia uchenogo soveta instituta narodov Afriki 30 iiunia 1961 goda, in ARAN, f. 2010, op. 1, d. 15, l. 155.

114. J.P. Hadengue, Note à l'attention de Monsieur le President de la République, le President de la Communauté, "Aides extérieures reçues por la Guinée," September 19, 1962, in AN, Fonds Foccart, 5/AG/F/1640.

115. Situation de l'Aide Extérieure Négociée ou a Négocier et possibilité de son utilisation, 1961, in ANM, USRDA(BPN)/CMLN/UDPM, Article 134: Procès-verbaux et rapports sur la situation économique du pays, 1961; Spravka ob innostrannoi pomoshchi Respublike Mali, December 1962, in AVP RF, f. 0607, op. 3, p. 5, d. 12, l. 43–48.

116. Cabinet Memorandum by the President, Subject: "Agreement on Trade, Economic and Technical Cooperation Concluded between the Soviet Union and the Republic of Ghana," February 1961, in PRAAD, SC/BAA/490; Office of the President, Republic of Ghana, "Agreements with the Soviet Union, Eastern European Countries, and the People's Republic of China," December 1962, in PRAAD, RG 6/6/1.

117. Effektivnost' ekonomicheskogo sotrudnichestva SSSR so stranami Afriki, June 20, 1963, in ARAN, f. 2010, op. 1, d. 37, l. 23–24.

118. This is an indicative and rudimentary calculation based on the GDP level in Guinea in 1960–1961 converted from 1990 US dollars to 1960 US dollars assuming an inflation rate of roughly 5 percent per year. See Maddison, *The World Economy*, 2:591.

119. Situation de l'Aide Extérieure Négociée ou a Négocier et possibilité de son utilisation, 1961, in ANM, USRDA(BPN)/CMLN/UDPM, Article 134: Procès-verbaux et rapports sur la situation économique du pays, 1961.

120. Memorandum From the Deputy Assistant Secretary of State for African Affairs (Penfield) to the Under Secretary of State (Bowles), February 17, 1961, in *FRUS*, 1961–1963, Vol. XXI, 341.

121. The Soviet bloc included the USSR, Bulgaria, Czechoslovakia, the German Democratic Republic, Hungary, and Poland. It excluded the People's Republic of China, Yugoslavia, Romania, and Albania. See Office of the President, Republic of Ghana, "Agreements with the Soviet Union, Eastern European Countries, and the People's Republic of China," December 1962, in PRAAD, RG 6/6/1.

122. Ekonomika Respublika Mali (spravka), August 25, 1961, in AVP RF, f. 0607, op. 2, p. 3, d. 7, l, 85–86.

123. Fiscal policy—taxes and revenues—is covered in chapter 5.

124. Harcourt Fuller, *Building the Ghanaian Nation State: Kwame Nkrumah's Symbolic Nationalism* (London: Palgrave, 2014), 68–80.

125. Sarah Stockwell, "Instilling the 'sterling tradition': Decolonization and the creation of a Central Bank in Ghana," *Journal of Imperial and Commonwealth History* 26, no. 2 (1998): 100–119; Zapis' besedy sostoiavsheisia v Banke Gany, November 6, 1962, in RGAE, f. 413, op. 13, d. 9448, l. 97–102.

126. W.A. Lewis, "The Par Value of the Ghana Pound" (note), May 9, 1958, in RBSC, W. Arthur Lewis Papers (MC092), box 20, folder 7.

127. Matthew Kofi Ocran, "A Modelling of Ghana's Inflation Experience: 1960–2003," *African Economic Research Consortium Research Paper* 169 (Nairobi: AERC, 2007), 6–7.

128. W.A. Lewis, "Budget Enquiry Committee" (memorandum), December 22, 1958, in RBSC, W. Arthur Lewis Papers (MC092), box 20, folder 7.

129. The World Bank provides data on the standard M2 set ("money and quasi money") growth rate since 1960. The data are available at http://databank.worldbank.org/data/.

130. Government of Ghana, "National Investment Bank Act," Act 163, March 22, 1963.

131. André Lewin, *Ahmed Sékou Touré (1922–1984) Président de la Guinée*, vol. 4: *1960–1962* (Paris: L'Harmattan, 2009), 47–73.

132. B. Reysset (French Embassy in Guinea), "Mesures monétaires guinéennes," March 4, 1960, in MAE, Guinée 1960–1965, vol. 65; Présidence de la Communauté, "Mesures monétaires prises par la Guinée. Reunion des Ministres des Finances des Etats d'Afrique de l'Ouest," March 14, 1960, in AN, Fonds Foccart, 5/AG/F/555; Sergei Mazov, *A Distant Front in the Cold War: The USSR in West Africa and the Congo, 1956–1964* (Stanford, CA: Stanford University Press, 2010), 130–132.

133. Vneshniaia zadolzhennost' gvineiskoi respubliki, January 1962, in RGAE, f. 413, op. 13, d. 9322, l. 5.

134. Government of Guinea, décret n. 0276/PRG/61, July 27, 1961; Lewin, *Ahmed Sékou Touré*, 4:62–63.

135. Pons (Ambassador in Guinea) to Couve de Mourville, "Deuxième session annuelle de l'Assemblée Nationale guinéenne," November 23, 1961, in AN, Fonds Foccart, 5/AG/F/1638.

136. Vladislav Brizek (économe et membre de l'institut de l'économie a Prague) et dr Mirko Svoboda (docteur en droit et candidat des sciences juridiques a l'Universite a Prague), "La République du Mali et les Questions Monétaires," January 1961, in ANM, BPN USRDA, carton 136, dossier 531: Création monétaire et note sur la dévaluation; Zapis' besedy c ministrom finansov Maiga ot 24 marta 1961 goda, in AVP RF, f. 607, op. 2, p. 1, d. 4, l. 36–37.

137. Jean Bénard, "L'organisation monetaire de la Republique du Mali," October 17, 1960, in ANM, BPN USRDA, carton 136, dossier 533: Organisation Monetaire en R. du Mali.

138. Keïta to De Gaulle, July 1, 1962, cited in Guia Migani, "L'indépendance par la monnaie: la France, le Mali et la zone franc, 1960–1963," Relations internationales 1, no. 133 (2008): 33.

139. Denezhnaia reforma v respublike Mali ot 30 iiunia 1962 g., August 23, 1962, in AVP RF, f. 0607, op. 3, p. 5, d. 12, l. 158–171.

140. According to the few estimates available, the cost of living in Mali nearly doubled between 1962 and 1968. See Jean-Paul Azam and Christian Morrisson, Etudes du Centre de Développement, Conflits et Croissance en Afrique, vol. 1: Le Sahel (Paris: OECD, 1999), 38.

141. Stenogramma zasedania uchenogo soveta instituta Afriki AN SSSR sovmestno s otdeleniem istoricheskikh nauk AN SSSR 13 dekabrya 1960 goda, in ARAN, f. 2010, op. 1, d. 4., l. 20.

142. Stenogramma zasedania uchenogo soveta instituta narodov Afriki 20 iiunia 1961 goda, in ARAN, f. 2010, op. 1, d. 16, l. 170.

143. D.D. Degtiar in Stenogramma zasedania uchenogo soveta instituta Afriki AN SSSR sovmestno s otdeleniem istoricheskikh nauk AN SSSR 13 dekabrya 1960 goda, l. 21.

144. Robert Wade, Governing the Market: Economic Theory and the Role of Government in the East Asian Industrialization (Princeton, NJ: Princeton University Press, 2004), 81.

145. Atul Kohli, State-Directed Development: Political Power and Industrialization in the Global Periphery (New York: Cambridge University Press, 2004), 109.

146. Albert Fishlow, "Brazilian Development in Long-Term Perspective," American Economic Review 70, no. 2 (1980): 104–105.

147. Kohli, State-Directed Development, 265–266.

148. Kohli, State-Directed Development, 263.

149. Wade, Governing the Market, 82.

150. Chong-Sik Lee, Japan and Korea: The Political Dimension (Stanford, CA: Hoover Institution Press, 1985), 66.

151. Tobias Rupprecht, "Socialist High Modernity and Global Stagnation: A Shared History of Brazil and the Soviet Union during the Cold War," Journal of Global History 6, no. 3 (2011): 505–528; Kohli, State-Directed Development, 183, 204.

152. Chalmers Johnson, MITI and the Japanese Miracle: The Growth of Industrial Policy, 1925–1975 (Stanford, CA: Stanford University Press, 1982), 10.

153. Kohli, State-Directed Development, 104, 109, 181.

154. Wade, Governing the Market, 113–158.

155. Kohli, State-Directed Development, 117.

156. Oscar Sanchez-Sibony, Red Globalization: The Political Economy of the Soviet Cold War from Stalin to Khrushchev (New York: Cambridge University Press, 2014), 125–172.

157. Zapis' besedy pervogo zamestitelia predsedatelia soveta ministrov SSSR, chlena Prezidiuma TsK KPSS A.I. Mikoiana s trudiashchimisia Gvinei, sdelannye

korrespondentami Moskovskogo radio vo vremia prebyvaniia A.I. Mikoiana v Gvineiskoi Respublike, 1962, in AVP RF, f. 575, op. 5, p. 6, d. 9, l. 16.

158. W.N. Hugh Jones to J.H.A. Watson, July 27, 1959, in TNA, FO371/138811; Pons to Ministère de la France d'Outre-Mer, December 14, 1961, in AN, Fonds Foccart, 5/AG /F/1640.

159. Ministère des Affaires Etrangères, Direction des Affaires Politiques Afrique-Levant, "Participation des pays communistes à la vie économique et à l'équipement de la Guinée," February 6, 1961, in MAE, Guinée 1960-1965, vol. 59; Ministère de la France d'Outre-Mer, "Situation économique et financier de la Guinée," August 20, 1962, in AN, Fonds Foccart, 5/AG/F/1638. On Sékou Touré's approach to "revolutionary" education, see James Straker, *Youth, Nationalism, and the Guinean Revolution* (Bloomington: Indiana University Press, 2009), 56-79.

160. Iz otcheta o poezdke molodezhnoi delegatsii SSSR v Gvineiskuyu Respubliku, 29 sentiabria–12 oktiabria 1959 g., in Davidson and Mazov, *Rossiia i Afrika*, 2:232–238.

161. On the brutal repression of tribal chiefs and spiritual leaders in Guinea, see Mike McGovern, *Unmasking the State: Making Guinea Modern* (Chicago: University of Chicago Press, 2012), 147–194.

162. Kratkaia spravka o poezdke po strane, August 20, 1959, in AVP RF, f. 575, op 2, p. 1, d. 8, l. 88–90.

163. Spravka, December 1960, in AVP RF, f. 573, op. 4, p. 5, d. 25; "Protocol on Cultural Exchange between the Republic of Ghana and the USSR in the years 1960–1961," August 25, 1960, in PRAAD, MFA/4/85.

164. Agreement on Cultural Cooperation between the Republic of Ghana and the USSR, August 25, 1960, in PRAAD, MFA/4/85; Davidson, Mazov and Tsypkin, *SSSR i Afrika*, 187–189.

165. Zamiatin (MID) to TsK, March 9, 1963, in RGANI, f. 5, op. 55, d. 54, l. 47–48; Davidson, Mazov and Tsypkin, *SSSR i Afrika*, 191.

166. Beseda s poslom Respubliki Mali v SSSR Mamadu Falila Keita, August 4, 1962, in GARF, f. r5446, op. 120, d. 1687, l. 12–28.

167. Priem A.I. Mikoianom posla Respublika Mali v SSSR Mamadu Fadiala Keita, August 11, 1962, in GARF, f. r5446, op. 120, d. 1687, l. 29–46.

168. Procès-verbal de négociations entre la délégation soviétique des spécialistes en formation professionnel technique avec l'effectif de 300 personnes (conformément á l'accord sur l'assistance économique á la République du Mali de la part de l'Union Soviétique), August 28, 1961, in ANM, BPN USRDA, carton 29, dossier 63: Conseil des Ministres II, 1961.

169. Zapis' besedy s Ministrom vnutrennikh del i informatsii Respubliki Mali Madeira Keita, 17 October 1961, in ARAN, f. 2010, op. 1, d. 9, l. 5–6; Séance du 7 novembre 1963: "Accord entre la République du Mali et l'Union des Républiques Socialistes Soviétiques relatif aux transportes aériens," in ANM, BPN USRDA, carton 30, dossier 65: Conseil des Ministres, 1963.

170. P. Siraud (French Ambassador in Conakry), "Rapports de la Guinée avec les pays du bloc communiste," October 22, 1959, in MAE, Guinée 1958-1959, vol. 20; Protocol on cultural exchange between the Union of Societ Socialist Republics and the Republic of Ghana in 1962, in PRAAD, RG 3/5/1948; Spravka o mezhdunarodnoi kooperatsii v sfere obrazovaniia, December 1961, in RGANI, f. 5, op. 14, d. 20, l. 27–40.

171. Julie Hessler, "Death of an African Student in Moscow: Race, Politics and the Cold War," *Cahiers du Monde Russe* 47, no. 1–2 (2006): 33–63; Nana Osei-Opare, "Uneasy Comrades: Postcolonial Statecraft, Race, and Citizenship, Ghana-Soviet Relations, 1957–1966," *Journal of West African History* 5, no. 2 (2019): 99–103; Sean Guillory, "Culture Clash in the Socialist Paradise: Soviet Patronage and African Students' Urbanity in

the Soviet Union, 1960–1965," *Diplomatic History* 38, no. 2 (2014): 271–281; Maxim Matusevich, "Expanding the Boundaries of the Black Atlantic: African Students as Soviet Moderns," *Ab Imperio* 2 (2012): 325–350; Ophélie Rillon and Tatiana Smirnova, "Quand les Maliennes regardaient vers l'URSS (1961–1991). Enjeux d'une coopération éducative au féminin," *Cahiers d'études africaines* 226 (2017): 331–353; Anika Walke, "Was Soviet Internationalism Anti-Racist? Toward a History of Foreign Others in the USSR," in *Ideologies of Race: Imperial Russia and the Soviet Union in Global Context*, ed. David Rainbow (Montreal: McGill-Queen's University Press, 2019), 284–311.

172. Spravka, f. 5, op. 14, d. 20, l. 27–40; Hessler, "Death of an African Student in Moscow," 35; Memorandum from Samuel E. Belk of the National Security Council Staff to the President's Special Assistant for National Security Affairs (Bundy) and the President's Deputy Special Assistant for National Security Affairs (Rostow), August 3, 1961, in *FRUS, 1917–1972, col. 6: Public Diplomacy, 1961–1963,* 126; Duvauchelle to MAE, "Rapports sovieto-guinéen," January 21, 1961, in MAE, Guinée 1960–1965, Vol. 59; TsK to Semichastnyi, November 16, 1962, in RGANI, f. 5, op. 33, d. 194, l. 99–102.

173. Cissé in Jorge García, "Entrevista con Souleymane Cissé," *El Amante Cine*, no. 207 (August 2009), 62.

174. Cissé in Olivier Barlet, "La masterclass de Souleymane Cissé à Dakar," *Africultures*, December 29, 2020, http://africultures.com/la-masterclass-de-souleymane-cisse-a-dakar-15042/.

175. Atukwei Okai in conversation with Gheysika Agambila, *Obsidian* 44, no. 2 (2018): 135–143. For more on African directors and writers in the USSR, see Rossen Djagalov, *From Internationalism to Postcolonialism: Literature and Cinema between the Second and the Third Worlds* (Montreal: McGill-Queen's University Press, 2020), 65–110, 137–172.

5. THINGS FALL APART

1. Emmanuel Tettey Mensah, "Ghana-Guinea-Mali," in E.T. Mensah and the Tempos, *King of Highlife Anthology*, Disc D, Track 16 (London: RetroAfric Records, 2015).

2. I.K. Kosolovskii in Stenogramma zasedaniia uchenogo soveta instituta narodov Afriki 30 iiunia 1961 goda, in ARAN, f. 2010, op. 1, d. 16, l. 134–135.

3. Kosolovskii in Stenogramma zasedaniia, l. 133.

4. Otsenka ekonomicheskogo polozheniia respubliki Mali i nekotorye voprosy sovetsko-maliiskogo ekonomicheskogo sotrudnichestva, January 17, 1962, in AVP RF, f. 0607, op. 3, p. 5, d. 12, l. 81–82.

5. William Taubman, *Khrushchev: The Man and His Era* (New York: W.W. Norton, 2003), 507–516.

6. Philip Hanson, *The Rise and Fall of the Soviet Economy. An Economic History of the USSR from 1945* (London: Routledge, 2014), 70–80.

7. Oscar Sanchez-Sibony, *Red Globalization: The Political Economy of the Soviet Cold War from Stalin to Khrushchev* (New York: Cambridge University Press, 2014), 173–244.

8. Hanson, *The Rise and Fall of the Soviet Economy*, 58–60; Taubman, *Khrushchev*, 523–525.

9. Hanson, *The Rise and Fall of the Soviet Economy*, 87–96.

10. This section is a brief overview of research on the Congo crisis. See Alessandro Iandolo, "Imbalance of Power: The Soviet Union and the Congo Crisis, 1960–1961," *Journal of Cold War Studies* 16, no. 2 (2014): 32–55; Alessandro Iandolo, "Beyond the Shoe: Rethinking Khrushchev at the Fifteenth Session of the United Nations General Assembly," *Diplomatic History* 41, no. 1 (2017): 128–154; Lise Namikas, *Battleground Africa: Cold War in the Congo, 1960–1965* (Stanford, CA: Stanford University Press, 2013); Sergei Mazov, *A Distant Front in the Cold War: The USSR in West Africa and the Congo, 1956–1964* (Stanford, CA: Stanford University Press, 2010), 77–129; Segei Mazov, "Soviet Aid to

the Gizenga Government in the Former Belgian Congo (1960–61) as Reflected in Russian Archives," *Cold War History* 7, no. 3 (2007): 425–437; Alanna O'Malley, *The Diplomacy of Decolonisation: America, Britain and the United Nations during the Congo Crisis, 1960–1964* (Manchester: Manchester University Press, 2018).

11. Rapport sur les Entretiens que Mamadou Madeira Keïta a eus en Union Soviétique, lors de son séjour d'un mois dans ce pays à la tête d'une délégation de l'Union Soudanaise-RDA, August 1964, in ANM, BPN US-RDA, Carton 86, Dossier 296: Rapports de missions à l'extérieur du Mali, 1962–1968.

12. I.K. Kosolovskii, in Stenogramma zasedaniia uchenogo soveta instituta narodov Afriki 30 iiunia 1961 goda, in ARAN, f. 2010, op. 1, d. 16, l. 128.

13. V.E. Semichastnyi to Presidium, March 26, 1963, in RGANI, f. 5, op. 55, d. 56, l. 92–118.

14. Philip Muehlenbeck, *Betting on the Africans: John F. Kennedy's Courting of African Nationalist Leaders* (New York: Oxford University Press, 2012), 223.

15. Fursenko and Naftali, *Khrushchev's Cold War*, 388–492; Pleshakov and Zubok, *Inside the Kremlin's Cold War*, 210–274.

16. R. Duvachelle (French Embassy, Conakry) to Minister of Foreign Affairs, "Séjour de M. Brejnev en Guinée," February 16, 1961, in AN, Fonds Foccart, 5/AG/F/1638.

17. Rech' Predsedatelia Prezidiuma Verkhovnogo Soveta SSSR L.I. Brezhneva na mitinge sovetsko-gvineiskoi druzhby v Konakri, February 12, 1961, in Ministerstvo Inostrannykh Del SSSR, *SSSR i Strany Afriki, 1946–1962 gg. Dokumenty i Materialy, vol. 1: 1946 g.–Sentiabr 1960 g.* (Moscow: Gosudarstvennoe Izdatel'stvo Politicheskoi Literatury, 1963), 167–179.

18. Nikita Khrushchev, "Disarmament, Colonialism and Other International Problems. Statement in the General Debate at the Fifteenth Session of the United Nations General Assembly," September 23, 1960, in Nikita Khrushchev, *Khrushchev in New York* (New York: Crosscurrent Press, 1960), 11–57.

19. Apollon Davidson, Sergei Mazov, and Georgii Tsypkin, *SSSR i Afrika, 1918–1960: Dokumentirovannaia Istoriia Vzaimootnoshenii* (Moscow: IVI RAN, 2002), 212–214.

20. Zapis' besedy L.I. Brezhneva s Seku Ture v Prezidentskom dvortse, February 15, 1961, in GARF, f. r5446, op. 120, d. 1736, l. 31–33.

21. Sergei Mazov, *Politika SSSR v Zapadnoi Afrike, 1956–1964: Neizvestnye Stranitsy Kholodnoi Voiny* (Moscow: Nauka, 2008), 150–151.

22. These disagreements are explored in detail later in this chapter.

23. Iz zapisi besedy s direktorom kabineta natsional'nogo obrazovaniia Gvinei, chlenom TsK Afrikanskoi Partii nezavisimosti Amessata Sarrom, June 12, 1960, in Davidson and Mazov, *Rossiia i Afrika*, 2:244–245; Seku Ture (kharakteristika), October 31, 1960, in AVP RF, f. 575, op. 3, p. 3, d. 24, l. 2–4; GKES to TsK, August 16, 1961, in RGANI, f. 5, op. 30, d. 371, l. 162–163, 221–226.

24. La situation économique en Guinée, March 25, 1961, in AN, Fonds Foccart, 5/AG/F/1638.

25. Sékou Touré to Khrushchev, December 14, 1961, in GARF, f. r5446, op. 120, d. 1736, l. 45.

26. J.-L. Pons to Minister of Foreign Affairs, September 29, 1961, in MAE, Guinée 1960–1965, Vol. 38; Priem A.A. Gromyko Al'fa Diallo, December 18, 1961, in GARF, f. r5446, op. 120, d. 1736, l. 47–52.

27. Priem tov. N.S. Khrushchevym Al'fa Diallo, December 18, 1961, in GARF, f. r5446, op. 120, d. 1736, l. 53–58.

28. Priem tov. N.S. Khrushchevym Al'fa Diallo, l. 53.

29. Direction of African Affairs, MFA to French Embassies in Washington, London, Bonn, Moscow, and Africa, January 26, 1962, in AN, Fonds Foccart, 5/AG/F/1638.

30. Priem A.A. Gromyko Al'fa Diallo, December 18, 1961, in GARF, f. r5446, op. 120, d. 1736, l. 49.

31. Nkrumah's writing became increasingly more radical in the 1960s. He began to question openly Western, including American, interference in Africa. See Kwame Nkrumah, *Neo-Colonialism: The Last Stage of Imperialism* (London: Nelson, 1965); Kwame Nkrumah, *Challenge of the Congo: A Case Study of Foreign Pressures in an Independent State* (New York: International Publishers, 1967).

32. Jeffrey Ahlman, *Living with Nkrumahism: Nation, State, and Pan-Africanism in Ghana* (Athens: Ohio University Press, 2017), 129–147, 156, 176–203; W. Scott Thompson, *Ghana's Foreign Policy, 1957–1966: Diplomacy, Ideology and the State* (Princeton, NJ: Princeton University Press, [1969] 2015), 265–304.

33. K. Nkrumah to L.B. Johnson, February 24, 1964, in PRAAD, SC/BAA/309.

34. Christopher Andrew and Vasili Mitrokhin, *The Mitrokhin Archive II. The KGB and the World* (London: Penguin, 2006), 434–438.

35. Vasilii Mitrokhin Papers, Churchill College, Cambridge, UK (henceforth, MITN), Series 2, Envelope K-8 (Part II), "US/Directorate S," p. 178; MITN 2, Envelope K-14 "Agents," 122, 166; MITN Series 1, Volume 6 "The USA," Part 5 "Intelligence Games" (henceforth, MITN 1/6/5), 450.

36. K. Nkrumah to N. Khrushchev, September 6, 1962, in PRAAD, SC/BAA/149.

37. Cabinet Meeting, February 13, 1961, in PRAAD, ADM/13/1/30; Cabinet Meeting, February 15, 1961, in PRAAD, ADM/13/1/30.

38. Mazov, *Politika SSSR v Zapadnoi Afrike*, 174.

39. Informatsiia o Gane, December 1961 in AVP RF, f. 573, op. 5, p. 8, d. 21, l. 12–18; Joint Intelligence Committee Memoranda 73, January 5, 1961, in TNA, CAB158/41.

40. APN Novosti to TsK, December 22, 1961, in RGANI, f. 5, op. 33, d. 181, l. 93–125. For Nkrumah's own definition of Nkrumahism, see K. Nkrumah to S.G. Ikoku (BAA), 2 March 1964, in PRAAD, SC/BAA/90.

41. Gregory Mann, *From Empires to NGOs in the West African Sahel: The Road to Nongovernmentality* (New York: Cambridge University Press, 2015), 8.

42. Baz Lecocq, *Disputed Desert: Decolonization, Competing Nationalisms and Tuareg Rebellions in Northern Mali* (Leiden: Brill, 2010), 135–180.

43. Lecocq, *Disputed Desert*, 181–226.

44. Kratkie fakticheskie o vnutropoliticheskom polozhenii respubliki Mali, April 24, 1962, in AVP RF, f. 0607, op. 3, p. 5, d. 12, l. 11–17.

45. For the Guinea version, see (in chronological order of appearance): "East and West Reach a Cold War Truce in Guinea," *New York Times*, July 24, 1964; Robert Legvold, *Soviet Policy in West Africa* (Cambridge, MA: Harvard University Press, 1970), 124; "Parkas and Snowplows," *Los Angeles Times*, February 26, 1987; Bartholomäus Grill, "Snowplows for Tropical Guinea: How We Can Learn from Failed Development Aid in Africa," *Spiegel Online*, March 6, 2008, https://www.spiegel.de/international/world/snowplows-for-tropical-guinea-how-we-can-learn-from-failed-development-aid-in-africa-a-539782.html; Stephen Kinzer, *The Brothers: John Foster Dulles, Allen Dulles, and their Secret World War* (New York: Time Books, 2013), 282; Philip Muehlenbeck, *Czechoslovakia in Africa, 1945–1968* (London: Palgrave, 2016), 161. David Laibman remembers having heard the same story, but set in Ghana, in 1978. See David Laibman, "Snow Plows, Cookies, and the Formation of Ideologized Consciousness," *Science & Society* 68, no. 4 (2004/2005): 389–395.

46. William Attwood, *The Reds and the Blacks: A Personal Adventure* (London: Hutchinson, 1967), 67; Marshall I. Goldman, "A Balance Sheet of Soviet Foreign Aid," *Foreign Affairs* 43, no. 2 (January 1965): 355.

47. Mazov, *A Distant Front in the Cold War*, 181–185, 212–214, 220–226.

48. Spravka ob obiazatel'stvakh Sovetskogo Soiuza po Sovetsko-Gvineiskomu soglash-eniiu i khode ikh vypolneniia, May 1960, in AVP RF, f. 575, op. 3, p. 3, d. 19, l. 29–31.

49. Stupashin (MID African Department) speaking at the Institute of Africa, in Steno-gramma zasedaniia soveta instituta narodov Afriki, June 30, 1961, in ARAN, f. 2010, op. 1, d. 16, l. 147.

50. Zapis' besedy Orlova, Alikhanova i Mordvinova s misistrom planirovania Gvin-eiskoi Respubliki Barri Ibragima, ministrom Ture i ministrom torgovli Keita N Famara, January 8, 1962, in RGAE, f. 365, op 2, d. 339, l. 17–41.

51. Zapis' besedy Parshina s Ture, March 26, 1962, in RGAE, f. 365, op. 2, d. 339, l. 73–74.

52. Zapis' besedy Parshina s Ture, l. 70.

53. S. Romanovskii (MID) to Gromyko, May 6, 1964, in AVP RF, f. 0607, op. 5, p. 8, d. 10, l. 121.

54. Goldman, "A Balance Sheet of Soviet Foreign Aid," 354.

55. Ministère des Travaux Publics des Mines, de l'Habitat & des Recherches Scienti-fiques, "Note sur le programme de prospection minière du plan quinquennal," 1961, in ANM, BPN US-RDA, Carton 29 Dossier 63, Conseil des Ministres II, 1961: Séance du 2 mai 1963; Project de Loi Minière en République du Mali—Expose des Motifs, in ANM, BPN US-RDA, Carton 30, Dossier 65, Conseil des Ministres, 1963.

56. S. Skachkov (GKES) to TsK KPSS, November 4, 1961, in AVP RF, f. 0607, op. 2, p. 3, d. 7, l. 10–12.

57. Zapis' besedy A.I. Alikhanova s ministrom obshchestvennykh rabot Respubliki Mali Mamadu Av, October 2, 1961, in RGAE, f. 365, op. 2, d. 278, l. 83–84.

58. Zapis' besedy ministra obshchesvennykh rabot Mamadu Av i predstaviteliami sovetskoi storony Orlovym, Alikhanovym i Mordvinovym v Bamako, January 18, 1962, in RGAE, f. 365, op. 2, d. 340, l. 75–76.

59. Ministère de Travaux Publics—Note sur le Projet de Révision du Plan Quinquen-nal, May 1962, in ANM, Fonds du USRDA(BPN)/CMLN/UDPM, Article 01: Plan Quin-quennal de développement économique et social de la République du Mali, 1962–1963.

60. Spravka ob okazanii tekhnicheskogo sodeistviia Gvineiskoi Respublike v stroitel'stve promyshlennykh predpriiatii i drugikh ob"ektov, March 24, 1961, in AVP RF, f. 575, op. 4, p. 4, d. 19, l. 3; Stenogramma sovmestnogo zasedaniia uchenykh sovetov Instituta Afriki i Instituta Geografii Akademii Nauk SSSR, May 23, 1961, in ARAN, f. 2010, op. 1, d. 15, l. 45–46; Parshin (Soviet Embassy Conakry) to A.I. Alikhanov (GKES), June 20, 1961, in RGAE, f. 365, op. 2, d. 298, l. 126.

61. A. Parshin (Soviet Embassy, Conakry) to S. Skachkov (GKES), May 23, 1961, in RGAE, f. 365, op. 2, d. 298, l. 189–190.

62. S. Skachkov (GKES) to N.I. Mel'nikov, June 6, 1961, in RGAE, f. 365, op. 2, d. 298, l. 188; Zapis' besedy Parshina s Ture, March 14, 1962, in RGAE, f. 365, op. 2, d. 339, l. 56

63. Zapis' besedy c poslom SShA v Gvineiskoi Respublike Uil'iamom Atvudom, Au-gust 12, 1963, in AVP RF, f. 575, op. 6, p. 8, d. 7, l. 6–6a.

64. Zapis' besedy Skachkova s Ture vo vremia priema 26 iiunia 1963, in RGAE, f. 365, op. 2, d. 394, l. 149–150.

65. Comments on Contract No. 393, November 1961, in PRAAD, RG 7/1/1692; Geo-logical Survey Department, "Russian Geological Team," October 9, 1961, in PRAAD, RG 7/1/1692.

66. Geological Survey Department, "Contract 393—Comments on the Proposed Scheme of Work," January 18, 1962, in PRAAD, RG 7/1/1692.

67. A. Golubkov (Soviet Embassy, Accra) to Krobo Edusei (Minister of Industries), February 21, 1962, in PRAAD, RG 7/1/1692.

68. N. Solovyev (Soviet Geology Team) to A. Awuah (Deputy Minister of Industries), March 22, 1962, in PRAAD, RG 7/1/1693.

69. N. Solovyev (Soviet Geology Team) to A. Awuah (Deputy Minister of Industries).

70. K.K. Apeadu (Ministry of Industry) to A. Golubkov (Soviet Geological Team), June 28, 1962, in PRAAD, RG 7/1/1694; Draft State Control Commission Memorandum by the Minister of Industries, "Funds for Soviet Geological Survey Team," February 1, 1963, in PRAAD, RG 7/1/1696.

71. M. Ananev (Ministry of Agriculture) to MID, "Spravka po voprosu okazaniia tekhnicheskogo sodeistviia Gvinee v stroitel'stve risovogo goskhoda na ploshchadi 7 tys. ga.," December 27, 1961, in AVP RF, f. 575, op. 4, p. 4, d. 19, l. 31–36.

72. Sékou Touré to Khrushchev, August 19, 1961, in AVP RF, f. 575, op. 4, p. 4, d. 19, l. 12–16.

73. Zapis' besedy tov. Parshina A.V. s Ministrom sel'skogo khoziaistva Gvineiskoi Respubliki g. Bari Sori Ibragima, sostoiavsheisia 29 avgusta 1961 g., v Ministerstve sel'skogo khoziaistva Gvineiskoi Respubliki, in AVP RF, f. 575, op. 4, p. 4, d. 19, l. 17–21; Khrushchev to Sékou Touré, September 25, 1961, in AVP RF, f. 575, op. 4, p. 4, d. 19, l. 27–28.

74. See chapter 4.

75. Zapis' besedy tt. Orlova, Alikhanova i Mordvinova s Misinform planirovaniia Gvineiskoi Respubliki Barri Ibragima, Misinform obshchestvennykh rabot i transporta Ismailom Ture i Misinform torgovli Keita N'Famara, January 8, 1962, in RGAE, f. 365, op. 2, d. 339, l. 39; Zapis' besedy s ministrom obshchestvennykh rabot Ismailom Ture, April 12, 1962, in AVP RF, f. 575, op. 5, p. 6, d. 9, l. 7.

76. Razvitie eksportnykh resursov gvineiskoi respubliki, November 15, 1962, in AVP RF, f. 575, op. 5, p. 6, d. 18, l. 84–85.

77. Zapis' besedy . . . , January 8, 1962, in RGAE, f. 365, op. 2, d. 339, l. 40.

78. Zapis' besedy s ministrom po delam ekonomicheskogo sotrudnichestva N Famara Skachkova, August 14, 1964, in RGAE, f. 365, op. 2, d. 454, l. 176.

79. Cabinet Memorandum, "Ghana/USSR agreement for economic and technical cooperation: contract no. 8406 on complex of fishing industries," October 15, 1963, in PRAAD, ADM/13/2/109.

80. Zapis' besedy Golubkova s torgovym attashe BNR Faildi i predstaviteliami CHSSR, PNR, GDR, BNR, KNR, SSSR, February 1962, in RGAE, f. 365, op. 6, d. 338, l. 191–192.

81. Protocol of the First Meeting of the Joint Soviet-Ghana Fisheries Commission, May 1964, in PRAAD, MFA/8/4.

82. Cabinet Information Paper by the Minister of Agriculture, February 14, 1962, in PRAAD, ADM/13/2/89.

83. Cabinet Meeting, February 14, 1962, in PRAAD, ADM/13/1/31; Report on establishment of state farms by USSR credit and technical assistance, April 17, 1962, in PRAAD, ADM/13/2/91.

84. Notes of a meeting held on Thursday, March 15, 1962 to discuss the proposals by the leader of the Soviet agricultural team in connection with the establishment of state farms, in PRAAD, RG/4/1/84.

85. V.P. Koranyshev to The Director of State Farms, Ministry of Agriculture, Accra, September 5, 1962, in PRAAD, RG/4/1/84.

86. Kratkaia zapis' soderzhaniia besedy sovetnika ministra sel'kogo khoziaistva Gany Bergamova G.G. S prezidentom Gany doktorom Kvame Nkruma, December 1964, in RGAE, f. 365, op. 2, d. 454, l. 142–143.

87. Ministère du Plan et de l'Economie Rural—Dossier Plan, 1962, in ANM, Fonds du USRDA(BPN)/CMLN/UDPM, article 01: Plan Quinquennal de développement économique et social de la République du Mali, 1962–1963.

88. Comité National de Planification et de Direction Economique—Procès-Verbal de la réunion du 14 mai 1962, in ANM, Fonds du USRDA(BPN)/CMLN/UDPM, article 01: Plan Quinquennal de développement économique et social de la République du Mali, 1962–1963.

89. Ministère de Travaux Publics—Note sur le Projet de Révision du Plan Quinquennal, May 1962, in ANM, Fonds du USRDA(BPN)/CMLN/UDPM, article 01: Plan Quinquennal de développement économique et social de la République du Mali, 1962–1963.

90. D. Pozhidaev (I African Department, MID) to Ya. A. Malik (Deputy Minister of Foreign Trade), November 25, 1964, in AVP RF, f. 0607, op. 5, p. 8, d. 10, l. 47–52.

91. Ob itogax vypolneniia pervogo goda Trekhletnego plana razvitiia Gvineiskoi Respubliki (spravka), August 22, 1961, in AVP RF, f. 575, op. 4, p. 5, d. 24, l. 96–101; O sessii natsional'nogo soveta revoliutsii v Konakry (kratkaia informatsiia), October 16, 1964, in AVP RF, f. 575, op. 7, p. 10, d. 14, l. 14–19; S. Romanovskii (Committee for Cultural Contacts with Foreign Countries) to A. Gromyko (Foreign Minister), May 6, 1964, in AVP RF, f. 0607, op. 5, p. 8, d. 10, l. 121.

92. Spravka, in RGANI, f. 5, op. 30, d. 371, l. 162–163, 221–226.

93. Ob itogakh vypolneniia . . . , August 22, 1961, in AVP RF, f. 575, op. 4, p. 5, d. 24, l. 107–109.

94. J.L. Pons (French Ambassador, Guinea) to Minister of Foreign Affairs, January 15, 1962, in MAE, Guinée 1960–1965, vol. 59: Relations avec l'URSS.

95. French Embassy, Conakry to Ministry of Foreign Affairs, Paris, April 6, 1961, in AN, Fonds Foccart, 5/AG/F/1638; Zapis' besedy tt. Orlova, Alikhanova i Mordvinova s Ministrom planirovaniia Gvineiskoi Respubliki Barri Ibragima, Ministrom obshchetvennykh rabot i transporta Ismailom Ture i Ministrom torgovli Keita N'Famara, January 8, 1962, in AVP RF, f. 575, op. 5, p. 7, d. 19, l. 1–25; Zapis' besedy sovetnika po ekonomicheskim voprosam posol'stva SSSR v Gane Aleksandrova G.Ia. s sekretarem kabineta ministrov E.K. Oko, July 13, 1963, in RGAE, f. 365, op. 2, d. 394, l. 101–103; Alpha Diallo (Minister of Foreign Affairs) to Soviet Embassy, Conakry, July 24, 1961, in AVP RF, f. 575, op. 4, p. 4, d. 18, l. 15–17.

96. Zapis' besedy sovetnika po ekonomicheskim voprosam posol'stva SSSR v Gane Aleksandrova G.Ia. s ministrom sel'skogo khoziaistva Respubliki Gana Krobo Eduseem, May 10, 1963, in RGAE, f. 365, op. 2, d. 394, l. 95–97; O khode vypolneniia sovetsko maliiskogo soglasheniia o kul'turnom sotrudnichestve i torgovogo soglasheniia, August 27, 1961, in AVP RF, f. 0607, op. 2, p. 3, d. 7, l. 38–42.

97. Zapis' besedy sostoiavsheisia v Ministerstve Torgovli i finansov Gany, January 25, 1962, in RGAE, f. 413, op. 13, d. 9448, l. 23–25; Zapis' besedy torgpreda SSSR v Gane t. Myshkova V.N. s General'nym direktorom Natsional'noi Torgovli Korporatsii Gany g. Adzhimanom, February 17, 1962, in RGAE, f. 413, op. 13, d. 9448, l. 29–30.

98. Doklad o sostoianii rabot po ob"ektam, vkhodiashchim v trekhletnii plan ekonomicheskogo i sotsial'nogo razvitiia Gvineiskoi Respubliki, vypolniaemykh pri tekhnicheskom sodeistvii i ekonomicheskoi pomoshchi Sovetskogo Soiuza, September 1962, in AVP RF, f. 575, op. 5, p. 7, d. 19, l. 70–75.

99. Zapis' besedy tt. Orlova, Alikhanova i Mordvinova s Ministrom planirovaniia Gvineiskoi Respubliki Barri Ibragima, Ministrom obshchesvennykh rabot i transporta Ismailom Ture i Ministrom torgovli Keita N'Famara, January 8 1962, in AVP RF, f. 575, op. 5, p. 7, d. 19, l. 25; Otchet o vruchenii veritel'nykh gramot Poslom SSSR Prezident Gvineiskoi Respubliki Seku Ture, February 1962, in AVP RF, f. 575, op. 5, p. 6, d. 9, l. 3–7; Zapis' besedy ministra obshchykh rabot Mamadu Av i predstaviteliami sovetskoi storony Orlovym, Alikhanovym i Mordvinovym, January 18, 1962, in RGAE, f. 365, op. 2, d. 340, l. 79–81; Zapis' besedy Ll. Brezhneva s Seku Ture v Prezidentskom dvortse, February 15, 1961, in GARF, f. r5446, op. 120, d. 1736, l. 31–33.

100. O novykh formakh sovetsko-gvineiskogo ekonomicheskogo sotrudnichestva, November 14, 1963, in AVP RF, f. 575, op. 6, p. 8, d. 13, l. 47.

101. Semiletnii plan ekonomicheskogo i sotsial'nogo razvitiia gvineiskoi respubliki (spravka), May 18, 1964, in AVP RF, f. 575, op. 7, p. 11, d. 15, l. 1–11.

102. Alain Faujas, "Des trains nommés désir," *Jeune Afrique*, March 17, 2019, 136.

103. The Niger flows west to southeast, from Sierra Leone to Nigeria, following an unusual curved shape that has fascinated both locals and visitors for centuries.

104. Otsenka ekonomicheskogo polozheniia respubliki Mali i nekotorye voprosy sovetsko-maliiskogo ekonomicheskogo sotrudnichestva, January 17, 1962, in AVP RF, f. 0607, op. 3, p. 5, d. 12, l. 79–86.

105. Otsenka ekonomicheskogo polozheniia . . . , in AVP RF, f. 0607, op. 3, p. 5, d. 12, l. 79–86; O reorganizatsii vnutrennei i vneshnei torgovli v Gvineiskoi Respublike (spravka), June 20, 1961, in AVP RF, f. 575, op. 4, p. 5, d. 24, l. 76–79; Zapis' besedy Skachkova s poslom gvinieiskoi respubliki Biro Bubakar Barri, October 16, 1962, in RGAE, f. 365, op. 2, d. 339, l. 82.

106. Rapport sur les Entretiens que Mamadou Madeira Keïta a eus en Union Soviétique, lors de son séjour d'un mois dans ce pays à la tête d'une délégation de l'Union Soudanaise-RDA, August 1964, in ANM, BPN US-RDA, Carton 86, Dossier 296, Rapports de missions à l'extérieur du Mali, 1962–1968.

107. O vnutripoliticheskom i ekonomicheskom polozhenii Federatsii Mali (spravka), February 18, 1960, in AVP RF, f. 607, op. 1a, p. 1a, d. 9, l. 2–21.

108. Accord sur la coopération économique et technique entre la République du Mali et l'Union des Républiques Soviétiques Socialistes [*sic*], March 1961, in ANM, BPN US-RDA), carton 45, dossier 126; Zapis' besedy sostoiavsheisia v "Somieks"e 23 marta 1961 g. (11:00–12:00), in RGAE, f. 413, op. 13, d. 9048, l. 6–7; Zapis' besedy sostoiavsheisia v "Somieks"e 23 marta 1961 g. (18:00–19:00), in RGAE, f. 413, op. 13, d. 9048, l. 4–5.

109. L. Ezhov (Africa Department, MVT) to Kolosovskii (African Department, MID), August 15, 1961, in AVP RF, f. 0607, op. 2, p. 3, d. 7, l. 20, l. 20; Zapis' besedy soostoiavsheisia v "Somieks"e, March 23 1961, in RGAE, f. 413, op. 13, d. 9048, l. 4–7; O khode vypolneniia sovetsko maliiskogo soglasheniia o kul'turnom sotrudnichestve i torgovogo soglasdeniia, August 27, 1961, in AVP RF, f. 0607, op. 2, p. 3, d. 7, l. 38–43.

110. The FOB clause in international trade means that the seller is liable only up to the border, and then the goods become the responsibility of the buyer. The CIF clause means instead that the seller is liable for the goods until they reach the final buyer, including domestic transportation.

111. N. Okonshenikov (Mashinoeksport) to V.B. Spandarian and S.A. Mkrutinov (MVT), June 8, 1961, in RGAE, f. 413, op. 13, d. 9049, l. 1–3; Comité National de Planification et de Direction Economique—Procès Verbal, Reunion du 24/1/1962, in ANM, BPN US-RDA, Carton 107, Dossier 409, Rapports et correspondances—Service Economie Rural Industrie et Mines, 1962–1968; V. Mordvinov (Director of Africa Department, MVT) to Avtoeksport, Aviaeksport, Mashinoeksport, and Traktoroeksport, December 12, 1962, in RGAE, f. 413, op. 13, d. 9049, l. 8.

112. Zapis' besedy sostoiavsheisia v Bamako 18 yanvarya 1962 goda mezhdu ministrom obshchestvennykh rabot, gornogo dela, zhilishch i energeticheskikh resursov Respubliki Mali - Mamadu Av i drugimi predstaviteliami Maliiskoi storony i predstaviteliami Sovetskoi storony tt. Orlovym, Alikhanovym i Mordvinovym, in RGAE, f. 413, op. 13, d. 9451, l. 3–9; Razvitie eksportnykh resursov Respubliki Mali i perspektivy pogasheniia ee vneshnei zadolzhennosti, January 1962, in AVP RF, f. 0607, op. 3, p. 5, d. 12, l. 99–123. Modibo Keïta to N.S. Khrushchev, 2 November 1962, in AVP RF, f. 0607, op. 3, p. 5, d. 12, l. 42.

113. Rapport sur les Entretiens que Mamadou Madeira Keïta a eus en Union Soviétique, lors de son séjour d'un mois dans ce pays à la tête d'une délégation de l'Union

Soudanaise—RDA, August 1964, in ANM, BPN US-RDA, Carton 87, Dossier 296, Délégation de l'US RDA en Union Soviétique, 1964; Zapis' besedy zamestitelia ministra vneshnei torgovli tov. Borisova S.A. s Sekretarem partii Sudanskii Soiuz (Respublika Mali) Madeira Keita, August 31, 1964, in RGAE, f. 413, op. 31, d. 95, l. 1–2; Memorandum o sovetsko-maliiskikh torgovykh peregovorakh, sostoiavshikhsia v dekabre 1964 goda, in RGAE, f. 413, op. 31, d. 338, l. 16–25.

114. Zamechaniia po razrabotke teoreticheskoi i prakticheskoi bazy tsen na gvineiskie tovary, 22 January 1960, in AVP RF, f. 575, op. 3, p. 2, d. 23, l. 79–93.

115. Razvitie eksportnykh resursov gvineiskoi respubliki, November 15, 1962, in AVP RF, f. 575, op. 5, p. 7, d. 19, l. 70–91; Situation économique et financière de la Guinée, August 28, 1962, in AN, Fonds Foccart, 5/AG/F/1638; Zapis' besedy zamestitelia ministra vneshnei torgovli tov. Kymykina P.I. s Ministrom torgovli Gvineiskoi Respubliki N'Famara Keita, February 21, 1962, in RGAE, f. 413, op. 13, d. 9322, l. 70–77; Zapis' besedy glavy sovetskoi delegatsii tov. Bakhtova K.K. s misinstrom torgovli Gvineiskoi Respubliki g-nom Keita N'Famara, January 24, 1963, in RGAE, f. 413, op. 13, d. 9712, l. 4–11; Zapis' besedy torgovogo sovetnika pri posol'stve SSSR v Gvineiskoi Respublike t. Pikuz A.N. s direktorom departmenta vneshnei torgovli Ministerstva torgovli Gvinei Berete, February 15, 1964, in RGAE, f. 413, op. 31, d. 69, l. 19–20.

116. Zapis' besedy nachal'nika vtorogo afrikanskogo otdela upravleniia torgovli so stranami Afriki t. Sizonenko V.G. s torgovym attashe posol'stva Gvineiskoi Respubliki v g. Moskve g-nom Bokumom Kh., May 30, 1964, in RGAE, f. 413, op. 31, d. 69, l. 38–40; Zapis' besedy zamestitelia ministra tov. Borisova S.A. s ministrom pri kantseliarii prezidenta Gvineiskoi Respubliki po voprosam ekonomicheskogo sotrudnichestva i ekonomicheskim problemam g. Keita N'Famara, August 14, 1964, in AVP RF, f. 575, op. 7, p. 10, d. 11, l. 47–51.

117. Zapis' besedy zamestitelia ministra tov. Borisova S.A. . . . , in RGAE, f. 413, op. 31, d. 69, l. 87.

118. Zapis' besedy zam. Ministra vneshnei torgovli tov. I.F. Semichastnova s glavoi gvineiskoi delegatsii g-nom F. Berete, 14 January 1964, in RGAE, f. 413, op. 31, d. 68, l. 12–14; Zapis' besedy zamestitelia ministra tov. Borisova S.A. . . . , in RGAE, f. 413, op. 31, d. 69, l. 87.

119. Rapport sur les Entretiens que Mamadou Madeira Keïta . . . , August 1964, in ANM, BPN US-RDA, Carton 87, Dossier 296, Délégation de l 'US RDA en Union Soviétique, 1964.

120. Memorandum o besede s ministrom promyshlennosti Gany g-nom Krobo Eduseem, January 15, 1962, in RGAE, f. 413, op. 13, d. 9448, l. 3–5; Zapis' besedy direktora kontory bakaleinykh tovarov V/O "Prodintorg" t. Gorshkova G.N. i upolnomochennogo "Prodintorg" t. Chernobrovogo B.G. s ispolniaiushchim obiazannosti upravliaiushchego "Koko Marketing Kompani" g-nom Koranteng, July 5, 1963, in RGAE, f. 413, op. 13, d. 9822, l. 32–36.

121. Zapis' besedy glavnyi Sovetskoi Torgovoi Delegatsii t. Borisova B.A. s Ministrom Finansov Gany Kvazi Amoako-Atta, December 10, 1964, in RGAE, f. 413, op. 31, d. 68, l. 37–38; Zapis' besedy zamestitelia ministra vneshnei torgovli SSSR tov. Borisova B.A. s Ministrom finansov Gany Amoako-Atta, December 11, 1964, in RGAE, f. 413, op. 31, d. 68, l. 39–40; Renegotiating of debts with the centrally planned economies with Eastern Europe, January 31, 1967, in PRAAD, RG/4/1/41.

122. Zapis' besedy torgovogo sovetnika v Gane t. Myshkova V.N. s nachal'nikom tekhnicheskoi slushby ganskoi armii polkovnikom Nikol'son (anglichanin), March 4, 1961, in RGAE, f. 413, op. 13, d. 9046, l. 6–7; Zapis' besedy torgpreda v Gane tov. Myshkova V.N. s Ministrom kommunikatsii i obshchestvennykh rabot Bensa, October 5, 1962, in RGAE, f. 413, op. 13, d. 9448, l. 70–73.

123. Zapis' besedy torgrepa SSSR v Gane t. Myshkova V.N. s Ministrom torgovli i fi-nansov Gany Goka, July 24, 1962, in RGAE, f. 413, op. 13, d. 9448, l. 74–77; Zapis' besedy s zamestitelem perdstavitelia Ganskoi Zakupochnoi Komissii Ababa, July 20, 1962, in RGAE, f. 413, op. 13, d. 9448, l. 80–82; Ghana National Trading Corporation, "Accounts with Soviet organizations," May 23, 1963, in PRAAD, RG/7/1/1691; Zapis' besedy torg-preda SSSR v Gane t. Myshkova V.N. s Ministrom sel'skogo khoziaistva Gany Abavina, January 10, 1963, in RGAE, f. 413, op. 14, d. 9448, l. 11.

124. Soviet Embassy, Accra to GNTC, "Pro Memory," September 1962, in PRAAD, RG/7/1/1699; Zapis' besedy sostoiavsheisia v Banke Gany, November 6, 1962, in RGAE, f. 413, op. 13, d. 9448, l. 97–102.

125. Zapis' besedy glavy sovetskoi torgovoi delegatsii tov. Borisova B.A. s upravliaiush-chim direktorom Ganskoi Natsional'noi Torgovoi Korporatsii Patrikom Fitzdzheral'dom, December 12, 1964, in RGAE, f. 413, op. 31, d. 68, l. 43–45; Soviet Embassy Ghana to I.S. Stepanov (Prodintorg), June 3, 1961, in RGAE, f. 413, op. 13, d. 9056, l. 27–28.

126. Obzor ekonomiki i vneshnei torgovli Gany za 1963 god, March 1964, in RGAE, f. 413, op. 13, d. 9824, l. 25.

127. Soviet development specialists' interest in conservative economic recipes in-creased in future decades. See Chris Miller, "The Bureaucratic Bourgeoisie: How the Soviet Union Lost Faith in State-Led Economic Development," *History of Political Econ-omy* 19, no. 1 (2019): 231–252.

128. Note sur la dévaluation, 1966, in ANM, BPN US-RDA, Carton 136, Dossier 531: Création monétaire et note sur la dévaluation.

129. Note sur la dévaluation, 1966, in ANM, BPN US-RDA.

130. Situation économique et financière de la Guinée, August 28, 1962, in AN, Fonds Foccart, 5/AG/F/1638; Spravka o valiutno-finansovoi sistem Gvineiskoi Respubliki, De-cember 1964, in AVP RF, f. 575, op. 7, p. 11, d. 15, l. 188–189; Semiletnii plan ekonomi-cheskogo i sotsial'nogo razvitiia gvineiskoi respubliki (spravka), May 18, 1964, in AVP RF, f. 575, op. 7, p. 11, d. 15, l. 6–7; Vneshniaia zadolzhennost' gvineiskoi respubliki, Janu-ary 1962, in RGAE, f. 413, op. 13, d. 9322, l. 16; Obzor ekonomiki i vneshnei torgovli Gany za 1962 g., in RGAE, f. 413, op. 13, d. 9449, l. 17.

131. Obzor ekonomiki . . . , in RGAE, f. 413, op. 13, d. 9824, l. 24.

132. Obzor ekonomiki . . . , in RGAE, f. 413, op. 13, d. 9824, l. 19; "Taxation," Note by Professor Lewis, January 28, 1958, in RBSC, W. Arthur Lewis Papers (MC092), Box 20, Folder 7; Finansoviye meropriiatiia maliiskogo pravitel'stva v kontse 1961 goda (spravka), in AVP RF, f. 0607, op. 3, p. 5, d. 12, l. 155–157; Vneshniaia zadolzhennost' . . . , in AVP RF, f. 575, op. 5, p. 7, d. 23, l. 2–15; La situation économique de la Guinée et les résultats de l'aide extérieure, March 16, 1965, in MAE, Guinée 1960–1965, vol. 63: *Assistance fourni par pays outre que la France.*

133. Finansoviye meropriiatiia . . . , in AVP RF, f. 0607, op. 3, p. 5, d. 12, l. 155–157; Vneshniaia zadolzhennost' . . . , in AVP RF, f. 575, op. 5, p. 7, d. 23, l. 2–15; La situation économique de la Guinée et les résultats de l'aide extérieure, March 16, 1965, in MAE, Guinée 1960–1965, vol. 63: *Assistance fourni par pays outre que la France.*

134. Meropriiatiia, sposobstvuiushchie razvitiiu Gvinei po nekapitalisticheskomu puti (kratkaia spravka), April 21, 1964, in AVP RF, f. 575, op. 7, p. 10, d. 14, l. 13–16; D. Pozhidaez (MID) to Ia.A. Malik (Deputy Minister of Foreign Trade), November 25, 1964, in AVP RF, f. 0607, op. 5, p. 8, d. 10, l. 47–52; Note sur la dévaluation, 1966, in ANM, BPN US-RDA, Carton 136, Dossier 531: Création monétaire et note sur la dévaluation.

135. This will be explored more in detail in the following chapter.

136. Spravka, November 1964, in AVP RF, f. 573, op. 8, p. 13–A, d. 7, l. 1–2; Note pour le Ministre, "Situation en Guinée," October 4, 1963, in MAE, Guinée 1960–1965, Vol. 62: Assistance fourni par pays outre que la France.

137. Rech' Pervogo sekretaria TsK KPSS, Predsedatelia Soveta Ministrov SSSR N.S. Khrushcheva v Kremle na mitinge druzhby mezhdu narodami SSSR i Mali, May 30, 1962, in *SSSR i strany Afriki*, 2:562–576.

6. THE END OF THE AFFAIR

1. Memorandum From the President's Deputy Special Assistant for National Security Affairs (Rostow) to President Kennedy, October 2, 1961, in *FRUS, 1961–1963*, 21:359–360; Memorandum of Conversation, November 19, 1963, in *FRUS, 1961–1963*, 21:390–391.

2. Memorandum from the Vice President's Military Aide (Burris) to Vice President Johnson, January 31, 1962, in *FRUS, 1961–1963*, 21:373.

3. John Esseks, "Political Independence and Economic Decolonisation: The Case of Ghana under Nkrumah," *Western Political Quarterly* 24, no. 1 (1971): 59–64.

4. Stenograficheskaia zapis' vystuplenii N.S. Khrushcheva na zasedanii Prezidiuma TsK KPSS, September 10, 1963, in *Prezidium TsK KPSS 1954–1964*, ed. Aleksandr Fursenko (Moscow: ROSSPEN, 2004), 1:753–754.

5. Memorandum from Secretary of State Rusk to President Kennedy, July 15, 1961, in *FRUS, 1961–1963*, 21:399–400; Memorandum of Conversation, May 10, 1962, in *FRUS, 1961–1963*, 21:404; Memorandum from the President's Special Assistant (Dungan) to President Kennedy, March 6, 1963, in *FRUS, 1961–1963*, 21:329–330.

6. Memorandum from Robert W. Komer of the National Security Council Staff to President Johnson, June 19, 1965, in *FRUS, 1964–1968*, vol. 24: *Africa*, 306–307. G. Mennen "Soapy" Williams was the assistant secretary of state for African affairs. MAP was the US Military Assistance Program.

7. Central Intelligence Agency, *Communist Aid Activities in Non-Communist Less Developed Countries, 1979 and 1954–79* (Washington, DC: CIA, 1980), 39; Zapis' besedy s poslom SShA v Gvineiskoi Respublike Uil'iamom Atvudom, August 12, 1963, in AVP RF, f. 575, op. 5, p. 8, d. 7, l. 6–6a.

8. Zapis' besedy s Poslom Frantsii v Gvineiskoi Respublike Ponsom, June 25, 1963, in AVP RF, f. 575, op. 6, p. 8, d. 7, l. 9–10; Les relations économiques et financières entre la France et la Guinée, September 20, 1962, in AN, Fonds Foccart, 5/AG/F/1640; Organisation de Coopération et de Développement Économique, Annexe statistique, "La situation économique de la Guinée et les résultats de l'aide extérieure," March 16, 1965, in MAE, Guinée 1960–1965, vol. 62: *Assistance fourni par pays outre que la France*; Koenig (French ambassador to Conakry) to Couve de Murville, May 8, 1964, in Ministère des Affaires Étrangères, *Documents Diplomatiques Français*, 1964, vol. 1: *1er janvier–30 juin* (Brussels: Peter Lang, 2002), 494–497.

9. Spravka ob inostrannoi pomoshchi Respubliki Mali, December 1962, in AVP RF, f. 0607, op. 3, p. 5, d. 12, l. 43–48; Politique du Mali, December 28, 1963, Ministère des Affaires Étrangères, *Documents Diplomatiques Français*, 1963, vol. 2: *1er juillet–31 décembre* (Paris: Imprimerie Nationale, 2001), 670–673; Rapport sur les Entretiens que Mamadou Madeira Keita a eus en Union Soviétique, lors de son séjour d'un mois dans ce pays a la tête d'une délégation de l'Union Soudanaise—RDA, August 1964, in ANM, BPN US-RDA, Carton 87, Dossier 296, Délégation de l'US RDA en Union Soviétique, 1964.

10. Zapis' besedy s glavoi delegatsii partii Sudanskii Soiuz Madeira Keita, August 4, 1963, in AVP RF, f. 0607, op. 5, p. 8, d. 10, l. 41–46; Jean-Marie Koné, "Compte Rendu de la Délégation du Mali a la Reunion Annuelle du Fonds Monétaire International (FMI), de la Banque Internationale pour la Reconstruction et le Développement (BIRD) et de ses Affilies," 1963, in ANM, USRDA(BPN)/CMLN/UDPM, Article 389.

11. Zapis' besedy s ministrom-upravliaiushchim Bankom Gvineiskoi Respubliki Diakite Mussa, May 23, 1962, in AVP RF, f. 575, op. 5, p. 6, d. 9, l. 15–16; H. Alphand (French

Ambassador to the US) to MAE, Paris, May 9, 1962, in MAE, Guinée 1960–1965, vol. 62: Assistance fourni par pays outre que la France.

12. Eboe Hutchful, ed., *The IMF and Ghana: The Confidential Record* (London: Zed Books, 1987).

13. Gregg Brazinsky, *Winning the Third World: Sino-American Rivalry during the Cold War* (Chapel Hill: University of North Carolina Press, 2017), 3.

14. On the Sino-Soviet alliance and the subsequent split, see Austin Jersild, *The Sino-Soviet Alliance: An International History* (Chapel Hill: University of North Carolina Press, 2014); Lorenz M. Lüthi, *The Sino-Soviet Split: Cold War in the Communist World* (Princeton, NJ: Princeton University Press, 2008); Sergei Radchenko, *Two Suns in the Heavens: The Sino-Soviet Struggle for Supremacy, 1962–1967* (Stanford, CA: Stanford University Press, 2009).

15. Brazinsky, *Winning the Third World*, 195–230; Jeremy Friedman, *Shadow Cold War: The Sino-Soviet Competition for the Third World* (Chapel Hill: University of North Carolina Press, 2015), 60–100.

16. Brazinsky, *Winning the Third World*, 133–165; Friedman, *Shadow Cold War*, 101–147.

17. OECD, "La situation économique de la Guinée et les résultats de l'aide extérieure," March 16, 1965, in MAE, Guinée 1960–1965, vol. 62.

18. Otnosheniia Gvinei s Kitaiskoi narodnoi respublikoi, December 12, 1962, in AVP RF, f. 575, op. 5, p. 7, d. 23, l. 111–115; Spravka ob inostrannoi pomoshchi Respublike Mali, December 1962, in AVP RF, f. 0607, op. 3, p. 5, d. 12, l. 43–48; CIA, *Communist Aid Activities in Non-Communist Less Developed Countries, 1979 and 1954–79*, 10.

19. Situation en Guinée, October 6, 1964, in MAE, Guinée 1960–1965, vol. 62: *Assistance fourni par pays outre que la France*.

20. Dokladnaia zapiska, February 1961, in GARF, f. R9540, op. 2, d. 39, l. 9–18.

21. W.W.K. Vaderpuye (BAA), "The Sino-Soviet Split," April 26, 1964, in PRAAD, SC/BAA/240.

22. Intelligence Memorandum, "Some aspects of subversion in Africa," October 19, 1967, in *FRUS*, 1964–1968, 24:383.

23. Agreements with the Soviet Union, Eastern European Countries and the People's Republic of China, 1962, in PRAAD, RG/6/6/1.

24. Activités Communistes en Afrique, Deuxième part, December 1965, in MAE, Afrique-Levant 1953–1959, vol. 25: *Pénétration Communiste en Afrique, 1961–1976*.

25. William Taubman, *Khrushchev: The Man and His Era* (New York: W.W. Norton, 2003), 609–611.

26. Taubman, *Khrushchev*, 3–17.

27. Nikita Khrushchev, *Memoirs of Nikita Khrushchev*, vol. 3: *Statesman, 1953–1964* (University Park: Pennsylvania State University Press, 2007), 877–884.

28. Iz doklada Pervogo sekretaria TsK KPSS L.I. Brezhneva na torzhestvennom zasedanii v Moskve, posviashchennom 47-i godovshchie Velikoi Oktiabr'skoi revoliutsii, November 6, 1964, in Ministerstvo Inostrannykh Del SSSR, *SSSR i strany Afriki, 1963–1970 gg.: dokumenty i materialy* (Moscow: Politizdat, 1982), 1:160–162.

29. Ministerstvo Vneshnei Torgovli, *Vneshniaia torgovlia SSSR za 1964 god: Statisticheskii obzor* (Moscow: Vneshtorgovizdat, 1965), 264–265; Ministerstvo Vneshnei Torgovli, *Vneshniaia Torgovlia SSSR za 1965 god: Statisticheskii obzor* (Moscow: Vneshtorgovizdat, 1966), 291–292; Ministerstvo Vneshnei Torgovli, *Vneshniaia Torgovlia SSSR za 1966 god: Statisticheskii obzor* (Moscow: Vneshtorgovizdat, 1967), 298–299; Ministerstvo Vneshnei Torgovli, *Vneshniaia Torgovlia SSSR za 1967 god: Statisticheskii obzor* (Moscow: Vneshtorgovizdat, 1968), 279–280; Ministerstvo Vneshnei Torgovli, *Vneshniaia Torgovlia*

SSSR za 1968 god: Statisticheskii obzor (Moscow: Vneshtorgovizdat, 1969), 265–266; Ministerstvo Vneshnei Torgovli, *Vneshniaia Torgovlia SSSR za 1969 god: Statisticheskii obzor* (Moscow: Vneshtorgovizdat, 1970), 260–261.

30. Memorandum From the President's Acting Special Assistant for National Security Affairs (Komer) to President Johnson, March 12, 1966, in *FRUS*, 1964–1968, vol. 24: *Africa*, 457.

31. Kwame Nkrumah, *Dark Days in Ghana* (London: Lawrence & Wishart, 1968), 46, 49.

32. See, for example, "Sobytiia v Gane," *Pravda*, February 25, 1966; "Miting v Konakri," *Pravda*, March 2, 1966.

33. Natalia Telepneva, "Saving Ghana's Revolution: The Demise of Kwame Nkrumah and the Evolution of Soviet Policy in Africa, 1966–1972," *Journal of Cold War Studies* 20, no. 4 (2019): 4–25.

34. A quick internet search will produce the more extravagant ones. For an idea of the "intelligence memoirs" genre, see John Stockwell, *In Search of Enemies: A CIA Story* (New York: W.W. Norton, 1978).

35. Memorandum from the President's Acting Special Assistant for National Security Affairs (Komer) to President Johnson, March 12, 1966; Memorandum from Robert W. Komer of the National Security Council Staff to the President's Special Assistant for National Security Affairs (Bundy), May 27, 1965; Memorandum From the Director of the Office of West African Affairs (Trimble) to the Assistant Secretary of State for African Affairs (Williams), February 11, 1964, in *FRUS*, 1964–1968, vol. 24: *Africa*, 414, 447, 457.

36. Memorandum from the President's Acting Special Assistant for National Security Affairs (Komer) to President Johnson, *FRUS*, 1964–1968, 457. The other place Komer was thinking about was Indonesia.

37. For an overview of Ghana after 1966, see Clifford Campbell and Kwasi Konadu, *The Ghana Reader: History, Culture, Politics* (Durham: Duke University Press, 2016), 299–360.

38. See, for example, Kwame Nkrumah, *Handbook of Revolutionary Warfare: A Guide to the Armed Phase of the African Revolution* (New York: International Publishers, 1969); Kwame Nkrumah, *Revolutionary Path* (London: Panaf Books, 1973). See also Ama Biney, "The Development of Kwame Nkrumah's Political Thought in Exile, 1966–1972," *Journal of African History* 50, no. 1 (2009): 81–100.

39. On the end of the Keïta government and the fate of its members in the camps, see Gregory Mann, *From Empires to NGOs in the West African Sahel: The Road to Nongovernmentality* (New York: Cambridge University Press, 2015), 214–216.

40. For a survey of Mali's foreign relations after the coup, see Philippe Decraene, "Deux décennies de politique extérieure malienne (1960–1980)," *Politique étrangère* 45, no. 2 (1980): 437–451.

41. André Lewin, *Ahmed Sékou Touré (1922–1984), Président de la Guinée*, vol. 5: *1962–1969* (Paris: L'Harmattan, 2010); André Lewin, *Ahmed Sékou Touré (1922–1984), Président de la Guinée*, vol. 6: *1970–1976* (Paris: L'Harmattan, 2010); André Lewin, *Ahmed Sékou Touré (1922–1984), Président de la Guinée*, vol. 7: *1977–1984* (Paris: L'Harmattan, 2010); Mike McGovern, *A Socialist Peace? Explaining the Absence of War in an African Country* (Chicago: University of Chicago Press, 2017).

42. Jean Allman, "The Fate of All of Us: African Counterrevolutions and the Ends of 1968," *American Historical Review* 123, no. 3 (2018): 728–732.

43. Spravka o Gvinei, December 1964, in AVP RF, f. 575, op. 7, p. 10, d. 7, l. 149; P. Baudet (French Ambassador to Moscow) to Couve de Murville, December 2, 1964, in MAE, Guinée 1960–1965, vol. 62.

44. Plan nauchno-issledovatel'skikh rabot instituta Africa AN SSSR na 1961 g., December 1960, in ARAN, f. 2010, op. 1, d. 11, l. 1–14; I.P. Yastrebova to P.A. Dolgov (Cen-

tral Accountancy, Academy of Sciences), February 2, 1963, in ARAN, f. 2010, op. 1, d. 24, l. 29–30; Nauchno-issledovatel'skie i opytnye raboty po estestvennym i obshchestvennym naukam na 1964–1965 gody, June 1964, in ARAN, f. 2010, op. 1, d. 43, l. 3.

45. For more information on Potekhin and his thinking, see Ivan Potekhin, *Afrika smotrit na budushchee* (Moscow: Izadatel'stvo vostochnoi literature, 1960); A.M. Vasil'ev, ed., *Chelovek na fone kontinenta: Materiali nauchnoi konferentsii, posviashchennoi 100-letiiu I.I. Potekhina* (Moscow: Institut Afriki, 2005).

46. Doklad V.G. Solodovnikova "O nauchnykh zadachakh i o novoi strukture Instituta Afriki AN SSSR" na zasedanii Uchenogo Sovieta Instituta, September 4, 1964, in ARAN, f. 2010, op. 1, d. 53, l. 59–78. For more on Solodovnikov's ideas, see V.G. Solodovnikov, *Afrika vybiraet put': Sotsial'no-ekonomicheskie problemy i perspektivy* (Moscow: Nauka, 1970).

47. W. Arthur Lewis, *Politics in West Africa* (Oxford: Oxford University Press, 1965).

48. Robert Tignor, *W. Arthur Lewis and the Birth of Development Economics* (Princeton, NJ: Princeton University Press, 2006), 179–267. See also Douglas Gollin, "The Lewis Model: A 60-Year Retrospective," *Journal of Economic Perspectives* 28, no. 3 (2014): 71–88.

49. François Denord and Xavier Zunigo, "'Révolutionnairement vôtre.' Économie marxiste, militantisme intellectuel et expertise politique chez Charles Bettelheim," *Actes de la recherche en science sociales* 3, no. 158 (2005): 8–29.

50. *Pravda*, October 16, 1964, cited in Taubman, *Khrushchev*, 620.

51. CIA, *Communist Aid Activities in Non-Communist Less Developed Countries, 1979 and 1954–79*, 38–9; Theodore Shabad, "Russians Pushing Output at Bauxite Mine in Guinea," *New York Times*, November 23, 1973.

52. Shabad, "Russians Pushing Output at Bauxite Mine in Guinea," 55; Stephen Fortescue, "The Soviet Union's 'Bauxite Problem,'" in *Aluminum Ore: The Political Economy of the Global Bauxite Industry*, ed. Robin Gendron, Mats Ingulstad, and Espen Storli (Vancouver: University of British Columbia Press, 2013), 138–157.

53. For the USSR's involvement in the former Portuguese empire, see Elizabeth Banks, "Socialist Internationalism between the Soviet Union and Mozambique, 1962–1991" (PhD diss., New York University, 2019); Natalia Telepneva, "Mediators of Liberation: Eastern Bloc Officials, Mozambican Diplomacy and the Origins of Soviet Support for FRELIMO 1958–1965," *Journal of Southern African Studies* 43, no. 1 (2017); Natalia Telepneva, "Our Sacred Duty: The Soviet Union, the Liberation Movements in the Portuguese Colonies, and the Cold War, 1961–1975" (PhD diss., London School of Economics and Political Science, 2015).

54. For an overview of Soviet activities in Africa and the Third World during the 1970s and 1980s, see O. Arne Westad, *The Global Cold War: Third World Interventions and the Making of Our Times* (New York: Cambridge University Press, 2005), 207–330. There is comparatively less literature on the USSR in Africa during the 1970s and 1980s than on Afghanistan. See Vladimir Shubin, *The Hot Cold War: The USSR in Southern Africa* (Scottsville: University of Kwa-Zulu Natal Press, 2008); Artemy Kalinovsky, *A Long Goodbye. The Soviet Withdrawal from Afghanistan* (Cambridge, MA: Harvard University Press, 2011); Timothy Nunan, *Humanitarian Invasion: Global Development in Cold War Afghanistan* (New York: Cambridge University Press, 2015).

CONCLUSION

1. Atul Kohli, *State-Directed Development: Political Power and Industrialization in the Global Periphery* (Princeton, NJ: Princeton University Press), 6.

2. Samir Amin, *Trois expériences africaines de développement: Le Mali, la Guinée et le Ghana* (Paris: Presses Universitaires de France, 1965), 230–232.

Bibliography

ARCHIVES

France

ARCHIVES DU MINISTÈRE DES AFFAIRES ÉTRANGÈRES (ARCHIVES OF THE MINISTRY
OF FOREIGN AFFAIRS)—MAE LA COURNEUVE, PARIS
Série: Afrique-Levant; Sous-série: Ghana/Gold Coast, 1953–1959
Série: Afrique-Levant; Sous-série: Guinée, 1953–1959, 1960–1965
Série: Direction des Affaires Africaine et Malgaches; Sous-série: Généralités, 1959–1979

ARCHIVES NATIONALES (NATIONAL ARCHIVES)—AN
Pierrefitte-sur-Seine, Paris
Fonds "Foccart," (AG/5/F), 1958–1962

Ghana

PUBLIC RECORDS AND ARCHIVE ADMINISTRATION—PRAAD ACCRA
Ambassadors' reports (RG/17), 1960–1971
Attorney General (RG/1), 1960–1962
Bureau of African Affairs (SC/BAA), 1957–1965
Cabinet agenda (ADM/13/2), 1957–1966
Cabinet papers (ADM/13/1), 1957–1966
Ministry of Agriculture (RG/4), 1960–1971
Ministry of Education (RG/3), 1961–1963
Ministry of Finance (RG/6), 1961–1983
Ministry of Foreign Affairs (MFA/4), 1959–1964; (MFA/8), 1964–1976
Ministry of Industries (RG/7), 1951–1963
National Council for Higher Education and Research (RG/11), 1961–1962

Mali

ARCHIVES NATIONALES DU MALI (NATIONAL ARCHIVES OF MALI)—ANM HAMDALLAYE,
BAMAKO
Fonds du BPN US-RDA, du Comité Militaire de Libération Nationale, de l'Union
Démocratique du Peuple Malien (USRDA-BPN/CMLN/UDPM), 1961–1968
Fonds du Bureau Politique National du US-RDA (BPN USRDA), 1961–1968

Russia

ARKHIV ROSSIISKOI AKADEMII NAUK (ARCHIVE OF THE RUSSIAN ACADEMY OF SCIENCES)—
ARAN MOSCOW
Fond 2010, Institut Afriki, 1959–1964

ARKHIV VNESHNEI POLITIKI ROSSIISKOI FEDERATSII (ARCHIVE OF THE FOREIGN POLICY
OF THE RUSSIAN FEDERATION)—AVP RF MOSCOW
Fond (0)573, Referentura po Gane, 1957–1966

Fond (0)575, Referentura po Gvinee, 1958–1968
Fond (0)607, Referentura po Mali, 1960–1968

GOSUDARSTVENNYI ARKHIV ROSSIISKOI FEDERATSII (STATE ARCHIVE OF THE RUSSIAN
    FEDERATION)—GARF MOSCOW
Fond R5446, Soviet Ministrov SSSR, 1959–1962
Fond R9540, Sovetskii komitet solidarnosti stran Azii i Afriki (SKSSAA), 1958–1964

ROSSIISKII GOSUDARSTVENNYI ARKHIV EKONOMIKI (RUSSIAN STATE ARCHIVE
    OF THE ECONOMY)—RGAE MOSCOW
Fond 365, Uchrezhdeniia po vneshneekonomicheskim sviaziam, 1960–1973
Fond 413, Ministerstvo vneshnei torgovli SSSR, 1957–1965
Fond 645, Degtiar' Dmitrii Danilovich, 1959

ROSSIISKII GOSUDARSTVENNYI ARKHIV NOVEISHEI ISTORII (RUSSIAN STATE ARCHIVE
    OF CONTEMPORARY HISTORY)—RGANI MOSCOW
Fond 5, Apparat TsK KPSS, 1957–1964
Fond 11, Komissiia TsK KPSS po voprosam ideologii, kul'tury i mezhdunarodnykh par-
    tiinykh sviazei XX sozyva, 1956–1961

United Kingdom

CADBURY'S ARCHIVES—CB BOURNEVILLE, BIRMINGHAM
British Cocoa and Chocolate Co Ltd minutes (series 101), 1961–1964

CHURCHILL COLLEGE ARCHIVES—MITN CAMBRIDGE
Vasilii Mitrokhin Papers, Series 1, Series 2, 1960–1966

THE NATIONAL ARCHIVES OF THE UNITED KINGDOM—TNA KEW, LONDON
CAB/158; CAB176: Cabinet Office, Joint Intelligence Committee (JIC), 1957–1966
CO/1029: Colonial Office, Production and Marketing Department, 1956
FO371: Foreign Office, Political Departments, 1955–1966

United States

RARE BOOKS AND SPECIAL COLLECTIONS, SEELEY G. MUDD LIBRARY, PRINCETON
    UNIVERSITY—RBSC PRINCETON, NEW JERSEY
W. Arthur Lewis Papers (MC092), 1958–1960

PUBLISHED PRIMARY SOURCES

Newspapers
    Los Angeles Times
    New-York Daily Tribune
    New York Times
    Pravda
    Der Spiegel

Internet Resources
Barlet, Olivier. "La masterclass de Souleymane Cissé à Dakar." *Africultures*, December 29,
    2020. http://africultures.com/la-masterclass-de-souleymane-cisse-a-dakar-15042/.
Cold War International History Project Digital Archive. "Transcript of a CC CPSU Plenum,
    Evening, 28 June 1957." http://digitalarchive.wilsoncenter.org/document/111990.

Cold War International History Project Digital Archive. "Transcript of a Meeting of the Party group of the USSR Supreme Soviet, 8 February 1955." https://digitalarchive .wilsoncenter.org/document/113336.

Dwight Eisenhower Presidential Library, "Top Women Appointments in the Eisenhower Administrations (1953–1959), 1959." https://eisenhower.archives.gov/research /online_documents/women_in_the_1950s/Top_Women_Appointments.pdf.

Dwight Eisenhower Presidential Library. "Women in the Foreign Service, 1959." https:// eisenhower.archives.gov/research/online_documents/women_in_the_1950s /Women_in_Foreign_Service.pdf.

Dwight Eisenhower Presidential Library. "Women in the United States Congress, 1959." https://eisenhower.archives.gov/research/online_documents/women_in_the _1950s/Women_in_US_Congress.pdf.

Grill, Bartholomäus. "Snowplows for Tropical Guinea: How We Can Learn from Failed Development Aid in Africa." *Spiegel Online*, March 6, 2008. https://www.spiegel .de/international/world/snowplows-for-tropical-guinea-how-we-can-learn-from -failed-development-aid-in-africa-a-539782.html.

US Department of State, Office of the Historian. "The Department Dddresses Inequality." https://history.state.gov/departmenthistory/short-history/inequality.

World Bank. "GDP per Capita (Current US$)." http://data.worldbank.org/indicator/NY .GDP.PCAP.CD.

World Bank. "Money and Quasi Money (M2) as % of GDP." https://databank.worldbank .org/reports.aspx?source=1277&series=FM.LBL.MQMY.GDP.ZS.

Documents Collections

Census Office of Ghana. *1960 Population Census of Ghana*. Vol. 1: *The Gazetteer: Alphabetical List of Localities with Number of Population and Houses*. Accra: Census Office, 1962.

Davidson, Apollon, and Sergei Mazov, eds. *Rossiia i Afrika: Dokumenty i materialy XVIII v.–1960 g.*, vol. 2: *1918–1960*. Moscow: IVI RAN, 1999.

Fursenko, Aleksandr, ed. *Prezidium TsK KPSS 1954–1964: Chernovye protokol'nye zapisi zasedanii stenogrammy*, 3 vols. Moscow: ROSSPEN, 2004–2008.

Government of Ghana. "National Investment Bank Act," Act 163, March 22, 1963.

Khrushchev, Nikita. *Khrushchev in New York*. New York: Crosscurrent Press, 1960.

Mensah, E.T., and The Tempos. *King of Highlife Anthology*, 4 Discs. London: RetroAfric Records, 2015.

Ministère des Affaires Étrangères. *Documents Diplomatiques Français, 1964*. 2 vols. Brussels: Peter Lang, 2002.

Ministère des Affaires Étrangères. *Documents Diplomatiques Français, 1960*. 2 vols. Paris: Imprimerie Nationale, 1996.

Ministère des Affaires Étrangères. *Documents Diplomatiques Français, 1956*. 2 vols. Paris: Imprimerie Nationale, 1988.

Ministerstvo Inostrannykh Del SSSR. *SSSR i strany Afriki, 1963–1970 gg.: Dokumenty i materialy*. 2 vols. Moscow: Politizdat, 1982.

Ministerstvo Inostrannykh Del SSSR. *SSSR i Strany Afriki, 1946–1962 gg.: Dokumenty i Materialy*. 2 vols. Moscow: Gosudarstvennoe Izdatel'stvo Politicheskoi Literatury, 1963.

Ministerstvo Vneshnei Torgovli SSSR. *Vneshniaia torgovlia SSSR za 1969 god: Statisticheskii obzor*. Moscow: Vneshtorgovizdat, 1970.

Ministerstvo Vneshnei Torgovli SSSR. *Vneshniaia torgovlia SSSR za 1967 god: Statisticheskii obzor*. Moscow: Vneshtorgovizdat, 1968.

Ministerstvo Vneshnei Torgovli SSSR. *Vneshniaia torgovlia SSSR za 1966 god: Statisticheskii obzor*. Moscow: Vneshtorgovizdat, 1967.

Ministerstvo Vneshnei Torgovli SSSR. *Vneshniaia torgovlia SSSR za 1965 god: Sstatisticheskii obzor.* Moscow: Vneshtorgovizdat, 1966.

Ministerstvo Vneshnei Torgovli SSSR. *Vneshniaia torgovlia SSSR za 1964 god: Statisticheskii obzor.* Moscow: Vneshtorgovizdat, 1965.

Ministerstvo Vneshnei Torgovli SSSR, *Vneshniaia torgovlia SSSR za 1959–1963 gody.* Moscow: Vneshtorgnzdat, 1965.

Ministerstvo Vneshnei Torgovli SSSR, *Vneshniaia torgovlia SSSR za 1957 god.* Moscow: Vneshtorgizdat, 1958.

TsK KPSS. *XX S"ezd Kommunisticheskoi Partii Sovetskogo Soiuza. Stenograficheskii otchet.* Vol. 1. Moscow: Gosudarstvennoe Izdatel'stvo Politicheskoi Literatury, 1956.

US Department of State. *Foreign Relations of the United States (FRUS), 1917–1972.* Vol. 6: *Public Diplomacy, 1961–1963.* Washington, DC: Government Printing Office, 2017.

US Department of State. *Foreign Relations of the United States (FRUS), 1964–1968.* Vol. 14: *Africa.* Washington, DC: United States Government Printing Office, 1999.

US Department of State. *Foreign Relations of the United States (FRUS), 1961–1963.* Vol. 21: *Africa.* Washington, DC: United States Government Printing Office, 1995.

US Department of State. *Foreign Relations of the United States (FRUS), 1958–1960.* Vol. 14: *Africa.* Washington, DC: United States Government Printing Office, 1992.

US Department of State. *Foreign Relations of the United States (FRUS), 1955–1957.* Vol. 19: *National Security Policy.* Washington, DC: United States Government Printing Office, 1990.

US Department of State. *Foreign Relations of the United States (FRUS), 1955–1957.* Vol. 28: *Africa.* Washington, DC: United States Government Printing Office, 1989.

US Department of State. *Foreign Relations of the United States, 1955–1957 (FRUS).* Vol. 14: *Arab-Israeli Dispute, 1955.* Washington, DC: United States Government Printing Office, 1989.

US Department of State. *Foreign Relations of the United States (FRUS), 1955–1957.* Vol. 8: *South Asia.* Washington, DC: United States Government Printing Office, 1987.

Index

www.ingramcontent.com/pod-product-compliance
Ingram Content Group UK Ltd.
Pitfield, Milton Keynes, MK11 3LW, UK
UKHW040849190325
456432UK00016B/91/J